Union Made

Union Made

*Working People and the Rise of
Social Christianity in Chicago*

———— ·◦◦· ————

HEATH W. CARTER

OXFORD
UNIVERSITY PRESS

OXFORD
UNIVERSITY PRESS

Oxford University Press is a department of the University of Oxford. It furthers
the University's objective of excellence in research, scholarship, and education
by publishing worldwide. Oxford is a registered trade mark of Oxford University
Press in the UK and certain other countries.

Published in the United States of America by Oxford University Press
198 Madison Avenue, New York, NY 10016, United States of America.

First issued as an Oxford University Press paperback, 2017

Chapter 5 draws significantly upon two previously published articles: "Striking Out On Its
Own: Labor and the Modern Church," *Chicago History Magazine*, Vol. 37, no. 2 (Summer
2011); and "Scab Ministers, Striking Saints: Christianity and Class Conflict in 1894 Chicago,"
American Nineteenth Century History 11, No. 3 (September 2010): 321–349. Reprinted with
permission © Chicago Historical Society and © Taylor & Francis respectively.

Library of Congress Cataloging-in-Publication Data
Carter, Heath W.
Union made : working people and the rise of social Christianity in Chicago /
Heath W. Carter.
pages cm
Includes bibliographical references and index.
ISBN 978–0–19–938595–9 (hardcover); 978–0–19–084737–1 (paperback)
1. Labor unions—Religious aspects—Christianity. 2. Labor unions—Illinois—
Chicago—History. 3. Labor movement—Religious aspects—Christianity.
4. Labor movement—Illinois—Chicago—History.
5. Christian sociology—Illinois—Chicago—History. I. Title.
HD6338.2.U52C553 2014
261.09773'11—dc23
2015000066

For Alan Bloom

Contents

Acknowledgments

I COULD NOT have completed this book without funding from a variety of institutions. I am deeply grateful for support from the History Department and Graduate School at the University of Notre Dame; the Andrew W. Mellon Foundation; the Charlotte W. Newcombe Foundation; and the Creative Work and Research Committee, Provost's Office, and College of Arts and Sciences at Valparaiso University. A grant from Notre Dame's Institute for the Study of the Liberal Arts went directly to the hire of five translators—Ian Rinehart, Jessica Szafron, Alex Meyer, Joela Zeller, and Stina Bäckström—whose able work opened an illuminating window into Chicago's vast foreign-language periodical literature.

My research benefited immeasurably from the resourcefulness of a number of archivists, librarians, and curators, including: Martha Briggs and Katie McMahon at the Newberry Library; Catherine Bruck at the Illinois Institute of Technology; Julie A. Satzik and Peggy Lavelle at the Archives and Records Center of the Archdiocese of Chicago; Elaine S. Caldbeck at Garrett-Evangelical & Seabury-Western Theological Seminaries; Richard Harms and Lugene Schemper at Calvin College; John Hoffman at the University of Illinois; James Holley at the International Brotherhood of Boilermakers; Eddie L. Knox, Jr., at Pullman Presbyterian Church (Chicago); Kevin Leonard at the United Methodist Church's Northern Illinois Conference Archives; Frank Levi at St. Andrew's Anglican Church (Tinley Park, Illinois); Patrick Gorman at the Lee County (Illinois) Historical Society; Dianne Luhmann at the First Presbyterian Church (Chicago); Ruth Tonkiss Cameron at Union Theological Seminary's Burke Library Archives; and Frances Bristol and Dale Patterson at the United Methodist Church's General Commission on Archives and History. I logged hundreds of hours in the Research Center at the Chicago History Museum and am thankful for its entire staff. I accrued especially large debts to Debbie Vaughan and Lesley Martin, expert guides to the collections, whose unremittingly good humor made CHM a delightful place to while away the days; to Michael Featherstone and Tom Guerra, whose diligent work made mine so much easier; and to Michael Glass, whose warm greetings brightened the beginning and end of nearly every day I was there.

Along the way I have been astounded by the kindness of academic colleagues. During my apprenticeship, which took me from Georgetown University to the University of Chicago, and finally to the University of Notre Dame, I was privileged to work closely with world-class scholars such as Beth McKeown, Scott Pilarz, Jim Walsh, Catherine Brekus, Dan Graff, George Marsden, and John McGreevy. I am indebted, above all, to my doctoral adviser, Mark Noll, whose generosity is justly legendary. Others shared invaluable insights and rigorously engaged my ideas in various stages of development. I am especially grateful to Rosemary Adams, Bruce Baker, Gail Bederman, Ed Blum, Dave Burns, Chris Cantwell, Kathleen Conzen, Joe Creech, Jake Dorn, Janine Giordano Drake, Bob Elder, Leon Fink, Tim Gloege, Danny Greene, Jim Grossman, Luke Harlow, Suellen Hoy, Kevin Kruse, Hugh McLeod, Emily Nordstrom, Susan O'Donovan, Dominic Pacyga, Laura Porter, Amanda Porterfield, Paul Putz, Jarod Roll, Nick Salvatore, Ellen Skerrett, Robert Weir, and David Zonderman, as well as the participants in the Colloquium on Religion and History at the University of Notre Dame, the Religions in America Workshop at the University of Chicago, the History Department Research Workshop at Valparaiso University, and the Urban History Dissertation Group and the Labor History Seminar at the Newberry Library. Eric Arnesen, Darren Dochuk, Ken Fones-Wolf, Paul Harvey, Tom Kselman, and Rima Lunin Schultz offered extensive comments on entire drafts, and in so doing helped to enhance greatly the quality of the ideas and narrative. It has been a delight to work with my editor, Theo Calderara, and the staff at Oxford University Press; together they have also, in ways large and small, made this a better book.

While many friends have sustained me through the writing process, a few have had a decisive impact on this book's shape. These include Lisa Cockrel, Keith Cox, Aaron Johnson, Marty LaFalce, Micah Lott, Adam Phillips, and John and Susan DeCostanza. I would never have had the opportunity to write in the first place had it not been for the unfailing support of my parents, Clyde and Jacque Carter, and for the love and nurture of my wider family, especially Primrose Langer, whom I still miss after all these years. I met Thais Pietrangelo Carter in the autumn of 2001 and soon intuited what I now know to be true: there is no one with whom I would rather walk through life. Our journey has been delightfully unpredictable and is the source of a singular joy, which has somehow, miraculously, increased with the arrival of three beautiful boys, Isaiah, Samuel, and James. Thanks be to God.

I started at Valparaiso University in the fall of 2012 and was immediately conscious of my great fortune to have ended up with such congenial colleagues, both in the Department of History and across the university. I remain ever grateful for them, and for the support I have received from Jon Kilpinen, the Dean of the College of Arts and Sciences, as well as the three different department chairpersons with whom I have worked to this point: Colleen Seguin, Alan Bloom, and Ron Rittgers. When I arrived three years ago I could never have imagined how fully Colleen and Alan, and their own brood of boys—Zeke, Jin, and Kuo—would invite me into their lives. Alan and I were different in many ways and yet, almost before I knew it, we had become the best of friends. He was a brilliant thinker, teacher, mentor, and conversationalist. He was a devoted father and citizen, who would always say that he was working to make Valparaiso the kind of town in which he wanted to raise his kids. In the spring of 2013 we took a group of students to Selma, Alabama, where we heard Martin Luther King III exclaim, "If, when you die, you haven't left the world a little bit better off than you found it, you should be ashamed." Alan loved that line. Alan lived that line. The fact that his ebullient spirit no longer walks this earth remains hard to fathom, let alone accept. I dedicate this book to him.

H.W.C.

Union Made

FIGURE I.1 Portrait of Agnes Nestor, circa 1913

Credit: Chicago History Museum, ICHi-67688. Photographer—Clinedinst Studio.

Introduction

"HOODWINKING CLERGYMEN," screamed the headline, emblazoned across the pages of dozens of American newspapers in the week leading up to Labor Day 1910. The sprawling text below explained, "Ministers of the gospel are essentially and fundamentally honest but, like all men who work for the public good, they are at times misled by false statements." The point of contention was an American Federation of Labor (AFL) press release entitled, "Interest in Labor Sunday," which appeared "harmless" but was in fact "as dangerous to the peace and liberty of the citizens as a coiled rattlesnake in the grass." The article went on to assert, "We see here a demand on the ministers of God, that they endorse and help build up the strike-producing, boycotting and violent American Federation of Labor." It was signed and syndicated by cereal magnate Charles W. Post, who was beside himself at organized labor's latest attempt to evangelize the churches.[1]

The idea for "Labor Sunday" was not new. An Episcopal organization in New York had pioneered a similar observance as early as 1890 and, in the intervening years, the Presbyterian Church had also taken up the initiative.[2] But the day had never amounted to much, so the delegates to the AFL's 1909 convention at Toronto had resolved to push for wider recognition.[3] The organization's many local affiliates responded in kind, though few with as much gusto as the Chicago Federation of Labor (CFL). Early in the summer of 1910, it appointed a seven-person special committee to oversee plans. Margaret Dreier Robins, a member of that body and the president of the local chapter of the Women's Trade Union League (WTUL), drafted a letter, sent out to six hundred Christian ministers across the city, inquiring as to whether, on September 4th, they would consider preaching on "What Has Organized Labor Accomplished for Social Progress." Or even better: allow a worker to do so in their stead. When more than three hundred clergymen replied in the affirmative, Robins and CFL President John Fitzpatrick were sent scurrying to find workers to speak.[4] Overwhelmed by the struggle to meet such high demand, they left it to the churches and wage earners to work out the details. Arrangements were still being finalized when Post's screed hit the newsstand. Who knew what Labor Sunday would bring?[5]

Remarkably, across the city that day union representatives, standing before congregations swelled by larger-than-usual numbers of workers, preached the word. To a person they insisted that the aims of the labor movement were fully consonant with the teachings of Christianity. At Sedgwick Street Congregational, Leopold P. Straube, the secretary of the Allied Printing Trades Council, argued that unionism was in fact just Christianity translated into concrete, practical form.[6] Many workers preached on "the workingman's alienation from the church," a subject weighing heavily on middle-class Christian minds.[7] In the estimation of Swedish painter A. C. Anderson, the source of this alienation was not especially mysterious. As he informed the respectable women and men of Ninth Presbyterian, "Some of the worst enemies organized labor has are very ardent church goers."[8] A. A. Allen, the editor of the *Union Labor Advocate*, made the point even more emphatically. He startled the people of Seventy-Seventh Street Methodist Episcopal Church by waving in their faces a contract that many Chicago employers forced female workers to sign; "No bill of sale of a chattel slave in ante-bellum days was as cruel or exacting," Allen exclaimed.[9] Yet too many church members were out of touch with such realities, lamented the lone female homilist this day, Agnes Nestor, secretary of the International Glove Workers Union (figure I.1). The Catholic Nestor unflinchingly informed the members of the North Shore's fashionable Winnetka Congregational Church, "You are so far removed from the life of the factory girl that you cannot understand the view she takes of life."[10]

While a number of Chicago divines stayed planted in the pews, soaking in these hard-hitting sermons, others assumed the prophetic role themselves. At Ravenswood Presbyterian, the Reverend Duncan Milner excoriated "organized capital," even while touting trade unionism as "one of the mightiest forces of today in the uplift of human society." Milner went on to offer his own thoughts on the vexed relationship between Chicago's churches and wage earners. Decrying "persistent and malignant efforts to persuade men that the churches are class institutions," he reminded his audience, "Jesus Christ was known as a carpenter, was born and reared in poverty and as a teacher, 'the common people heard him gladly'"; as a result, Milner insisted, "a true church of Jesus Christ cannot be a class church."[11] While the Reverend Austin Hunter of Jackson Boulevard Christian saw Jesus in a similar light, he was not as quick to let the churches off the hook. "The reason why workingmen are not found in larger numbers in the church," he declared, "is not due to the coldness of the church, nor to the dress parade, but primarily to the fact that the church has been more often upon the side of capital than upon the side of labor."[12] Milner and Hunter were not the only ones to raise their voices. Across the city, ministers of nearly every confession—Catholic, Congregational, Episcopal, Reformed Episcopal, Methodist, Presbyterian, Lutheran, Swedenborgian, Baptist, Disciples of Christ, and Unitarian—addressed the labor question this day.[13] The next morning the *Tribune* announced, "Gospel of Unions Told in Pulpits."[14]

That was news indeed. Historically, the churches had favored capital over labor and many leading Christians still harbored suspicion of trade unions. This hostility sprung in part from close and long-standing ties between the Protestant and industrial elites.[15] In Chicago, the newspapers failed to mention that Labor Sunday was not celebrated in any of the city's most exclusive churches. While the local Episcopalian bishop urged his priests to observe the day, there is no record that the patricians at St. James did; nor did those at upscale First Congregational or Second Presbyterian.[16] At Winnetka Congregational, meanwhile, Agnes Nestor encountered capital's strong hand when, after her sermon, she was accosted by a member of the church wielding anti-labor propaganda.[17] Nestor's own Church had an uneasy relationship with labor in its own right. While the Catholic hierarchy's rhetoric was often friendly, its worries about the creeping influence of radicalism had long precluded a more fulsome embrace.[18] Labor Sunday found Chicago Archbishop James E. Quigley on his way to Montreal, but in his absence he would have been gratified to hear that the bishop of nearby Rockford had taken the occasion to declare, "Catholic men, I admonish you to fight against socialism in the labor unions."[19]

Even given these countervailing currents, there could be no mistaking the change. Workers were preaching to ministers, and a strong, self-critical voice was emerging within the churches themselves. Seeing reason for optimism, the CFL's Fitzpatrick, also a Roman Catholic, observed, "The number of churches that had special services Sunday in observance of Labor day preliminaries was an excellent sign."[20] For working people, it was evidence that social gospels—which they had espoused for decades—were gaining long-sought legitimacy.

This book recasts the history of social Christianity. Scholars have long used this catchall category to describe the myriad reform impulses that together constituted the progressive Christian response to industrial capitalism.[21] The earliest histories of the movement placed white, male ministers and theologians such as Washington Gladden, Walter Rauschenbusch, and John Ryan at the vanguard.[22] More recent scholarship has vastly expanded the cast of characters, recovering the ample contributions of both white women, who powered the settlement house and home mission movements, and African Americans, whose pioneering work at the intersection of racial and economic justice helped to humanize the Great Migration of southern blacks to northern cities.[23] But until very recently one feature of the literature has remained constant: an almost uniform emphasis on the centrality of the middle classes.[24] I do not dispute that middle-class reformers supplied some of the impetus for social Christianity's rise. In Chicago, the likes of Jane Addams, Reverdy Ransom, Ellen Gates Starr, Graham Taylor, and Mary McDowell made heroic contributions to the cause of social reform. But I do contend that working people played a much more essential role in this story than they have typically been accorded.

Indeed, social Christianity was "union made"—and in at least two crucial senses. The first pertains to the history of ideas. Throughout the Gilded Age, the clergy largely failed to muster a critical analysis of the nation's changing economic life. As vehemently as conservatives and liberals disagreed on matters of biblical interpretation, they were often of one mind on "the labor question," attributing the vast disparities of wealth in their midst to the poor's individual failings. As the pioneering modernist Reverend David Swing wrote in 1874, "The conflict between classes in the cities of our country is not a conflict between labor and capital, but between successful and unsuccessful lives."[25] Countless working people begged to differ and, during this same era, their communities proved hotbeds of theological innovation. Wage earners fashioned the words of scripture into searing critiques of both the emerging industrial order and the churches that so readily accommodated it. In the generation before Rauschenbusch published *Christianity and the Social Crisis* (1907)—"the magnum opus of [the social gospel] movement"—workers hammered out social gospels in union meetings, socialist publications, and anarchist demonstrations.[26] They were not systematic theologians. But, in addition to being "lived," their religion was *thought*; and this book is in part an exploration of their intellectual history.[27]

It is also more than that, for workers did not sit back on their theological laurels, but rather threw themselves into the politics of church. They could sense the anxiety emanating from northern sanctuaries, as leading Christians struggled to absorb the shock of the industrializing city. Protestants were long preoccupied with the prospect of a prodigal generation: would the unprecedented numbers of people pouring into new boomtowns fall prey to the myriad temptations to be found there?[28] By the late nineteenth century, the specter of lost sheep had influential divines of nearly every denomination on edge. Catholic priests and bishops worried constantly about their flock's susceptibility to socialist incursions. Meanwhile, evangelical ministers were ever more distraught about the paucity of working people—and especially working men—in the pews. Were the churches, long the nation's cornerstone, on the verge of becoming irrelevant?

This "crisis" was belied by the facts on the ground: rates of urban church attendance were on the rise and the American faithful had been overwhelmingly female for centuries.[29] But working people were only too happy to add fuel to the fire. In the decades following the Civil War, they consistently threatened to leave the fold unless the churches warmed to labor. Workers backed these threats with concerted resistance to "scab ministers," generating clashes that, especially when picked up by the press, only intensified clerical anxieties. A select subset of the working classes—namely, white, skilled men—wielded disproportionate influence in this unfolding cultural process. The clergy were especially desperate to secure their allegiance, as it seemed not only the antidote to the feminization of the churches but also the guarantor of their ongoing relevance. Across the nation at the turn of the century, Protestant ministers turned to this population for help, conducting surveys designed to identify the sources of their disenchantment. The churches' hostility to labor topped nearly every list. This empowered scattered reformers on the inside, who insisted that the hope of a Christian society would soon be altogether dashed if the churches did not find a way to embrace trade unionism. In the first decade of the twentieth century, as entire denominations did just that, there could be no doubt that social Christianity was ascendant—and that it had emerged from below.

The rise of the AFL as a major force expedited this sea change. With its focus on achieving incremental gains for comparatively privileged workers, the organization advanced a vision of labor reform that was increasingly palatable to church leaders. So long as Samuel Gompers and his allies could hold the socialists within the organization at bay, the Christian elite could imagine its rising support for trade unionism as a crucial prong of its ongoing battle against radicalism. The middle-class Social Gospel was, in this and every sense, a real but distinctly moderate accommodation of working-class religious dissent. It was almost inevitably so. While historians of the modern conservative movement have been combing the archives for evidence of collaboration between churches and corporations in the mid-twentieth century, the hunt could easily begin a century before.[30] The churches' patrons in the industrial elite did not wield as much clout during the Progressive Era as they had during the Gilded Age, but they remained formidable. Their enduring strength pushed many of the more radical middle-class Social Gospelers to pursue their visions outside the confines of the institutional churches. Those reformers who remained had to tread carefully, as was clear on Labor Sunday 1910, when the very prospect of friendly gestures toward the AFL's labor aristocrats made some leading Christians nervous and others irate.

If social Christianity was not often revolutionary, it was nevertheless among the most important American reckonings with industrial capitalism.[31] Long after the First Amendment disestablished religion, Christianity remained the dominant ideological framework within which the nation's diverse peoples debated public questions.[32] Thus, the lively, late nineteenth-century exchanges recounted here were not merely of religious significance. When believers wrangled over the modern implications of Jesus's command, "Thou shalt love thy neighbor as thyself," the contours of the national conscience were at stake.[33] For many Americans of the day, questions about what the Lord meant when he said, "the laborer is worthy of his hire," and whom he had in mind when he declared, "Woe unto you that are rich!" were gripping.[34] The answers to these questions had major ramifications for public policy, not to mention the country's longer term political economy. Indeed, in repositioning working people as makers of social Christianity, this study locates them at the very center of

fierce fights over how to reconcile democracy and capitalism in the industrializing United States.[35]

American workers were also players in a wider and longer story: namely,
the history of Christianity. The vigor with which many pressed their theological case—in the papers, the pews, and the streets—underscored their
investment in the shape of this fractious, transnational, two-millennia-
old movement.[36] To be sure, there was no monolithic "working-class
Christianity," let alone a "religion of the working classes." Some wage
earners were altogether indifferent toward religion.[37] Countless others
found meaning and solace in the ideals propounded by their pastor or
priest. But class was nevertheless among the most important lines of
demarcation running through the Gilded Age church and workers were
far more likely than their social betters to believe that God sides decisively with the poor. While the documentary record is most robust for
white Protestant men, fragmentary evidence suggests that myriad others,
including working-class women, Catholics, and African Americans,
shared this intuition.[38] In defending their conviction that God would lift
up the lowly—which had ancient roots, but was not always embraced by
Christian institutions—wage earners joined a line of believers, stretching
back for millennia, who sought to reform the churches themselves.[39]

The action here is set in nineteenth and early twentieth-century
Chicago, which emerged from the swamps to become an industrial behe-
moth. In 1830 the settlement numbered some 100 persons. In 1900 it
boasted nearly two million, making Chicago the world's fifth largest city.[40]
The speedy transformation of a frontier outpost into a modern metropolis
reflected tectonic shifts in the global economy, for what was happening
on the southwestern shores of Lake Michigan was intricately connected
to developments in Manchester, Bombay, and the far corners of a world
ever-more woven together by the flow of capital and commodities.[41] In
addition to its significance for industry, Chicago was a global epicenter of
working-class organization, of anxiety, experimentation, and often violent
confrontation over the labor question. The city was moreover a hub of
religious innovation and activity, home to a breathtaking array of ethnic
parishes, as well as to many of the greatest revivalists and reformers of
the age.

While the decision to concentrate on a single locale introduces inevitable limitations, it also opens up new interpretive vistas. Here—in the geog-
raphies, habits, conversations, and conflicts of a specific place—the lines
between intellectual, social, religious, and political history are blurred,

and the push-and-pull between working people and church leaders comes into full view. This more focused lens allows me to track not only what a minister had to say about a strike but also who was sitting in the pews when he said it, what transpired in the immediate aftermath, and what were the longer term reverberations. Only when these various layers of the story are accounted for do the working-class origins of social Christianity become clear. Developments in Chicago were not entirely representative. However, the fundamental dynamics driving historical change here can be found across the industrializing north, suggesting that this story's implications extend well beyond its geographical scope.[42]

Leading economists have taken to calling ours "a new Gilded Age," and not without reason, as the widening chasm between rich and poor in the contemporary United States approaches historic proportions.[43] Yet readers may find that the analogy only goes so far. In the world evoked in these pages, unlike today, concerns about the experiences of workers and the fate of the working classes saturated public conversation; devastating recessions elicited fundamental questions about the shape of the nation's economic life; and believers, both ordinary and elite, could hardly help but be drawn into freewheeling debates regarding the morality of capitalism. It is a world familiar and yet strange.

I

"Is the Laborer Worthy of His Hire?" Christianity and Class in Antebellum Chicago

"IS THE LABORER WORTHY OF HIS HIRE?" read a July 1858 headline in the *Chicago Press and Tribune*. "As an abstract question, every person would answer 'Yes,'" the article began, "but in practice there are thousands who answer 'No.'" For readers attuned to the news of the day, the workers at Chicago's McCormick Harvesting Machine plant might have come immediately to mind. The company had slashed wages that very month, accelerating a dismal trend: in 1849 the average pay rate had been 12.5 cents per hour; by 1859 it was down to 6.2.[1] But the writer had something else in mind: "We do not here particularly refer to the exactions of grasping employers and hard taskmasters, who wring from humble toil their own ill-gotten gains." Rather, "we would speak for a moment of the great fault of Christian communities everywhere, the inadequate payment of Christian ministers."[2]

This particular problem had roots in the nation's constitutional order, which forbade tax support for churches and thereby rendered ministers dependent upon the largesse of their congregations.[3] The transition to the voluntary system proved financially rocky for many clergy families and more than a generation after disestablishment Christian leaders found themselves still in the position of having to plead for better support. Luke 10:7—"for the laborer is worthy of his hire"—was a favorite scriptural touchstone of these pleas. The religious press worked this verse into countless columns bemoaning congregations' failures to adequately pay their ministers. "Go throughout the sparsely settled districts of the country, and though store-house, granary and cellar be full and overflowing with the rich bounties of Providence, yet the minister of Christ is often found in suffering want," wrote one correspondent.[4] The going was especially tough for Baptist farmer-preachers, who were paid with irregular free-will offerings, and Methodist itinerants, whose salaries were capped at subsistence levels through the mid-1840s.[5] As late as the mid-1850s, the average minister earned roughly $400 a year, the same as the average laborer and nowhere near enough to afford the trappings of a comfortable middle-class life.[6] In at least one case, frustrated divines—inspired by the growing militancy of their fellow workingmen—organized a Preachers' Protective Union. "NO PAY—NO PREACH," avowed an 1853 circular published in Boston's *Independent*.[7]

As much as ministers may have resented their plight, it had, if anything, a salutary effect upon their work. In the wake of independence, many Americans became enamored with the idea that the truth was as accessible to the common man as to any learned divine. Ruffled collars and Harvard degrees became, in many cases, liabilities. Indeed, in the early decades of the nineteenth century crowds flocked to hear plain-folk revivalists, who developed innovative techniques to popularize an evangelical tradition that was rapidly—and improbably—converging with the dominant political and moral philosophies of the day.[8] Remarkably, this unrefined, ill-educated class of preachers accomplished what their aristocratic, colonial-era predecessors had not: the mass Christianization of the people.[9] In cities, boomtowns, and far-flung rural regions ordinary persons converted in record numbers and to spectacular result; in the years between 1776 and 1850, rates of Christian adherence more than doubled.[10] American Christianity had become the people's religion by becoming, first, a religion of-and-by the people.

By 1858, however, when the *Chicago Press and Tribune* ran its column on ministers' salaries, the religious landscape had begun to shift dramatically once more. The article's author was well aware of the changes. They were, he asserted, what prompted him to write: "We have been led to think upon this subject by the numerous accounts which have gone the rounds of the papers lately of particular instances of liberality of certain congregations to their pastors."[11] The qualifying adjectives—"*particular* instances"; "*certain* congregations"—served his rhetorical purpose, which was to impart a sense of ongoing urgency to Christian givers elsewhere. But the delicate prose hid a striking development on the ground: that leading churches in many a northern city were evolving into exclusive clubs dominated by an emergent industrial elite.[12]

Chicago was no exception, as underscored by dramatic shifts in two key indices: the amount of ministers' salaries and the cost of church buildings. In the city's earliest years even the most prominent congregations met in simple frame buildings and paid their ministers only marginally more than local artisans and tradesmen earned. But as Chicago grew from outpost to metropolis, elite merchants and industrialists financed the construction of ornate cathedrals and underwrote lucrative salaries to secure the most renowned ministers. In so doing, Chicago's wealthiest Christians sowed the seeds of working-class resentment, though notably, these did not sprout into militancy during the antebellum period. Throughout these years many of the city's ordinary believers remained hopeful that they, too, would soon enjoy the fruits of modern industrial society. The pervasive evangelical revivalism of the earlier nineteenth century had unpredictable consequences for class relations, fueling antipathy at particular moments and diminishing it at others. But so long as an expanding frontier economy churned out a better standard of living for its citizens—as it did, more or less, up through the Civil War—it held class conflict in check, both within the churches and without.[13] Only in the postbellum era, as a northern consensus on the dignity of free labor devolved into industrial warfare, would the churches, having sown the proverbial wind, reap the whirlwind.

In 1830, Chicago looked much the same as when Louis Jolliet and Jacques Marquette first laid eyes on the area in 1673: to the west lay an expansive swamp, separated from Lake Michigan by a ribbon of dry prairie several miles wide. The north and south branches of the Chicago River ran sluggishly toward one another through the terrain, uniting a mile or so west of the Lake before emptying their combined waters into it. The most conspicuous change was that, since 1803, the local Indian trails had converged at Fort Dearborn, a military post positioned alongside the River and just a short walk east of where its branches joined. As late as 1830 fewer than a hundred people lived in the shadows of the Fort. But when federal investment in the improvement of the harbor signaled renewed commitment to a long-proposed Illinois and Michigan Canal, a wave of new settlers descended. By 1837, nearly 4,000 persons resided in the newly incorporated city, including a handful of merchants, doctors, and lawyers, a smattering of "gentlemen speculators," and a large cohort of ordinary laborers, many hard at work upon the canal.[14]

These early white settlers confronted the attendant challenges of life on the frontier. To be sure, some accumulated vast fortunes during these years: in one 1836 auction, 186 undeveloped lots sold for $1,041,344.[15] But the nouveau riche had to traverse the same roads—"about as bad as could be imagined"—and endure the same smells—"putrid meat"; "green putrid water and decaying vegetable matter"; "nauseous fumes . . . from the sink-holes and sloughs of the town"—as everyone else.[16] Recurrent waves of cholera and consumption afflicted the local population. Housing was so scarce, one settler recalled, "[that] in many instances families were living in their covered wagons while arrangements were made for putting up shelter for them."[17] Meanwhile, food prices fluctuated wildly in accordance with unpredictable supply and demand. In December 1833, flour cost roughly $5.50 a barrel; in one three-week span in 1836, it spiked from $12.00 to $20.00 a barrel.[18]

Throughout the 1830s religious life, too, bore the unmistakable mark of the frontier. One of the first Christian preachers to settle in the area was William See, a regularly ordained Methodist who in 1831–1832 preached sermons in a log hut on Wolf's Point.[19] One early history remembers See as a "gunsmith to the Indians occasionally, [who] held forth to the 'igno-ramusses,' (as he termed the unbelievers)," while another recalls, "he was by trade a blacksmith and poor in purse, but of good moral character and highly esteemed."[20] See's preaching did not impress the refined likes of Juliette Kinzie, who disparaged it as "less to the edification of his hearers than to the unmerciful slaughter of the 'King's English.' "[21]

But outside of such rarefied circles, rough-hewn revivalists more than sufficed. Consider the success of the Reverend Peter R. Borein. Two years after his conversion at an 1828 camp meeting in Tennessee, the 20-year-old Borein moved to Illinois, worked in a brickyard, and made an abortive attempt to get an education before becoming a circuit rider. In 1837 he was called to Chicago's First Methodist Episcopal Church, where no one seemed to mind his common pedigree. During his two-year tenure, by one count, "about three hundred united with the Church; the young city containing at the time a population of about three thousand."[22]

Some of Chicago's earliest divines boasted more impressive credentials, but their lives were none the easier for it. The city's first Catholic priest, a Frenchman by the name of John Mary Irenaeus St. Cyr, completed a classical course of study at the Grand Seminary of Lyons before migrating across the Atlantic. Dispatched to Chicago in May 1833, St. Cyr marveled at the warm welcome he received from Catholics and Protestants alike. But in a letter to his superior in St. Louis the following month, he underscored the hardships he faced:

> I should have reason to complain, Monseigneur, were you not to send me some assistance at the start to relieve my needs; for I should not have money enough even to pay postage on a letter were I to receive one, nor do I know how I am going to pay the transportation charges on my trunk, when it comes, unless I have some help from you beforehand. I cannot say Mass every day, as I should like to, for I cannot always obtain the wine and candles.[23]

St. Cyr's fledgling congregation gathered initially in a parishioner's log cabin and then in a small room on State Street before finally, in 1836, building a proper sanctuary. Completed at the corner of Lake and State Streets for $400, St. Mary's Catholic Church did not exactly inspire heavenly thoughts. The unpainted, 25' x 35' wood exterior became recognizable as a church only after a bell tower was added several years later (figure 1.1). Inside one found row after row of crude benches, already insufficient to seat the area's fast-growing, multiethnic Catholic population.[24]

Function trumped form even in those churches that were home to early Chicago's most prominent citizens. The founding generation of the First Presbyterian Church, established in 1833, included the families of William Brown, a banker and financier, George Dole, the city's first meat packer, Philo Carpenter, a leading pharmacist, and Philip F. W. Peck, a real estate tycoon. Nevertheless, throughout its first year the congregation shared a single, two-story, frame building on Franklin and South Water Streets with the Baptist and Methodist societies.[25] When First Presbyterian dedicated its own place of worship in the early days of 1834, it was also conspicuously plain. Constructed for just $600, the 30' x 40' wooden structure remained in use all the way up through 1849.[26] In the 1830s, in fact, the sole exception to the Spartan rule was St. James Episcopal, whose exclusive congregation financed the city's first brick sanctuary in 1837. Outfitted with a bell tower and an organ, the building showcased as well a mahogany altar screen that alone cost between $2,000 and $2,500. In total, for materials, labor, and furnishings, the members expended $15,000, an extraordinary amount considering that a common laborer in Chicago was lucky to make $18 a month.[27] But even the well-heeled parishioners at St. James could not entirely escape the reigning ethic of simplicity: in 1843, a new rector ordered that the altar screen be dismantled and its beautiful mahogany refashioned into a less ostentatious pulpit.[28]

FIGURE 1.1 St. Mary's Catholic Church
Credit: Chicago History Museum, ICHi-37096.

The original Episcopalian extravagance was especially inappropriate in the wake of the 1837 panic, which burst Chicago's speculative bubble. But by the mid-1840s the city had rebounded. Farmers from around the Midwest powered the turn-around, in part, by lugging their surplus to the southwesterly shores of Lake Michigan, where they found high prices for grains, lumber, and meat. But even more pivotal were Eastern financiers, whose interest in interior markets sustained those prices and whose capital furnished an expanding network of waterways and, after 1848, railways to-and-from Chicago. The trend in wheat exports illustrates the city's rising importance to the national economy. In 1842, Chicago exported 586,907 bushels to eastern markets; in 1844, 891,894 bushels; and in 1847, 1,974,304 bushels.[29] By mid-century the city had become—as William Cronon, the foremost historian of these developments, so aptly puts it—"the link that bound the different worlds of east and west into a single system. In the most literal sense . . . it was where the West began."[30] Migrants from all over flocked to its bustling streets: in 1850, the city counted nearly 30,000 residents.

Amidst this astounding growth, Chicagoans' disparate fortunes were etched more deeply into the emerging urban landscape.[31] Vast numbers of Irish—the largest and poorest subset of the foreign-born, which already in 1850 comprised more than half of the city's population—lived in ramshackle buildings situated next to slaughterhouses and factories in unsanitary Bridgeport.[32] More fortunate workers—usually native-born, or of Scandinavian or German descent—resided in simple cottages, sometimes with an adjacent garden or barn. Meanwhile, a small elite, composed almost entirely of native-born families from New England and the mid-Atlantic, congregated in several elegant preserves.[33] Some settled in the sparsely populated district north of the Chicago River along Pine Street (now North Michigan Avenue), where their homes sat on large plots of land, enclosed by picturesque picket fences.[34] Others lived just south of the central business district along Michigan and Wabash Avenues, where eminent architects designed luxurious dwellings that sold in the 1850s for tens of thousands of dollars. Still others preferred the bucolic surroundings of the West Side's Union Park, which was only a two-mile carriage ride from downtown and yet a world away from the congested intersection of State and Madison.[35]

The city's leading citizens soon decorated these exclusive neighborhoods with magnificent cathedrals. North of the river, the denizens of St. James Episcopal brought their brief flirtation with austerity to a decisive end in 1857, upgrading to a stone sanctuary that—excluding lot and tower—cost $60,000.[36] Out in Union Park, the First Congregational Church met in frame buildings from 1852 to 1855, when it moved into a new, $40,000 home, hewn out of Illinois marble. The most dramatic transformations were closer to the city center. First Presbyterian remained in its original (1834) frame building until 1849, when the members invested $28,000 to fashion an impressive brick structure at Clark and Washington Streets. Just a few short years later encroaching commercial development prompted many within the church to move further south and First Presbyterian followed along.[37] In 1857 the church dedicated a highly ornamented, marble structure, finished in the Norman architectural style, on Wabash Avenue, between Van Buren and Congress. It cost $115,000.[38] The church's younger sister, Second Presbyterian, started out in 1842 in a "plain frame edifice" on Randolph Street, constructed for $1,000. Less than a decade later, it spent $90,000 on a building at Wabash and Washington that seemed to some "the most imposing and inviting church edifice in the city."[39] Figures 1.2 and 1.3 underscore just how stark the contrast was.

SECOND PRESBYTERIAN CHURCH—RANDOLPH STREET NEAR CLARK.

FIGURE 1.2 Second Presbyterian's Original Building
Credit: The Newberry Library.

THE SPOTTED CHURCH.

NORTHEAST CORNER WABASH AVENUE AND WASHINGTON STREET.

FIGURE 1.3 Second Presbyterian's Second Building
Credit: The Newberry Library.

Even as they commissioned these elegant buildings, the vestries and boards of elite churches secured eminent divines to preside within them by offering salaries of which the average workingman could only dream. Second Presbyterian's founding pastor, Robert W. Patterson, started out making $600 a year in 1842. This represented a handsome wage in those lean years—more than triple the earnings of the average canal worker—but was not so impressive in wider perspective: before the 1837 panic, the average bricklayer had taken in more than $900 a year.[40] In the ensuing thirty years, however, relative equality gave way to eye-opening disparity. By the time Patterson retired in 1873, he was collecting $5,000 annually, while the bricklayers were embroiled in a fight for $4.00/day, which—assuming impeccable health and a six-day week—worked out to $1,252 a year.[41] The trend was the same in leading churches across the city. Upon opening its doors in 1851, First Congregational could only afford to pay its minister $800 a year. As a result, it failed to secure a permanent pastor until 1854, when the board finally upped its offer to $1,500/year. In 1867 the church lured the Reverend Edward P. Goodwin away from First Congregational in Columbus, Ohio, with what was undoubtedly a far more lucrative package. By 1874, Goodwin was drawing a salary of $5,000, plus the use of the parsonage.[42]

During these same mid-century decades, Chicago's Catholic leaders went to great lengths to keep pace with their Protestant counterparts. To be sure, there was no comparable market for priests' salaries, which were fixed by the bishop, and the diocese struggled at first to muster the funds for adequate buildings. As late as 1844, when St. Mary's—still the only Catholic parish in the city—finally upgraded to a sturdier home, the need for frugality remained pressing: while the structure included a few decorative touches, it cost only $4,000.[43] But in the two decades that followed, the hierarchy summoned vast capital from donors around the nation and the world in order to finance an impressive construction spree.[44] In 1846 St. Patrick's began serving the city's West Side out of a ramshackle $750 building on Desplaines between Randolph and Washington Streets. In 1856 it moved just more than a block north into "one of the finest church edifices in the city," a Romanesque cathedral outfitted with stained glass windows, an elegantly frescoed interior, and seating for 1,200.[45] Starting in 1849, the near north side's Irish flocked to the Church of the Holy Name, which met in two different temporary buildings until 1854, when it dedicated a $100,000, Gothic cathedral made of Milwaukee brick with a steeple rising 245 feet into the sky.[46] Chicago's first Jesuit parish enjoyed a similar rags-to-riches story. From 1857 to 1860 the Church of the Holy Family met in a large frame chapel on 11th Street, which is depicted in figure 1.4. At that point the congregation moved into the building pictured in figure 1.5: a stunning $130,000 cathedral a block further south on 12th Street (now Roosevelt Road).[47] In 1856 Bishop Anthony O'Regan went so far as to splurge on a sparkling new residence at the corner of Madison Street and Michigan Avenue. The *Tribune* immediately identified "the Bishop's Palace"—a four-story stone building, constructed for $25,000—as "the most princely private residence in the city."[48]

All in all, the transformation was dramatic. Working people had once been accustomed to seeing their minister as a social equal. Now they learned of preachers commanding salaries ten times that of the average wage earner.[49] Ordinary believers had once worshiped in simple buildings, where they gathered with others wearing the same plain, albeit dignified, garb. Now they looked on as elegant carriages deposited ladies and gentlemen clad in finery at the doorstep of gilded cathedrals. To step inside, meanwhile, was to walk into a world structured by social distinctions. Many churches in nineteenth-century Chicago determined the order of pew selection at an annual auction.[50] The highest bidder won his choice of seats, followed by the next highest, and on down. The proud holder of each pew paid, in addition, a set rent: the better the seat, the higher the premium.[51] In Protestant circles, the most prominent pews often fetched an extravagant price (in 1865, one of the seats in Henry Ward Beecher's New York City church went for a grand total of $520).[52] Seats in Catholic parishes were usually more affordable, though the sanctuary remained a stratified space, as the late nineteenth-century diagram of Holy Family featured in figure 1.6 makes clear.

There were occasional grumbles about this state of affairs. In an 1857 letter to the *Tribune*, for example, a Catholic layman by the name of John Floyd lambasted Bishop O'Regan and his newly palatial estate. "Such was the dignity and majesty of his person," Floyd complained, "that an ordinary house was entirely insufficient. He looked for a house somewhat adequate, and the result is, that the present building, instead of indicating the residence of an Apostle of Christ, is that of some extravagant Lord who did not know what to do with the public moneys."[53] Two years later, when the Protestant elite supported a drive to shut down the city trains on the Sabbath, some sparks of class consciousness flew. One *Tribune* reader interpreted the proposal as a flagrant encroachment upon working people's opportunities for recreation. In contrast with the poor, he wrote,

TEMPORARY CHURCH, ELEVENTH STREET, NEAR MAY
First used July 12, 1857; burned May 10, 1864

FIGURE 1.4 Holy Family's Original Building
Credit: The Newberry Library.

FIGURE 1.5 Holy Family's Second Building
Credit: The Newberry Library.

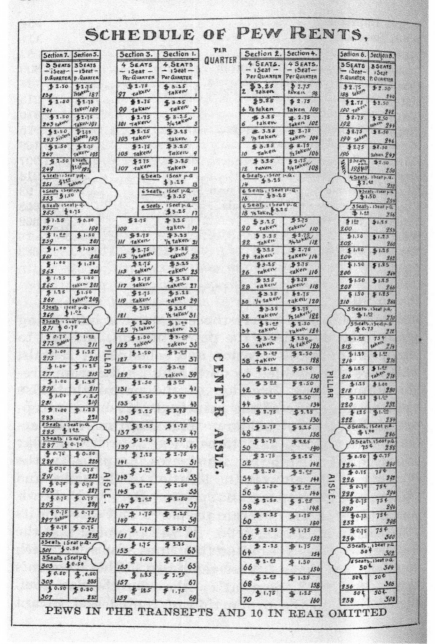

FIGURE 1.6 Schedule of Pew Rents for Holy Family, 1896

Credit: The Newberry Library.

"Salaried clergymen can keep a horse and carriage, or afford the luxury of an occasional bill at the livery stable, and as their pay is principally for Sabbath day services, they can well afford to take their holidays during the week. Capitalists can also take a gala day among the trees and flowers with those they love during the week."[54] But notwithstanding such instances of protest, there was no general outcry on the part of the city's working-class Christians. Their muted response reflected the strength of a free labor consensus, which had, for some time, reinforced the harmonizing legacies of the nineteenth-century revivals.

The Second Great Awakening exerted complicated, even contradictory, effects on relations between social classes. By the 1830s the evangelical churches had spawned an array of voluntary associations whose collective cultural power exceeded that of the federal government.[55] This "Benevolent Empire" championed moral discipline as the linchpin of social reform. Organizations such as the Society for Bettering the Condition and Increasing the Comforts of the Poor taught that poverty sprang from individual—not systemic—defects: thrift and hard work would, over time, remedy even the most stubborn of cases. Thus, even as revolutions in transportation and communication accelerated the demise of an older, agricultural patriarchy, evangelicalism supplied the sinews of a new, interiorized social order. Many working people who experienced new life in Christ came to see industriousness as a vital expression of godliness. Their ethic resonated with the Whig program for economic development, which was based on a belief that if individuals seized the chance, they could become self-directing entrepreneurs. The new ethic also promised to reward diligent workers with the comforts of modern life. For those believers who held, with the Whigs, that America was a land of limitless social mobility, the notion of class seemed a relic of the feudal past.[56] From one angle of vision, freedom in Christ fit naturally with the freedom of markets.

But if awakened religion could militate against class consciousness, countless thousands nevertheless discovered in the crosscurrents of evangelicalism and republicanism a powerful critique of the emerging market order.[57] In early national New York City, the artisan-preacher with an egalitarian message was a common sight. Few were better known than Johnny Edwards, a Welsh master scalemaker, who would park his scale-beam wagon in the most crowded boulevards and preach against, among other things, the sinful divide between the city's rich and poor.[58] In Jacksonian Baltimore, it was evangelical craftsmen who spearheaded the rise of the local labor movement. Journeymen coopers cited the Book of Isaiah in support of their cause, striking hatters drew on biblical rhetoric to critique their employers' greed, and church-going laymen occupied prominent positions in most trade associations.[59] Parallel developments could be found across antebellum America, in villages such as Fitchburg, Massachusetts, and boomtowns such as Rochester, New York, as well as in newly industrialized suburbs.[60] In 1830s Manayunk, just outside of Philadelphia, a Baptist and Presbyterian revival disrupted the textile industry when new converts galvanized a movement against the bosses.[61]

The tensions present within evangelicalism existed also among antebellum Catholics. Consider, for example, the experience of Irish canal diggers. Canal operators often cultivated partnerships with priests in the hope that they would keep rough-hewn workers in line. Sometimes the strategy worked. With unrest mounting along the Gallopes Canal near Williamsburg, Ontario, in 1845, Father James Clarke assured management, "any assistance in my power to preserve order among the labourers is at your service." The day after Clarke rebuked the strikers, they were back at work and "perfectly peaceable." Yet other diggers flocked to priests who denounced companies' oft-inhumane labor practices. In 1849 Father John McDermott implored the trustees of the Wabash and Erie Canal to take action when a contractor fled the line without paying the men. His letter relayed that they had been left in a "wretched and miserable condition . . . without food, without raiment, without shelter, without those common necessaries, the absence of which will press heavily upon them during this cold and inclement season," and went on to urge the trustees "to see that [the men] will be treated with kindness and I will add from myself, with justice."[62]

In early 1850s Chicago, the *Western Tablet*, an archdiocesan paper marketed to the Irish, played a similar, watchdog role. It amplified the voices of workers like Patrick Staunton and Patrick Roe, who wrote in March 1853 that a contractor for the Wisconsin and Chicago Railroad Company had summarily dismissed them without even proper compensation for work already performed. "We deem it a sacred duty to publish the particulars," the two relayed, "that fellow-workmen may not be deceived and victimized by the specious promises of callous hearted and self contractors." The editors added this comment: "Amid such a state of affairs, patience ceases to be a virtue, and silence becomes a crime. It is the duty of the press to expose the system, and bring down punishment on the offenders."[63]

Thus Christian faith—a growing force in everyday life—did not translate inexorably into a single posture toward the nation's industrializing economy. The gospel's implications for the evolving market order remained contested, though in most parts of the antebellum north these battles were not especially fierce. By the 1850s many northern believers had embraced a free labor ideology that mediated between the liberal capitalist and artisan republican extremes. It maintained the Whig faith in personal responsibility, progress, and social mobility, but nurtured alongside it a suspicion of disproportionate wealth and a respect for the dignity of labor, broadly defined to include all producers.[64] Those who embraced this *Weltanschauung* earnestly believed that hard work would ultimately yield economic independence, even in the face of increasingly stubborn facts: by 1860, nearly 60% of American laborers worked for someone else.[65] Significantly, though, the dynamic northern economy did offer many wage workers a rising standard of living, a consolation that temporarily bolstered the attractions of the free labor paradigm.[66] So long as ordinary believers entertained dreams of personal advancement, they would not protest ecclesial excess.

Throughout these years, Chicago's working people enjoyed mostly cordial relations with the churches. This was evident at the annual festivals of the Chicago Typographical Union (CTU), held each January 17th, on the anniversary of Benjamin Franklin's birth. Like a number of the unions founded in the 1850s, the CTU in its earliest years embraced a conciliatory approach to class relations, welcoming everyone from proprietors to journeymen into its ranks.[67] Craftsmen of all different statures were present at the 1855 feast, when then-president Francis A. Belfoy delivered a speech that showcased the interpenetration of Christianity and artisan culture. "The primordial principle of the Press, sprung from the very soul of the Divinity Himself," he declared. Noting that "[God] did not disdain to designate His own Humanity by the title of 'The Word made Flesh,'" Belfoy went on to describe the press's mandate: "Being sent of God, it must account to God, and to His principles of eternal Truth for all the actions of its life. But the mission of all teachers being to improve, to regulate, to return again the lost wanderers in the paths of life; to prepare the world for a nobler and higher state; to so order human society and human endeavor, that they shall aim at perfection in all their efforts at advancement." In fulfilling this grand purpose, Belfoy concluded, "[the press] not only unites man to man by the ties of common brotherhood; but it also unites man to God by the links of the chain of truth which it is ever so busily engaged in reform-ing." By this point it was clear that Belfoy's gospel contained no hard, class-driven edges. If anything, its upbeat, post-millennial emphasis underscored that the faith of respectable antebellum workers was not so different from that propounded at the grandest cathedrals on any given Sunday morning.[68]

The resonance was even more apparent at the CTU's 1861 banquet. As some two hundred ladies and gentlemen gathered to celebrate the benefits of free labor, the news from around the nation was grim. In the preceding weeks the sectional crisis had boiled over into outright secession. South Carolina, Mississippi, Florida, and Alabama had already withdrawn from the Union and seven other Southern states were not far behind. The Civil War that commenced with the firing of shots at Fort Sumter later that spring would have significant implications for Chicago and its working people, but this cold January night inside the Briggs House, one of the city's most elegant hotels, a festive mood prevailed.

Just before 9 o'clock the Great Western Band struck up a tune that signaled the arrival of the dinner hour. When all had found their way from the parlors to the dining room the Reverend Henry Cox—seated at the head table, just to the left of Union president Alfred M. Talley—rose to bless the meal. The 39-year-old Englishman was the pastor of Wabash Avenue Methodist Church, whose congregation boasted some of Chicago's leading men, including John V. Farwell, leading partner of Marshall Field in the dry goods business, and Orrington Lunt, one of the trustees of the fledgling Northwestern University.[69] His church possessed also one of the city's most breathtaking buildings, a gleaming, early gothic struc-ture, completed at the corner of Wabash Avenue and Harrison Street in 1857 for $61,000.[70] But however impressive the structure, it hamstrung the congregation with debt and made it impossible for Wabash Avenue Methodist to afford the salaries proffered by many churches with similarly extravagant sanctuaries. As a result, though Cox served at the pleasure of the rich, he was not one of them. He estimated the value of his personal estate at only $1,000 in 1860, well below the national mean of $2,580 for free white men and paltry in comparison with Farwell's $60,000.[71] Cox was considerably poorer even than many members of the Typographical Union, whose membership included, for example, *Tribune* publisher William Bross, worth $15,000. The reverend's salary, somewhere in the neighborhood of $600 a year, was more comparable to that of journeymen compositors who earned roughly $1.67 a day.[72]

Following Cox's prayer, the feast commenced. Eventually, President Talley called the room back to order and read fraternal greetings from printers across the northeast:

From Baltimore: "Chicago and Baltimore—May they be united in the cause of truth and justice, and ever hold out the beacon light to our weary fellow craftsmen";

From Washington D.C.: "Union of States, and the Union of Printers, Let the people stick to the one, and the craft stand up to the other, and liberal institutions and well organized labor will rule the world";

From Boston: "The Prairie State—To her gallant chieftain the Union now holds as the greatest succor in time of need."[73]

Next came the toasts. "[To] The Occasion we Celebrate—The remembrance of our Patron Saint and the love feast of the craft," went the first. Glasses clinked and the band broke into "Hail to the Chief," as Andrew Cameron, a 29-year-old Scot employed at Wilbur Storey's *Times*, rose to deliver the response. The printers went on to applaud the National Typographical Union, the federal government, the press, and Chicago. At their invitation, the Reverend Cox even toasted "the ladies." Eventually the speeches wound down and the dancing began. The next day's *Tribune* observed, "The closing scene . . . was that of a brilliantly lit hall, where very many good looking couples were joining in what Mr. Swiveller might call 'the mazy,' with very much of an air of oblivion as to the passage of the hours."[74] Amidst all the revelry in that crowded ballroom, one imagines it might have been easy—as in times past—to mistake the good reverend for just another one of the men: laborers all, and all worthy of their hire.

"Undefiled Christianity"

THE RISE OF A WORKING-CLASS SOCIAL GOSPEL

ON 6 JULY 1867, some ninety miles west of Chicago in the railroad town of Amboy, a company of Illinois Central men broke into the home of the Reverend Daniel J. Holmes. The 36-year-old minister, who had moved to the area the previous year at the call of the local Methodist church, was away for the evening at a camp meeting in neighboring Dixon. He was shocked to discover, upon his return, the parlor rug ripped from the floor, the sofa and chairs gone. He was even more shocked to find in their place an elegant new carpet, a set of oiled walnut furniture, a marble-top table, and a mirror, collectively valued at $260—just less than what the average workingman earned in a year.[1] The intruders had also left behind a note, which read, "We regret . . . that our friends are so few; but feel gratified in being able to prove by this, that among the few, we esteem you the highest." It went on, "your action in the matter has proved that you are among those, who, regardless of the opinions of mankind, practice what they preach."[2] "The matter" to which they referred: the battle over the eight-hour day, which had consumed all of Illinois throughout the spring of 1867.

The fight, centered in Chicago, had been brewing since at least 1865, when the General Trades Assembly and its flagship newspaper, the *Workingman's Advocate*, inaugurated a campaign for shorter hours. By commissioning smaller task forces known as Eight-Hour Leagues to raise awareness at the grassroots, the movement saw its candidates for city council to victory in five of sixteen wards.[3] Then, in the early months of 1867, organizers seemed to achieve the crucial breakthrough, coaxing the Illinois legislature into passing the nation's first statewide eight-hour law.[4] But the bill included many loopholes and as countless employers vowed to circumvent it, it became clear that the fight was far from over.[5] On May 1st, the day the new law went into effect, workers around the state went on parade, unfurling banners emblazoned with the emblems of their trade and waving signs inscribed with slogans like, "In God we trust" and "We abide by the law." In Chicago, the procession wound its way to the lakeshore, just north of what is now Roosevelt Road, where a throng beheld speeches in both German and English, including one by Republican Mayor John B. Rice, who urged the crowd to proceed with "reason, calmness, and conciliation," while adding, "I will stand by you as long as I can," to deafening applause.[6] The cheers gave way to grim resolve the next day, as, faced with persistent recalcitrance on the part of major employers, workers across Illinois declared a general strike.

Out in Amboy, the Reverend Holmes had already made clear where he stood on the question. At a mass meeting of Illinois Central employees on 24 April, he avowed, "That part called the shirt tail, is as good as that part called the collar."[7] The following week an assembly of local eight-hour men stopped deliberating about their next move long enough to tender him a sincere "vote of thanks."[8] But Holmes was far from done. Once the strike commenced, he delivered a series of memorable speeches, suffused with biblical rhetoric, in defense of the "honest and industrious laboring men of America." "[The aristocrats] must have a fall," he insisted, picking up on the theme of Mary's song (Luke 1:52). The *Chicago Tribune*—once a bulwark of the fight against slavery—had "like Judas betrayed his master for thirty pieces of silver."[9] Over the course of this campaign Holmes, who was not a rich man himself, but whose church was home to some of the wealthier employers in town, won the affection of a wide range of local workers.[10] These included native-born craftsmen such as William French, a carpenter, and Swain Hughes, a grocer; Canadian transplants like William Rigby, a machinist, and Abijah Brown, a farm laborer; and even Irish Catholics such as Patrick Corcoran, a boilermaker.[11] The reverend's labor-friendly gospel had ecumenical appeal.

While the *Republican*, affiliated with that party's radical wing, carried regular updates on Holmes's campaign to Chicago, the churches there produced no such champion. Leading ministers eyed the whole affair skeptically, with some characterizing the eight-hour campaign as noble and yet quixotic. "That is Utopia—this is Chicago," harrumphed the Reverend Daniel M. Graham, editor of the Freewill Baptists' *Christian Freeman*.[12]

Others countered the movement's moral claims, construing the Illinois law as unjust because it impinged upon a man's right to run his business as he saw fit. "Special legislation which operates even indirectly with such a result, is simply oppressive," the Baptist *Christian Times and Witness* warned.[13] However much Protestant pundits differed on the details, they agreed on this: the notion that labor's interests diverged from those of capital was "utterly false."[14] Mayor Rice's affirmation of this idea at the lakeshore rally provoked a flash of anger from the Methodist divine Arthur Edwards, editor of the *Northwestern Christian Advocate.* "Is the mayor a demagogue, an ignoramus, or intentionally an incendiary orator? No sentiment or invective can be more productive of revolt," he fumed.[15]

Capital would win this particular day. Lax discipline and faltering morale undercut everywhere the strike's effectiveness. In Chicago, orderly protest quickly devolved into general mayhem, as roving bands of unskilled laborers stormed the streets, crude weapons in hand, forcing proprietors to shutter businesses and workers to desert posts. When organizers' calls for an immediate end to the marauding were to no avail, it became clear that the movement was in disarray. By mid-May, when the police finally subdued the last of the rioters, workers' hopes for a shorter day were effectively dashed.[16] But even as Chicago's workingmen retreated for the time being on the eight-hour question, they trained their sights on the turncoats in their midst: the leaders of the city's churches.

In the years preceding the Civil War, Chicago's elite churches had decisively forsaken simplicity. Boards and vestries had begun spending unprecedented dollars on towering cathedrals and top-dollar ministers, untroubled by how closely the internal life of the city's Christian communities was coming to mirror the growing inequalities without. But through the end of the antebellum era, a common faith in the dignity and destiny of free labor united the city's rich and poor Christians, who did not yet understand themselves to be, respectively, upper- and working-class.

That consensus dissolved abruptly in the earliest postbellum years, as the clergy's failure to rally behind the eight-hour movement in 1867 inaugurated an era of intensifying class conflict within the city's churches. Workingmen had counted on the fact that their ministers would support their cause, as the Reverend Holmes did in Amboy. When they encountered instead ardent opposition, the lens through which they viewed the religious establishment shifted. While leading clergymen—still desirous of the common man's affections—continued to laud the dignity of labor, many ordinary believers now dismissed such statements as empty platitudes. As they walked by majestic sanctuaries and heard tell of ministers' princely salaries, they gritted their teeth: these standbys of the antebellum era seemed, suddenly, clear signs of the churches' obsequious relationship to the city's most elite.

In the months and years following the failed general strike, labor went on the offensive against the brand of Christianity propounded in many of Chicago's churches. The battle was not between Christianity and secularism, but rather between competing interpretations of the Christian gospel. Leading trade unionists insisted that wealthy churches' willingness to abide the emerging industrial system exposed them as apostates. In the process of calling for a return to the true religion of Christ, working people would create the city's earliest social gospel. Indeed, it would be up to them, it seemed, to see that "undefiled Christianity" did not drown in Gilded Age excess.

By the time of the Civil War, the traces of Chicago's frontier past were gone. The city had become, seemingly overnight, one of the nation's five largest, growing at a rate that had few precedents in human history. In 1840 Chicago counted just over 4,000 persons, while in 1870 it boasted nearly 300,000.[17] With this explosive growth came new cachet. The Republican Party chose Chicago as the site of its 1860 convention and the Democrats followed suit in 1864. Just two weeks after Abraham Lincoln's first general election victory, he returned to the city. Though inundated with meetings, the president-elect found time to worship with William B. Ogden, Gurdon Hubbard, and their patrician friends at St. James Episcopal.[18] That church's elegance remained conspicuous. Despite skyrocketing municipal expenditures, the city's makeshift infrastructure could not keep up with the needs of its booming population.[19] While in 1850–51 local authorities allocated only $3,700 for maintaining the sewage system, they sunk $1,204,100 into it in 1869–70. This investment had been sorely needed, for as late as 1866 the system served only one-eighth of the city.[20] Water was another perennial problem. While Chicago abuts one of the world's largest freshwater lakes, residents endured, in the words of one, "brackish, fishy, glutinous, dirty, odoriferous fluid," until the completion of a pipeline two miles beneath the bottom of the lake in 1867. Even then, most still relied on water drawn from backyard wells.[21] The reach of public transportation expanded dramatically in these same years, though the system's extensive dependence on horses—which were susceptible to theft, disease, and unpredictable mood swings, and produced piles upon piles of foul-smelling waste, known better in the vernacular as "road apples"—proved a source of considerable unpleasantness.[22] Like other "shock" cities of the age, Chicago was not for the faint of heart.[23]

But what the city lacked in beauty it increasingly made up for in economic might. The Civil War only hastened the pace of Chicago's development into an industrial juggernaut. In the first year of hostilities alone, the city's grain exports increased by more than 60%, from thirty-one million to fifty million bushels. An accompanying wave of speculation more than doubled the membership of the Board of Trade, from 665 to 1,462 persons.[24] The meatpacking sector's fortunes also soared. In the early 1850s, Chicago had packed just 20,000 hogs a year, a number that paled in comparison to the 334,000 packed by Cincinnati. But the thickening web of rail lines that connected the city to the rest of the nation—not to mention to Union soldiers fighting at Fort Donelson, Vicksburg, and far-flung other battlegrounds—threw the game to the city's meatpackers, who rapidly overtook their competitors in older, river-based cities.[25] Chicago became the nation's official Porkopolis in 1862, celebrated the opening of the Union Stockyards in 1865, and never looked back: by the early 1870s it was slaughtering more than a million hogs each year.[26]

The means of this astounding production were concentrated, notably, in the hands of an ever-dwindling few. By 1870 just three meatpacking firms—owned by Philip Armour, Gustavus Swift, and Nelson Morris—employed the lion's share of the industry's 2,119 local employees, a ratio that reflected wider trends. As Chicago transitioned from a commercial to manufacturing center, ascendant corporations in a variety of industries gobbled up smaller companies, resulting in a significant increase in the average number of workers employed by any given firm. In the 1860s alone, the percentage of Chicago workers employed by large firms (those with more than twenty-six in their employ) rose from 54% to 75%.[27] Taking full advantage of the surplus help generated by an internationally consolidating labor market, industrialists in many cases paid meager wages.[28] Meanwhile, they reconfigured the division of labor, breaking skilled positions into multiple unskilled ones, and thereby further eroded workers' bargaining position.[29]

Developments such as these derailed countless wage earners' hopes of economic independence and, consequently, destabilized the prevailing free labor consensus. The early years of the war only compounded matters, introducing skyrocketing inflation—the cost of clothing increased 80% and rent 66%—and a labor shortage to boot, as more than one-third of Chicago's workforce (some 15,000 men) was pulled into the fight.[30] It was hardly a coincidence that, in the city and across the nation, working people began to organize at a more rapid clip. While some local tradesmen had founded unions and *vereins* in the 1850s, these remained small and fragmented through the mid-1860s, when, in one four-year stretch, nineteen new multiethnic unions emerged on the scene.[31] The year 1864 witnessed two particularly momentous developments. When the *Times* and *Tribune* took a stand against the Typographical Union, a Scottish printer by the name of Andrew Cameron (see figure 2.1) seized the opportunity to found an opposition paper, the *Workingman's Advocate,* "devoted exclusively to the interests of the producing classes."[32] The *Advocate* soon became the voice of the General Trades Assembly, a fledgling conglomerate of unions, which by 1865 represented some 8,500 wage earners (roughly 28% of the total).[33] For the first time in Chicago's history, labor might be described, without exaggeration, as a movement.

While this initial organizing push bespoke deteriorating relations between workingmen and their employers, there were few signs as yet of

FIGURE 2.1 Andrew Cameron
Credit: Chicago History Museum, ICHi-69615.

a comparable downturn in wage earners' relation to the churches. With the eight-hour campaign in full tilt during the days leading up to the 1866 municipal election, the Trades Assembly set aside an evening to host a lecture by the Reverend William H. Ryder. Ryder boasted an honorary Master of Arts from Harvard and was then serving as the minister at St. Paul's Universalist, whose impressive building sat just north of First Presbyterian on the most fashionable stretch of Wabash Avenue. But there was not a trace of condescension in the esteemed doctor's speech, which he devoted to the "dignity of labor." Ryder began by heralding "organizations like the present . . . as the product of Christian civilization" and built on this winning line by finding countless ways to restate his main theme. He lionized "the mechanic," who had "formed so large a part of the Union armies"; exalted the "industry and thrift of the common people," in which "the strength and hope of the people lies"; and insisted that "all the great enterprises of their day have their roots in the masses, not the few." The delegates to the Trades Assembly could not have helped but exit Smith & Nixon Hall with more than the usual pride in their step.[34]

Many returned the following month, still basking in the glow of the eight-hour campaign's recent electoral gains, to hear the Reverend Robert Collyer of Unity Unitarian, the Assembly's latest distinguished guest. Collyer had come to Chicago in 1859 to take charge of First Unitarian's benevolence work. He set about the position with conspicuous verve, writing a letter to the *Tribune* shortly after his arrival to spread the word about his ministry and also to advertise the services of a disabled Dutch painter desperate for work. He concluded that missive, "Other cases are waiting to be noticed. Boys of sixteen who come eagerly to seek work; men who will be worth anything to the right man, but either do not know how to find him or have lost hope. I am their Pastor, they are members of *my* church."[35] It was not merely Collyer's advocacy but also his fraternal manner that won him friends among the city's working people. The moment he accepted the position as First Unitarian's "minister at large" he moved unquestionably into the professional class; his $1,200 starting salary made him, in his own words, "well to do."[36] But when news of the exceptionally bloody Battle of Shiloh hit the city, Collyer was among those who rushed to Tennessee to nurse the wounded. Throughout the Civil War, moreover, he advocated tirelessly for more relief funds to be funneled to ordinary soldiers and their families.[37]

Collyer's regard for workingmen sprung, he was quick to point out, from his own experience of having been one. He began his lecture to the

Trades Assembly on 10 May 1866 in this vein, declaring, "I am in the most literal sense a workingman myself." He proceeded to give an account of his twenty-two years as a blacksmith and bi-vocational minister: "for ten years I preached once every Sunday, often twice, and my pay for preaching averaged seventy-five cents a year, or seven dollars and a half for the whole job."[38] Collyer did not mention that, between his salary from Unity and assorted publishing and speaking ventures, he now earned roughly $5,000 a year; but the men of the Trades Assembly, who must have had an inkling, did not seem to mind.[39] The Painters Union had announced in advance that it would attend the lecture as a body and the *Workingman's Advocate* had urged other organizations to follow its "noble example."[40] Those who made it to the lecture heard Collyer articulate the best hopes of the once-regnant free labor ideology: that, through thrift and hard work, workingmen would gain their economic independence. Although he disparaged strikes as "the most risky and unprofitable thing," he nonetheless enjoined the audience to "unite wherever and whenever it is possible, in such a way as to be your own employers, your own storekeepers, and to do whatever others do for you now."[41] The message resonated with the Trades Assembly's members, who promptly tendered the good reverend a vote of thanks.[42]

Labor may have been on especially good terms with liberal divines like Ryder and Collyer, but its relationship to the religious mainstream remained cordial enough in the years before the 1867 general strike. To be sure, as the eight-hour movement gained steam, a growing consciousness of class was changing the way some workers interpreted the religious landscape. The 25 August 1866 edition of the *Workingman's Advocate* included this lament:

> The plain buildings in the wilderness where our forefathers listened to the words of truth have long since passed away, and in their stead have sprung up magnificent edifices with marble and granite fronts, on aristocratic avenues, where fashionable women have private boxes and rival each other in displaying the latest styles. . . . Members of boards of swindle, sometimes called boards of trade, flourish there. . . . How are thy temples fallen, O, King of Israel![43]

But if workers harbored such criticism in their hearts, they only rarely expressed it; and they could sometimes cheer the sentiments emanating from even the most fashionable pulpits.[44] On the morning of Sunday,

25 February 1867, the Reverend Robert M. Hatfield stood beneath the spandrel arches and ornamental pendants that decorated Wabash Avenue Methodist Church's majestic ceiling and condemned the pursuit of undue wealth.[45] Expounding upon the parable of the rich fool who meets an early demise in Luke's gospel, Hatfield observed that "the earth worm was blind and deaf to all" and argued moreover that "he should have used the money to relieve the poor, feed the hungry, clothe the naked, and thus lay up treasures in Heaven."[46] Meanwhile, at the regal First Baptist Church the Reverend William W. Everts went so far as to mount an argument in favor of the eight-hour day, reasoning that workingmen had invented a number of time-saving technologies and were entitled to reap the benefits of them.[47]

But the long-harmonious relationship between the churches and labor quickly soured in the wake of the failed 1867 general strike. At the height of the action Chicago's workingmen could read in the pages of the *Republican* telegrams from Amboy, where the Reverend Holmes was at the center of the scrum, arguing, as they very much believed, that the eight-hour movement had the Bible on its side.[48] Meanwhile, closer to home they watched as their ministers lined up behind their bosses. It was a betrayal that working people would not soon forget, though if they could have peered into the future, they might have seen the Protestant elite's reaction to this episode as mild. While in the years to come leading ministers would respond to industrial upheavals with violent calls for blood, there was no such rhetoric deployed in the spring of 1867.[49] It required no prescience to see that leading ministers were, moreover, eager to forgive labor's purported transgressions. Just two weeks passed before the *Northwestern Christian Advocate*'s Arthur Edwards, who had been among the divines most riled by the strike, urged employers and employees to come together once more "in the spirit of conciliation."[50]

While the clergy's comparatively restrained, even forgiving, posture fell far short of workers' hopes, it made clear that in immediate postbellum Chicago the churches were concerned about more than just pleasing their benefactors in the industrial elite. Leading ministers enjoyed strong ties to "capital," which predisposed them to oppose any eight-hour bill—let alone, strike—which would restrict an employer's right to run his business as he saw fit. But these same ties bound them, somewhat paradoxically, also to "labor," if by that one means the organized fraction of the overall wage-earning population. The native-born comprised just over 50% of Chicago's population in the immediate postbellum years, and yet predominated within both the uppermost economic echelon—those 10% of families that controlled 80% of the total wealth—and the Trades Assembly.[51] Indeed, as much as the latter purported to speak for the average working man, it represented mainly skilled, Anglophone workers, who as a group constituted only 18% of the local workforce.[52]

These "labor aristocrats" had more than nativity in common with the city's upper classes, as the example of Andrew C. Cameron—founding editor of the *Workingman's Advocate*—makes clear.[53] Cameron emigrated from Scotland in 1851, at the age of 15, and worked his way up through the printing trade. He served as an apprentice for a local penny paper and then as a printer for the *Chicago Times*, before going on in 1865 to establish the *Advocate*.[54] Throughout his life he remained firmly within the orbit of respectable society. He served two terms as president of the Illinois St. Andrew's Society and was a faithful member of the Caledonian Society, the Old-Time Printers Association, and the Chicago Press Club as well. His politics were firmly rooted in a recognizable brand of free-labor republicanism. He rejected all forms of state-centered socialism and moreover denounced force as a means to achieve labor's ends.[55] As the architect of the local eight-hour movement, he was also the lead signer of the "Appeal to Workingmen"—published in all the major daily papers on 6 May 1867—that enjoined those in the streets to end the reign of "mob violence."[56] While Cameron and leading businessmen disagreed vehemently on the appropriate length of the workday, they concurred on the legitimate bounds of politics. In the earlier 1860s, numerous men of Cameron's ilk had served in the Union army, putting their lives on the line to save the republic. Maintaining their allegiance was, for the churches, which had long fashioned themselves the cornerstone of the nation, imperative.

Consequently, in the earliest phase of Chicago's unfolding industrial conflict, leading churches occupied an uncomfortable middle ground. Intent on keeping both industrialists and workers in the fold, some leading ministers practiced a kind of rhetorical acrobatics. Consider the Reverend Everts's sermon on "Labor and Christianity," delivered within the confines of the First Baptist Church's $175,000 building the autumn following the collapse of the eight-hour movement.[57] Everts, who had previously gone on record in favor of the shortened workday, began this discourse in a similarly encouraging vein, underscoring Jesus's humble origins—"His father was a carpenter and He worked in his shop. He mingled with the lowly, and gave them many kindnesses, and comforted them in their need"— and then proceeding to ask, "Was there no meaning in this?" From his vantage the ramifications seemed clear: "if [the Church] draws her hand from the good work [of welcoming the poor]," he avowed, "she loses her right to the title of the true Church." Everts then brought this moral to bear upon the mounting strife between employers and employed, making the striking claim, the *Republican* reported, "[that] if he had to choose between labor and capital, he dare not go against labor, for Christ himself would have gone with it." Yet such clear overtures to working people now came paired with derogatory comments about labor reform. Everts observed at one point, "one of the bad signs of the late movement for making 8 hours a day's work was, that the saloon keepers were all in favor of it"; and declared at another, "[that] Trades Unions [were] productive of evil. From them had sprung murder, arson, and drunkenness, and all kinds of debauchery."[58] The wealthiest members of Everts's congregation—men like James E. Tyler, noted banker and real estate maven—could rest assured that his "choice" of labor would not interfere with their bottom line.[59]

Still seething from the spring, eight-hour men resented such attempts to play both sides. In the following week's edition of the *Workingman's Advocate*, Cameron took Everts to task, contending, "When [he] asserts that Trades' Unions are, or have been 'the parent of murder, debauchery, and drunkenness,' we may be excused for informing him that he uses an expression *altogether unwarranted by facts*." The column went on to articulate a critique of the religious establishment that was more thoroughgoing than anything Chicago's working people had yet mustered. "The Church has too frequently ranged itself on the side of the oppressor," Cameron wrote. "In all reforms, in which labor and capital have been directly interested, the Church has thrown its influence in behalf of the money changers." Just beneath the surface of his indignation lay bitter disappointment that the city's clergy had failed to rally behind the movement. Indeed, Cameron was incredulous "that a Christian gentleman occupying Dr. Evarts' [sic] position would gratuitously insult the workingmen of this city" precisely because "one of the best eight hour discourses we ever listened to we heard from the doctor's own lips."[60]

Such feelings of betrayal were fundamentally altering the way many working people viewed the churches, as was evident in the pages of the *Workingman's Advocate* throughout the autumn of 1867. The ink had barely dried on Cameron's retort to Everts when he read, in the newly founded Congregationalist *Advance*, a scathing indictment of labor reformers like himself. "For several years past preconcerted and systematic effort have been made by demagogues and so-called friends of American mechanics and laboring men, to cause them to be dissatisfied and discontented with the position to which the Supreme Ruler of all has assigned them in this world," wrote the editor, the Reverend William W. Patton, who had just completed a ten-year stint as minister at Chicago's First Congregational Church.[61] Cameron was incensed. Lambasting Patton in the *Advocate* two days later, he related, "We have some respect for the highwayman, who revealing his true character, demands 'Your money or your life'; we have none for the individual who, presuming on the sanctity of his office, prostitutes the function of a minster of the gospel to . . . sustain a villainy against which the vengeance of heaven is assured." In Cameron's view, the problem was much bigger than Patton. "It is this superlative cant and truckling to mammon which has brought the modern church into disrepute, and caused the working classes to look upon its teachings with suspicion and distrust," he generalized.[62] His anger would not subside easily. Over the course of the ensuing month, he penned a total of four responses to Patton, which collectively shed much light on labor's emerging critique of the churches.

Central to Cameron's response was his conviction that leading churches had perverted the true message of Christianity. "[Patton's] sentiments, sentiments too which are promulgated in nine-tenths of our sanctuaries, are repugnant alike to the teachings of Christ and the enlightened spirit of the age," he avowed.[63] Construing Patton's "great chain of being" account of poverty as both inadequate and immoral, Cameron asserted his own producerist alternative, "Poverty exists because those who sow do not reap; because the toiler does not receive a just and equitable proportion of the wealth which he produces." If it was clear to Cameron that Patton's view did not hold water, it was nevertheless also clear why Patton held it: the churches proffered no critique of industrial capitalism because they depended so heavily upon the generosity of industrial capitalists.[64] Cameron insisted at one point, "[Poverty exists] because the Church, through the paid toadies of employers, has denounced every attempt on the part of the working classes to assert their rights and remove the curse which has bound them hand and foot, and has prostituted the high and holy calling of a minister of Christ to the level of a village pettifogger."[65] In a similar vein elsewhere, he declared, "The connection between the Church and the existence of the evils complained of is simply this: Two-thirds of the establishments who employ women at wages which drive them to prostitution, are members of our churches, and while our political parsons are filling the role of pettifoggers, they dare not, and do not show the hypocracy [*sic*] of these whitened sepulchers."[66]

While such salvos reflected profound disenchantment with the present state of the churches, Cameron was quick to clarify that his grievances were not with Christianity itself, writing, "In what we have said we refer only to the *perversion* of the truth by those who profess to be its authorized expounders."[67] He longed for the reform of the church and for the advance of true religion. In fact, he announced, "we believe as sincerely as Dr. Patton does, that upon the spread of the gospel depends the perpetuation of the American republic."[68] It was not too late for the churches to redeem themselves, Cameron suggested, though any such redemption would require an about-face on the part of the ecclesiastical elite. "If ministers, instead of being the slick-spittles and apologists of wrongdoers . . . would emulate the example of the master they profess to serve, and denounce sin in high places; know no distinction between the mechanic and the millionaire, would preach the simple story of the cross . . . the evangelization of the world [would soon be] accomplished," he declared.[69] He appended to this advice a warning: "when [the ministers of the gospel] espouse the cause of mammon and oppression and attempt to sustain their apostasy by the words of divine inspiration, we shall denounce and expose them on all occasions, with what ever little energy God has endowed us."[70]

Cameron stayed true to his word and, in so doing, carried on a much wider and longer working-class fight to preserve "true" Christianity in the industrializing world. Growing up in the Scottish border town of Berwick-upon-Tweed, he may well have heard his parents and neighbors discussing Chartism's challenge to the established Church. Galvanized by masses of ordinary women and men, the Chartist movement is best known for its role in pressing for political and economic reform in 1830s and 1840s Britain. But it was also a religious insurgency, which protested the religious establishment's ties to wealth and power in a variety of ways. Chartists showed up early to Sunday morning worship services and occupied rented pews, refusing to rise when their proper owners arrived. They also made a habit, on such occasions, of submitting in advance scriptures on which they hoped the presiding reverend would preach. When one divine opted instead to cite the words of St. Paul, "I have learned, in whatever station of life, therewith to be content," the Chartists in the sanctuary cried out, "You get $200 a year—Come and weave bombazines."[71] The movement sponsored camp meetings, founded churches, and even produced its own hymns, one of which declared, "God himself is on our side."[72] That religious authorities disputed this point came as no surprise to the Chartists. As one of the movement's countless lay preachers, Abram Duncan, a quill dresser by trade, declared at Aberdeen: "The Tories are all religious men. They talk much about religion. They want more new churches and more stupid blockheads for ministers and each person for telling the truth is to have a bond in exchequer. The Tory parsons are our modern Pharisees; they make long prayers; they pray at the corner of the streets but devour widows' houses."[73] When Cameron was a young boy nearly every town in Scotland boasted a Chartist church, some of which enjoyed strong ties to the very printing trade from which his family derived its livelihood.[74]

He emerged out of that milieu with a profound sense of Christianity's leveling possibilities and went on to become one of the foremost proponents of an egalitarian, pro-labor gospel in his generation. To be sure, Cameron's views reflected his times. The language through which he understood and with which he expressed his support for greater equality was thoroughly gendered, as underscored by the very title of his newspaper. Cameron was a firm believer in the ideas and ideals of the artisan republican tradition, which grew directly out of the experiences and hopes of skilled male workers in the generations immediately following the American Revolution.[75] Yet, in the context of the post–Civil War years, when countless unions explicitly excluded women, Cameron might be considered something of a progressive on such matters. At the 1868 convention of the National Labor Union, which he helped to found, the delegates urged female workers to "join our labor unions or form protective unions of their own, and use every other honorable means to persuade or force employers [to] do justice to women by paying them equal wages for equal work."[76] Cameron sounded similar notes in the *Workingman's Advocate*, contending, "Workingmen *and workingwomen* are justly entitled to enough of the funds of their labor to enable them to live comfortably" (emphasis added).[77] He even went so far at one point as to argue that his male readers' masculinity was contingent upon their willingness to enter into solidarity with their female counterparts, declaring, "Every claim of honor, every dictate of true manhood insists that in the future [workingmen] shall throw aside the selfish apathy or petty jealousy which has heretofore characterized their treatment of workingwomen—and make the grievances of which they complain, their own."[78]

The name of Cameron's paper would have also had an implicitly racial resonance for countless nineteenth-century Americans. If the artisan republican tradition was deeply gendered, it was also thoroughly bound up with white supremacy; and just as women found themselves barred from many a union, so too did African Americans.[79] In Civil War era Chicago, tensions between white and black workers had flared into outright hostilities on a number of occasions.[80] Consequently, those who cracked the pages of the *Workingman's Advocate* may have been surprised by what they found: namely, that its editor was a major proponent of treating African Americans as co-equals in the labor movement. Even while the National Labor Union as a whole was slower to warm to black workers than it had been to female, its leadership—including Cameron as well as his collaborators Richard Trevellick and William Sylvis, who were major figures in their own right—was intent upon organizing them.[81] Cameron stated his views on the issue in no uncertain terms and in language that seemed in places to be almost ripped from the New Testament, writing, "What is wanted, then, is for every union to inculcate the grand, ennobling idea that the interests of labor are one; that there should be no distinction of race or nationality; no classification or Jew and/or Gentile, Christian or Infidel; that there is but one dividing line—that which separates mankind into two great classes, the class that labors and the class that live by others labor."[82] Notably, Cameron's relatively open perspective did not extend so far as to permit the inclusion of Chinese workers into the polity. He published a series of troubling pieces, often titled simply "The Chinese Problem," which amplified the concerns of labor leaders across the country, who almost to a man deplored the fact that "the Mongolian hordes" had come to these shores.[83]

While the *Workingman's Advocate* was based out of Chicago, it quickly grew into one of the nation's premier labor organs even as Cameron developed into "the greatest labor editor of his time."[84] Throughout the late 1860s and 1870s, he used this expansive platform to ferociously criticize the churches' entanglement with bankers, industrialists, and the like. Never one to shy away from brash generalization, he wrote in one issue, "It is a startling fact that the modern pulpit has arrayed itself on the side of the oppressor; has almost invariably defended the aggressions of the monied power; and used its high and holy mission to pervert the ways of the Lord"; and in another, "the ignorance of the religious press, in dealing with the Labor Movement, is only equaled by its mamonized servility."[85]

Nor did he refrain from lampooning leading churchmen. When a Catholic bishop in Montreal refused to permit a deceased printer a Christian burial on the grounds that he was a member of the Typographical Union, Cameron labeled him an "ecclesiastical bigot."[86] Meanwhile, in the wake of one prominent New York minister's announcement that he opposed the eight-hour movement, Cameron roasted him as "a gemmen who preaches Christ crucified to the Wall street gamblers and Madison Avenue belles, for $10,000 per annum."[87]

Closer to home, even labor's one-time friend, the Reverend Collyer, did not escape censure. Back in 1865, when Collyer lectured before the Trades Assembly, purporting to be a workingman himself, his congregation's plain building had bolstered his credibility. Constructed in 1859 for a mere $4,000, it was something of an embarrassment in elite circles: "a rude, uncouth wooden structure . . . one of the barest specimens of ecclesiastical architecture in the city."[88] But Unity Unitarian did not lag behind its fashionable sister churches for long. In 1869, the congregation—comprised, in Collyer's own words, "of men and women of education; editors, lawyers, etc."—sunk $210,000 into a spectacular new temple at Dearborn Ave. and Whitney St. (now Walton St.) that better reflected its leading position in Chicago's liberal religious circles.[89] Meanwhile, Collyer's own income by that point, roughly $8,000, illustrated the jaw-dropping, still-widening disparity between the most in-demand divines' salaries and the earnings of the average minister, which remained comparable to those of the city's workingmen.[90]

Having observed the former blacksmith's ascent into the upper echelons of society with growing dismay, Cameron finally lashed out in 1873, responding to a letter Collyer wrote the *Tribune* that called for the abolition of the minister's half-fare discount on railroad tickets. Aware that many on the lower end of the ecclesiastical pay scale deeply appreciated this benefit, Cameron declared, "Now this would come with a better grace from an impecunious colporteur who is really benefited by this system; who lives, or rather tries to live, on $400 per annum, and support a wife and three or four children on that amount, than from a metropolitan clergyman receiving $5,000 or $8,000 per annum, who gets two or three months holidays from his ardent admirers."[91] His prose exuding a depth of disappointment and resentment that comes only with familiarity, he concluded, "Robert, the wheel of fortune is a fickle wheel, and you should have been one of the last men to have made the suggestion. Fifteen years ago you would not have done so."[92]

Cameron was hardly alone in his conviction that the city's elite churches were forsaking ordinary people and, in the process, Christ himself. This belief resonated with the many thousands who read his paper and with countless more beyond, including any number of working women. They had, in many cases, even greater cause for resentment: whatever her opinions on trade unionism, a woman who worked often endured censure within religious circles on that basis alone. In the most fashionable Protestant churches she risked being totally shunned. One *Tribune* correspondent recounted how, on the way to church one Sunday morning, she ended up in the same public car as a prominent Protestant minister and a female milliner who had once crafted her bonnets. She reported that the latter "modestly, and with no apparent temper, informed me that she had always attended that pastor's church, had rented a pew there several years, had communed there, but had never spoken to the Reverend gentleman or any of his people." The author of the letter went on, "I glanced across at the minister as she finished. He sat with his brow drawn into a pious frown, and his lips tightly closed. 'Thinking of his sermon,' said a dimpled girl on my right. 'More likely on real estate,' retorted a dark-browed woman on her left." Such cynicism was earned the hard way. Indeed, the writer insisted, "This is not a solitary instance; there are thousands of them in every woman's experience, if they would only tell them."[93]

A number of women could not help but vent their frustrations when, in 1874, several leading ministers panned a proposal for a women's industrial home and training facility. The Reverend Collyer's exhortation for more native-born "girls" to instead join their immigrant sisters in the kitchen proved particularly galling, and he soon found himself back at the center of a firestorm.[94] One woman wrote sardonically to the *Tribune*, "Not much wonder that those who have paid their annual dues to hear Brother Collyer preach the simplicity, and charity, and love of the religion of Christ, have no particular desire to blacken themselves against the pots and kettles of his kitchen."[95] Another, who described herself as a "homeless working girl" and signed her name Miranda Meane, drove to the heart of the matter. "We did not imagine such were the feelings of Christian ministers (especially those marching under the banner of *liberal* Christianity) towards our class," she declared, "while claiming, as they do, to represent the teachings and principles of Jesus of Nazareth. We could but feel that we were indeed outcasts; that all we had been taught in childhood, about the Savior choosing the meek and lowly for his companions and followers, was but an idle fable; that Heaven was but for the rich; that its massive gates would open only to those coming in their fine coaches, with liveried attendants."[96] While as a woman Meane confronted distinctive challenges, she and Andrew Cameron nevertheless drew upon a similar theological well. Both envisioned Jesus as the ordinary person's champion, and it was this conviction that steeled their common critique of churches awash in wealth.

In postbellum Chicago no woman articulated this critique so publicly and so frequently as Maria Darker Wynkoop. Like Cameron, she grew up in Great Britain during the heyday of the Chartist movement. She was born in 1827 in the village of Quorndon (now Quorn), England, where she and her siblings were all baptized into the Church of England. The Darkers had long roots in Leicestershire and were a respectable, land-owning family, though not members of the local aristocracy. Maria's father, John Darker, was a farmer and brewer; in their early years her sister, Elizabeth, was a dressmaker and her brother, John, a butcher. Maria worked as a school-mistress until, in 1851, the family immigrated to the United States, where they eventually settled in Dixon, Illinois, just over a hundred miles west of Chicago. There she married an American-born carpenter and Civil War veteran by the name of Legrand Wynkoop, who was active in both local civic and religious institutions. Throughout their early married years, they participated in the life of the local Methodist Church, but by 1870 they relocated to the West Side of Chicago.[97]

Upon arriving there, Mrs. M. D. Wynkoop, as she signed her name, soon became known as a forceful advocate for the city's working people. Within a handful of years, she had turned the family home at 1003 W. Lake Street into the headquarters for a fledgling organization known as the Advocates of Justice. For an apparently brief period of time, this intentionally inclusive group brought together women and men who sought to reform an economic system that seemed increasingly stacked against producers.[98] Some of their myriad goals included: "to resist the oppressions of centralized capital"; "to overthrow the credit system"; "to settle all disputes as much as possible by arbitration"; "to provide for the education of the ignorant"; and "to form Co-operative societies wherever and whenever practicable, for buying, selling, manufacturing."[99] When a *Tribune* reporter inquired about the society's more precise mission, Mrs. Wynkoop, its "Grand Matron," informed him matter-of-factly that it was to bring glory to God in the highest and peace to people of good will.[100]

As the comment suggested, a deep Christian faith animated Mrs. Wynkoop's advocacy. Hers was not the theology of the churches, however.

In fact, she often rebuked the city's Christian elite in her regular column for the *Tribune*. In one piece she recounted the story of a common "rag man" who had been interested in renting a pew at one of Chicago's more exclusive churches. An usher inquired about the location of his workplace and, when informed that "he had no particular place of business," showed him to a pew in the far rear of the sanctuary. When the rag man indicated that he would like to sit closer to the pulpit, the usher made clear that those seats cost $15 a quarter and added, "Our terms are strictly in advance." The rag man produced the money the very next week but was treated rudely by the church's other members, who looked down upon his rented house and line of work. Mrs. Wynkoop reported, "They went to another church, where they met with a more cordial reception . . . and have since been considered amongst its most valuable members—living consistent Christian lives, and doing good service in the church."[101]

If the moral of that story was clear enough, Mrs. M. D. Wynkoop was in other columns even more direct. In one she declared, "Did the ministers of the Gospel perform their duty and maintain the cause of the struggling poor as did Christ, our beloved country would not be in the condition it is to-day." She went on to say, "the poor do not believe in a Gospel that is only for the rich and from which they are excluded," and moreover to offer this advice to "well-disposed clergymen": "visit the laborer at his home, attend the workingmen's meetings, be on hand among striking mechanics, and learn the true condition of things."[102] Inspired by those words, one of her female readers, signing only her initials, H. G. C., elected to share her thoughts on the theme. "At present the workingman is rather repelled than otherwise by the grand church, the grand people who are there, and the grand rent marked on the empty pew he finds his way into," she related. She had her own ideas about how to remedy the problem. "Ministers [would] have a greater influence for good if they opened wide their doors, saying, 'Come one, come all' . . . And let those that are already there, overlooking all differences in their worldly circumstances, say, by act, and word, and look: 'We be brethren.' "[103]

Many a workingman heartily agreed. That same year one "Worker" wrote to the *Tribune*, "It is a well-known fact that the salaries of our city pastors range from $3,000 to $5,000 per year, and, as I attend church occasionally, I feel compelled to contribute something toward its support, and generally give from $20 to $25 per year." "Notwithstanding this," he went on, "there is a continual begging almost every Sunday . . . and the writer is getting sick of it, and does not feel like taking much stock in a concern where the leader gets from three to six times as much for services as himself." The writer's complaint was not only directed at ministers, nor was it purely financial; it had to do, also, with the more basic matter of respect. Having noted the prevalent "rustling of silks" and "nodding of plumes" in the city's fashionable sanctuaries, he rued, "it is poor consolation for a man with an unfashionable suit to attend church, and be passed coldly by, by the well-to-do in the world, as though they considered it a favor to notice him at all." Yet even still, he held out hope for the restoration of the churches to their original purity. "Let some one designate a church where the poor will be treated as well and made as much of as the rich," he wrote, "and I think it safe to say that that church will be filled to its fullest capacity, with such a rejoicing as has not been seen in a long time."[104]

Cameron, too, kept the faith. While cognizant of widespread associations between working-class protest and infidelity, he persistently denied any necessary link between the two, insisting, "Our fight is not against Christianity, but against those who use it as a cloak to secure their selfish purposes."[105] In fact, until it ceased publication in 1877 the *Workingman's Advocate* radiated what its editor called "undefiled Christianity."[106] Biblical language permeated his editorials, with their freewheeling allusions to the Psalms ("How long O Lord! How long!") and the gospels ("the laborer is worthy of his hire"); and so did biblical themes of neighborly love and divine judgment.[107] In the *Advocate*'s Thanksgiving 1875 edition, for example, he thanked God for the "belief that there is a good, old fashioned, orthodox hell" and then promptly consigned "species resumption knaves and robbers" to it.[108] Cameron did not triumph a particular sect or creed. He eagerly published and praised Catholic supporters of the labor movement, even as his paper carried forward many of the impulses and emphases of the antebellum era's broad evangelical Protestant coalition.[109] Unabashedly biblical, its faith was also deeply activistic, kindling a desire for reform akin to that which once animated crusades against slavery and Indian removal. Cameron viewed the labor movement in a similar light, as an instrument of God's justice in the world, and wrote to this effect, "the Gospel of Christ sustains us in our every demand . . . the volume of Divine inspiration is the rock of truth upon which our 'pretensions' are founded."[110]

Thus, it was that, in the decade immediately following the Civil War, ordinary believers in Chicago fashioned the city's first social gospel. This vein of Christianity—critical of both the industrial order and the churches place within it—had no proponents in leading seminaries or pulpits. It sprung from the experiences of respectable working-class persons, both male and female, and was cultivated and sustained by the same. As deeply social as labor's gospel was, it was not to be confused with the Social Gospel innovated by the likes of the Reverend Washington Gladden. In fact, when Gladden published *Working People and their Employers*, a touchstone of early middle-class social Christianity, in 1876, Cameron tore it apart in the *Workingman's Advocate*, writing, "The author ought to have put the Englishmen's motto in front: 'You keep 'em pious and we'll keep 'em poor.' " Gladden's proposed answer to the labor question—faithful observance of the Golden Rule—was no answer at all, Cameron insisted: "Employers have rebelled against Christ's teachings too often and too persistently to hope for a solution of the trouble in this way." Heralded by some as a tract for the times, the book seemed to him "worthless."[111] The implication was clear: if the churches were to have any hope of keeping working people in the pews, they were going to have to do better.

3

"It Pays to Go to Church"

MINISTERS, "THE MOB," AND THE SCRAMBLE
FOR WORKING-CLASS SOULS

THE REVEREND EDWARD P. GOODWIN, for one, had no patience for labor's grousing. While he had not moved to Chicago until the year following the failed 1867 general strike, he was well aware that some of the city's working people had nursed hard feelings toward the churches ever since. Goodwin could moreover tell that ordinary believers' complaints had unsettled some of his colleagues. It was one thing for a leader of the abstemious Freewill Baptists to denounce churchly extravagance.[1] It was quite another for the Congregationalist *Advance*, edited by Goodwin's long-time predecessor at Chicago's fashionable First Congregational Church, the Reverend William W. Patton, to run an editorial worrying about the exclusivity of wealthy congregations. The column suggested the abolition of pew rents—a staple of nineteenth-century church financing—as a promising way forward. Observing that "the Romanists" had managed to stay on good terms with the city's wage earners, Patton posed the rhetorical question, "Must Protestantism bear the stigma of contradicting the spirit of the gospel by so selling out the house of God as to exclude the poor?" A handful of reforming Chicago ministers had founded "free" churches in the preceding decade and Patton had come to see the sensibility of this novel strategy.[2] He exhorted his readers, "Let us have city churches that will hold from two to three thousand persons, magnificent enough for the rich, but open equally to the poor," adding, "Let the sittings be rent free; at least let the seats be at so cheap a rate that the poorest may be accommodated with eligible places."[3]

By the spring of 1869, Goodwin had grown tired of reading such drivel. Intent on setting both disgruntled workingmen and overly anxious clergy straight, he penned an article of his own for the *Advance*, entitled "The Cost of Churchgoing." In it Goodwin contended, matter-of-factly, "it costs people more habitually to stand away from the churches than habitually to attend them." If the piece seemed at first a relatively straightforward defense of the pew rental system, it was in fact far more. Consider Goodwin's tack. "Why, on the face of the matter," he reasoned, "the very fact that a man has a pew in church and is in it every Sabbath, is one of the prime influences that enters into and shapes his business relations, and directly affects his income. Insensibly to himself he gets character and credit out of it." He elaborated this line of argument with a hypothetical: "Let any two men equally unknown make application to any firm wishing to hire, and who doubts that, other reasons being balanced, if one was certainly known to rent a pew in a church and to be regularly in it, and the other as regularly to stay away, the church goer would get the situation?" Goodwin pressed the case still further. "More than that," he declared, "In nine cases out of ten that single difference in his habits would secure for the church goer a better credit than he could have without it. And with reason. Church going, hearing the gospel, being consistently an observer of the Sabbath, is coupled in the nature of things with temperance, honesty, integrity, economy, thrift." Driving to the heart of the matter, he concluded, "And so it pays to go to church, pays, I mean, in actual dollars and cents."[4]

From the vantage of Goodwin's perch at First Congregational, the connection between church membership and financial success must have seemed self-evident. Founded in 1851, it was one of the oldest religious societies in the West Side's Union Park neighborhood (figure 3.1), which during the mid-century decades had offered well-to-do residents a quiet, exclusive retreat from the bustle and grime of the city center. In the years after the Civil War, many of the area's early settlers still faithfully attended First Congregational, whose governing council could easily have been mistaken for a sub-committee of the Board of Trade.[5] Goodwin himself could attest to the material benefits of associating with such a congregation. His annual salary, somewhere in the vicinity of $5,000, was ten times the amount earned by the average wage earner.[6] But in these postbellum years, the question, increasingly, was whether working people would find the good reverend convincing.

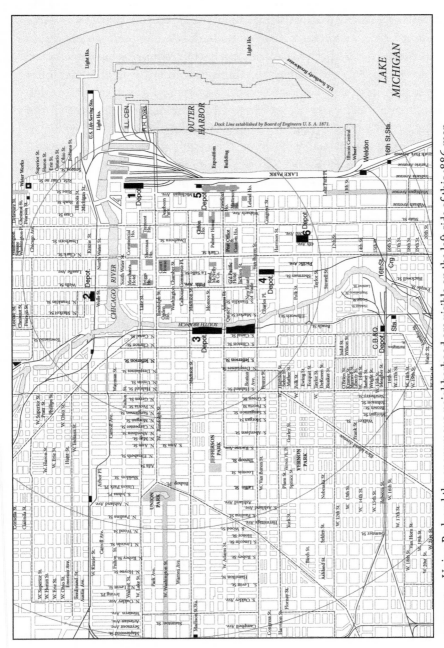

FIGURE 3.1 Union Park and the eponymous neighborhood are visible on the left side of this 1886 map

Credit: Chicago History Museum, ICHi-31337.

Indeed, the Union Park neighborhood was shaping up to be a crucial battleground in the Protestant churches' fight to maintain the allegiance of increasingly restive workers. Throughout the 1870s, this district was—like the larger city—in a state of flux. As industrial development surged across the Chicago River, the area became less bucolic, a process hastened by the Great Fire of 1871, which displaced thousands from the incinerated inner city to the intact West Side. Union Park's class profile diversified considerably during these years, as artisans and mechanics moved into the new cottages that were popping up alongside leading bankers' and merchants' sprawling estates. Notably, however, the neighborhood's ethnic composition remained steady. Even as Chicago's foreign-born population exploded in the 1870s, the district bounded by Ashland Avenue on the west and Halsted Street on the east, Lake Avenue to the north and Jackson Street to the south, remained a bastion of anglophone peoples.[7] As late as 1880, more than 75% of Union Park's residents were native-born; another 15.9% were of British, Canadian, or Irish vintage.[8]

More than just a monoglot enclave in a polyglot city, Union Park was contested religious terrain. It was, in the first place, a major hub of middle- and upper-class evangelicals, who interpreted their own experience as confirmation of the old Whig teaching that prosperity was available to anyone willing to work for it. Far from problematizing their privileged status atop the industrializing economy, their faith explained it. As Goodwin so aptly put it, "it pays to go to church." Yet the neighborhood was also home to an increasing number of respectable working people, whose loyalty the clergy very much coveted. In many cases, they had it. Numerous Union Park laborers still believed that they, too, would soon gain their economic independence and, with it, the fruits of the bourgeois lifestyle enjoyed by their better-off neighbors. No matter their income or occupation, these workers were middle class by aspiration. But some wage earners found themselves increasingly alienated from the institutional churches and the press increasingly reported, in the words of one *Tribune* column, "that [the Protestant laborers—the men and women who work with their hands] rarely attend divine service."[9] Such news had many a local minister on edge. It did not help that still other laborers—including Andrew Cameron and Maria Wynkoop, who lived in close proximity to one another on Union Park's western outskirts—had begun to espouse a working-class social gospel, which decried the emerging industrial system and the churches that underwrote it.[10] What hope was there of Christianizing the foreign masses if the churches could not hold on to their own?

The question took on additional urgency in light of the Protestant elite's eroding position within the larger city. By the early 1870s, Chicago's growing immigrant populations had begun to realize their electoral strength, loosening the long-standing Yankee grip on City Hall. Meanwhile, during these same years a prolonged depression contributed to mounting unrest within the city's increasingly foreign-born workforce.[11] By 1873, much to the clergy's horror, socialists had gained a lasting foothold. As the decade marched on, angry and insecure church leaders closed rank with their friends in the business community.[12] Their strengthening alliance produced vicious results in the summer of 1877, when restive working-class persons took once more to the streets and leading Protestants—who had responded negatively, but mildly, to a similar episode in 1867—now cried for blood. Strikingly, though, even as they spewed venom at "the mob," these same clergymen reiterated their faith in the dignity of "labor," a term now reserved for those workers who most closely resembled themselves. With the city's soul at stake, the churches desperately hoped God's (Anglo-Protestant) people would stick together. There were signs they just might.

"Developments made within the last few days in this city . . . show that communism, that dangerous exotic from the hot-beds of the continental cities of Europe, has taken root in this country," exclaimed the Reverend Justin A. Smith, editor-in-chief of the Baptist *Standard*, on New Year's Day in 1874.[13] That same week a headline in the Methodist *Northwestern Christian Advocate* read "Are We to Have a Commune?", while the Congregationalist *Advance* ran editorials entitled, "Communism—From What It Comes" and "Communism—To What It Leads."[14] A sequence of late December events had inspired the hubbub. On the 21st several thousand workers attended a meeting at Turner Hall near Halsted and Twelfth [now Roosevelt] Streets. The speakers that night called for the city to implement an aggressive new public works program or else provide direct relief to the multitudes left unemployed by a reigning panic. The national economy had been contracting sharply ever since the previous September, when the nation's most powerful banking firm, New York City's Jay Cooke & Co., went under. Chicago fared better than most eastern cities in the months that followed, but suffering was nevertheless rife due to widespread layoffs and wage reductions, as well as draconian cuts in city services.[15] The day after the Turner Hall meeting some ten thousand persons marched in two silent columns from the West Side's Union Park to City Hall. There, outside the makeshift two-story building that the city had thrown up following the 1871 fire, they watched as German attorney Francis A. Hoffman, Jr., presented their petitions to the mayor and city council. Contemporaries were struck by the orderliness of the whole affair. The *Times* observed, "The assembly was not a mob, for it was as quiet as a funeral procession."[16]

Why, then, did Chicago's Protestant leadership react so much more frantically than they had responded to the 1867 general strike? After all, neither the Turner Hall rally nor the march on City Hall involved the kinds of intimidation and violence in the streets that had been hallmarks of that earlier upheaval. The answer to this question lies not in these specific events but rather in the shifting contexts within which they unfolded. Only six years had passed since Cameron's failed eight-hour campaign, but in the meantime Chicago had been remade.

This was in no small part due to what happened more than 4,000 miles away, in Paris, in the spring of 1871. In late March of that year working people briefly seized control of the city, capitalizing on the central government's weakness as a result of the Franco-Prussian War, which had turned out disastrously for France, the aggressor. On the strength of the National Guard, a citizens' militia several hundred thousand strong, disgruntled proletarians exiled the head of the provisional government, Adolphe Thiers, as well as the duly-elected National Assembly, to Versailles. In its place they elected a 92-member Common Council, comprised largely of skilled workers, which became the governing authority of the newly established Paris Commune. In the euphoria of the moment, Karl Marx heralded these developments as the beginning of a much grander revolution, but it was not to be: by the end of May, the ousted Thiers government had regained control of the city.

However ephemeral its reign, the Commune left a deep imprint on the consciousness of an aroused western elite, which in places as far away as Chicago was transfixed by mounting fears of proletarian uprising. Throughout the spring of 1871, Americans devoured the daily papers' lurid reports on the situation in Paris.[17] In Chicago these stories, like one in the *Chicago Tribune*, which detailed how "the reckless and unprincipled mob, arms in hand, rule the streets," irrevocably altered the way leading citizens imagined their own city.[18] Socialism and communism, once foreign exotics, seemed now to pose an immediate threat. In fact, when the Great Chicago Fire incinerated a wide swath of the city some four months after the Commune's demise, one swirling explanation of the catastrophe blamed it on an exiled-Communard-turned-arsonist.[19] Such paranoia had yet to subside more than two years later: it helps to explain why Chicago's Protestant leaders so vigorously decried the 1873 demonstration, which in their view advanced "Communistic principles." More than one warned that if such disorder went unchecked, Chicago would soon be like "Paris, with its streets running with blood."[20]

Such sensational comparisons evinced the sway of conspiratorial thinking, though beneath layers of hysteria there lay a kernel of truth: socialism had indeed gained a lasting foothold in Chicago. A small but vocal cadre of foreign-born radicals led the charge. Among the most influential of these was Carl Klings. He arrived in Chicago in 1869 and quickly ascended through the ranks of the German-speaking labor movement, which was even then in the process of breaking away from Cameron and other Anglo reformers. Klings served as the editor of the German Trades Assembly's weekly paper, *Der Deutsche Arbeiter,* until both suddenly collapsed in 1870. At that point he partnered with other German socialists to found the Sozial-Politischer Arbeiterverein, which promptly affiliated with Marx's First International.[21] It was these "internationals," as they would come to be known, who had organized the 1873 rally and demonstration. In the days following, they, predictably, came under intense Protestant fire. The religious press accused Hoffman and his co-collaborators of having been "schooled in the fauborgs of Paris," and insistently cast them in the role of "designing demagogues" who were needlessly stirring up the people.[22]

Yet in truth the political and economic problems for the city's industrialists ran much deeper than the presence of a band of determined socialists. In the November 1873 municipal election, the balance of power had shifted decisively away from the city's Anglo-Protestant elite, as the upstart People's Party gained control of both the mayor's office and the Common Council. The defeated incumbent, Lester L. Bond, had been mayor for only three months, having assumed the office when a battle-weary Joseph Medill suddenly resigned. Medill, the longtime editor of the *Chicago Tribune,* had stormed to victory in the immediate wake of the 1871 fire on a promise to outlaw wood construction within the city limits. But from the very beginning he found himself embroiled in conflict with the foreign-born. Medill's "Union-Fireproof" ticket alienated many immigrant homeowners, who could not afford brick or stone construction and feared that new restrictions would thus prevent them from rebuilding. In the months after the election a popular uprising, galvanized and financed by German boss Anton Hesing, managed to stymie the new mayor's fireproofing agenda. Medill struck back in kind, however, choosing to enforce a long-neglected Sunday-closing law, which targeted the saloons and beer halls so much beloved by the city's Germans and Irish. Outraged, they banded together under the new umbrella of the People's Party, once more underwritten largely by Hesing. Its surprising triumph in the 1873 election showcased the growing power of Chicago's vast ethnic communities, and signaled the arrival of a new day in a city long controlled by Yankees.[23]

Leading Protestants glowered in defeat. The *Standard*'s Reverend Smith remarked, "The result of the city election on Tuesday of last week was to throw the entire control of the municipal government into the hands of the vicious elements of society."[24] In fact, the People's Party had won largely on the strength of middle-class immigrants, entrepreneurs and shopkeepers who treasured the freedom to drink a beer on Sundays but had little interest in radical social upheaval. Protestants who interpreted this group's ascendance as a new nadir for Chicago soon faced other setbacks. Just a few weeks later the internationals and their impoverished base—some of whom *were* radicals—began banging on the door of City Hall. Flush with anger and resentment, Protestants lashed out at the foreign-born, who seemed everywhere emboldened. The *Standard* insinuated that the Turner Hall rally had no place in the United States, noting, "all the addresses were in a foreign tongue; the voice of an American, using the language of the country, was not heard."[25] In the wake of the next day's demonstration, meanwhile, both the *Northwestern Christian Advocate* and the *Advance* scorned, in the latter's words, "[the] multitude of skeptical foreigners from the Continent, who are as easily duped and led by godless agitators and demagogues, as are the Papal Irish by their priests, or by Democratic politicians."[26] Trying times had once more awakened nativist demons.

But Chicago's Anglo-Protestants were nowhere near as beleaguered as their resort to name-calling made it seem. To be sure, they had suffered an electoral setback. Yet they retained a number of civic strongholds, including the Chicago Relief and Aid Society (RAS), which in the winter of 1873 proved more strategically important than City Hall. A private organization, wholly unaccountable to the electorate, the Society had nevertheless overseen the administration of public relief funds ever since the Great Fire. Consequently, when Hoffman presented Mayor Harvey Colvin and the Common Council with petitions for immediate aid to the unemployed, they urged him to apply instead to the RAS. The suggestion had merit. While the city was swimming in over $2,000,000 of debt, the Society boasted more than $600,000 in undistributed donations in its coffers. Showing genuine enthusiasm for the idea, the Council went on to pass a resolution calling for the RAS to "distribute the funds in their hands liberally," even as Mayor Colvin agreed to set up a summit with the organization's board of directors.[27]

The meeting proved bitterly disappointing. On 26 December, the mayor, a delegation of aldermen, the RAS's executive committee, and representatives from the Workingmen's Committee convened downtown. Following introductions, Hoffman entreated the RAS to turn its substantial reserves over to the city government for redistribution to the poor, or else to reconstitute its board of directors to reflect the ethnic composition of the city.[28] The organization resolutely declined to do either, a decision that was no surprise. As it stood, the RAS's twenty-two member board was not a diverse group. All were white men, and all but two were leading attorneys, entrepreneurs, or industrialists. In addition, twenty were Protestant and fully fifteen attended one of four churches: Second Presbyterian, Fourth Presbyterian, St. James Episcopal, and the Church of the Messiah, all of which ranked among the most exclusive in the city.[29] These were men who had limited interaction with the masses and who were moreover steeped in the doctrines of scientific charity, which distinguished sharply between the "worthy" and "unworthy" poor.[30] Thus, in asking for the Society to dole out aid irrespective of a person's lifestyle, Hoffman and his fellows had not only made an unreasonable request; they had affronted the board's moral sensibilities.

Chicago's Protestant elite fully sympathized. The religious press was indignant on the RAS's behalf, underscoring the close ties between the organization and the churches. The *Northwestern Christian Advocate* declared defensively, for example, that the Society was "controlled by a board of strong, honest unpaid men."[31] Protestant pundits moreover parroted the claims of the RAS's executive committee, denying the existence of "extreme destitution or suffering" and insisting "not a single worthy applicant is turned away."[32] "Worthy" was, of course, the crucial word. What poverty did exist they attributed to the travesties of idleness and drink. The *Standard*'s Smith wrote, "We have fifteen millions of dollars, ten millions at least, of which are expended by these anti-temperance working men for intoxicating liquors."[33] But the demonstrators' petitions were more than unfounded, Protestants insisted. They were dangerous, threatening, and communistic: "in violation of our theory of government."[34] This latter conviction stemmed in part from Protestant anxieties about the shifting politics and demographics of Chicago's working classes, as described above; but it sprung also from Protestants' deep misgivings about the actual substance of the demonstrators' demands. While the internationals believed that the plight of the unemployed generated a moral imperative for the RAS to liberalize its distribution policies, the churches inhabited an ethical universe in which the reverse seemed true.

Indeed, to aid the unworthy poor was to commit an act of rankest injustice, as the Reverend David Swing—one of the nation's most famous modernist preachers—wrote in an illuminating editorial. However liberal his theological views, Swing remained throughout his life an arch-conservative on labor issues. As the illustrious pastor of Fourth Presbyterian, he was well acquainted with many members of the RAS's board; and in a 3 January contribution to the *Alliance*, a new publication under his editorial direction, he came rushing to their defense. Rejecting one of the demonstrators' central assumptions—that poverty was often the product of circumstances beyond an individual's control—Swing crafted an impassioned defense of Whig economics. He declared,

> The reason the man who raves about the relief fund is not in as easy circumstances as, for example, George Armour, is because he did not come here thirty years ago, and heave trunks at a hotel and invest each ten dollars in a town lot. The reason why Mr. Hoffman's poor man is not as wealthy as Wirt Dexter, is because he did not go to a country school as Dexter did, and then bend down to twenty years of bondage at the law, studying cases far into the night.

Swing believed that every man had an equal opportunity in the nation's "open, free arena" and that some took better advantage than others. Elaborating the obvious corollary, he explained, "The conflict between class in the cities of our country is not a conflict between labor and capital, but between successful and unsuccessful lives." Because Chicago's poor perennially squandered their God-given time and talents, no amount of undeserved aid would ever produce an egalitarian society. "Instead of bothering the city council, there is a large part of Mr. Hoffman's reform that would be better suggested to the Maker of the Universe direct," he dryly concluded.[35]

However flippantly Swing had intended the comment, it proved on the mark. Certainly the demonstrators could have fared no worse with the Almighty than they did with the RAS. Incensed by the summit, Hoffman and his fellow organizers called for the unemployed to flood the Society with applications. Over the course of the next week thousands waited in line outside RAS headquarters on LaSalle Street, prompting the Society to hire sixty additional staff to conduct the home visits needed to verify the applicants' worthiness. But even with the added help, it proved unable to keep up with the pace of new requests. Rather than ease its standards, the RAS clamped down. On 3 January it declared that all men, regardless of their situation, were henceforth ineligible for assistance. Before the end of that month, meanwhile, it added the further stipulation that all initial requests for aid had to be made in writing, a requirement that proved a significant hardship for the many poor who could not speak—let alone write—English. The more people turned away, of course, the more rigorous the scrutiny of those remaining: it was an outcome perfectly in keeping with the Society's philosophy of relief. And if the new restrictions dovetailed with the board of directors' moral outlook, they had the added benefit of reducing its fundraising responsibilities: the $600,000 of remaining fire donations bankrolled the Society's operations for the next eleven years.[36]

The Protestant elite was not alone in its worries about the ways that Chicago was changing. To be sure, throughout the dispute between the mostly foreign-born workingmen and the RAS, Maria Wynkoop and Andrew Cameron sympathized with the former. "Capitalists," who had "done their best to introduce cheap labor among us," bore the responsibility for the plight of the poor, Mrs. Wynkoop argued in one column.[37] She wrote in another, "Under a government like ours, when a few men amass colossal fortunes in a short time, while the majority have barely enough to support life . . . there is something wrong in that government."[38] Cameron, meanwhile, quickly cast aside the prevailing caricatures of Hoffman and his co-collaborators as demagogues, declaring, "those who have taken hold of this movement are not politicians, but men who love humanity and desire to relieve its impoverished condition."[39]

But many evangelical wage earners saw things differently. One "workingman," the son of a Presbyterian minister, wrote to the *Tribune*, "I protest against the use of the name of American workingmen in connection with this French-named robbery, Communism." He went on, "I believe the Relief and Aid Society amply able and willing to do their whole duty, and totally disbelieve any stories of starvation."[40] Another worker by the name of Jake Flake was amenable to labor reform but not, he declared, "with such leaders as addressed the crowd in the North Side Turner Hall. In no sense have they expressed the views of the honorable and intelligent mechanics." Condemning the likes of Hoffman as "parasites on the body politic," he went easy on capital. In the end, he confessed, "We are all after the almighty dollar."[41]

Even Cameron harbored some reservations about the way things were going. In the years since the 1867 general strike his influence within local labor circles had declined precipitously, as the movement fractured down ethno-cultural lines. The 1869 municipal election cycle proved a pivotal turning point. That year Cameron opted to abandon independent labor politics in favor of the Citizens' Party, which had vowed to root out corruption within the city government; such promises appealed to his reforming sensibilities, but not at all to those of working-class Germans, who saw his decision as a betrayal of workingmen. In the ensuing months many in their number broke off from the Anglo-American-dominated Trades Assembly to form an independent German Trades Assembly, and by 1870 the original organization had withered and died.[42] Relations between the Anglo and foreign-born wings of the labor movement only deteriorated further in 1871, as Cameron endorsed Medill, once more choosing a respectable Yankee reformer over the candidate favored by the city's immigrant populations. If Cameron's shifting political allegiances distanced him from many foreign-born workers, they brought him into closer alignment with the city's Protestant mainstream. For example, when the "wet" People's Party upended Medill's successor in the 1873 election, Cameron—a teetotaler himself—rued the day. Echoing the sentiments of the religious punditocracy, he harrumphed in the *Workingman's Advocate* that the victorious coalition represented a "canker worm . . . gnawing at the city's vitals."[43]

More common ground emerged in response to the formation of a local socialist party. The unsatisfactory outcome of the City Hall demonstration, as well as more thoroughgoing disenchantment with the People's Party, prompted the internationals—led still by Klings—to form the Workingmen's Party of Illinois (WMPI) in January 1874. Its signature issue was a call for state operation of major infrastructure components: railroads, telegraphs, canals, savings banks, and fire insurance companies. By March the Party had made significant inroads into the city's ethnic neighborhoods and even into some English-speaking communities, forcing Cameron to stake out a position. He had first-hand experience with radicalism, having been selected as the National Labor Union's delegate to the Fourth Congress of the International Workingmen's Association in Basle, Switzerland, in the spring of 1869. Cameron returned from that meeting—where he rubbed elbows with the disciples of Karl Marx and the Russian anarchist Mikhail Bakunin—more convinced than ever that, in contrast with Europe, the United States did not require a revolution, but rather "a just administration of the fundamental principles upon which the government is founded."[44] Back in Chicago he joined the Protestant establishment in opposing the WMPI, arguing that its centralizing scheme would erode "the noblest ambition in man, that of independence, and he would become a simple pensioner."[45] But even as Protestants converged across classes, the extent of their alliance remained in flux.

This became eminently clear in the summer of 1874, when yet another major fire reconfigured Chicago's unstable political landscape once more. The 14 July blaze consumed sixty acres south and west of Van Buren Street and Michigan Avenue, and aroused the National Board of Fire Insurance Underwriters to issue an ultimatum: its subsidiaries would suspend all coverage in Chicago unless the city took immediate steps to fireproof itself.[46] Aware of the economic havoc this pull out would entail, the city's property holders—including everyone from Marshall Field to Anton Hesing—united behind a ban on wood construction. The city council, still controlled by the People's Party, which had coalesced in part around opposition to just such a measure, acquiesced, though over the protests of Cameron and the WMPI—more strange bedfellows, brought together by circumstance. But this new legislation was not enough to satisfy wealthy Yankees, already rankled by a year of immigrant rule and now more motivated than ever to protect their interests. Aware that the steady influx of foreign-born posed intractable electoral difficulties, they threw their collective weight behind a new strategy, not dependent on the whims of the people.[47] On 24 July they formed the Citizens' Association of Chicago, designed to represent "the best part of the community," which had been "disenfranchised" by the political ascendance of "the baser part of the community."[48] With an executive board comprised entirely of leading merchants and manufacturers, the Association became the phalanx of the city's consolidating bourgeoisie. The military metaphor fits, for in addition to advocating for the upper classes the upstart organization funded a businessmen's militia, used to intimidate WMPI demonstrators and other radicals. Militarization bred only more of the same, as German socialists went on to found their own militia, the Lehr- und Wehr-Verein, in April 1875; and Bohemian socialists to establish theirs, the Bohemian Rifles.[49] Two years later the deadly consequences of this arms race would be devastatingly realized in Chicago's streets.

Class warfare erupted first in Martinsburg, West Virginia, where on 14 July 1877 the employees of the Baltimore and Ohio Railroad shut down all train service, pending the reversal of the latest wage cut. The nation remained in the clutches of a fierce depression, and the railroad companies had made a habit of balancing their books on the backs of working people, even while continuing to pay dividends to stockholders. No longer willing to abide the trend, workers found themselves confronted by state militias and federal armies. Violence in Martinsburg soon spread to Baltimore, Philadelphia, Reading, and Pittsburgh. In every case the authorities met threats to property with assaults on life, a pattern reproduced also in East St. Louis, Illinois, starting on 21 July. Chicago lay just over three hundred miles away, waiting.[50]

Political power had continued to shift since the founding of the Citizens' Association. In the spring of 1876, with both Anton Hesing and the People's Party embroiled in separate corruption cases, the Republican Party, with the strong support of the Yankee elite, recaptured City Hall. Incoming Mayor Monroe Heath's three-year term would be marked by tumult, due in part to the activities of Chicago's increasingly assertive socialists. The same year that Heath assumed office the WMPI joined forces with the newly established Workingmen's Party of the United States (WPUS). While Klings remained at the vanguard of the local party, which was still heavily German, new leaders had also emerged. With George Schilling, Thomas Morgan, and Albert Parsons—all English-speaking— having joined the cause, socialists sought to attract more native-born workers into their ranks. In mid-July 1877, as they devoured reports of the battles unfolding across the nation, they sensed an opportunity.[51]

The unrest finally came to Chicago on Monday, 23 July. That day, even as local switchmen convened to discuss a possible walkout, the WPUS distributed a notice in working-class neighborhoods that read, in part, "Have You No Rights? No Ambition? No Manhood?" The flyer also announced a mass meeting at Market and Madison Streets later that evening, which ended up drawing more than 10,000 persons. They listened to a number of impassioned speeches, including one by Parsons, a native-born printer and member of the very same Typographical Union local as Andrew Cameron. A Southerner with family roots extending back to the Revolutionary era, Parsons had in the course of his early life developed, remarkably, into an abolitionist with Radical Republican sympathies. In 1873, no longer safe in Texas, he fled for Chicago with his wife, Lucy, who was almost certainly a former slave.[52] Now, standing before a throng that

Parsons strategically dubbed the "Grand Army of Starvation" (the play on Grand Army of the Republic, a fraternal organization populated by northern Civil War veterans, would have been lost on no one), he enjoined them to save the nation from overweening capitalists. Such language was calculated to resonate especially with the many anglophone wage earners who could be found in the crowd that night.

The next day the strike began in earnest, as first railroad workers and then others deserted their posts; soon many of these were roaming the city's industrial districts, seeking to shut down other factories, mills, and shops. In the streets the scene looked much as it had in 1867, when the general strike devolved into acts of intimidation and vandalism. But this time the authorities' response was much harsher. On Wednesday, 25 July, Mayor Heath dispatched local militia and called respectable citizens to arm themselves, even as two regiments of the US army, pulled away from the Indian wars, arrived from the Dakotas. Open-air battles raged, with the bloodiest transpiring the next day, when the police fired repeatedly into a crowd of thousands of workers at the viaduct near Halsted and 16th Streets (Figure 3.2). By Friday, when peace was for the most part restored, at least two hundred and thirty working people lay dead or maimed. The police counted not a single casualty.[53]

Most of those workers who were in the line of fire were Catholic and what little evidence remains suggests that their religious leaders deplored the authorities' violent tactics. Father Edward J. Dunne, whose Irish parish, All Saints, was in the heart of the riot zone, could not move fast enough to keep up with the needs of his people. But in between administering last rites and anointing the wounded, he took time to express his chagrin at Mayor Heath's response.[54] Meanwhile, with bullets still flying, the editor of Chicago's German Catholic paper, *Katholisches Wochenblatt*, took the railroad magnates in his sights, declaring, "If the rail companies want to save money, they ought to begin saving at the top. For what reason do the presidents and directors need such fabulous salaries? Why must the president of most rail companies earn $40,000 to $50,000 in a year, live in a luxurious home, waltzing around in velvet and satin, while the lowly worker is oppressed beyond belief, to the point where he may even take his own life?" If local Catholic leaders were indignant about labor's plight, however, they remained apprehensive about its strategies. In that very same column the editor made a point to say, "We are not friends of strikes, and we don't intend to lessen the atrocities that the strikers so often turn to during their demonstrations."[55] Whatever the hierarchy's

FIGHT BETWEEN THE MILITARY AND THE RIOTERS AT THE HALSTED STREET VIADUCT.

THE GREAT STRIKE—SCENES OF RIOT IN CHICAGO.—From Sketches by C. and A. T. Sears.—[See Page 641.]

FIGURE 3.2 *Harper's Weekly* published this iconic, if somewhat deceptive, depiction of the Battle of the Viaduct. It was not the military but the police who fired into the crowd.

Credit: The Newberry Library.

reservations, its attitude toward the workingmen in the streets appeared downright cordial compared with that of its Protestant counterparts.

On Sunday, 29 July, leading ministers in evangelical bastions such as Union Park positively celebrated the violent suppression of the uprising. At Park Avenue Methodist Church the Reverend Simon McChesney insisted it was not always best to leave vengeance to the Lord, avowing, "When mob-rule threatens the civil power, when the dire necessity is upon us, we must recover the reins of government at all hazards, if it takes artillery to do it."[56] McChesney's language reflected a decisive shift. In 1867 when Cameron and the Trades Assembly orchestrated a general strike, the Protestant elite took exception to their tactics but said nothing about "mob-rule," even when the *Tribune* did. The tumultuous events of the ensuing decade had fostered increasing solidarity within the city's upper classes, however; and in 1877, with socialists and foreign-born workers now leading the charge, Protestants, too, saw a mob in the streets. Thus across the city endorsements of retribution echoed from sanctuary walls: "Trust in God, and keep your powder dry," one minister advised; "they should have been put down at whatever cost," another resolved.[57] Influential Protestants painted fallen workers not as victims but rather as sinners, who had come under divine judgment. As one reverend grimly put it, "The soldiers, the police, the militia, and all the forces were but mediums for the translation of God's will."[58]

The Reverend John M. Caldwell lamented only that more had not died. Indeed, at Ada Street Methodist Church, the 36-year-old minister declared: "One of the worst features of the riot is, it did not cost enough human lives. . . . Something like twenty fell under that first volley; it were better if it had been 200. It would have taught those lawless beings the cost of human lives, that it cost them something to defy the law."[59] Apparently, the congregation reveled in Caldwell's words. The *Times* reported that throughout the sermon, "the people turned to each other with looks of approval; and occasionally a movement of that sort commonly described in brackets by the intelligent reporter as 'sensation,' swayed them."[60] Who were these saints, several hundred in all, who cheered Caldwell's lusty cries for the blood of the "lawless"?

They were not the patricians who flocked to Union Park's most fashionable churches. Nestled between Lake and Fulton Streets, just over a mile west of where the Chicago River divides into north and south branches, Ada Street Methodist was nowhere near as flush as First Congregational. From 1870 to 1873, the congregation managed to pay the Reverend

Thomas R. Strobridge $1,800 a year, a more than respectable salary, but only a quarter as much as his best-paid colleague.[61] Under Strobridge, the church flourished, growing to a membership of 250 persons, with weekly attendance frequently double that number. Caught up perhaps in the promise of these developments, the Board of Trustees began to manage Ada Street as though it had the buying power of its wealthier sister churches, when in fact it did not. By 1874, only a year after the completion of a $100,000 building project and the hiring of a new minister at $3,000 a year, the church was taking out loans just to pay its bills.[62] The Reverend Caldwell entered this deteriorating situation in the autumn of 1875 and proceeded to right the ship: within a year the church's membership, which had dipped all the way to 150, swelled to 300.[63]

Caldwell's rapport with a wide variety of middle-class persons proved the linchpin of Ada Street's resurgence. To be sure, the church boasted a few of the old-time aristocrats who once predominated in Union Park, men like George Drinkwater, a charter member of the Chicago Board of Trade.[64] But most of the congregation was of the middling sort that increasingly gravitated to the neighborhood.[65] Ada Street's members remained overwhelmingly anglophone, with many having been born in the United States and many others having immigrated from England, Canada, Scotland, and the Isle of Man. Nearly half of the church's membership lived in white-collar households. Some, like Ebenezer Jennings, who owned a gentleman's furnishings store, had risen into the upper tiers of the middle classes, but most hailed from the ranks of the petit bourgeoisie, working as clerks, bookkeepers, and the like. The other half worked with their hands. While some of these, like Kate Grant, a 23-year-old domestic servant, were unskilled, the vast majority were artisans and craftsmen: machinists, carpenters, shoemakers, and such.[66] They were, in other words, the very demographic that Cameron sought to reach through the *Workingman's Advocate* and on which socialists like Albert Parsons had set their sights.

The fact that working people comprised such a significant segment of Ada Street's community recasts the scene that Sunday morning, 29 July 1877, in a surprising light. After all, if the newspaper reports are to be believed, it was not merely aristocrats like George Drinkwater and Ebenezer Jennings who applauded Caldwell's macabre rhetoric: "It was quite evident that in all essential points *his congregation* was with him emphatically" (emphasis added). This included James Dickson, a teamster, Anna Quayle, a milliner, and hundreds of others of their stature.[67] Perhaps it was one of these laborers who raised his voice against Caldwell—in what the *Times* called "a slight sibilant demonstration"— but more striking is the fact that no others followed suit.[68] Indeed, the question arises, how was it that so many wage earners became caught up in the "sensation" the reverend's words induced? Why would working people have taken heart in cries for the blood of other working people? The answer lies, in part at least, in the rest of what Caldwell and his Protestant colleagues around the neighborhood had to say on the Sunday following the uprising.

Ministers and pundits alike took great care, for one, to make clear who was and was not included in "the mob." Dickson and Quayle could rest easy, he being from Ohio and she from the Isle of Man. In leading Protestants' view, the anglophone were practically beyond reproach, even if they came from abroad. As the Reverend McChesney pointed out at Park Avenue Methodist, "many of our best citizens have come to us from across the waters." This was a prudent way to preface the remarks that followed, for McChesney's church—located, like Ada Street, just blocks from Union Park—would have been home to many British immigrants.[69] He wanted to communicate that they constituted the exception to his withering generalization, "Europe has been emptying her criminal classes upon our shores."[70] The Reverend Norman F. Ravlin harped on nativity as well. The following Sunday, 5 August, at the Free-Will Baptist Church, which sat at Jackson and Loomis Streets on the southernmost edge of the Union Park neighborhood, he declared, "The mob was composed entirely of foreigners."[71] It was of course true that the foreign-born had predominated in the crowds that initiated the street protests, but Ravlin and his peers were not content to make this factual point. The Protestant elite extrapolated a nativist calculus that moved unreasoningly from foreign birth to a lengthy list of pejorative phrases: "communistic offscourings," "disorderly classes," "dangerous classes," "roughs and thieves," "lowest rabble," and "vicious element," to name a few.[72]

Thus, the foreign-born "mob" bore the brunt of Protestant outrage, though unionized workers—regardless of national origins—came under censure as well. Indeed, it was immediately evident that Protestant opposition to organized labor had hardened in the decade since the 1867 general strike. The Reverend William Gray, editor of the Presbyterian *Interior*, spoke for many when he painted unions as bastions of "unreasonableness, injustice and tyranny."[73] This judgment sprang in part from venerable ideological roots. The Protestant elite retained its faith in the fundamental harmony of capital and labor. At Second Baptist Church, located at the intersection of Monroe and Morgan Streets, just a few blocks southeast of First Congregational, the Reverend Galusha Anderson proclaimed, "these unions are founded on the false assumption that capitalists are the enemies of laborers. The interest of both parties is identical."[74] Increasingly, though, leading Protestants focused on the ways that union tactics impinged upon the freedom of the labor market. Some ministers granted that an individual had the right to strike—to refuse to sell his labor—but all regarded interference with strikebreakers as anathema.[75] The Reverend Anderson resolved, "When these unions stop the work of those who do not wish to join them, they become outrageous tyrannies—they smite down the most fundamental liberties of the people."[76] Free-Will Baptist's Reverend Ravlin heartily agreed. The *Tribune* reported, "[he] denied [trade unions'] right to drive off any man from work who was laboring for the wages which the others had refused to accept. This, he held, threatened the very foundation of our free institutions."[77] But the mob and the unions were not the only such threats abroad in the land.

Significantly, Chicago's Protestant establishment also insisted that the railroad companies were just as menacing to the nation's well-being. The *Interior's* Reverend Gray accused the industry's leadership of being "an irresponsible and tyrannous oligarchy," while at the Holland Presbyterian Church the Reverend Jacob Post exclaimed, "the destructive war of the different railroad corporations is the sole and simple cause of all our trouble."[78] Such criticisms were widespread and bespoke a major shift since 1867, when pulpits and presses had stood unwaveringly behind a corporation's right to act as it pleased. To be sure, not all had entirely abandoned this high view of corporate privilege. At another Union Park church, St. Paul's Reformed Episcopal, the Reverend William J. Hunter opined, "the employer is the best judge of his own ability and resources, and the employe [sic] should go a long way to meet the difficulties of the case."[79] But leading Protestants were no longer willing to write railroad executives a blank check, believing that they had abused their prerogative by trampling upon their employees' dignity. "The grievances urged by the strikers are real and serious," the Reverend Smith acknowledged in the *Standard*, going on to say, "The rights of the employe [sic], in the eager rush of competition, are much too often treated as if they had no existence."[80] The *Northwestern Christian Advocate* concurred, declaring, "The railways have not done justice to the workmen, whatever may be the present condition of the railways' treasury."[81]

When assessing the nation's industrialization as a whole, Protestant ministers saw at the root of the injustice a great evil: monopoly. The major rail lines had, for one, cornered the labor market by colluding to suppress wages. Gray fulminated against this practice in the pages of the *Interior*, writing, "W. H. Vanderbilt, Thomas Scott, Mr. Garrett and a few others, not over eight in all, control, and dictate the terms of the labor of 100,000 men. They meet and agree together—if they were poor men we should say, conspire together—to the effect that the wages of the hundred thousand men shall be reduced ten per cent."[82] Leading Protestants objected to such collusion for the same reason that they rejected union tactics; in Gray's words, it rendered the laborer only "theoretically, not practically [free]."[83]

There was yet another problem with monopoly, namely, that it unduly enriched a few at the expense of the many. At Calvary Tabernacle, located just a mile southwest of Union Park but in a poorer, more heterogeneous section of the West Side, the Reverend Henry M. Paynter pronounced, "The great financial men, the Jay Goulds, Tom Scotts, Vanderbilts, and others were avaricious. They had their millions. They wanted millions more. They ground the face of the poor man in the dust to enrich themselves at his expense. God never intended that any one man should be worth $1,000,000."[84] These words rang with conviction from the mouth of Paynter, paid just $17.57 a week for his labors at the church.[85] But criticisms of excessive wealth were heard also in the more upscale environs of Union Park proper, where divines paid exponentially more than railroad workers railed against industrialists paid exponentially more than them. At Park Avenue Methodist the Reverend McChesney decried those who would "oppress and paralyze whole communities to pour a broader current of wealth within the control of the grasping, absorbing, engulfing, covetous monopolist."[86] Even at regal First Congregational, meanwhile, the esteemed guest preacher, the Reverend William W. Patton, acknowledged, "It is not without a degree of reason that the managers of railroads have been charged with sometimes conducting them in the interest of a few leading stockholders, or of prominent officials with enormous salaries, ranging from $10,000 to $25,000."[87]

Such words must have heartened the proud workers who crowded into Ada Street Methodist and other Union Park churches the Sunday following the railroad riots. Their enthusiastic response to the Reverend Caldwell's words reflected the fact that they, too, resented the railroad bosses' exorbitant salaries, and moreover that they, too, looked askance at the foreign-born "mob." Wage earners like James Dickson and Anna Quayle would have appreciated their minister's assurances that they were not guilty by association. The editor of the Methodist *Northwestern Christian Advocate* insisted, for example, "many of the workingmen protested against injuring or destroying property, and abandoned the procession, but the mob continued its march."[88] But leading Protestants did more than merely exonerate non-unionized, native-born workers.

In strong continuity with the past, ministers also lavished praise upon "labor." At Ada Street Methodist the Reverend Caldwell tapped into the same rhetorical vein that the Reverend Everts had a decade earlier. "Being of a democratic spirit, though I sympathize with both capitalist and laborer, if I had to choose between the two," he confessed, "it would be with the laborer, because the latter are poor."[89] Across Union Park pastors issued similar endorsements. At St. Paul's Reformed Episcopal, the Reverend Hunter proclaimed, "Labor is a divine sacrament, a sacrament of life. The plowman in the fields, the blacksmith at his anvil, the merchant at his store, the lawyer at his brief, the student at his desk, the physician anxious to save a precious life, the minister watching, praying, studying for his people, all these are noble orders of labor."[90] Meanwhile, at Park Avenue Methodist, the Reverend McChesney relayed, "The bible, as I read it, is the friend of the workingman. In every department of human toil, it says, 'The laborer is worthy of his hire.'" McChesney went on to frame the labor question as central to the fate of both the churches and the nation, declaring, "Of the two millions of Methodists in our country, a large portion of them are laboring men. . . . This country cannot afford to fall out with its workingmen. . . . It was our workingmen largely who gave us Gettysburg and the victories of the Wilderness, and a nation redeemed by their blood cannot afford to allow its workingmen to grow restless and discontented, and at length desperate."[91]

Given the stakes, the Protestant elite needed to toe a delicate line. By 1877 it had turned fiercely against the institutions and leadership of Chicago's working classes. Leading Protestants had never cared for unions, even when the likes of Andrew Cameron had been the chief organizers. With the foreign-born now ascendant and socialism on the move, organized labor looked only more and more reprehensible. Yet the city's Protestant establishment still coveted the friendship of "labor," understood more narrowly to describe the Anglo craftsmen and artisans who crowded into neighborhoods like Union Park. The fate of the republic and its churches had long rested upon their sturdy shoulders, and to lose them now to the unions or the socialists would surely spell disaster. The applause at Ada Street Methodist betokened hope that the city's Anglo-Protestant peoples might hang together, even as mounting class conflict threatened to pull them apart. But there were countervailing signs as well.

Union Park's ministers would hardly have been surprised to learn that, in the pages of the *Workingman's Advocate,* Cameron—a known quantity by this point—deplored both the violence against workers during the late riots and the underhanded dealings of the railroad magnates that catalyzed them.[92] Far more disconcerting was a letter published in the *Daily News* several weeks later, which suggested how precarious the Protestant foothold among the ordinary masses had become. The writer began, "I was at the Second Baptist Church prayer meeting last week, and one of the deacons rose and made the remark that he liked to see a young man come to church and drop a nickel in the box and pay for a seat upstairs. Such men were talented young men. Well, I am not a talented young man of that church, but would like to be." He went on to explain, "I am trying to live the life of a Christian, but when I look at my bosses, who are members of the Christian denomination, I shudder and wonder how they can impose upon us poor miserable creatures throughout the week; and Sunday you will see them out with their coachman and fine span of horses, going to church, while thousands like myself are plodding along foot sore and hungry." The writer made clear he was no radical, nor even a trade unionist. "I do not believe in these strikes at all," he declared. But he grew increasingly despondent about his situation. "I have submitted my case to the proprietor personally, asking for a promotion or more wages," he related; "the reply was, 'if you do not want to work for what I am paying you, there are thousands who will.'" The letter closed, "Let some Christian answer this."[93]

FIGURE 4.1 August Spies

Credit: Chicago History Museum, ICHi-30017.

4

"With the Prophets of Old"

WORKING PEOPLE'S CHALLENGE
TO THE GILDED AGE CHURCH

MOMENTS BEFORE BEING led to the scaffold on the morning of 11 November 1887, one of the condemned Haymarket anarchists told the First Methodist Church's Reverend Henry W. Bolton, "Now, I die like Jesus died—at the hands of my murderers."[1] The speaker was almost certainly August Spies (figure 4.1), who had first made this "blasphemous comparison" in an impassioned courtroom speech just before his sentencing in early October 1886.[2] He went on to explain it in considerable detail in a letter to his fiancée, Niña Clarke Van Zandt, later that year. "[You] will probably remember the crucifixion of a young, bright, generous and noble-hearted Jew, by the name of Jesus," Spies wrote, "And in connection with this incident you will likewise remember that a few days prior to his 'legal' murder, he had entered the temple of Jerusalem, which he found occupied by the Board of Trade men of that city." He quoted the passage from Matthew's gospel that recounts how Jesus overturned the money changers' tables and then went on to say, "And when the Jerusalem Board of Trade men saw their 'respectable business' thus exposed by this 'foreign, half-distracted, wild-eyed, ranting agitator,' and when they saw that his words were listened to eagerly by the people, they . . . formed a conspiracy, 'drummed up' some charges against the 'lawless fiend' and—crucified him as a 'convicted felon.'" Spies concluded, "You will readily see the analogy of this and our own case."[3]

Chicago's clergy *did not* see the analogy. In the wake of the anarchists' execution, ministers of nearly every denomination rejoiced in the justice secured by the hangman's noose.[4] The Reverend Bolton took a week to gather his thoughts before joining in the general revelry. Bolton had spent more time with the condemned—Spies, Albert Parsons, Adolph Fischer, and George Engel—than perhaps any of his colleagues, having offered in their final days to be their confessor. While all four turned down his services, they did engage him in conversation, with Spies proving particularly garrulous.[5] By the end of their talk Bolton clearly understood the anarchist's view of Jesus. On the day of the execution the reverend elaborated it for the benefit of the *Tribune*'s readership, "Jesus, [Spies] said, had undertaken to reform the world at that time, and as a result was nailed upon the cross and caused to suffer death. He compared his own case with that of Christ, and said they were both martyrs for the cause of the laboring classes."[6] But however well Bolton comprehended Spies's interpretation, he still utterly rejected it, as he made abundantly clear in a sermon at First Methodist on 20 November. Taking as his text the crucifixion narrative in Luke's gospel, he countered Spies's analogy with one of his own: the executed anarchists were like that hell-bound thief who hung on the cross next to Jesus and relentlessly mocked him in their final hours. Bolton reflected, "They die, unrepentant, recklessly, without hope, and 10,000 will take courage to do their works of violence and die in sin as these men died. But remember, 'he is a fool who saith there is no God.'"[7]

The reverend's antagonism comes as no surprise: historians have long known that the nation's religious authorities opposed radicalism at every turn. What has been less often accounted for is the presence of competing Christianities on the ground. Indeed, far from idiosyncratic, Spies's subversive interpretation of Jesus was common in sundry labor circles. The month following the anarchists' 1886 conviction the *Knights of Labor*—Chicago's most widely circulated newspaper—published a letter from "A Christian Woman," who had recently attended a revival meeting at Farwell Hall and had left dismayed: "The church member of to-day quite forgets in his scramble for wealth and prominence the words of his divine Master, 'Blessed are ye poor, for yours is the kingdom of God.' He (of Chicago) also forgets that those who are lying in the dungeons of the Cook county jail await the same fate that was meted out to the humble carpenter of some 1800 years ago!"[8] The writer went on to invoke a vision of the Kingdom of God, in which "there will be no death penalties for men of honest purposes." "In that day," she insisted, "elders of churches will not say, 'hang them first, and pray for them afterwards. Hell is too good for them;' (the anarchists)."[9] Letter after letter in this same vein poured in to the city's leading labor papers. "[These seven] men have been condemned to die upon the scaffold for exactly the same offense for which Christ died upon the cross," declared one.[10] Another contended that the anarchists' respectable accusers were "as much crazed as were those of eighteen centuries ago, when they cried out 'Away with him! Crucify him! Crucify him!' "[11]

Such correspondence suggests a central fact about Chicago's diverse working-class communities: by the mid-point of the Gilded Age, they had become hotbeds of alternative Christianities. To be sure, many wage earners were faithful churchgoers who eschewed class activism. One particularly pious bricklayer informed the press, "I did not want [to join a union] because I was part of a Christian church, and I considered it wrong according to my conscience to become part of an organization which governed the rights of my fellow men."[12] He was not alone in this conviction. Exasperated by the challenges involved with mobilizing the city's seamstresses, labor activist George Schilling explained, "The difficulty in organizing the girls lies in that most of them are Swedish and very religious and that their employers through the ministers are preventing them from joining labor associations."[13] But even so, what had begun in the 1860s and 1870s as a narrow stream of working-class discontent with the institutional churches widened during the Great Upheaval of the mid-1880s into a churning river. Throughout those turbulent years, trade unionists, radicals, and Knights of Labor all challenged the cozy ties between the city's Christian and industrial elite. Championing more egalitarian readings of the gospel, in which Jesus, a carpenter, stood in judgment over industrial modernity, they sustained and elaborated a growing tradition of working-class social Christianity. For the time being, church leaders would continue to shrug off wage earners' criticisms. But as the chorus of dissent grew louder in the years leading up to the century's end, even the most recalcitrant of divines would be forced to take heed.

By the 1880s, Chicago had become one of the world's leading urban centers. In the two decades between 1870 and 1890 its population jumped from 298,977 to 1,099,850 persons, and by the latter date it had surpassed Philadelphia to become the second largest city in the United States. A series of annexations accelerated this astounding growth. Between 1871 and 1893 the city engulfed a number of smaller, neighboring municipalities, expanding nearly fivefold geographically, from 35 to 185 square miles.[14] But the single most important factor contributing to Chicago's population explosion was a continuous stream of migrants, both from other parts of the Old Northwest and from abroad. This latest wave of immigration included especially large numbers of Germans and Scandinavians, as well as many transplants from the British Isles and a small but growing contingent of Poles, Bohemians, Italians, and others from Eastern and Southern Europe.[15] Notably, the proportion of native- to foreign-born residents rose steadily throughout these years, though many of the former remained only one step removed from their European roots: by 1890, a remarkable 77.9% of the city's people were of foreign parentage.[16]

Newcomers to Chicago vacillated between awe and alarm as they encountered a city that exemplified the best and worst of industrializing society. "An overhanging pall of smoke; streets filled with busy, quick-moving people; a vast aggregation of railways, vessels, and traffic of all kinds; and a paramount devotion to the Almighty Dollar are the prominent characteristics of Chicago," observed a visiting correspondent from the *London Times* in 1887.[17] The conspicuous devotion of which he wrote produced serious dividends for the factory-owning elite. By 1880 Chicago had become the nation's third-largest manufacturing center; with 15% of all residents employed in factories, the city boasted the largest industrial workforce west of the Appalachians.[18] What Chicago failed to produce was a pleasant existence for most of its inhabitants. Tens of thousands dwelt in overcrowded and unsanitary homes. Life in the city was, for countless children, tantamount to a death sentence. In the early 1880s, the odds that a baby born in Chicago would live to see her fifth birthday were only 50–50.[19]

It was such grim conditions that energized ongoing protest movements within the city's fractious working classes. While the authorities managed to quash the 1877 railroad riots, they proved unable to suppress an intensifying radical impulse. If anything, the riots strengthened the socialist Workingmen's Party of the United States: it won 13% of the local vote in the following November's election. By that point the socialists had gained control of the city's labor movement, capitalizing on the trade unions' persisting weakness. Throughout 1878, meanwhile, socialist militias—the German Lehr- und Wehr-Verein and Bohemian Sharpshooters—took to the streets, performing provocative public drills. Not until the 1879 election of Carter Harrison, a Democrat, to the mayor's office did the threat of radicalism seem to subside. Harrison was convinced that the Democrats would retain power only as long as they kept both the trade unionists and the socialists in their camp, and he went to considerable lengths to make that happen. He appointed socialists to prominent municipal positions, gave the city's printing business to the radical *Arbeiter Zeitung*, allowed the Lehr- und Wehr-Verein to march unmolested, and ordered the police to stop aggressively suppressing strikes and other labor disruptions. While his lax policies infuriated some of the city's leading citizens, Harrison had by the early 1880s forged an uneasy truce between the classes.[20]

The peace did not last long. After several years of relative prosperity, a sharp economic downturn starting in 1883 left tens of thousands of Chicagoans unemployed.[21] This latest bust reinvigorated working-class organizations, which did not speak with one voice, but which by the mid-1880s spoke increasingly for themselves—not as factions within the Harrison regime. Among the three main groups vying for working people's allegiance were, first, the anarchists, who gained a local foothold in 1883 and who sought a fundamental overhaul of the emerging industrial order. By 1886 there were still only 2,800 anarchists in the city. However, they held considerable sway within the Central Labor Union, the largest body of German trade unionists, and so their influence far outstripped their numbers.[22] Second, the Trades and Labor Assembly (TLA) remained Chicago's leading association of conservative labor reformers, who tended to be skilled, native-born, and—like Andrew Cameron—hostile to all forms of revolutionary and state-centric socialism. Third, and situated ideologically between the anarchists and the TLA, were the upstart Knights of Labor, whose local assemblies incorporated labor reformers, socialists such as Albert Parsons, and others besides. The Knights had established a presence in the city in 1877 but remained a non-factor in local politics until 1885, when they entered a season of phenomenal growth: from 1,906 members in July 1885 to 10,000 by March 1886; from 18,000 members in July 1886 to 36,000 members by that very same autumn.[23] This trajectory had parallels across the nation, as the order's aggregate membership skyrocketed from a mere 104,000 in 1885 to fully 729,000 in 1886.[24]

The Knights' surge coincided with a dramatic uptick in the frequency of labor disruptions across the United States. Chicago averaged 35 strikes, involving an average of 6,357 workers, in the years 1881 to 1885; in 1886 there were 307 strikes involving 88,000 workers. This Great Upheaval sprang from a complicated array of social and macroeconomic sources, one of which was the growing militancy of Chicago's upper classes.[25] Long incensed by Harrison's passive response to labor conflict, the business elite gained a new champion when the mayor—who had barely eked out a victory in the recent municipal election—consented to allow police captain John Bonfield to guard the West Side's streetcar lines during a July 1885 strike. Bonfield packed half of the city's police force into a ten-car train, which moved slowly along Madison Street through a series of barricades and large crowds of strikers. His men arrested anyone who shouted "scab" and assaulted all who dared to obstruct the cars' path, brutally implementing their leader's self-proclaimed philosophy: "the club today saves the bullet tomorrow." When in the strike's wake Mayor Harrison appointed Bonfield to the second highest post on the police force, the probability of a catastrophic confrontation increased exponentially.[26]

The moment arrived on the evening of 4 May 1886, when a crowd of some three thousand workers and radicals gathered at the intersection of Randolph and Des Plaines Streets, in what was then known as Haymarket Square. Peaking tensions between employers and the employed had escalated to a breaking point on 1 May, as 30,000 Chicago workers—native- and foreign-born, skilled and unskilled—joined with 170,000 more across the nation in a mass strike designed to win, finally, the eight-hour day.[27] On 3 May, at the McCormick Reaper Works, 200 policemen fired on a crowd of strikers, killing six. In the heat of the moment, the city's leading radicals wavered between a longing for vengeance and a desire to maintain their movement's broad appeal. They distributed a flyer calling for a mass meeting in Haymarket Square, "to denounce the latest atrocious act of the police, the shooting of our fellow-workmen yesterday afternoon." One version included the words, "Revenge! Workingmen, to Arms!!!"

The meeting was peaceable until the police showed up. Mayor Harrison left shortly after 10 p.m., as the event appeared to be winding down and it seemed certain that there would be no bloodshed that evening. But then twenty minutes later hundreds of policemen marched into the square and their captain, with Inspector Bonfield by his side, shouted, "I command you in the name of the people of the state of Illinois to immediately and peaceably disperse." The anarchist who was speaking at the time eventually assented, saying, "All right, we will go." But then, in the next instant, there was a flicker of light and an explosion. The bomb threw the Square instantly into chaos. Shots were exchanged and by the end of the melee dozens lay injured, though in the eyes of many respectable citizens there was only one number that mattered: 7 mortally wounded policemen. A backlash commenced within twenty-four hours, as law enforcement raided the offices of the anarchist press, saloons and beer-halls where militant workers were known to congregate, and the homes of many known radicals. Over the course of the ensuing two months, the police arrested more than 200 suspects, eight of whom eventually stood trial for the murder of the fallen policemen. In November 1887, having appealed their case to no avail all the way up to the Supreme Court of the United States, four of these men were hung. Across the nation, many reveled in the news. Had he been alive to behold the reaction, August Spies would hardly have been surprised—after all, it had been much the same some eighteen centuries before, when the Jerusalem Board of Trade men had found a way to eliminate a certain troublemaking Jew.[28]

In the decade following the 1877 railroad riots, Chicago's leading Protestants and Catholics joined with the business elite to create a united phalanx against radicalism. Throughout the late 1870s, harangues against socialism reverberated regularly within the city's most fashionable sanctuaries, including those near the central business district, such as Wabash Avenue Methodist, St. James Episcopal, and St. Paul's Universalist; as well as those which lay further west in the Protestant hub of Union Park, including Centenary Methodist, St. Paul's Reformed Episcopal, and First Congregational.[29] At the last of these the Reverend Edward P. Goodwin called, in the summer of 1878, for 5,000 federal soldiers to stand always at the ready in case disorder once more engulfed Chicago's streets.[30] Catholic divines were less inclined to issue threats, though they were no less committed to defeating radicalism. Upon assuming the Holy See in 1878, Leo XIII almost immediately issued an encyclical entitled *Quod Apostolici Muneris*, which condemned "the plague of socialism" and pronounced that "the right of property and ownership . . . stands inviolate."[31] His subordinates in Chicago took the cue. In the Bohemian neighborhood of Pilsen on the city's near southwest side, church officials fought relentlessly—and most often futilely—throughout the late 1870s and early 1880s to halt the mass defection of Czechs to freethinking and socialist societies.[32]

By the mid-1880s, the growing restiveness of the working classes, not to mention the emergence of a vibrant anarchist movement, had pushed Chicago's Christian elite into a near-constant state of alarm. Catholics and Protestant pundits waxed indignant about the city's tolerance of black flags and "incendiary speeches."[33] Meanwhile, prominent pulpits propounded messages even more confrontational than the scenes in the streets. During the 1885 streetcar strike, the Reverend Goodwin launched into a sermon at First Congregational by announcing, "My sympathies are with the laborers. I know what it is to toil with the hammer." Such nods to the dignity of working people were a venerable Union Park tradition. But so, increasingly, were Christian celebrations of violence. Goodwin went on, "The police should clear the streets if they leave a corpse at every step. Capt. Bonfield has been cursed for his conduct with the crowds, but if we had more men like him we should have less trouble with the strikers. These are times for heroic remedies, and if I were Mayor of the city of Chicago, tomorrow morning I should protect this company if I had to mow down the crowds with artillery."[34] Such sentiments were anything but exceptional in 1885; in the tumultuous run up to Haymarket they became only more and more commonplace.[35]

But Goodwin's distinction between "the laborers" and "the strikers" was telling. Even as Chicago's Christian leaders prosecuted their ferocious assault on radicalism, they remained as determined as ever to retain the allegiance of respectable working people. The worry that the churches were failing at this essential task was in the 1880s becoming more and more pronounced, especially in Protestant circles, across the industrializing world. Speculation as to "Why the Masses Do Not Go to Church" filtered into Chicago from eastern cities such as Cincinnati, Philadelphia, and New York, while strategies for "Reaching the Artisan Classes with the Gospel" arrived from as far away as Birmingham, England.[36] Meanwhile, local ministers' associations took up the question of "city evangelism" with renewed urgency and individual pastors preached sermons with titles such as "The Masses and the Classes."[37] The continued expansion of working-class neighborhoods where life carried on irrespective of the Protestant elite's wishes seemed to some sure evidence of the devil's work. In the autumn of 1885, the *Interior* published a dispatch entitled "Satan on the West Side," in which the author lamented that the district bounded by Halsted on the west and Canal on the east, Madison to the north and Harrison to the south, was "destitute of the gospel."[38] Four years later two ambitious women, Jane Addams and Ellen Gates Starr, would go on to establish the city's first settlement house in this very vicinity, just south of Harrison on Halsted St. While Addams and Starr were not nearly as interested in evangelizing the city's immigrant peoples, their remarkable success at building inroads into the neighborhood only underscored the failures of the city's leading churchmen to do the same. Some still held out hope for the souls of the foreign-born, but on the whole, paralysis and even resignation prevailed.[39]

The case of the sturdy but wayward American workingman was altogether different, as Protestants sought as urgently as ever to draw him back into the fold. In the eyes of some, this work did not seem to require innovation so much as the correction of devious misinformation. One editorial in the *Interior* reflected, "How snake-like, cold and venomous is that spirit which crawls among the working men, lifts up its head in their shops and homes and club rooms, and above all in the saloons, and hisses in their ears, 'The church is the ally of the capitalist and the oppressor, the Bible is the rich man's book.'"[40] But others were beginning to think that the churches' medium was getting in the way of its message. These reformers called for the abolition of pew rents and the removal of all other stumbling blocks to the workingman's participation in worship: fancy carriages, elegant clothes, and the like. In the same spirit, they even endorsed trade union campaigns to secure Sundays off, though their views on the larger labor question rarely differed much from those of their more traditional colleagues.[41]

In Gilded Age Chicago, the aims and aspirations of this reforming camp were most clearly embodied in the work of evangelical preacher and institution builder Dwight L. Moody. The one-time shoe salesman arrived in the city just in time to be caught up in the "businessman's revival" of 1857, an experience which reinforced his long-standing discomfort with the formality and luxury of the established churches.[42] By the time Moody set out on the revival trail he had developed a full-throated critique of churchly excess. So long as urban congregations remained little more than "aristocratic clubs for the few rich and respectable," workingmen would stay beyond their reach, an outcome with potentially catastrophic implications: "Dynamite or gospel," as one 1885 headline in the *Record of Christian Work* framed it.[43] Just months before the Haymarket affair, Moody showed forth a different way at a Chicago revival meeting, allowing the poor to enter and select their seats first, while "Mr. and Mrs. East-of-Clark-Street" awaited their turn.[44] When the bomb exploded that same spring it corroborated his worst fears:

> I am not speaking disparagingly of the different churches and missions now attempting to reach this class but anyone with their eyes open can't fail to see that the masses are not reached. One of two things is absolutely certain: either these people are to be evangelized, or the leaven of communism and infidelity will assume such enormous proportions that it will break out in a reign of terror such as this country has never known. It don't take a prophet or the son of a prophet to see these things. You can hear the muttering of the coming convulsion even now, if you only open your ears and eyes.[45]

Haymarket bolstered Moody's efforts to raise funds for a Bible institute that would equip lay missionaries for the formidable task of converting the city's workers. Notably, what the upheaval did not do is change the revivalist's mind on matters of political economy. Moody enjoyed close ties to a number of the city's leading families, including the McCormicks, at whose plant the violence had begun. Like them and so many of his fellow divines, he never could "see how a man can follow Christ and not be successful."[46]

A handful of Chicago ministers did call for a more wholesale renovation in the churches' posture toward the poor. Most persistent was a middle-aged Methodist by the name of Charles H. Zimmerman, who published a wide-ranging series of essays during these years, calling for systemic changes to both the economy and the churches. In an illustrative column in the *Interior* entitled "How to Reach the Masses" he declared, "Jesus Christ and his disciples had no social status in Jerusalem, and would have none now in Chicago or New York, or Boston. It is useless to try to disguise the fact that the church has got a long way off from Christ's spirit and method in dealing with the poor." Emphasizing the contrast, Zimmerman continued, "[The church] gravitates toward the 'upper circles,' [Christ] worked among the lower strata of society. It conforms to social distinctions based upon culture, wealth, clothes; he ignored them. Its members extend their sympathy by proxy, pay an almoner to distribute their charities, instead of going themselves, as Christ did, to the homes of squalor and misery."[47] It is intriguing that the *Interior* published Zimmerman's work, for among the city's religious papers, it was one of the most consistently hostile to organized labor. This hostility sprang from material roots: the McCormicks significantly underwrote the paper's operations. Wary of upsetting his patrons, the editor made sure to publish a letter or note alongside Zimmerman's column that better represented the *Interior's* editorial point of view. An exemplary one of these accused the Methodist divine of "rank socialism."[48]

Zimmerman was well outside the religious mainstream, which eyed not just radicalism but also organized labor with suspicion throughout the 1880s. To be sure, Chicago's leading Christians were not of one mind. Some reviled trade unionism altogether. At a gathering of clergy in the wake of Haymarket, the Reverend Robert Hatfield declared, "Just in proportion as men were drawn into trade-unions they were drawn away from Jesus Christ."[49] Chicago readers of the *Knights of Labor* learned that high-ranking Catholics such as Minnesota Bishop John Ireland shared the worry. At St. Paul's Cathedral, he placed the blame for the riot not only on anarchists but also on the "labor element," declaring, "By striking, they became idlers and allowed seditious and communistic leaders to incite them to deeds of lawlessness."[50] At the level of the local parish priest, responses to labor varied. Father Patrick Flannigan—whose Southside parish, St. Anne's, encompassed many a stockyard laborer—enjoyed work-ingmen's trust and confidence, which was more than could be said for some of his colleagues. In 1878 the priest at Nativity Church in Bridgeport had befriended a butchers' local, only to betray it the very next year, pub-lishing a devastating letter in the *Tribune* that undermined the union's campaign for a closed shop.[51] In general, Catholic leaders regarded con-servative labor reform more favorably than their Protestant counterparts, though a smattering of the latter also discerned that trade unions had a constructive role to play: as a counterbalance to monopoly and, moreover, an agent of uplift through campaigns for shorter hours and Sunday clos-ing, and against child labor and the sweating system.[52]

But even those who expressed support for labor did so cautiously. Consider the particulars of Christian leaders' posture toward the resur-gent eight-hour movement of the mid-1880s. Those ministers who backed the campaign rallied almost to a man behind its most conservative wing, which called for corresponding wage reductions. "If anybody thinks he can make as much money as he needs by working eight hours a day, he ought to have full liberty to try the experiment," the *Interior* harrumphed.[53] Even the Reverend Daniel J. Holmes, who now pastored a Chicago church but who had previously been stationed in Amboy, Illinois, where in 1867 he campaigned vigorously on behalf of the eight-hour movement, demurred as to the details. The *Tribune* reported that at a meeting of Methodist clergy on the matter, "[he] also spoke, saying the question was a very seri-ous one and those present ought to give it their deepest consideration."[54] The Knights of Labor offer another particularly interesting case study. By disavowing the saloon and discouraging frequent strikes, Terence V. Powderly, the Knights' national spokesman, earned the admiration of both Catholic and Protestant leaders in Chicago.[55] But Powderly was himself unpopular in many of the Knights' Local Assemblies in Chicago, which regularly ignored his counsels and employed aggressive tactics that in turn raised the ire of many religious leaders.[56] After all, in the view of almost all leading churchmen, strikes, boycotts, and other coercive mea-sures were entirely beyond the pale.[57]

Unwilling to rally behind workers' organizations and yet desirous of their affections, church leaders pushed forward with a rhetorical strategy, first developed in the mid-1870s, of leavening their denigration of "socialists, loafers, and communists" with high praise for "intelligent" and "sensible" wage earners. The latter renounced the saloon, radicalism, and aggressive trade union tactics, and were assumed to be native-born or—at the very least—thoroughly Americanized. Such upstanding workers had the churches' professed sympathy. As the editor of the Methodist *Northwestern Christian Advocate* put it, "The New Testament is the magna carta of the rights of labor, and invests with highest dignity all honest labor and laborers."[58] Just as in 1877, church leaders paired such commendations of labor with denunciations of monopoly. Even the *Interior* mustered the declaration, "The accumulation of wealth by the railway speculators is sheer robbery," in January 1886.[59]

Such friendly rhetoric did, in many cases, resonate with Chicago's working people. Throughout the 1880s, the city's working-class editors eagerly touted any hint of support from church leaders, reproducing, sometimes in full, sermons and speeches that endorsed labor causes.[60] When in 1882 Archbishop Feehan spoke favorably of the Knights of Labor, *The Progressive Age*, the Knights' flagship journal at the time, seized immediately upon his words.[61] Four years later, when representatives of the Eight-Hour League coaxed a heavily qualified resolution of support out of Chicago's Baptist ministers, publications as various as the Swedish daily *Svenska Amerikanaren* and the German socialist *Vorbote* carried the news to the city's working-class neighborhoods.[62] Labor even warmed to Washington Gladden, the increasingly renowned Columbus, Ohio, divine whose name would become synonymous with the Social Gospel. While Andrew Cameron had panned *Working People and their Employers* (1876), the *Knights of Labor* published a glowing review of *Applied Christianity* (1886), a collection of sermons that reflected the latest developments in Gladden's thought on industrial questions, including his newfound enthusiasm for profit sharing as a possible way forward through the thicket that was the labor problem.[63] The editor declared, "It is needless to say also that had the church done what Dr. Gladden declares it her duty to do there would have been no such landslide of workingmen away from her portals as the last twenty years has witnessed."[64] But as the very structure of that compliment made clear, wage earners' long-standing desire for the churches to be their champion remained far from satisfied.

Consequently, over the course of the 1880s, Chicago's working people broadened their campaign to save Christianity from those churches that appeared to have abandoned Christ. The fight had first broken out in the years following the Civil War, when Andrew Cameron, the editor of the *Workingman's Advocate*, led a charge against ecclesial collaboration with the captains of industry. The *Advocate*'s run ended in the late 1870s but throughout the following decade a "gray-whiskered" Cameron, still a stalwart of the Trades and Labor Assembly (TLA), remained active in the battle for a more egalitarian Christianity.[65] In an 1883 speech before the TLA he lamented, "that for reasons best known to itself the pulpit has seen fit to use its influence to antagonize the demands of the laboring classes." Fully sixteen years had passed since the great betrayal of 1867 and yet the churches' conduct during that episode still stung. He went on to recount:

> A few years ago, when the eight-hour system was made a prominent issue, the churches of Chicago rang with denunciation of those whom they were pleased to style the demagogues who urged its adoption, while one divine fortified his opposition to the movement by the text, "The poor ye have always with you," and broadly intimated that those who sought to lessen the gulf between the rich and the poor were working directly against the decrees of Divine Providence.[66]

Cameron was nothing if not persistent. Still five years later, in 1888, he continued to indict the city's Christian leaders. At a conference on the "social question," he declared, "Instead of the gospel of Christ, their audiences are regaled with tirades against labor, about which they know as little as they do about the Master whom they claim to serve. They have become the apologists of the oppressor instead of the advocates of the oppressed." An editor at *The Unitarian Review* seemed taken aback by the depth of the Scottish labor reformer's faith. Reporting on the speech, he observed, "From his language it was evident that Mr. Cameron was a religious man."[67]

Cameron's suspicions of radicalism had calcified into outright hostility by the mid-1880s. In the wake of the bomb, his beloved Chicago Typographical Union resolved, "C.T.U., No. 16, condemns in unmeasured terms the heinous acts of the mob at the hay market May 4. And we declare the men who have, by their uncivilized teachings, caused this red letter day in the history of our great city to be the greatest enemy the laboring men has."[68] It was thus all the more notable that during these same years socialists and anarchists joined conservative labor reformers of Cameron's ilk in their fight against the institutional churches. The city's radical communities are widely associated with freethinking and anti-clericalism, and to be sure there were few regular churchgoers in their midst.[69] But Gilded Age Chicago's socialists and anarchists nevertheless participated vigorously in the construction of a "radical historical Jesus." As historian David Burns writes, "freethinkers, socialists, and anarchists found a wealth of material in the Bible that they could use to present Jesus as a radical bent on overthrowing the prevailing order"; and in the process of marshaling this evidence they "contested the authority of the clergy and theologians to determine the parameters of religion."[70] If Cameron's religious activism was tinged with feelings of hurt and betrayal, which reflected a deep emotional connection to the life of the churches, radicals' tended to be more dispassionate. Yet there was no mistaking their profound investment in battles over the meaning of Christianity for industrial modernity. Indeed, their most common critique of church leaders was that they were hypocrites, who did not live up to the example of Christ.

During his tenure as the editor of the English-language, anarchist *Alarm*, Albert Parsons (figure 4.2) regularly raked the clergy over these coals. When the minister of Eighth Presbyterian preached vociferously against monopoly, Parsons deemed it not enough, responding, "With all due regard for the very reverend gentleman, we must accuse him of that sin of which Christ spoke when he denounced the hypocrits [sic] of his day for 'trying to serve both God and mammon.' For are not the wealthy classes of to-day the money changers in the Temple?" He went on, "This reverend fraud, however, claims that 'the laborer is worthy of his hire,' but upholds the system which withholds it from him—the private ownership of capital." Unveiling his own subversive reading of the Christian story, Parsons declared, "The reverend hypocrite says he is 'not a communist,' but Christ, the man he pretends to follow was and his Apostles *sans culotte*."[71] The anarchist editor targeted more than just well-heeled Protestants. He rained down similar criticism upon the Vatican when, in 1885, it once more vocally expressed its opposition to socialism. "The Pope has conveniently overlooked the fact that Jesus Christ, the founder of Christianity, was a Socialist, and that his apostles were of the *sans culotte*," he avowed, going on to say, "They preached the gospel of humanity without money or price." As Andrew Cameron had long done, Parsons underscored what he took to be the material roots of the Vatican's position. "The

FIGURE 4.2 Albert Parsons, circa 1880
Credit: Chicago History Museum, ICHi-03695.

Pope, on the contrary, resides in a palace, with the revenue of a king, and this, no doubt, accounts for his defence of the privileges of aristocracy, and the capitalistic class," he declared.[72]

Lucy Parsons held a similarly low view of "Christian Civilization." In a satirical 1885 contribution to the *Alarm* she told a story about some "barbarians," who embarked on a visit to America, excited to experience the wonders of its advanced society. At one banquet, where "sparkling wine from vine-wreathed cups was freely drunk," and where the celebration "made the silken draperies quiver and fairly rent the magnificent frescoed ceiling," these visitors beheld a strange apparition. "[It] was the wretchedest of women . . . 'Ladies and gentlemen, Christian people,' said she, 'while at your banqueting board will you hear the prayer of the widow, the cry of the orphan?'" The woman went on to tell of her desperate plight, but her testimony produced not an ounce of compassion in the hearts of the well-heeled guests. "From the ladies side could be heard . . . 'Pshaw! Such management, as to let such a creature make her way into the banqueting hall. . . . From the gentlemen we could hear . . . 'Those fancied grievances from the improvident lower classes, in venting their supposed wrongs and annoying decent people, is becoming all too frequent.'" Parsons proceeded to describe the barbarians' visit to church, where "the minister very sanctimoniously declared that 'we are faithful followers of the meek and lowly Jesus, who had nowhere to lay his head,' then mounted his gorgeous pulpit." Among the lessons these "heathen" came away with: "in their religion they are hypocrites, inasmuch as they preach one thing and practice another."[73]

In 1885 the *Alarm* published a poem by another native-born radical, Dyer Lum, entitled, "In Church," which echoed the above criticisms while striking distinctly elegiac tones:

> *I sat in church with reverential sadness*
> *To hear no words that to our wants applied,*
> *No word that could in feeling be allied*
> *With that which filled the birds without with gladness;*
> *This life's a vale of tears, in which all badness*
> *Is by the unchurched infidels supplied,*
> *And we must look without the 'fold' for pride*
> *And luxury, greed and stock gambling madness;*
> *O'er each fair sinner's head rich plumes were waving.*
> *And prayers on scented air were borne to heaven*
> *In scheduled form what Wall street souls were craving,*
> *Then rose a jeweled hand and blessing given;*
> *While musing if such 'souls' were worth the saving,*
> *By prancing steeds they were to dinner driven.*[74]

The longing for a true church, in which a minister's "words" would be applied to the people's "wants"; in which "the unchurched" would not be conceived as "infidels" but as fellow travelers through this "vale of tears"; in which the saints would eschew "jeweled hand(s)" and "prancing steeds" as impediments to the realization of a common good, was palpable in every line. Indeed, the primary thrust of Lum's poem was not to champion the secular, but rather to lament Christians' failure to live up to their founder's good name.

Such feelings were not the unique province of native-born radicals. While anti-clerical currents ran deep in communities of foreign-born socialists and anarchists, they often framed their criticisms of Chicago's actual churches with respect to an imagined ideal of the church.[75]

When the editor of the Bohemian socialist *Svornost* got wind that an American missionary society had set its sights on the "infidel" community of Pilsen, he bristled with righteous indignation. "We have recognized your infamy," he wrote, "and this deterred us from attending your churches and services, which allow such thieves, impostors and libertines to be seen and honored as holy men; holy men that despise poor, honest workingmen." Contrasting the Christian elite's hypocrisy with the Bohemian worker's virtue, he continued on, "You American Pharisees, who are hiding your vice and knavery in places that are meant for prayers, go among the Bohemians and learn how to pray simply but sincerely."[76] Here again the implication was that, were the churches not so "infamous"; their congregations not so full of "impostors"; and their ministers not so "pharisaical," there might be more Bohemian Christians.

A similar intuition animated the German socialist *Vorbote*'s religious commentary. The paper's contributors consistently highlighted the disingenuousness of Christian leaders who purported to stand with the people, even while receiving handsome paychecks from the powerful. When, during the 1885 streetcar strike, Second Presbyterian's Reverend John Barrows proclaimed himself a "Christian socialist," an editor reproduced an excerpt of the sermon, "delivered to his aristocratic flock and Pharisee comrades," and then went on, his words dripping with irony, "So this is Christian socialism! We hear that the shareholders of the streetcar monopoly have avowed themselves to the latter and are about to found an organization."[77] Meanwhile, when the rector at St. Matthew's Reformed Episcopal Church lambasted the wealthy in the abstract, an editorialist in *Vorbote* took him to task, reporting, "Jay Gould received a side blow and in very vague bursts he then had a go at exploiters who he called with undefined words only, so none of his rich church members felt addressed." The writer took the opportunity to make also a larger point, declaring, "the worst human beings—McCormick for example—are pious Christians, and even though the Bible and teachings of Christianity equate the suppression of the poor and the withholding or privation of the day's or week's salary with sodomy and murder, and call it a blatant sin, the rich and noble form nowadays the core of the pious."[78]

As this last quotation suggests, writers for *Vorbote* often assumed that Jesus himself and the true "teachings of Christianity" were in fact allied with the radical cause. Whereas "the preachers of Christendom today are

the watchdogs of capitalism," one wrote, "a traveler's carpenter's apprentice was the founder of the Christian religion." In stark contrast with
Chicago's "elegantly dressed, over-sated" ministers, "[Jesus] did not have
anything himself and amongst all the poor devils he was the one who
was worst off."[79] Another article exalted "Jesus, the vagabond carpenter, who was nailed to the cross because he agitated the people," adding, "It seems that there was a similar kind of freedom at that time in
Palestine as in America today, for look at the fate of the deliverer of this
diatribe [against the Pharisees]."[80] Still another column, sparked by the
arrival of the traveling evangelist Sam Jones, waxed nostalgic about how,
"once, being a Christian was similar to being a Socialist, it was being an
antagonist of the respectable ones."[81] How far the churches had fallen,
the author suggested, expressing a view that was ubiquitous in Chicago's
radical circles.

Socialists and anarchists were not content to lob such criticisms only in
print. Some attended ministerial meetings, where they could confront the
clergy face to face. At one such gathering German-born socialist George
Schilling—accompanied by his Bohemian friend Prokop Hudek as well
as Albert Parsons—offered some professional counsel to the Methodist
divines in attendance. The *Tribune* reported, "He did not think, as some
did, that it was a minister's duty to preach exclusively about the joys of
Heaven. A minister's duty, as he conceived it, was, in addition to that, to
make a paradise out of earth. If that were done, he thought it pretty sure
that there would be a paradise throughout all eternity." Schilling went
on to give a theological lesson as well, arguing that the socialist "distinction between what was personal and what was common property" had its
foundation in holy writ. Indeed, "this principle that the earth was man's
and the fullness thereof was founded on the plain teachings of the Bible,"
he declared.[82]

However much Schilling may have irked his listeners, the offense paled
in comparison to that committed by the 2,000 anarchists who protested
the grand opening of the new Board of Trade building (figure 4.3). The
city's Christian elite helped to orchestrate the celebration surrounding
the construction and completion of the $1,500,000 structure. At the cor-
nerstone laying ceremony in mid-December of 1882 Reformed Episcopal
Bishop Charles Edward Cheney prayed an "impressive prayer," saying in
part, "We thank Thee that Thou has blessed the efforts of those who have
been instrumental in the commercial prosperity of this great city."[83] At the
1885 dedication for the building, meanwhile, Episcopal Reverend Clinton

THE NEW BOARD OF TRADE IN CHICAGO.—DRAWN BY H. F. FARNY.—[SEE PAGE 318.]

1. Opening Exercises in the New Hall, April 29.   2. Free-Place.   3. Promenade Concert, April 28.   4. The New Building.   5. Communist Demonstration on the Night of April 28.

FIGURE 4.3 News of the anarchist demonstration spread far and wide, especially after it was featured in this *Harper's Weekly* spread on the opening of Chicago's new Board of Trade building

Credit: The Newberry Library.

Locke petitioned God for favor, announcing before a crowd of 4,000, "We are met here to dedicate to the trade and commerce of this city this noble temple, and as our forefathers ever did, and as we pray Thee our descendants may ever do, we would first ask Thy blessing on our work."[84] That same day, just a handful of blocks away, Parsons riled a massive crowd of protesters, crying aloud, "A temple was being dedicated to the god of mammon, to be devoted exclusively to the robbery, the plunder, and destruction of the people. When the cornerstone was laid Bishop Cheney was there to baptize it." He went on, "What a truthful follower that man must be of the tramp Nazarene Jesus." The crowd erupted into laughter and then into cheers when Parsons added, "who scourged the thieves from the board of trade of Jerusalem." The crowd laughed once more when Parsons needled the Reverend Locke, noting that "another pious man was to take part in the ceremonies," but Chicago's leading Christians were not amused. The *Northwestern Christian Advocate* raged against "the mob," while the *Interior* abhorred "the extreme stupidity of the men led by the communists in Chicago."[85]

Radicals such as August Spies compared the scene that day to Jesus's overturning the tables of the moneychangers in the Temple.[86] Their subversive interpretation of the gospel would never filter into Chicago's Christian mainstream, but many nevertheless took such views with them to the grave. Spies died believing himself, a convicted anarchist, to be like Christ. Albert Parsons pulled the final lines of his autobiography, crafted while he awaited his fate in prison, directly from scripture. They begin, "To [the monopolists] With the prophets of old we say," and then quote from the fifth chapter of the Epistle of James: "Go to now, ye rich men, weep and howl for your miseries that shall come upon you. Your riches are corrupted, and your garments are moth-eaten. Your gold and silver are cankered; and the rust of them shall be a witness against you; and shall eat your flesh as it were fire. Ye have heaped treasures together for the last days."[87] Long after Parsons's 1887 execution, his indomitable widow, Lucy, carried on the fight. In one 1889 lecture before a Knights of Labor local assembly she decried "the Christian civilization of Chicago, [which] permits the heart's blood of your children to be quaffed in the wine cups of the labor robbers." Had the churches taken up the fight of the city's widows and orphans, instead of "tickl[ing] the ears of the Board of trade robbers," then Parsons might have sung a different tune. But things being as they were, she assured those gathered, "Socialism is the 100-cents-on-the-dollar religion."[88]

In the decade following the 1877 railroad riots, the Knights of Labor became yet another vehicle for the production and dissemination of dissenting Christianities. Their diatribes against the established churches rang out across the Gilded Age United States.[89] In Chicago, their criticisms often echoed those of trade unionists and radicals. They resented, on the one hand, ministers' fealty to the industrial elite. One L. S. Oliver wrote a letter to the *Knights of Labor* indicting, among others, First Congregational's Reverend Goodwin: "the silk stocking board of trade preacher waxed quite eloquent during the street car strike, and said that the police should be called out first, then the militia, and if that didn't answer, that canon ought to be placed at every street crossing to mow the strikers down till the pavement should be covered with their blood and these remarks from our leading clergy. And to use a familiar quotation of Sam Jones, 'Hell is full of just such Christians as that.'"[90] Many Knights objected, on the other hand, to the very presence of so many capitalists in the pews. Drawing on venerable producerist ideas, one Mrs. B. R. Root wrote to the *Labor Enquirer*, "How many ministers can look over their vast wealthy congregations and see only those who have produced nothing themselves, but have amassed their wealth from the work of their poorly paid fellowmen? It is a crime against divine law to possess the birthright of others."[91]

Countless Knights agreed with Mrs. Root that to become rich off others' labors was to become also apostate. This controversial conviction lay at the heart of a remarkable 1886 polemic in the *Knights of Labor* between the wholesaler John V. Farwell, one of Moody's leading patrons, on the one hand; and one-time Chartist Matthew Trumbull, writing under the pseudonym "Wheelbarrow," on the other. It began with a letter from Farwell, who enjoined, "Let the true Knight of Labor . . . be a thorough student of the four gospels of the New Testament . . . and become a true follower of Christ."[92] Bristling at both the tone and substance of the merchant's missive, Trumbull recounted the gospel story of the rich young ruler who refused Jesus's mandate to sell all his possessions and give the money to the poor. He went on to elaborate a contemporary application, saying, "As a 'student of the four gospels' I have learned that there is a fair prospect for the Knights of Labor to reach the kingdom of heaven, but I can hardly see any chance at all for Mr. Farwell. It would be easier for a camel to go through the eye of a needle than for him to get there. That is the decision of the 'New Testament.'" Driving home the point, Wheelbarrow continued, "Mr. Farwell, of course, does not believe the New

Testament, and the evidence of his infidelity is this, that although he is a richer man than any man that lived in Judea at the time of Christ, yet he is trying to be richer still. He is working very hard and very successfully to make him ineligible for a place in the kingdom."[93]

In the succeeding months a barrage of letters poured into the paper's editorial offices to the same effect. One E. J. Paul wrote, "To hear the professed followers of Christ denounce communism in their churches is sickening. Their Christ was an avowed communist, the only man or God I ever read of who was good enough to be a communist. And they who run the church, men like Farwell, place themselves in the place of the people and divide all the products of labor, above a mere subsistence, among themselves."[94] Not all were so earnest. The *Knights of Labor* reprinted the following satire from the *Decatur Labor Bulletin* under the heading, "Chicago Church Wit":

DEACON—Brother Farwell, I have the solution of the Labor Problem; it is a simple one.

J. V.—(Haughtily) Ah, so; that's good news; what is, pray?

DEACON—(Chuckling) So simple, sir; so simple. A priest, a shooting squad and coffin; very simple, sir.

J. V.—(Thoughtfully) Damn the Priest and the coffin; the shooting squad might do some good if I was governor.

The Knights followed trade unionists and radicals in drawing a stark distinction between the corrupted Christianity of the churches and the true religion of Christ. Underscoring the incommensurability of the two, one writer in the *Progressive Age* declared, "The Savior of the World, who scourged the usurers, gamblers, and speculators from the Temple, would stand a mighty poor show if he were to make his appearance on earth at this time. He would be denounced as a Greenbacker, a Communist, a Socialist, a Nihilist, or a Trades-unionist."[95] Another Knight struck similar notes, writing: "Do not think we would say a word against religion. To the writer religion is life, and Christian religion Christian life. We never can enough praise and glorify the teachings of Jesus." He went on, "but those who pretend to be His ministers and see the enormity of the crimes committed against the poor by the rich, and open not their mouths in protest, are unworthy to take his name, much less to minister in His name."[96] Others insisted, variously, "We believe everything in the Bible"; and, "True Christianity—the religion of Sinai and Calvary—has a deeper, stronger hold upon the hearts of the masses than ever." But the converse of the latter was also true: "the churchly charlatancy, the blasphemous buffoonery, the mendacity, venality, hypocrisy, and cant which are characteristic of the high-toned churches of the period have no attractions for true disciples of the One who scourged from out the temple of God the prototypes of the modern pillars of the church."[97] In other words: the churches were losing the masses.

Over the course of the 1880s, the Knights pressed this claim with growing vigor. In doing so they were, in one sense, just parroting what the ministers themselves were saying. As the *Labor Enquirer* reported, "there is a great complaint made by the priests over the decline of religious sentiment, especially among the working class."[98] But there was more to it. Having observed the clergy's manifest anxiety, the Knights sought to capitalize upon it. Indeed, they almost always paired any assertion of working-class disaffection with a corresponding rationale. When the Archbishop of New York removed Father Edward McGlynn, a disciple of the reformer Henry George, from his parish, one letter in the *Labor Enquirer* construed it as "a case in point" of why working people were losing interest in the Catholic Church.[99] In a similar vein, one John H. Allen wrote to the *Knights of Labor*: "The reason the working people are leaving the churches is because the ministers do not preach the Bible truth. The Bible says the rich man cannot enter the Kingdom of Heaven. If that be true how many church members are going there? Not one out of a hundred." The corollary, of course, was that if the churches would only change their ways, they might still regain workers' trust. Allen was among those who made this implication explicit, writing, "If the ministers will start in and preach the gospel as the Lord commanded them the churches will be filled with the working classes." [100] In this way the Knights dangled their allegiance before church leaders in a gambit designed to make them think hard about the consequences of maintaining their accommodating relationship to capital. Their foothold among the people hung in the balance.

An editorial in an 1888 edition of the *Knights of Labor* reframed the issue in a way that would have resonated with trade unionists and radicals as well, asking, "Have the working classes fallen away from the churches or have the churches fallen away from the working classes?" Over the course of the 1880s, Chicago's working people had left no doubt about where they stood on the question. The hope that the churches could be redeemed was not yet extinguished. As the author of this column put it, "Whenever in fact they return to the pure and simple teachings of the 'despised Nazarene' they will not have to complain of the lack of interest manifested by the workingman."[101] But as it stood, the Christian elite remained unrepentant, prompting even some of those workers who still attended church to wonder whether the time had come to strike out on their own. After all, the logic went, would not Christ have done the same?

5

"The Divorce between Labor and the Church"

WORKING PEOPLE STRIKE OUT
ON THEIR OWN IN 1894 CHICAGO

WHEN ENGLISH JOURNALIST and reformer William Stead came to Chicago in 1893, he was dismayed to find that deep suspicion—in some quarters, outright hostility—had grown up between the churches and organized labor. Stead was on a mission to convince the city's religious, working-class, and business leaders to collaborate together on a sweeping municipal reform campaign; and his brief visit yielded impressive results, including most notably the still-active Civic Federation of Chicago.[1] But the following year he reflected in a sensational, muckraking book, *If Christ Came to Chicago* (1894), "the divorce [between labor and the church] has gone much further here than in the old country." Both sides were worse off as a result. "The labor unions are suffering from the lack of the support which the church should give them," he wrote, "and the church is vaguely and painfully conscious that it is not ministering to those who need her most." Putting a finer point on the second of these observations, Stead related, "Not five per cent of the members of labor unions in Chicago, I was assured on my first visit to the Trades and Labor Assembly, ever darken the doors of a place of worship."[2] Given that membership in urban churches was skyrocketing across the United States, that 5% figure was almost certainly inaccurate—and perhaps intentionally so.[3] After all, the TLA member's point had not been to relay an objective sociological fact but rather to execute a strategy for social change: the more loudly that laborers played on the clergy's anxieties about working-class attrition, the more the leverage that stood to be gained.

Stead's visit generated plenty of opportunities for Chicago's working people to air their religious grievances. Socialist Thomas J. Morgan was never one to pass up the chance. Earlier that year he had made the most of his testimony before Congress on the question of whether the World's Columbian Exposition should close on Sundays, turning to the ministers who were also present and snapping, "You have never been the friend of labor, and you have no right to speak for the workingmen."[4] Now, having heard Stead's call for increased cooperation between church and labor, Morgan reflected, "the union of labor organizations and ministers is a very doubtful possibility." Elaborating, he articulated the kinds of concerns that had troubled so many workers for decades: "These merchant princes, employers, and landlords . . . are the financial foundation and social pillars of the churches, and the employers of the ministers who occupy their pulpits. Ministers thus environed have not joined and cannot (except by forfeiture of their positions) join with the Trade Unions."[5] When several months later *If Christ Came to Chicago* hit the stalls, an editor at the *Railway Times* sounded similar notes, riffing cynically on the book's title:

> If Christ did come to Chicago his ministrations would be exercised in jail. If one were to appear on the streets of Chicago and lay the blessed hand of love and mercy on any of the heads of the thousands of ill-fed, rag-clothed, morally-stunted, haggard-eyed and prematurely wrinkled-cheeked, miserable little wretches necessary to modern prosperity as a contrast to set off its beauty, he would be arrested and clubbed on sight as a disturber of family and public peace, and plutocracy might again, as once before in the past, chip in big purses to the police to raise an anarchy scare and have him hanged on general principles.[6]

The offensive seemed to be working, at least to the extent that ordinary people were gaining leading churchmen's ears. Case in point: an essay in the Baptist *Standard* on "The Church and the Workingman" reproduced Stead's reproduction of the TLA member's 5% remark.[7] This echo effect both reflected and generated alarm, fanning the flames of middle-class Christian angst across the industrializing world in the 1890s. Chicago's Reverend Edward P. Goodwin was one of a hundred American ministers who attended an 1891 Congregationalist conference in

London, England, where one of the most pressing matters to be taken up was that of working people's faltering allegiance to the church. The same *Tribune* article that carried news of Goodwin's participation in the meeting included also a summary of English labor leader Ben Tillet's stern speech, which heaped ridicule upon "parsons [who] denounce the Prince of Wales for playing baccarat [while] they shut their eyes to the operations of the sweaters and heartless capitalists who rob the laborers of body and soul."[8] The news from New York and Newcastle-on-Tyne, Minneapolis and Milwaukee, and countless other places was much the same: "the laboring classes are drifting away from the church," as one Methodist preacher at a conference in Omaha put it.[9]

While the language used to frame the crisis was sometimes gender neutral, the prospect of losing workingmen increasingly gripped the clergy with special force. As the same minister at Omaha had gone on to lament, "Our church is made up of women to a large extent."[10] This was hardly a new phenomenon: "in actuality," as historian Gail Bederman writes, "the American Protestant churches had been two-thirds female ever since the 1660s."[11] That this long-standing arrangement struck many American divines as a novel crisis bespoke much larger changes afoot, and in particular the ways in which structural shifts in the national economy were unsettling Victorian gender norms. Feminized religion, which had once seemed the perfect counterbalance to the masculine world of commerce, was now a problem to be fixed; and in the light of this new day, workingmen's criticisms of the churches were resonating in a new way.[12]

To be sure, in Chicago some did express worries about the flight of "working girls" from the fold and many more stressed the class over the gender dimension of the problem, entitling their sermons, for example, "Reasons Why People Do Not Go to Church"; "The Charge of Exclusiveness Made Against the Church"; and "Has Christianity Lost its Grip on the People?"[13] Yet it was no accident that the clergy increasingly devoted their meetings to consideration of "The Relation of the Church to the Workingmen."[14] Nor is there any doubt that when, at one such gathering, a German tailor rose to explain why he no longer bothered going to church, his testimony was all the more distressing just by virtue of being "his." This particular workingman cited a personal experience of having been "sat down upon" when he attempted to "speak for labor," and went on to convey his disgust with the hypocrisy of Chicago's leading Christians. He pointed to the example of a sweatshop, owned by a professed believer, on the very same city block in which the day's meeting was being held.[15]

The tailor's story made its way into the *Tribune*, and through that conduit into the minds and conversations of many other local Christian leaders, who found themselves buried under an avalanche of analogous accounts.

But even as leading ministers fretted about the possibility of an ugly "divorce" between workingmen and the church, most still stood their ground on the labor question. The travails of 1894—a year marked by class upheaval, both across the nation and within Chicago's churches—would test their resolve. Frustrated by the clergy's recalcitrance, the city's workers brought their dissenting religious ideas to life in the world in new and creative ways. In the early months of that year, they established the "Modern Church," which was organized, funded, and run by the city's Trades and Labor Assembly. Though its life was brief, this labor church fixated the public's eye on the working classes' religious disaffection. It would remain there throughout the strike and boycott against the Pullman Palace Car Company, which became an occasion for remarkable religious unrest. At the height of the summer-long conflict a handful of young, little-known Protestant pastors bucked conventional wisdom by forging partnerships with the strikers. Many wage earners rallied around these dissenting ministers, while others rose up against the conservative divines presiding over their own religious communities, turning "company churches" into theaters of class conflict. Such uprisings did not produce an immediate shift in the attitude of the Christian elite toward labor: on the contrary, the city's leading Protestants and Catholics formed a united front against Eugene Debs's American Railway Union (ARU). But nor did leading Christians emerge unscathed. By year's end, their confidence seriously shaken, they were on the lookout for a new way forward.

Worry creased the wind-whipped faces of many who braved Chicago's streets on the evening of 22 January 1894. A fierce winter storm was on the way and already the city was locked in the most trying season in memory.[16] The failure of the Philadelphia and Reading Railroad the previous February had sent a shock wave through the nation's financial markets, and by early May the destructive reverberations were felt everywhere. As hundreds more corporations collapsed, a tidal wave of unemployment engulfed the United States, leaving destitution in its wake. In Chicago, the whirr of activity associated with hosting the World's Columbian Exposition temporarily forestalled the depression's worst psychological and economic effects. Throughout the summer of 1893 millions of visitors had traveled to the city to behold Daniel Burnham's majestic White City and to traipse through the exotic worlds of the Midway. But the Fair closed in October and by January seemed a distant memory, as tens of thousands of Chicagoans now waited in blocks-long bread lines and slept on stone floors inside City Hall.[17] From their vantage, the future appeared as bleak as the gray skies looming over Lake Michigan.

But inside the Grand Pacific Hotel—a monument to opulence, even in the best of times—the world seemed as genial as ever. It was there, at the corner of State Street and Jackson Boulevard, just across from the Board of Trade, that Chicago's Congregationalist Club convened this night.[18] As hundreds of men in their finest attire sauntered in, they looked forward to a feast. In years past the menu had featured Blue Point oysters and cream of farina to start; Boston baked beans, steamed brown bread, chicken salad, and potatoes anglaise to accompany tenderloin of beef jardinière and small patties a la Toulouse (puff pasta shells filled with calves' brains, chicken, and mushrooms); and a panoply of after-dinner treats, including pumpkin pie and vanilla ice cream, as well as cakes, doughnuts, fruit, crackers, cheese, and coffee.[19] This crowd demanded nothing less. The Congregationalists boasted several of the most impressive church edifices in the entire city, including the New England Church at Dearborn Avenue and Delaware Street; Plymouth Congregational on South Michigan Avenue between Twenty-Fifth and Twenty-Sixth Streets; and First Congregational, which towered over the West Side's Union Park.[20] Such buildings projected the power and prestige of those who worshiped in them, men like Major E. D. Reddington, the vice-president of the Chicago Life Underwriters' Association, who as the meeting got underway was elected the club's president.[21]

This year's annual meeting was devoted to a discussion of the "Relation of the Church to the Laboring World." The Club had invited two prominent working-class leaders to speak on the theme: Louis W. Rogers, the editor of the *Railway Times*, which was the new beacon of Eugene V. Debs' fledgling ARU, and L. T. O'Brien, the president of the retail clerks' union.[22] Rogers and O'Brien may have seemed relatively safe choices. Over the course of the previous year, O'Brien had worked with local ministers to rally support for a proposed Sunday-closing ordinance and had helped to found the respectable Chicago Civic Federation.[23] Both men had close ties to the Trades and Labor Assembly (TLA), which represented the roughly 20% of Chicago's workforce that most closely resembled—ethno-culturally, at least—the Congregational Club's members. The TLA tended to attract skilled, Anglo-American workers, who sought to reform the existing economic system, not overthrow it.[24] From the perspective of the Protestant

elite, any rapprochement with the working classes would have to begin
with this group. Those affiliated with the more ethnically and religiously
diverse Central Labor Union (CLU), which harbored revolutionary ambitions, would have seemed already too far beyond the pale.[25]

Within moments of Rogers assuming the podium, however, the organizers' strategizing looked more like a strategic miscalculation. "What,
your committee asks, does [the class known as 'the laboring people']
want?" he began. "It wants an honest share of the wealth it creates. It
wants such conditions as shall permit a fair distribution of what is produced. It wants to abolish the conditions that enforce idleness. It wants
free access to the resources of nature." Rogers's litany went on. "It wants
the abandonment of our wretched inequalities. It wants a place at nature's
banquet. It wants an equal chance." Rogers's rhetoric, which admitted no
fissures in the working class, was more radical than his labor politics. Later
that year, at an ARU meeting in which delegates voted to exclude African
Americans from membership, Rogers spoke up "in favor of admitting the
negro to the general body, but they should be given a separate organization, as was the case in many churches in the South."[26] White supremacist
views and practices permeated northern churches as well, of course, and
represented one more basis for common ground between Rogers and the
members of the Congregational Club. Yet some of them may well have
shifted uncomfortably in their seats as he forged ahead, asking, "Where
on this [labor] question does the Church stand?"[27]

Rogers paused here to contrast "the ideal Church" with "the Church
as it is," a familiar distinction for those attuned to the longer history of
working-class religious protest and one that structured the remainder
of his speech. With the former Rogers had no grievance: "I know where
Christ stood," he declared. "He was for the poor. He warned the rich, he
denounced force and wealth and usury. He toadied to no monopolist, he
preached from no palaces, he sold no pews! He was of and for the people."
His enthusiasm for Christianity's founding vision, however, was exceeded
only by his outrage at its present state. "The spirit of Jesus is absent from
the modern Church," he proclaimed. Instead of siding with the poor, it
had befriended the rich. Its close ties to "the Carnegies and Rockefellers"
had financed a charitable empire, but this amounted to "the pouring of
a little balm on the surface, while the cancer eats at the heart." What the
nation really needed was a wholesale renovation of the economic system,
Rogers contended, and yet this the church would never support: "it is not
for labor, and cannot be for labor because it is a pensioner on the system

from which labor suffers," he avowed. By the time he resumed his seat, an icy silence prevailed in the Grand Pacific Hotel.[28]

Undaunted, O'Brien picked up where his colleague left off, rattling off a list of reasons why laborers found themselves increasingly estranged from the churches. In the first place, low wages prevented them from keeping up with the fashions of the church-going crowd. Additionally, they were tired of hearing about how their poverty stemmed from abusing alcohol. As O'Brien went on it became clear that in his view wage earners' alienation sprung more from social than doctrinal roots. He referenced a recent gathering where workers had cheered the name of Jesus but hissed at the very mention of the church and recounted at length the testimony of a clerk he had interviewed, who rued: " 'When I go to church I see in the front pew a man who snatched the bed from under a widow, and in another pew a man whose real estate is used for immoral purposes. If the church bore any resemblance to Jesus I would be a church-goer, but it does not.' " Building on this last point, O'Brien jested that local churches should post the Ten Commandments in their sanctuaries so that their members might familiarize themselves with them. His audience was not amused.[29]

If they did not make friends at the Congregational Club meeting, Rogers and O'Brien did earn some notoriety. As far away as New York City, the editor of the *Christian Intelligencer*, a Dutch Reformed weekly, sneered that their accusations amounted to "the fruit of ignorance and thoughtlessness."[30] Closer to home, the Presbyterian *Interior* issued a predictably withering retort. "According to labor," an anonymous editorialist observed, "the Christianity of Christendom is not the Christianity of Christ." He went on: "Labor does not know what it is talking about." Rogers and O'Brien fundamentally misunderstood Jesus's identity and mission, the writer argued. "The Carpenter of Nazareth" had not come to bring "safety from poverty," but rather "salvation from sin." The kingdom of which Jesus spoke "is not material but spiritual, not bread and meat but righteousness and peace and joy in the Spirit." For evidence one need look no further than the fact that "Christ found himself environed by economic and political and social conditions infinitely worse than those that beset labor at the end of the nineteenth Christian century," and yet "never said a word against institutional or material conditions." Driving to the heart of the matter, he continued, "[Christ] warned rich men against the dangers of wealth, but he said not one word against wealth itself." If "modern thinkers, Christian and sociological" were to take this example seriously, the writer concluded, "[they] may well ask themselves whether they are right and wise in demanding that the church champion any economic scheme and broach projects for remaking society."[31] So went the theological argument in defense of the economic status quo.

Its anonymous exponent was almost certainly William Cunningham Gray, who had been the driving editorial force behind the *Interior* ever since the Great Fire. The 64-year-old Ohio native had studied law before making his way into the journalistic profession and was one of the few laymen of the period to exercise exclusive editorial control over a leading Protestant paper.[32] He excelled at the job. Over the course of his twenty-three-year tenure the *Interior* had grown from a locally circulated, financially insolvent weekly to the most widely read Presbyterian periodical in the nation.[33] Gray's editorial savvy helped spark this turnaround, as his substantial coverage of current events and staunch support of evangelical causes won the hearts of a wider Protestant public.[34] But just as transformative was the financial backing of McCormick, who poured tens of thousands of dollars into the *Interior* after purchasing it in 1873.[35] The industrialist's investment would have seriously constrained Gray's ability to champion labor had Gray been so inclined. He was not. In fact, Gray's own loyalties to the financial elite ran as thick as blood: in 1879 his only daughter, Anna, had married Charles A. Purcell, a prominent member of the Chicago Board of Trade.[36] Little wonder, then, that the *Interior* had no patience for labor's critique. But it would not have the last word.

A week later Rogers returned Gray's volley in the pages of the *Railway Times*. Rogers had already discussed the Congregational Club meeting at length in the paper's 1 February edition, recounting in rich detail the "viands" and "diamond shirt studs" that belied the church's purported sympathy for the laboring poor.[37] Now, in the wake of the *Interior's* salvo, he fired back, writing, "The soul of its article is that Jesus tolerated the extremely rich and insufferably poor, so the Church has no right to meddle with fixed institutions. It says the foe of Labor is Labor itself, and flaunts the old insult and falsehood that drinking is the cause of Labor's misfortune." Indignant, he asked, "Why does the Church do this?" and answered, "Because it instinctively feels the shame of its silence on the wrongs of Labor and hastens to throw the responsibility upon an alleged fault of the workingmen."[38] It was this view of the churches—as both corrupted by and complicit in economic injustice—that led Rogers and other working-class believers to the conclusion that it was time to strike out on their own.

On the afternoon of Sunday, 11 February 1894, with the tempera-
ture in the twenties, a variety of freethinkers, trade unionists, and curi-
osity seekers—not to mention four choirboys from the Moody Bible
Institute—headed toward Bricklayers' Hall, traversing along the way
the streets of the rapidly developing West Side. In the years leading up
to the Great Fire, many of the city's well-to-do had flocked to the area
bounded by the Chicago River on the east and Ogden Avenue on the
west, Randolph Street on the north and Congress Boulevard on the south.
Stretching across the northern section of fashionable Union Park, the
elegant Washington Boulevard became during these years home to some
of Chicago's most upscale churches, including the Episcopal Cathedral of
Saints Peter and Paul (1861) at Peoria Street, First Congregational (1870)
at Ann Street (now Racine Avenue), and Union Park Congregational (1871)
at Ashland Avenue. But as early as the mid-1880s, single-family homes
began to give way to sprawling warehouses and factories. By the time the
bomb exploded on 4 May 1886, in the West Side's Haymarket Square, it
was clear that the district's future belonged not to the landed aristocracy
but to the working poor—the Germans, Bohemians, Irish, and Eastern
European Jews who increasingly called it home.[39]

Bricklayers' Hall showcased the fruits of their labors. Completed in
1889, the same year Jane Addams and Ellen Gates Starr commenced their
settlement house work, the three-story brick structure sat at the corner
of Peoria and Monroe streets, roughly a mile due north of Hull House.
The building's $50,000 price tag—approximately $1.18 million in today's
dollars—testified to the rising power of the city's construction trades. So
did its magnificent cupola and its impressive third-floor auditorium; outfitted with lofty ceilings, fine woodwork, and seats for 800 persons, the
auditorium seemed in the *Tribune*'s estimation "finer than any of its kind
in the country."[40] The city's Trades and Labor Assembly held its meetings
there every other week on Sundays, but this wintry February afternoon
happened to fall on an off-week.[41]

Those who braved the elements had come, instead, for the first-ever
service of the Modern Church—a church by and for Chicago's working classes. The impetus for this new organization sprung from the
question-and-answer session that followed Rogers's and O'Brien's speeches
to the Congregational Club. Among those in the audience that night was
William Rainey Harper, the young president of the University of Chicago,
who by that point in the program had heard quite enough. Turning dourly
to Rogers and O'Brien, he asked, "Why not found a church of your own?"[42]

Following several weeks of intense conversation and planning with other working-class leaders, they were prepared to call his bluff. The new organization broke with the customs of the Protestant establishment on several key points: it was to be entirely funded by the TLA, with no weekly collection or auctioning of pews; its executive board was to be chaired not by an attorney or financier but instead by William C. Pomeroy, the TLA's vice president; and it would have no set creed, serving instead as a platform from which practitioners of all different traditions could proclaim the truths of "pure religion."[43] In these ways Chicago's trade unionists sought to spring Christ from the corrupting confines of the contemporary church.

They were not the first to try. A Unitarian minister by the name of John Trevor had founded the inaugural labor church in Manchester, England, in 1891; within three years there were at least twenty-four sprinkled throughout the industrializing cities of Great Britain.[44] Meanwhile, the movement was gaining steam on the other side of the Atlantic as well. In 1892 William Dwight Porter Bliss, an Episcopal priest, founded the Church of the Carpenter in Boston as "an effort to carry out, in church life, the principles of Christian Socialism."[45] Bliss's ministry resonated with an upstart 25-year-old minister named Herbert N. Casson, who had become disillusioned with the Methodist Church's lack of outreach to the working classes and left the denomination.[46] In 1894 in Lynn, Massachusetts, Casson founded the Labor Church, which like its Chicago counterpart spurned the weekly collection and curried to wage earners, proclaiming "the more unfortunate a man is, the warmer will be his welcome."[47] There was, however, at least one major distinction between these efforts and the Modern Church: it emerged not from the mind of a sympathetic cleric, but from the initiative of labor itself.

The inaugural service was a smashing success. The audience at Bricklayers' Hall, which included representatives from all of Chicago's leading trade unions, heard a sermon from Jenkin Lloyd Jones, organizing spirit of the previous year's World's Parliament of Religions and pastor of All Souls' Unitarian Church. Jones's usual parish sat just a few blocks northeast of Michigan Avenue's 3400 block—known to locals as the "Avenue of Mansions"—and at first it appeared he had not recalibrated his message.[48] His exhortation to "welcome to your reading and thinking the lives and thoughts of Lincoln, Newton, Agassiz, Longfellow, Whittier, Lowell, and Bryant" might have fared better with the well-heeled residents of the Near South Side. But when he proclaimed, "You can build a church where the millionaire and tramp may worship together," he was greeted by rousing cheers; and as he unleashed several more applause-worthy lines in succession, the audience forgave his awkward start. Indeed, about the only people dismayed by the meeting's end were the four Moody choirboys, who felt they had been hoodwinked into singing Unitarian hymns.[49]

The reactions of the press were mixed. While the *Railway Times* gushed that the Modern Church would be a bellwether for labor–church relations, the German-language socialist paper *Die Fackel* observed dubiously that it "will come up against many that believe there is absolutely no need for it."[50] These contrasting responses reflected the ongoing fractures within Chicago's working classes. As much as those in the TLA might welcome the advent of a workingmen's church, it had little appeal to those who comprised the base of the Central Labor Union. Also predictably negative were the leading Protestant papers. Responding to the news of the church's founding, the Congregationalist *Advance* opined, "[the members] will very quickly develop more sympathy with the other churches in their attempts to overcome the imperfections so freely criticized."[51]

However vocal its detractors, the Modern Church continued to build on its auspicious start. On 25 February, nearly a thousand people came to watch Pomeroy debate local Methodist preacher William A. Burch. The topic: Pomeroy's recent address before the American Federation of Labor's 1893 Chicago convention, in which he had roasted "the church which has strayed from the paths marked out for it by its twelve immortal walking delegates, under the supervision of the Grand Master Mechanic of the universe."[52] Moderating the debate was none other than William Stead, who must have relished the charged atmosphere inside Bricklayer's Hall. The Reverend Burch declared at the outset his sympathy for laboring people. Much to the audience's chagrin, however, he went on to denounce wage earners' "hostile attitude" toward the church as "a fearful mistake." Pomeroy, meanwhile, had nothing but kind words for Christianity's founder. In continuity with what labor leaders had been saying for a generation, he exulted, "Christ . . . whose every act was fathered by His mighty love and pity for the poor, the weak, the persecuted and the helpless—love for every man, woman, child and beast of the field." But the churches were another matter altogether. Pomeroy quipped, "In order to get good out of wheat we thrash it. In order to get good out of the Church we must thrash it." The *Tribune* characterized the conversation as "bold, honest, and at times almost bitter." The *Advance* resented the bitterness. Reprimanding all those who would "kick and cuff the church up and down all the streets," it declared, "It is all fun for the critics. But it is about as unlike Christianity, in whose name it indulges itself, as anything could well be."[53]

Those who sympathized with the *Advance* could take heart: this trade union church did not last. In fact, all traces of the organization disappear from the historical record within a month of its founding. On 11 March, during its last recorded gathering, social reformer Graham Taylor lectured on "Society" and L. T. O'Brien announced a new Sunday school program geared toward inculcating trade union principles in children. The church may have met several more times or not at all, but either way its lifespan was short and in this way representative. Labor churches rarely survived more than a year.[54] However ephemeral its existence, the Modern Church showcased labor's peaking dissatisfaction with Chicago's religious establishment. In the process, it also focused the public's attention on that dissatisfaction in ways that made the religious elite squirm. As much as the organization's rapid demise pleased the city's leading Christians, any feelings of relief were premature. Labor had retreated on this front but was preparing to advance on myriad others.

As winter turned into spring and no end appeared to the working classes' deprivation, unrest mounted across the nation. On Easter Sunday, Jacob S. Coxey and an "army" of 100 jobless men began a march from Massillon, Ohio, to Washington, DC, where they hoped to present their grievances to Congress. The District's police force brought Coxey's crusade to a speedy and violent end, but by late April a plethora of similarly disgruntled bands had cropped up across the American countryside. That same month 180,000 bituminous coal miners across five states laid down their picks, demanding that wages be restored to pre-panic standards and administering another shock to the nation's beleaguered economy. Especially shocking were the violent confrontations between strikers and law enforcement that broke out in places like La Salle, Illinois, just over ninety miles from the heart of Chicago's central business district.[55] The city had problems of its own, convulsing throughout March and April, as nearly two-dozen strikes erupted in industries ranging from upholstery to canal-digging, iron-molding to cloak-cutting. Most disruptive of all was the brawl between the Central Building League and the Building Trades Council, which prompted the bricklayers, carpenters, plasterers, gas fitters, plumbers, painters, hoisting engineers, tile layers, and roofers to leave their posts.[56]

Chicago's Protestant elite had never looked kindly upon such aggressive working-class mobilization. To be sure, it was in the habit of trumpeting the dignity of "labor" in the abstract, a vein of rhetoric that remained alive and well in 1894. At the First Presbyterian Church sympathy proved the mother of irony on the morning of 29 April, when the Rev. John H. Barrows pronounced, "there is no ethics that will justify all the inequalities now apparent in the distribution of wealth." Barrows's salary netted him nearly $10,000 a year, even as the average American income hovered in the $450 range. Just down the road at the Second Presbyterian Church that same Sabbath, meanwhile, Princeton-educated Reverend Simon J. McPherson delivered a sermon in which he declared that he saw "much earnestness" in industrial armies, which were "symptomatic of widespread uneasiness and of equally widespread determination that some solution of the pressing problems must be found." But there were distinct limits to his fellow feeling: he punctuated his rejection of "their *novel* and *grotesque* methods" (emphasis added) with crowd-pleasing adjectival embellishments. As much as Barrows and McPherson pitied the workingman in the abstract, they could not abide the gritty realities of working-class protest.[57] Some of their colleagues chose not even to feign compassion. In the pages of the *Interior*, Gray harpooned Coxey as a "demagogue" and denounced strikes altogether as "a signal failure."[58] In a series of seething columns, he rushed to the defense of old economic orthodoxies, arguing variously that hard work inevitably produced prosperity; that those fated to be poor should accept their lot with aplomb; and that the interests of capital and labor were one and the same.[59] The most vituperative of Protestant commentaries were, in keeping with a venerable pattern, tinged with nativist undertones.[60] *The Advance* blamed prevailing unrest, for example, on "the kind of dangerous elements that lie loose in a country like ours, wherever the representative forces of Christian civilization have failed in the due enlightenment and moral cultivation of the people."[61]

When Protestant leaders felt obliged to offer an intellectual justification for their opposition to strikes and boycotts, they increasingly resorted to theories about contracts. Abolitionists had equated freedom with the ability to enter voluntarily into contracts, and in the wake of Emancipation this rhetoric blossomed into a legally sanctioned regime of contract freedom.[62] This paradigm's ominous implications for the labor movement went on display on 15 April 1894, when two prominent divines conceded wage earners a theoretical right to organize even as they criticized the very tactics that made organization effective. At St. Paul's Reformed Episcopal Church, Bishop Samuel Fallows denounced interference with strikebreakers, elevating a man's ability to sell his labor at whatever price he deemed fit to the status of an "inalienable, God-given right." That same day the Reverend Kittridge Wheeler announced to the congregation at Fourth Baptist that when unions prevented men from crossing the picket line, "they infringe on the laws of God and man."[63] Ironically, even as influential Protestants insisted that the right to enter voluntarily into contracts should never be compromised, they also scolded workers for refusing to sign on the dotted line. The Methodist *Northwestern Christian Advocate* bristled, for example, when the building trades' unions rejected the offer of a stipulated wage, claiming such action would obstruct a much hoped-for building boom.[64]

Nor could wage earners depend upon the local Catholic hierarchy for support. They continued to trust some individual priests, including the likes of Father Maurice J. Dorney of St. Gabriel's Church—"the busiest priest in Chicago"—who was renowned for his work on behalf of the residents of the stockyards' district.[65] But fears about socialism nurtured anti-union sentiment among many immigrant Catholic leaders. At a mass meeting of German Catholics in 1887 a priest had lashed out at the "labor societies in which followers of Marx and other Jewish defenders of social economy are leaders. Those labor societies are working toward a revival of slavery, trying to dictate to their bosses," he declared.[66] More recently, commentary in Chicago's archdiocesan weekly, *the New World*, provided further reason for caution. On the positive side, the paper steered clear of the nativism that increasingly saturated so many of its Protestant counterparts. An editorial on the coal strikes in Pennsylvania put in a good word for immigrant miners, declaring, "foreigners and imported laborers though they be, such work as they perform should demand good payment—which they do not always get."[67] Yet in the very same column the writer went on to criticize the miners for obstructing strikebreakers and thereby disregarding "the natural right of men to sell their skill and labor at their own price."[68] Here he, too, baptized contractual ideology as "natural."[69] On this much at least, Chicago's leading Protestants and Catholics could agree.

The New World's resort to this contractual paradigm underscored the tenuous connection between Vatican pronouncements on the labor question and everyday practice on the shores of Lake Michigan. Nearly three years before the Pullman Strike, Pope Leo XIII had issued *Rerum Novarum*, an encyclical on the "Rights and Duties of Capital and Labour," which stipulated, among other things, "there is a dictate of nature more imperious and more ancient than any bargain between man and man, that the remuneration must be enough to support the wage-earner in reasonable and frugal comfort."[70] In the months and years that followed, leading American prelates endorsed this countercultural conviction. As recently as September 1893, at a labor gathering in downtown Chicago, Archbishop John Ireland of St. Paul had declared, "The term labor market, free labor, freedom of contract are specious terms to induce a man to step aside when a cheaper one is found to take his place."[71]

Yet *Rerum Novarum* largely failed to galvanize broader support for labor within the American church and in some cases had the opposite effect, as conservative bishops and priests latched onto its anti-socialist provisions while neglecting its progressive aspects.[72] The *New World* had not gone to this extreme, but on the ground in Catholic immigrant communities, priests often sought to organize church-sponsored societies as safe alternatives to labor unions. The latter were too susceptible to radical infiltration, the leaders of St. John Cantius Parish explained, while unveiling the newly formed Catholic Society of Polish Workers (*Twoarzystwo Katolickie Polskich Robotnikow*) in March 1894.[73] With such worries mounting, none of Chicago's official religious voices were prepared to take the side of labor, even as its battle with capital rose to fever pitch.

The Pullman Palace Car Company had fared better than most through the first six months of the 1893 panic, in large part thanks to the high demand for train cars generated by the World's Columbian Exposition. Shortly after the Ferris wheel stopped running on 30 October 1893, however, George Pullman began to cut costs. Closing down his Detroit plant and consolidating production in Chicago was only part of the solution: wage reductions soon followed. Journeymen mechanics were hit the hardest, suffering a 33% reduction, but others were severely affected as well. Making matters worse, Pullman—the sole landlord in his namesake town (figure 5.1)—refused to lower housing rents. Even with nearly a quarter of the employees now making less than $31.00 per month, monthly rents remained a stiff $14.00. On 9 December 1893 simmering tensions boiled over, as the company's steamfitters and blacksmiths walked out, demanding higher wages. This small-scale strike could not alone disrupt the massive Pullman operation, though, and within a matter of days—sensing the futility of their efforts—most had returned to work. The company blacklisted the rest.[74]

By the spring of 1894, however, financial distress had galvanized newfound unity among Pullman employees. Destitute workers yielded a ripe harvest for union organizers, and by early May the shop locals boasted

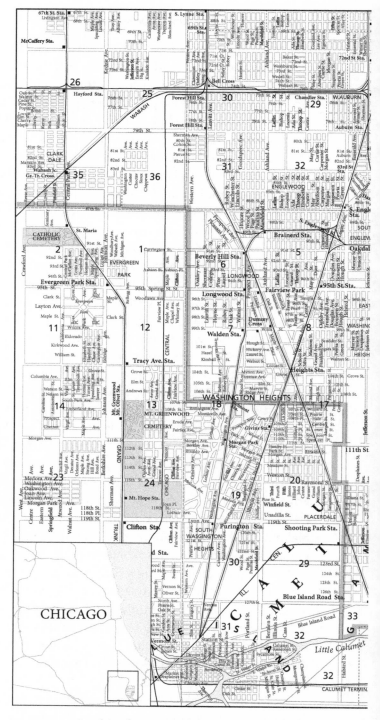

FIGURE 5.1 As this 1892 map shows, the town of Pullman was of downtown Chicago *Credit*: Map reproduction courtesy of the Norman

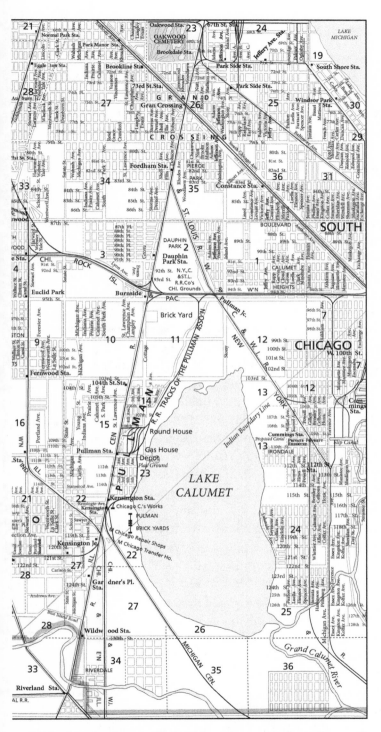

established on the shores of Lake Calumet, some twelve miles south
B. Leventhal Map Center at the Boston Public Library.

a 35% enrollment rate. More important, as common concerns prompted increased communication between the leaders of the various guilds, their collaboration produced during these same months a shop-wide union of locals organized under the umbrella of Eugene V. Debs's American Railway Union. This new coalition dramatically changed matters. Suddenly, the workers had achieved new leverage: namely, the capacity to bring the work of the entire Pullman Company to a grinding halt. With burgeoning confidence, the ARU elected a committee of forty-six men to negotiate on the employees' behalf. Mutual distrust, combined with Pullman's absolute unwillingness to compromise, doomed these talks, however; and in the middle of the morning on 11 May, the workers walked out the gates of the Pullman complex to much fanfare.[75]

True to form, Chicago's leading religious voices did not join in the celebration. The Catholic priest in Pullman emphasized the need for decorum, urging the strikers to "preserve good order."[76] Meanwhile, the New World hemmed and hawed, admitting that "the men had grievances" but arguing that it was "premature to decide the question" since "as a rule, a strike is justifiable only as a last resort."[77] The Archdiocese's non-committal response appeared decidedly favorable in comparison with the Protestant backlash, however. At First Methodist of Evanston, for example, the Reverend Frank M. Bristol denounced the strike. The illustrious minister had never looked kindly upon working-class mobilization. Two years earlier, while serving at Chicago's Trinity Methodist Church, he had criticized the workers of Homestead, Pennsylvania, for "bringing into contempt the laws of God and man and making our young men believe that the individual or the mob is superior to the law."[78] The evening of Sunday, 13 May, his rhetoric climbed to the same lofty heights. "Strikes are un-American, un-democratic, oppressive, and law-defying," he resolved.[79] What Bristol did not know was that the worst lay still ahead.

On 26 June, the ARU took dramatic action, turning its local battle against George Pullman into a nationwide war. The preceding six weeks had passed with little change in the negotiations. While the company was in a financial position to wait out the stalemate, the workers were not. With savings already depleted by the panic, more than eight hundred workers' families found themselves in need of aid by early June. These anxiously awaited the ARU's second national convention, which convened in Chicago's Uhlich Hall in the middle of that month. Men from around the west were in a fighting mood and many wanted to declare a national boycott against all trains carrying Pullman cars. Eugene Debs remained deeply concerned about the potential risks involved in such a gambit, but on 20 June, having been rebuffed yet again in a final plea for arbitration, the ARU served this notice: "Unless the Pullman Palace Car Company does adjust the grievances before . . . June 26, 1894, the members of the American Railway Union shall refuse to handle Pullman cars and equipment." On 25 June, the General Managers' Association (GMA), a body that represented the interests of twenty-four Chicago-based railroads, met in emergency session and elected to "act unitedly" in opposition to the ARU. Any worker bucking orders was to be immediately fired and replaced. The terms of engagement were now set.[80]

The boycott commenced on 26 June, as promised, and within a matter of days the upstart ARU commanded the attention of citizens across the nation. Debs had given careful instructions about how to proceed with this collective action and had insisted, above all, that the boycotters refrain from violence: they would need public opinion on their side. The boycott's potency became immediately apparent, as clogged steel arteries induced commercial convulsions. Across the nation, precious staples became suddenly scarce. The bleak view from the White House sent President Grover Cleveland and his cabinet scurrying for solutions, and within a week Attorney General Richard Olney had fashioned one. Noting that the boycott interfered with the distribution of US mail, Olney coaxed an injunction against the strike out of the Circuit Court in Chicago on 2 July. With the federal government now standing staunchly behind the General Managers' Association, it appeared that Goliath would crush David after all. Running out of options, the ARU vowed to persevere.[81]

Predictably, Chicago's leading Catholic and Protestant pundits rushed to the side of the GMA. The *New World* reiterated the Archdiocese's reservations regarding labor's tactics. "It is a thousand pities," one editorial declared, "that in this enlightened age there should be no way of settling such disputes but the barbarous one of strikes, which are ruinous to both sides, whichever wins."[82] The Protestant papers concurred, casting the ARU's boycott as a violation of economic laws and a challenge to the powers-that-be. The Methodist *Northwestern Christian Advocate* protested that "striking railway men have no . . . right to determine whether or not a certain road shall haul a car of a given kind," while the Congregationalist *Advance* described the boycott as "an act of the rankest injustice."[83] The Baptist *Standard* construed the battle's stakes in gravest terms, writing, "The result ought to be to settle, once for all, whether there is a government in the American republic."[84]

Within the week, Chicago had metamorphosed into a literal battle-ground. Federal troops marched into the city in the wee hours of the morning on Wednesday, 4 July, and set up encampments such as the one shown in figure 5.2. That evening hundreds commemorated the holiday by overturning train cars, committing the first major acts of vandalism since the strike began. The situation deteriorated rapidly. By the next day, with more than ten thousand people now impeding, assailing, and torch-ing trains, the city's vaunted railway system ground to a breathtaking halt. Only three of twenty-six lines could carry freight, and so no livestock entered and no packaged meat left the usually frenetic Union Stock Yards; meanwhile, the bustling open-air market on Water Street withered, even as a plentiful harvest began to rot in train cars stalled just outside the city limits. That same night brought a terrible portent, as Daniel Burnham's glorious White City burned to the ground. But Chicagoans had little time to ponder signs and symbols. On 6 July, even as the state militia arrived en masse, the mob destroyed more than $340,000 worth of railroad property, including the overturned cars pictured in figure 5.3. Then, on 7 July, a roiling crowd assaulted a company of state troops at the corner of 49th and Loomis Streets, in the heart of the gritty stockyards' district. The besieged soldiers cleared the streets with bayonets and rifles, and by the time the blood soaked into the earth, four rioters were dead and twenty more wounded. Not since the Haymarket explosion of 1886 had Chicagoans seen anything so fearsome.[85]

For the city's aghast religious elite, in fact, it proved difficult to remember a more horrific turn of events. On Sunday, 8 July, sanctuaries resounded with sober pleas for law and order.[86] In the days that followed, meanwhile, the editors of religious newspapers, huddled away in office buildings downtown, painted the disorder outside in historic proportions. "At no moment since the civil war of 1861 has the public danger been so great," the *Northwestern Christian Advocate* rued.[87] The *Standard* could find only one other parallel: the 1871 fire, "which saw so much of the city laid in ashes."[88] If the pundits were shocked, however, they were hardly speechless.

The *New World* expressed more sympathy for labor than it had in the preceding months. In its 7 July edition, it came belatedly to the defense of local strikers, avowing, "In the original fight at Pullman, right and jus-tice were entirely on the side of the employees."[89] The following week it grew bolder still. Even as respectable opinion turned decisively against the ARU, the Archdiocesan paper pinned the blame on management,

FIGURE 5.2 A military encampment in Chicago's Lake Front Park, 7 July 1894

Credit: Chicago History Museum, ICHi-61450.

OVERTURNED CARS ON THE MICHIGAN SOUTHERN AND LAKE SHORE
TRACKS, BETWEEN THIRTY-NINTH AND FORTIETH STREETS, JULY 6TH.
Photographed by F. E. Read.

FIGURE 5.3 Overturned cars on the Michigan Southern and Lake Shore Tracks, between Thirty-Ninth and Fortieth Streets, 6 July 1894
Credit: The Newberry Library.

writing, "It is a scandal that a company like this should be able to keep the whole country in hot water by refusing the very reasonable demand of their employes [*sic*] for an arbitration."[90] While these strong words marked a decisive shift in the paper's assessment of the conflict, it continued to qualify its support for the ARU.

For Chicago's Catholic elite there were at least two main sticking points, the first being the absolute sanctity of contracts. The *New World* criticized the boycott as "unfair and unreasonable" and was joined in this sentiment by the city's main Polish-language Catholic weekly, *Gazeta Katolicka*.[91] Second was President Cleveland's decision to send federal troops. The *New World* emphatically endorsed this strategy, dismissing Debs's insistence that it was intended not just to quell the violence but also to undermine the boycott.[92] This endorsement received a powerful second from Archbishop Ireland of St. Paul, who happened to be in Chicago during the outbreak of violence. From within the plush confines of the

Grand Pacific Hotel he applauded the federal government's martial intervention, going on to explain, "[The Catholic Church] abhors and forbids all approach to lawlessness and anarchy; she commands obedience to law and stern loyalty to country and to its institutions."[93]

The hierarchy's conflicted attitude reflected the challenges of the Church's location within the broader society. On the one hand, its flock was predominantly working class and so to side with capital would be to alienate its primary constituency. Fears that socialists or secularists might lay claim to wayward sheep already lurked in the back of many a bishop's mind. On the other hand, the Church had a serious public relations issue on its hands, as the long postbellum depression had catalyzed a new and virulent wave of anti-Catholicism. Opposition to federal intervention would only confirm the suspicions of those who insisted the Church was inherently undemocratic. Such concerns would have weighed especially heavily on someone like Ireland, a leading progressive voice, who sought to expand Catholic influence through adaptation to the American context.[94] He would have been pleased with the papers' coverage of his response: "Speaks as a Patriot," the headline in the *Daily Inter Ocean* read. If his words disappointed countless workers, they would have been even more chagrined at the Protestant reaction.[95]

Throughout the climax of the Pullman affair, Chicago's Protestant editors lauded the forces of law and order, while unleashing fury upon the unruly masses. "The violent strike has begotten the soldier," the *Northwestern Christian Advocate* observed matter-of-factly in one column, while remarking in another, "Force is needed only when hasty un-Americanized men misconstrue liberty and resort to violent license."[96] Much of the anger was directed at the ARU and its leadership. The *Living Church* opined, "is it possible that the members of the American Railway Union do not recognize that the strike inaugurated by them is tyrannical in the extreme," while the *Advance* declared, "the worst foe to the cause of labor, especially that of organized labor, is the self-protrusive and conscienceless demagog."[97] Only one man rivaled Debs as villain: John Altgeld, the Democratic governor of Illinois, who had vehemently objected to the Cleveland administration's decision to dispatch federal troops to Chicago. Altgeld had made enemies of many leading Protestants when, shortly after taking office in 1893, he pardoned the living Haymarket anarchists. Now the editor of the *Standard* was one of many who took a fresh swipe at him, writing, "It was an immense relief to millions of people when the government at last began to stir in the matter, and it was once more seen that law and order in America are not, after all, a delusion."[98]

Meanwhile, Chicago's preeminent Protestant preachers heaped on the criticism, delivering a round of rousing patriotic sermons.[99] The most stirring performance was John Barrows's at First Presbyterian, where the pageantry began even before the sermon. The *Inter Ocean* reported, "back of the pulpit . . . was a great American flag, whose silken folds and the supporting clusters of red, white, and blue roses supplied an object lesson of the pastor's subject." Barrows reiterated the Protestant establishment's main talking points. He belittled the "mostly imagined" grievances of the Pullman strikers, championed Cleveland and the federal troops, and denounced "the un-Americanized rioters, among them Bohemians, Poles, and Slavs, and other alien nationalities, who were bent on killing and burning." The service closed with a theatrical flourish, as Barrows invited President Marvin Hughitt of the Northwestern Railroad onto the stage while the congregation sang, appropriately, "America."[100]

Throughout the spring and summer of 1894, countervailing voices were scarce in the ranks of the Protestant elite. Charles H. Zimmerman remained the most notable. In sharply worded contributions to the *Northwestern Christian Advocate*, the Methodist minister faulted Christian philanthropy for being "alleviative rather than preventive," charged the churches with a failure to produce "economically righteous men," and heralded the controversial notion of compulsory arbitration as one appropriate solution to the labor question.[101] Meanwhile, at the Methodist ministers' gathering on 11 June, Zimmerman hijacked a conversation about the appropriateness of dancing, contending, the *Tribune* reported, "The question of minor morals should be laid aside and that the attention of the church should be directed to the question of 'economic righteousness.' "[102] At 54 years old, Zimmerman was both a full-fledged participant in the local Protestant establishment and its most vociferous internal critic on matters of economic justice. Yet he was no social radical, and in many ways, even in his exceptionality, reflected the rule. In the first place, there is no reason to think that his personal contact with the working poor was any more extensive than that of other elite ministers and pundits. This helps to explain why he spilt far more ink on the criticism of middle- and upper-class Protestant practices than on advocacy for working-class causes. In fact, Zimmerman never openly declared his support for the ARU's strike, let alone the boycott, which garnered the support of not one leading Protestant in all Chicago. Despite the industrial "earthquakes" of

1877, 1886, and now 1894, the city's Christian establishment remained, on the labor question, unwilling to budge.[103]

Yet their intransigence was not the whole story. However static the conversation in the ballrooms and sanctuaries where the elite congregated, change was afoot within other Protestant churches. Among its proponents were a handful of young, little-known ministers, stationed not in downtown cathedrals but rather in neighborhood churches. At least one of these hailed from the city's much-maligned immigrant communities. In early July, with battles raging in the streets, Thorvald Helveg brought down fire at the Danish Lutheran Trinity Church, declaring, "Mob rule threatens to take the power. But where is this mob found? Is it found only in the miserable pest-infected huts . . . ? No, the mob may also be found in the gilded palaces."[104] But the others—and there were not more than three or four—were native-born Baptists and Methodists, only a few years removed from seminary.

The most rhetorically radical of these was the Reverend Herbert G. Leonard, the 33-year-old pastor of First Methodist Church in the sleepy suburban village of Wilmette. In late winter the upstart minister, a recent graduate of Evanston's Garrett Biblical Institute, had arraigned the city's Methodist clergy.[105] He argued that Moses, not Marx, was the progenitor of socialism, and furthermore that the churches had betrayed Christ by neglecting the downtrodden. Ministers who offered working people little more than vague visions of the afterlife were to blame for this sad situation, Leonard insisted.[106] He returned to this theme several months later, but this time at an ARU meeting in south-suburban Kensington, which lay just on the other side of the Illinois Central tracks from Pullman. Most respectable men would not have dared set foot near the place, which was a notorious haven for gambling, drunkenness, and brawling.[107] But Leonard appeared comfortable enough, raking his colleagues over the coals once more with the declaration, "Men are needed at the present time who will do something more than feed the public with spongy oratory and make faces at the devil from behind the pulpit."[108]

The Reverend John M. Lockhart fit the bill. The 31-year-old was still taking classes at the University of Chicago Divinity School while he labored as the pastor of First Baptist Church in Harvey, another settlement neighboring Pullman. He quickly gained a name for himself when, in a late July sermon, he denounced "organized capital," contending it had "banded together to oppress the common people." He singled out, among others, the Pullman Company. His words so angered one Mr. J. W. Matthews, proprietor of a local boiler foundry, that in the middle of the worship service he arose and accused Lockhart of spreading propaganda. The situation threatened to spiral out of control when another member of the congregation then stood up to rebuke Matthews, but Lockhart quieted the crowd and coolly requested that all who sympathized with him come forward to shake hands at service's end. Only Matthews and his family declined. The drama spilled into the following week, however, as Matthews and several others petitioned the church's board of deacons to terminate the pastor. The diaconate refused, the *Times* reported, "as it has strongly favored Mr. Lockhart's stand."[109] These votes of confidence suggested that at the grassroots level there might be broader support for an overhaul of the churches' posture toward labor, a possibility confirmed by the experience of the Reverend William H. Carwardine.

Over the course of the strike and boycott, Carwardine rose from being the obscure pastor of Pullman Methodist Episcopal Church to the city's most prominent religious advocate for the working classes. This unexpected trajectory began on 17 May, when at strike headquarters in Kensington he took many aback by announcing his support for the ARU; his ascendance continued throughout the following weeks, as his campaign gained national renown.[110] Record crowds, swelled in part by throngs of strikers, came to hear Carwardine make the case against Pullman. It was not just his advocacy but also his familiar style that endeared him to the workers.[111] "*We* have common interests and a common enemy—the company" (emphasis added), he declared in his first sermon on the strike.[112] Yet even as Carwardine began to persuade the strikers that he was their man, he also made a series of concerted appeals to a wider middle-class audience. On 22 July, he spoke to pastors, businessmen, and ordinary citizens at the West Side's Congress Hall, defending his view that "Mr. Pullman [is] responsible for the whole situation."[113] Carwardine buttressed such speeches with a furiously written book, *The Pullman Strike*, which he hoped would further advance the "gospel of applied Christianity . . . of mutual recognition, of co-operation, of the 'brotherhood of humanity.' "[114] In a letter to fellow reformer Henry Demarest Lloyd, Carwardine confided, "[I] have written it in the hope of reaching the class of people who are so prejudiced against the strikers."[115] His sensational campaign irked the businessman's papers, and yet it also energized those who had been looking for change.[116]

Indeed, dozens of ordinary Chicagoans penned letters to Carwardine indicating that his version of "applied Christianity" resonated with what they had long believed. One thanked him for "taking the part of the 'under dog' in this fight," while another announced, "One hundred and fifty thousand workers in this city respond to your noble position." Still another relayed, "Tears of delight burst from my eyes on reading your sermon of last Sunday." Such feelings were shared by myriad other working-class believers around the city, who longed for the churches to champion their cause but had grown tired of waiting.[117]

Throughout the summer of 1894, the feud between the Company and the ARU spilled over into the churches of Chicago's far South Side and southern suburbs. During this season religious communities became, in fact, crucial battlegrounds in an intensifying class war. Roseland was no stranger to such travails. Just a mile west of Pullman, this Dutch settlement long frustrated union organizers. The men there were exceptionally committed to their churches, which were in turn exceptionally hostile to unionization. These dynamics were dramatically displayed during the Knights of Labor's 1886 strike for the eight-hour day, when every Hollander employed by the Pullman Company crossed the picket line.[118] In the summer of 1891, Chicago's gaze had once more fixed upon Roseland, where a showdown was playing out between the unions and the First Christian Reformed Church. Initially the fight centered on the fate of John W. Bloomendahl, who upon joining the bricklayers' union was summarily expelled from the congregation. The Reverend Henry Vander Werp matter-of-factly explained: "The rules of our church are against any of its members belonging to secret societies. Bloomendahl was told to take his choice between the church and the union. He took the latter."[119] But before long the conflict took on much larger proportions. Even as the church attempted to ward off the infuriated bricklayers on one flank, it became embroiled with the local carpenters' union on another. In early August reports surfaced in the *Tribune* that the church's diaconate, which included several prominent contractors, had formed an association to obstruct unionization among the Hollanders. One outraged organizer vocalized the suspicions of many, declaring, "There seems to be more of a personal interest on the part of the deacons as contractors than any religious objection to union men belonging to the church."[120] Three years later, the memory of this incident remained fresh in the minds of many Roselanders.

Consequently, when on 29 May 1894, the *Times* published word that the pastor of the town's largest church was aiding the Pullman Company's efforts to entice striking Hollanders back to work, the reaction was swift and severe. On Sunday, 27 May, the Reverend Balster Van Ess of the First Reformed Church of Roseland announced to his congregation of well over a thousand persons that a mass meeting would be held on the 30th to discuss the formation of a patrimonium, a religious association of workingmen that would have impelled the men promptly back to their posts. As the news spread, American Railway officials scrambled to make sure their Dutch allies remained in solidarity. Seven female strikers pursued less diplomatic tactics, sending a letter to Van Ess threatening retribution should he continue to collaborate with the company. The meeting went forward regardless, though the men resoundingly rejected the patrimonium idea. Meanwhile, a stung Van Ess contended that he had made the announcement merely as a favor to his colleagues at the First and Second Christian Reformed Churches of Roseland.[121]

Even in these more conservative bodies, however, church authorities treaded more carefully than Vander Werp had done just three years previously. By the time he resigned his pastorate at the First Church in 1892, it had grown to the point that lay leaders decided to spin off a daughter congregation.[122] The Second Christian Reformed Church was born in tumult, installing its first pastor the same day the railroad strike began. Indeed, the Reverend Henrik Van Hoogen arrived from the Netherlands just in time to shepherd a flock torn between its economic needs and its religious convictions. While the average Dutch worker remained skeptical about unions, many in this church joined the ARU, hoping it would allow them to continue to pay the bills. Van Hoogen chose pragmatism over principle. He held the congregation together by avoiding sweeping pronouncements about the strike, a strategic decision that was also a tacit nod to the growing power of the people in the pews.[123]

Clerical opposition to the strike was met by lay support for the same in yet another immigrant church toward the end of July. The city's Swedish Lutheran leadership had opposed the ARU's walk-out from the very beginning; the denomination's local beacon, *Fosterlandet*, called it a "tedious and sad affair."[124] When the pastor of Pullman's Swedish Evangelical Lutheran Elim Church, the Reverend Henry O. Lindeblad, spoke in the same vein in a Sunday morning worship service, however, it quickly became apparent that his flock had gone astray. Lindeblad rehearsed the tenets of contractual orthodoxy, saying, "I don't dictate to you or say to you whether you shall go to work or not . . . but you must not hinder anybody else wanting to work from doing so." As with the situation at Roseland back in May, rumors rapidly proliferated. That very afternoon word reached strike headquarters at Kensington that Lindeblad had ordered his people back to work and, even worse, that he had approached some strikers' wives in an underhanded attempt to undermine the men's perseverance. The Central Strike Committee immediately took up the issue, with some arguing that the minister should be run out of town, while others called for violent retribution. In the end, cooler heads prevailed. A delegation was appointed to call upon Lindeblad and insist that he allow the Committee's president, Thomas Heathcote, the opportunity to address his congregation. The pastor flatly declined the request, prompting Heathcote to call for a boycott of the "scab minister's" church. Soon enough Lindeblad consented to meet with the delegation himself.[125]

At this intense gathering, and with several members of the congregation present, the divisions within the church were laid bare. Lindeblad refused to recant, explaining that he answered only to God and his conscience. Some of the Swedes stood by him, while others tearfully declared that if he must be shot or lynched, they would take part. By meeting's end, the minister had managed to convince the delegation that the rumors were in fact nothing more than that, though if the strikers were satisfied, he was not. Afterwards, still bristling in an interview with the press, he quoted a New Testament passage that reads, in part, "if any would not work, neither should he eat." He went on to say, "If Paul should appear before a crowd of these strikers at Kensington now and utter such words they would hang him."[126] The *Tribune* dourly assessed the situation, writing, "things are coming to a pretty pass when in a land of liberty a preacher . . . [is] rated by a 'walking delegate' as having no right to live when [he] preaches the gospel."[127] Of course, it was the very content of "the gospel" that these working-class Swedes had called into question.

Perhaps the most striking instance of working-class resistance was at Pullman Presbyterian Church, where the Reverend Engelbert C. Oggel sided decisively with George Pullman. In mid-April, amid heightening tensions, the 53-year-old Dutchman preached a sermon entitled, "George M. Pullman, his services to his age, his country, and humanity," in which he recommended the railroad tycoon be nominated for the presidency, which prompted one laborer to grumble to the press, "Why, it has come to such a pass that one of the ministers had to preach a sermon on the virtues of George M. Pullman—just as if there wasn't enough in the bible to talk about." [128] Unfazed, Oggel went on, the Sunday following the strike's inception, to condemn the ARU's action, declaring at one point, "there is a maxim that half a loaf is better than no bread, and in my judgment the employees were getting two-thirds of a loaf." The headline in the next day's *Tribune* conveyed both the tone and substance of Oggel's message, observing that the strikers had been "Chided by a Pastor."[129]

Oggel's sermon disrupted the tenuous equilibrium within what had long been a class-integrated community. First- and second-generation Americans predominated at Pullman Presbyterian, which had grown from a founding membership of twenty-six in 1882 to a more robust two hundred and fourteen by the spring of 1894.[130] One key to this expansion had been the congregation's ability to assimilate both the town's most affluent residents as well as its respectable working-poor. Among the luminaries who belonged were Alexander McLachlan, who owned a construction business responsible for some of the most lucrative building contracts in town; Mrs. Sophia Van Blissengen, whose husband Arthur sat alongside George Pullman on the Pullman Savings Bank's board of directors; and Mrs. Nellie Sessions, whose husband Henry was not only George Pullman's close friend and chief inventor but also the head overseer of all Pullman Works through 1893.[131] Yet most of the church's members worked in the Company's mills, shops, and yards as cabinetmakers, draftsmen, steamfitters, upholsterers, carpenters, and the like. Worship services functioned, then, as a rare site of contact between someone like Irving Hirt—a 19-year-old iron molder whose parents had immigrated to the United States from Switzerland—and Nellie Sessions.[132]

But now a working-class exodus was underway. The *Mail* announced, "The Presbyterian church has come to be looked upon in Pullman as 'the company church,'" while the *Advertiser* alluded to its "diminishing congregation."[133] The *Journal* went so far as to announce on 30 May, "the kirk stands silent, shut, and deserted."[134] Even allowing for some hyperbole, the fact was that pews long filled now sat empty. Within three weeks of Oggel's exaltation of Pullman, Francis and Villiamine Gunn left with their brood of eight children, as did the Spanglers, the Hamiltons, and John Seymour. The minister's denunciation of the strike catalyzed another round of exits, with Lottie Wilson and her beau Calvin H. Swingle transferring their membership almost immediately; by the close of May, Myrtle Plant, John and Carrie Van Clay, and Edna and Myrtle Williams had followed suit. The trend continued the following month, as Theressa Harvstrawser and Mrs. James Kennedy left the church, along with the Maher, Kanegon, Larson, Warner, and elder Swingle families. And the fallout only snowballed: by mid-autumn, Pullman Presbyterian had lost fully 42 of its 214 members, or roughly 20%. This was a remarkably steep decline for what had long been a stable congregation, and yet the actual situation was likely gloomier. Indeed, assuming that the attrition rate among attendees—a far more transient population to begin with—approached that among members, the gross drop in Sunday morning attendance would have been nothing short of devastating.[135]

What is especially remarkable is the extent to which the church cleaved along class lines. Among those who left were at least three carpenters, two dressmakers, two carbuilders, a cabinetmaker, a railroad clerk, an iron molder, a bricklayer, a teacher, a bookkeeper, a teamster, a homemaker, the wife of a switchman, and an issues clerk.[136] Meanwhile, virtually all of the most affluent congregants remained.[137] The well-known sculptress, Mrs. Ellen Rankin Copp, and her precocious 6-year-old son, Hugh Dearborn Copp, already a world-travelling artist himself, continued to be faithful members. So did Ellis Morris, the vice-president of the Pullman Sound Money Club; Fred Bendle, a banker; the venerable physician Andrew C. Rankin and his wife, Susan; as well as the aforementioned Alexander McLachlan, Sophia Van Blissengen, and Nellie Sessions.[138] Thus, it seems clear that the exodus amounted to a working-class walk-out.[139] By taking Pullman's side, Oggel had severed the bonds holding this diverse congregation together. Whereas before the strike Irving Hirt and Nellie Sessions had worshiped alongside one another in relative peace, that no longer seemed possible: or at least to Hirt, who left along with so many others.

Whatever the destructive consequences for Pullman Presbyterian, the departure of these working-class believers had a decidedly constructive edge. At least forty of the forty-two people who left immediately reaffiliated with other congregations.[140] This 95% reenlistment rate made clear that their anger was not directed at *the* Church but rather *this* church, which had become too closely identified with capital. As they bolstered the rolls of religious communities more amenable to their values, they threw themselves into the contests over the meaning of Christianity for industrial society. The vast majority went to neighboring Reformed churches in Englewood, Harvey, or Chicago. One woman, Mrs. Mary Warner, joined Carwardine at Pullman Methodist.[141] As far away as Madison, Wisconsin, a former member of Pullman Presbyterian, Daniel T. Averill, gave voice to their longing for the churches to be their champion, writing to Carwardine, "I wish there were more ministers that would stand for God and the right and the common people."[142]

What Averill could not have anticipated is how central the activism of Chicago's working-class believers would be to the eventual realization of his wish. While the city's Christian elite had arrayed itself against both the Modern Church and the American Railway Union, these battles had taken their toll. Leading Christians found themselves increasingly beholden to fears of a working-class exodus from the churches, fears stoked by the fact that some wage earners were in fact exiting the fold—and in many cases, doing so as conspicuously as possible. In the years ahead anxious church leaders would reach out to working people, wondering what could be done to retain their allegiance. They were only too happy to answer: become labor's champion. A middle-class social gospel was finally in the offing.

6

"To Christianize Christianity"

LABOR ON THE MOVE
IN TURN-OF-THE-CENTURY CHICAGO

ON THE MORNING of 22 November 1895, Eugene V. Debs awoke in a jail cell in Woodstock, Illinois. At 9 p.m. that evening, having gained his freedom, he walked into the main hall at Battery D on Chicago's lakeshore, where a jubilant throng of more than ten thousand greeted the workers' champion. The *Tribune* reported, "Men and women climbed upon chairs and waved hats and handkerchiefs and yelled themselves hoarse with enthusiasm."[1] Cheers soon turned to hisses, though, when Debs, in one of the many rhetorical flourishes scattered throughout his speech, asked, "Where does the church stand with reference to labor?" The rapt crowd chanted in unison, "Against it! Against it!" Debs went on to confirm their suspicions, declaring that he and others had seen the "money power enter the church, touch the robed priest at the altar, blotch his soul, freeze his heart and make him a traitor to his consecrated vows . . . or, if true to his conviction, ideas and ideals, to suffer the penalty of ostracism, to be blacklisted and to seek in vain for a sanctuary in which to expound Christ's doctrine of the brotherhood of man."[2]

Debs had reason to harbor bitterness toward the churches. During the Pullman strike and boycott of 1894 the city's religious leaders had arrayed themselves against his American Railway Union (ARU). Even the local Catholic hierarchy, which took a more charitable view of Debs's character, had championed the Cleveland administration's decision to dispatch federal troops to Chicago. In addition, long after the ARU's defeat, leading Protestants continued to attack its leader. At an 1894 union Thanksgiving service, the Reverend Edward P. Goodwin of First Congregational Church had directed a thinly veiled blow at Debs, declaring, "It is matter for great thanks that labor has had too much sense to be swept from its feet by an unscrupulous leader in an attempt to redress grievances it knew not of."[3] Nearly a year later and with the ARU president ensconced in jail, some influential Protestants were still grinding their axes. At a gathering of Methodist ministers in late September of 1895 the Reverend William E. McLennan denounced Debs as one "who . . . would sacrifice his country to win a temporary victory for that small portion of workingmen that look to him for leadership." While these words miffed two members of the audience, who stormed conspicuously out of the room, they earned thunderous applause from the rest.[4]

Such enduring hostility makes it all the more striking that in early January 1896 this same union leader could be found standing behind the pulpit of Erie Street Methodist Church. It was no coincidence that the invitation to speak there arrived ten days after his speech at Battery D: Debs's denunciation that night had struck a nerve among leading churchmen, many of whom were growing increasingly alarmed about a perceived exodus of workingmen. The editor of the Catholic *New World* reacted defensively, writing, "To brand the Church as hostile to the interest and welfare of the toiling masses is not to know her."[5] The Sunday following the Battery D meeting, meanwhile, the Reverend Clifford Barnes preached at Sedgwick Street Congregational Church on "Debs and the Church." While Barnes resolutely asserted that the churches were the friends of working people, he spent most of the sermon worrying aloud about why, according to a statistic he cited, wage earners comprised only 10% of all the people in the pews.[6]

That same week the Reverend Jackson Stitt Wilson mailed an invitation to Terre Haute, Indiana, in the hopes that Debs would come speak at Erie Street Methodist on the relation of the churches to labor. The 27-year-old Wilson was then in the process of finishing his BA at Northwestern University, even while serving as the pastor of this church, situated near the corner of Erie and Robey Streets in bustling but impoverished West Town, a neighborhood home to many German, Polish, and Ukrainian immigrants.[7] During his studies he came upon the writings of George Herron, a Christian socialist whose stringent criticisms of industrial capitalism helped the young minister to make sense of the poverty that surrounded his church. Wilson would eventually leave Methodism to organize a Christian socialist movement of his own, but at this moment in early 1896, he was merely a young and open-minded divine who shared many of his colleagues' concerns about working-class attrition.[8]

Debs accepted the invitation. In fact, between January and April of 1896 he spoke at least three times at Erie Street Methodist.[9] Transcripts of these speeches did not make it into the major dailies, but the content of another address he delivered on one of these trips suggests that he probably rehashed many of the same themes as at Battery D. At Twelfth Street's Turner Hall on 10 April, Debs spoke before thousands of striking garment workers, straying at one point from questions about wages to comment on the role of the church vis-à-vis the labor question. The next morning's *Tribune* reported, "He said if Christ was on earth today he would be on the side of the striking garment workers. He said he opposed the church of today, not because it was Christian, but because it did not advocate the principles Christ taught."[10] These were, of course, the kinds of claims that Chicago's working people had been making since the Civil War. The difference now was that disaffected wage earners had church leaders' full attention.

Indeed, by the turn of the century, leading Protestants and Catholics had become completely absorbed in a crisis of working-class attrition. Convinced that respectable workingmen were leaving their churches at a rapid clip, Protestants conducted a series of surveys to find out what they could do to get them back. The answer, time and again: "Be our champion." The city's Catholic leadership harbored worries of its own. Increasingly fearful that socialists were stealing the Church's sheep, the hierarchy embarked on a concerted campaign against radicalism that would eventually drive it solidly into the conservative American Federation of Labor's camp. In both the Protestant and Catholic cases, intensifying anxieties about a purported working-class exodus were beginning to exert an overwhelming pressure on church leaders to reconsider their posture toward organized labor.

Andrew Cameron, who died in the late spring of 1892, with his mission to save Christianity from the churches woefully incomplete, would have taken heart in the fact that it remained alive and well in a rising generation of trade unionists.[11] To be sure, not all were interested. The city was home to a sizable freethinking community, concentrated especially in immigrant wards, and it was moreover true that in the 1890 census 43% of the city's entire population declared no religious affiliation.[12] But outright hostility to religious belief, while common on the other side of the Atlantic, was notably scarce on the shores of Lake Michigan.[13] In an 1895 poem entitled, "I am only a Working Girl," one of the leading women in Chicago's labor movement, Elizabeth Morgan, articulated a kind of skepticism, but one that resonated deeply with ancient Jewish and Christian reflections on human suffering: "But the good Lord isn't merciful, for some are born to hell / While some are born to heaven here, and afterward, as well."[14]

Meanwhile, many other working people remained convinced that God was on their side. One of Debs's associates, Colonel Jacob B. Maynard, gave eloquent voice to this view in an 1895 contribution to the *Railway Times*. He wove a theological narrative in which the same God ("Grand Master Workman") who had seen fit to send Moses ("a labor agitator") to liberate the Israelites ("subjected to numberless indignities") from Pharaoh ("a heartless employer") had enlisted, in the context of contemporary industrial battles, "on the side of the workingmen."[15] The 76-year-old Maynard was one of the chief editorialists for the Democratic *Indianapolis Sentinel*; his "theology of labor" bore the marks of a well-read newspaper man.[16] But the basic intuition animating his piece remained widespread among Chicago's rank-and-file, some 15,000 of whom showed up to hear Democratic nominee William Jennings Bryan hold forth at an 1896 Labor Day picnic sponsored by the Building Trades Council. Just two months before Bryan had electrified the delegates to the Democratic National Convention, gathered in the Chicago Coliseum, with his historic "Cross of Gold" speech. His efforts to win the election by forging an insurgent coalition of farmers and workers would fall flat, in large part because northern labor never fully warmed to his "popocratic" politics. But Bryan was also the foremost national proponent of a dissenting stream of agrarian Christianity that paralleled in many ways urban workers' own. His most rousing applause line at this 1896 Labor Day celebration: "Yet the meek and lowly Nazarene, who was rejected by those who robbed widows' houses, and then said long prayers, was heard gladly by the common people."[17]

Chicago's clergy remained more circumspect as to where God came down on the labor question. It had always been easiest to forge partnerships with local ministers when the matter at hand fit under a broader reform rubric, and this continued to be the case during the fin-de-siècle period.[18] Labor leaders had little trouble garnering clerical support for their work on temperance, child labor, sweat shops, and the six-day work week.[19] When in 1895, for example, some of the city's barbers redoubled their long-running efforts to get Sundays off, they won endorsements from an array of Protestant, Catholic, and Jewish divines, including several who had vociferously opposed the Pullman strike and boycott.[20] Reveling in the good news, Michael J. Carroll, the Irish-Catholic editor of the *Eight-Hour Herald*, "extend[ed] the compliments of the season to the reverend gentlemen."[21] That same week the pastor of Fulton Street Methodist, John P. Brushingham, a strong proponent of sabbatarianism, invited Trades and Labor Assembly (TLA) President Thomas J. Elderkin to deliver an address at his church. Brushingham would have listened approvingly as Elderkin warned "those who persist in making the laborer work on Sunday" that "another world shall call you to an accounting on the day when the sea and the land give forth their dead, and the countless millions meet again." But the minister may have been irked when Elderkin went on to issue a further call for the institution of the eight-hour day, for this was one of a number of items on labor's agenda about which Christian leaders remained uneasy at best.[22] No sticking point loomed so large as the status of strikes. Throughout the previous decades the city's Protestant and Catholic clergy had almost universally opposed the practice, though some exceptions were beginning to emerge on the scene.

This was especially the case in Chicago's small but growing African American community. In 1890 the city boasted 14,271 black residents, nearly four times as many as in 1870, though still only 1.2% of the total population.[23] Prior to the Great Migration African American ministers tended to be well-educated and middle class, though they were also unusually open to supporting workers' causes.[24] In the late 1880s, Bethesda Baptist's Reverend Bird Wilkinson made headlines when he declared, "Christ went further than socialism. He preached and practiced communism." Wilkinson insisted, "There are no millionaires in heaven who have succeeded in stealing the fairer portions and renting them out or in driving the poorer angels into the lower quarters," but did not leave it there. He wanted to "see true Christianity rule on earth" and closed by enjoining his congregation, "Suppose we try to start it. Brother Jones has $600; Sister Smith has $2000 in the bank; Brother Johnson has a house and lot. They give their worldly possessions to the church and we all share alike." Wilkinson's words won the approval of local labor leaders, one of whom praised him for "thundering the truth from the church rostrum."[25] In the early 1890s, meanwhile, the Reverends John T. Jennifer and John F. Thomas, senior pastors at Quinn Chapel and Olivet Baptist, two of the city's oldest and most respectable African American churches, lent material support to strikes instigated by a bi-racial waiters' union.[26]

For decades, their white counterparts had refused to do as much, though by the fin-de-siècle years there were indications that the ground was finally beginning to shift.

A handful of young Protestant ministers had, of course, rallied to the side of the ARU during the Pullman imbroglio and in the months that followed it became apparent that more change was in the works. Given the Reverend Carwardine's extensive involvement in the affair, the US Strike Commission called him to testify on 17 August 1894. In the course of the proceedings one commissioner asked, "Are you in favor of strikes?" Carwardine responded that he had "deplored" the Pullman strike and considered it "unwise," though he went on to add that in his "private opinion" the railroad men had few other realistic options. He was understandably cautious, for as his interrogator went on to ask, "You have been charged with being both a socialist and an anarchist?" Carwardine bristled at the very suggestion of the latter, declaring, "That charge would be so low that I really don't feel like answering it." Nevertheless, he went on to reply, "I might be what you would call a Christian socialist, but as to anarchy, I repudiate it entirely." The commissioners granted Carwardine an opportunity to further explain his position, which he did, closing with these noteworthy words:

> I will also say that there has been a good deal said on the part of the clergy about reaching the masses, getting hold of the workingmen and getting them into our churches, and I have thought if as clergymen, without endorsing all that the workingmen do, we would show our sympathy for them in their desire to better their condition we would probably be able to reach them on other lines if we would help them practically on these lines.[27]

In making explicit the connection between the churches' position on the labor question and their relationship to the nation's workingmen, Carwardine had reframed the industrial battles of the day in a way sure to catch the attention of even his most anti-union colleagues.

This altered perception became evident within a matter of weeks, for when the city's Methodist ministers gathered on 10 September for one of their regular business meetings, the question arose once more as to whether Carwardine's support for the ARU betrayed anarchist sympathies. The very fact that the charge was deemed serious enough to warrant discussion served as evidence for how unusual it was to see an upstanding member of the clergy support a strike. But after a brief debate, his colleagues rallied unanimously to his side, resolving, "[we] express our utmost confidence in the Rev. Mr. Carwardine's loyalty to Americanism, Methodism, and Christianity in the manly sympathy he has expressed in word and deed for the law-abiding people of Pullman."[28] While hardly a definitive endorsement, this carefully worded commendation—approved even by those who had decisively opposed the strike—nonetheless betokened increasing latitude for the denomination's ministers in their dealings with labor. Within ten days, meanwhile, the city's Methodist beacon had made Carwardine's interpretive frame its own. Commenting on the significance of the whole episode, the Reverend Arthur Edwards declared:

> The Methodist Church must keep close to the people. Industrious, mistaken, and sometimes designing labor leaders preach the error that the workingman is neglected by the church, and it is therefore immensely important that the misstatement should be corrected. Rev. W. H. Carwardine, our pastor at Pullman, has been true to his people, and has insisted that the rights of workmen should be respected, even while he plainly insists that he is not responsible for whatever mistakes may be made in the heat of word and action.[29]

Edwards's statement reflected, among other things, a growing sensitivity to workingmen's criticisms of the churches, which were as insistent as ever in the wake of the Pullman strike. The following year, when Chicago's Methodist ministers invited the British socialist and parliamentarian Keir Hardie to address them, they got far more than they bargained for. Hardie was born in Scotland a generation after Andrew Cameron and was, if anything, even more of a theological incendiary.[30] He opened his speech with an implicit comparison of the earliest Christians and the executed Haymarket anarchists that culminated in the question, "Is it not possible the men hanged in Chicago a few years ago may be pioneers of a new gospel?" At this juncture a number of the preachers present shouted "No!" even as the Reverend Daniel J. Holmes—the very same man who had, in 1867, championed the eight-hour movement at Amboy—exclaimed, "Those fellows should have been hanged."[31] Holmes had joined forces with John Caldwell—the very same reverend who in 1877 had so viciously denounced the mob from the pulpit of Ada Street Methodist—in vocally opposing the decision to invite Hardie on the grounds that they considered him an anarchist, but Carwardine had won the day, stating, "I do not agree with him in his views, but still he should be given a hearing."[32] One can only imagine how the latter felt now, though once the presiding officer restored order, Hardie veered in a somewhat more conciliatory direction, declaring, "All present, I believe, will be agreed that whatever prevents the people from coming to church should be removed." Those in the audience who had managed to regain their focus could hardly have been surprised by his analysis of the predicament: "If asked the cause of this lack of communion between the preachers, and his flock I would reply, 'want of Christianity in the church.' "[33]

The American Railway Union's Charles A. Keller sounded similar notes when, amidst the hubbub following Debs's speech at Battery D, reforming divine Graham Taylor challenged him to a debate on the question, "Is the Church Against Labor?" Taylor was in far closer touch with working people than his colleagues: he lived in a working-class, immigrant neighborhood on the city's northwest side and had recently founded the Chicago Commons, an institution modeled after Hull House.[34] He would have had a good idea of what to expect in this debate, given that both Debs and the *Railway Times* had more than tipped the ARU's hand, with the latter publishing a spate of editorials lashing out at "temples [where] the poor are strangers."[35] Following suit, "Mr. Keller led off with a severe and sweeping denunciation of the church," the next morning's *Tribune* reported. It went on to observe, "He quoted scripture and pulpit utterances in support of his argument." Trade unionists had long used Christian categories and concepts to formulate their critique of the churches, which most often had a constructive edge. As the ARU operative declared, "The great move for the laborer will be to reform the reformers, civilize civilization, Christianize Christianity, and redeem the 'redeemers.' "[36] But no matter how often Keller and his fellow wage earners reiterated their faith in what TLA leader William C. Pomeroy called "the teachings of true Christianity," church leaders fell deeper into despair over the godlessness of the working classes.[37]

By the turn of the century, Chicago's Protestant elite was gripped by a sense of full-fledged crisis. Looking out at what had once been their city, they saw entire neighborhoods given over to foreigners, drunkards, and radicals.[38] Out of these dens of iniquity came the likes of Michael Britzius, a prominent labor leader and one-time socialist candidate for mayor, whose funeral incorporated no hymns, no scripture, and no references to a god of any kind.[39] But as leading Protestants well knew, the German-born Britzius had never been within their fold. Much more painful was the mounting perception that native-born wage earners—the descendants of those who had fought in the Union army—were losing interest in the church. It was this very worry that prompted the Reverend Brushingham's Fulton Street Methodist Church to host a "workingmen's dinner" in the spring of 1895. The church's location at the corner of Fulton and Artesian Streets, roughly a mile west of Union Park and in a neighborhood still home to many artisans, rendered it well positioned for such an outreach. The congregation promised to cover the small price of admission for all unemployed attendees and meanwhile arranged for Clarence Darrow and a handful of other dignified persons to speak on the question, "Is the World Growing Better for the Average of Mankind?" As auspicious as the idea may have sounded, the event itself only compounded rising anxieties. Around the city the following morning many of Brushingham's colleagues would have read in the *Tribune*, "The dinner was an entire success as a dinner, but the workingmen did not materialize."[40]

In 1896 the Reverend Henry F. Perry, a student at the University of Chicago and Baptist minister in the prosperous Englewood neighborhood, set out to investigate the roots of the crisis. He sent a letter to three different classes of person—"Representative leaders of the wage-earners," "Workingmen who are churchgoers," and "Laboring Men who are alienated from the church"—asking two questions:

1. What reasons would be given by your associates, who do not attend church, for their absence from the church?

2. What remedies would you propose to bring your associates into closer touch with the church?

Perry was not the first to conduct such a survey; in fact, the practice dated back at least to the mid-1880s. In 1885 a minister in Montclair, New Jersey, had queried members of labor organizations about their church attendance and had been dismayed to find that less than 10% of Protestant workers regularly made it to worship.[41] During these same years Washington Gladden, too, had set out to understand why the percentage of working-class families in his congregation (10%) was so much smaller than that in the community at large (by Gladden's lights, somewhere between one-fifth and one-fourth). Yet another study in Pittsburgh had produced similarly troubling results: while professional men comprised only one-tenth of that city's population, they constituted over 60% of the local Protestant churches' membership.[42]

In March 1899 Perry published his own findings in the *American Journal of Sociology* in an article entitled, "The Workingman's Alienation from the Church." While he had done the interpretive work of sorting the various responses he received into different categories, the article was not densely analytical; it was, in the main, a reproduction of choice excerpts from those letters. These made clear that, for many ordinary working-men, alienation from the churches sprung from an attachment to what they deemed "true" Christianity. Perry received a number of replies from prominent leaders in the trade union world, including Samuel Gompers of the American Federation of Labor, but was most interested in what the non-churchgoing worker had to say for himself. "We should here, if anywhere, strike the root of the matter," he observed. Many in this class of respondent cited a perception, in the words of one man, "the churches are opposed to the workingman." Yet even those who seemed most disaf-fected articulated a deep attachment to Jesus. One declared, "Jesus Christ is with us outside the church, and we shall prevail with God," while another opined, "most of the ministers are muzzled by their masters and dare not preach the gospel of the carpenter of Nazareth." Perry summed up some of their proposed remedies: "Apply the Sermon on the Mount"; "Preach Christianity instead of theology"; "Let the pastor have a personal relation with the needs of labor. Be our champion." If these respondents understood themselves as true believers, Perry, for one, was not con-vinced. The article's final words read, "The Jesus who is applauded by the average workingman is a minimized Jesus Christ, a fictitious person, not the Christ of the gospels."[43]

Perry's condescension did not matter. It was significant, rather, that these workingmen had not only taken the time to respond but had also articulated terms on which the churches could regain their trust. By broadcasting their views to a wider audience, Perry raised the national profile of the issue and heightened proliferating anxieties, thereby inad-vertently increasing working people's leverage. Indeed, the article intensi-fied the pressure on Protestant leaders to recalibrate their stance on the nation's industrial crisis. They could ill afford to be perceived as "opposed to the workingman" any longer. Far from just a gauge of working-class disaffection, Perry's article became part of an unfolding cultural process that was bolstering the influence of both the churches' working-class crit-ics and their clerical allies.

Across the nation at the turn of the century, Protestant leaders con-ducted a spate of similar investigations. In St. Louis in 1901 a young Presbyterian divine named Charles Stelzle sent out letters to 200 labor leaders asking analogous questions. The *Tribune* relayed his finding, "that the 'wide gulf' is not 'between the workingmen and the church of Jesus Christ,' but between the 'workingmen and the church of today,' which is alleged to 'preach the doctrines' not of its founder but 'of the high and mighty ones of this earth.' "[44] Meanwhile, in 1902 fifteen Protestant clergymen on Chicago's West Side—long a hub of respectable working- and middle-class evangelicalism—elected to conduct their own survey. The results proved virtually identical to what Perry had found. At a gathering on 2 October, the Reverend Roy B. Guild listed the reasons why workingmen avoided church: "Churches are for the rich"; "Churches do not favor the poor"; and "Churches are antagonistic to labor unions" were the top three. The *Tribune* went on to report, "The Rev. Mr. Guild found, however, that the nonattendance of the workman, as a general thing, is not from absence of religious feeling . . . the majority of the replies indicated a deep lying spirit of reverence [for Jesus Christ]."[45] As more and more studies yielded more data like this, the pressure on the churches continued to mount.[46]

Meanwhile, trade unionists pressed the advantage. At a meeting of the Chicago Federation of Labor (CFL) on 2 June 1901, epithets flew when a delegate named Ingram read aloud a resolution passed at the Reformed Presbyterian synod's recent meeting, which upheld the denomination's ban on union membership. "I move that this assembly take action upon this," Ingram declared, going on to say, "They are not teaching the principles of Christianity, and if Christ came to Chicago today the first rebels against him and his doctrines would be found in the pulpits." One of the Federation's socialist delegates, Bernard Berlyn, came to the cloth's defense, but it was Ingram who carried the day. At his urging, the CFL sent a telegram, dripping with irony, to the synod, requesting prayers for the success of the eight-hour movement.[47]

Whatever Berlyn's objections to the telegram, the city's leading English-language socialists generally echoed workingmen's complaints. In the wake of Debs's 1897 conversion to socialism, his new beacon, the *Social Democrat*, picked up where the *Railway Times* had left off. In an editorial later that year, it proclaimed, "The truth is that the church has repudiated Christ and the great need of the hour is a new John the Baptist to prepare the way for his second coming."[48] Meanwhile, when in 1899 the local branch of the Socialist Labor Party named Algie M. Simons editor of a new weekly targeted at the city's workingmen, *The Workers' Call*, the churches gained yet another tough critic. Having grown up in a poor Wisconsin farming family, Simons had scraped together enough money to attend the state's flagship university in Madison, where he studied under Frederick Jackson Turner and Richard Ely. He left there convinced that the churches could be the "mightiest force for social regeneration," but found the realities on the ground in Chicago to be bitterly disappointing.[49]

Throughout a decade-long editorial tenure at three different socialist publications, Simons skewered the city's Protestant elite, which he perceived to be firmly in league with capital. Some evangelicals came under particular fire. He styled the otherworldly message preached at the Moody Church, for instance, "an up to date Gospel—that of capitalism."[50] But he was most fiercely critical of the well-heeled modernists whose handsome salaries came courtesy of pious industrialists like John V. Farwell, the dry-goods wholesaler whose brand of Christianity Simons labeled "spiritual chloroform."[51] Among his favorite clerical targets was the Reverend Frank W. Gunsaulus, pastor at the Loop's Central Church and vocal opponent of both unions and socialism. Simons rarely missed an opportunity to underscore the material underpinnings of Gunsaulus's "pulpit puerilities," observing in one editorial, "the author of this pitiful twaddle enjoys a greater annual income than the combined wages of half a dozen skilled mechanics."[52] At the root of all the vitriol lay not a hard-core materialism but rather a conviction that leading Protestants had ceased to preach the true gospel, propounding instead a false religion engineered, above all, to quiet a restless proletariat. When the *Tribune* reported that one Indiana factory owner, who did not himself attend church, had hired a Presbyterian minister to preach a fifteen-minute sermon to his employees at the beginning of each work day, Simons verged on apoplectic. "These employing classes have noticed these effects produced by this sham 'religion,'" he wrote, "and see in its spread and influence a long vista of peaceful and uncomplaining wage slavery, and uninterrupted profit."[53]

Foreign-born socialists—and especially those of Northern European descent—harbored similar grievances. Frithiof Malmquist habitually highlighted the transgressions of "the mediocre, lazy, egotistic, reactionary" clergy in his paper, *Svenska Nyheter*.[54] But his criticisms, too, had a constructive edge. In the very same editorial he went on to call for "a general conversion . . . among the clergy in order that the priests might gain a clearer understanding of the spiritual significance of the teaching of the Nazarene, 'Come unto me all ye who labor.'"[55] Fellow Swede A. A. Patterson created a stir in nearby Rockford in 1904 when he challenged Swedish Methodist Reverend P. M. Alfvin to a debate. Patterson was among a number of radicals who had heard Alfvin preach on the question

"Was Christ a Socialist?" He answered decisively in the negative. In an ensuing letter to the minister, Patterson wrote, "as to your arguments that all the Socialists are going to hell and that there is no chance for any of them to get into heaven, I must say that I am not well enough informed in theology to discuss that question and will therefore take your word for it."[56] It was not just Swedish radicals who expressed such exasperation. In the fragmented documentary record, one finds evidence that Danish, Dutch, and Norwegian socialists were also dissatisfied with the state of the Protestant churches.[57] Many of these yearned—like countless others around the city—for a return to the Christianity of Christ.

By the first decade of the twentieth century, then, Chicago's Protestant leaders had a serious dilemma on their hands. They found themselves increasingly beholden to fears that working people—and particularly native-born workingmen—were losing interest in the churches. They gathered from wide-ranging sources that this disaffection sprung in large part from their position on the labor question. How should they respond? By changing their attitude toward organized labor? If they did so, it would entail not only a revision of the laissez-faire ideology they had embraced long ago, in the days of the early republic, but also a potential reckoning with their patrons in the industrial elite. The alternative, they worried, was an irrevocable loss of cultural influence.

At first glance Chicago's Catholic elite seemed, by comparison, buoyantly confident. Throughout these turn-of-the-century years, William Dillon, the editor of the archdiocesan *New World*, and his successor Charles O'Malley worked to turn news of Protestant anxieties to their advantage. They were only too happy to confirm that the Episcopal Church was, indeed, "the church of plutocrats" and that "the [Protestant] parsons have little sympathy with the man who works."[58] Archdiocesan leaders maintained, meanwhile, that their church had no workingman problem. Dillon boasted in 1896, "Every Catholic Church in this and other large cities is filled to overflowing each Sunday four, five, and frequently six times, and the attendance is chiefly made up of working people and their families."[59] In contrast with Protestantism—"self-confessedly the church of the classes"—the Church of Rome was "the church of the poor."[60]

It was true that, in the wake of the Pullman strike, a fragile peace began to emerge between Chicago's Catholic and trade union communities. This rapprochement sprang in part from the Church's increasing willingness to talk about the nation's industrial economy as an unjust system. Even while many within the Protestant mainstream still refused to acknowledge any difference between capital and labor, Catholic leaders boldly named the structural disadvantages facing American workers. They asserted that court injunctions sometimes indulged "blind corporate greed"; that vast disparities of resources gave employers a decisive leg-up in nearly every strike; and that if an unfettered market were allowed to dictate wages, only "ruin and chaos" would result.[61] By 1900 the local hierarchy cast trade unionism as an absolute necessity: "organization of labor, in our present system of capitalistic production, is the only agency that can stand between labor and the degradation and ruin which is the inevitable result of unchecked competition between those who are in desperate need," Dillon declared.[62] But whatever the high-minded rhetoric, the Church's stance on a number of industrial questions had not fundamentally changed. At the turn of the century, leading Catholics continued to embrace the principle of contract freedom, which rendered their support for working-class causes deeply qualified: they opposed not only the use of violence but also boycotts, sympathetic strikes, and enforcement of the picket line, to cite just a few examples.

Such positions provoked labor's more radical wing to anger. When the *New World* condemned the ARU's widening of the fight against George Pullman, a number of readers stopped their subscriptions. Many more wrote to the editor, including one striker, who declared, "I think it a pity that, as you go as far as you do, you cannot see your way to go a little further and taking sides with the men heartily and without reserve or qualification."[63] These differences did not subside. In 1896 Dillon found himself in a protracted exchange with a Mr. W. J. Thomas, who wrote to the paper, "I am personally convinced that as individuals have the right to resist encroachment on their private property, even to the extent of using force, so laboring men, under present circumstances have the right, ethically speaking, to keep others from usurping their places made vacant by the exigencies of a just strike!" Dillon once more emphatically rejected this "very radical doctrine."[64] In the spring of 1897, meanwhile, the editor looked on as William E. Burns, a member of the ARU's board of directors, locked horns with St. Anne's Father Patrick M. Flannigan at a meeting in Washington Park's Werkmeister Hall. In response to Flannigan's plea for the repeal of a law prohibiting the pooling of railroad funds, Burns "took a slap at him," the *Railway Times* reported, "by quoting Daniel O'Connell's statement that he took his religion from Rome but his politics from the people."[65] At the turn of the century, then, influential Catholics and militant trade unionists remained at loggerheads.

Meanwhile, the hierarchy's worries about socialism were on the rise. The specter of radicalism had preoccupied the Vatican from the moment Leo XIII assumed the Holy See in 1878. That very year he issued an encyclical entitled *Quod Apostolici Muneris*, which condemned "the plague of socialism" and pronounced that "the right of property and ownership . . . stands inviolate."[66] He developed these themes further in his 1891 encyclical *Rerum Novarum*, which articulated a fuller response to the crises of industrialization. The document broke decisively with core aspects of laissez faire economics, issuing a clarion call for workers to be paid "what is justly due [them]."[67] But the pontiff made clear throughout that socialism was not the answer to the industrializing world's problems. Rejecting calls for an equal distribution of wealth as both unattainable and undesirable, he reiterated, "Private ownership must be preserved inviolate."[68] American prelates latched on to *Rerum Novarum*'s anti-socialist provisions especially and it was to these that Leo returned once more in 1901.[69] In *Graves De Communi Re*, he lamented "the growing power of the socialistic movement" and called for the officers of both Church and State to array themselves against those who are "working incessantly on the multitudes of the needy which daily grow greater, and which, because of their poverty are easily deluded and led into error."[70]

Echoes of these teachings could be heard in Chicago, though under the watch of Patrick A. Feehan, archbishop from 1880 until 1902, the local hierarchy made no systematic attempt to root out socialism. To be sure, when the faithful transgressed acceptable boundaries, the clergy left no doubt about where the Church stood. Throughout the upheavals of the 1880s Czech priests battled to reverse socialism's advance among their people, while Irish-Catholic officials used a variety of archdiocesan platforms to criticize all forms of radicalism.[71] Toward the end of Feehan's tenure this sort of sporadic policing activity became more regular. In the spring of 1899, Father T. F. Cashman vehemently denied a rumor that his parish, St. Jariath's, had authorized a circular crafted by a group calling itself the Roman Catholic Socialistic Society of Chicago.[72] Meanwhile, in the wake of the pope's 1901 encyclical, the *New World* published a scathing review of Kentucky socialist and priest Thomas McGrady's new book, declaring, "the work is revolutionary in its doctrines, and its dangerous influence is enhanced by the beauty of its diction and the enchanting character of the story."[73] Later that same year, the archdiocese commissioned the mass distribution in churches of an anti-socialist pamphlet entitled "The Crying Evil of the Hour."[74]

But even at this late date the *New World* indulged dissenting views. In the spring of 1900, it reproduced without comment the full text of three letters from a socialist correspondent, "S. T.," who wrote in one of these, "Socialism is still as 'the voice of one crying out in the wilderness,' but from millions of oppressed souls the prayer continually ascends, 'Thy kingdom come, Thy will be done on earth as it is in heaven,' and its realization when the people act accordingly as they pray may end in socialism."[75] Several months later it published a forceful apologetic from card-carrying socialist M. J. Weis, as well as a variation on the cooperative commonwealth theme from one "M.K."[76] Even six months after the promulgation of *Graves De Communi Re*, Dillon ran another "plea for socialism," this time from a reader rankled by the negative review of McGrady's book. "[It] will be a beacon light to many an intelligent man and woman who realize that their established rights are fast being undermined by a system of capitalism more beautiful in theory than in practice," wrote one "P.J.C."[77] But this era of relative openness came to an abrupt end in the autumn of 1902, when Feehan died and Dillon resigned his post.

As the Pope weighed different candidates to succeed Feehan, he eyed the advance of socialism in cities like Chicago with increasing concern. While the movement remained marginal across the United States, its fortunes were on the upswing by 1902.[78] The founding of the Socialist Party of America (SPA) the previous year had generated new enthusiasm and new recruits, both of which the Socialist Labor Party (SLP) had long failed to produce. By welcoming populists and radicals of all different stripes—including leading personalities such as Debs and Algie Simons—the SPA rapidly eclipsed the doctrinaire SLP, attracting a total of 229,762 votes in 1902 congressional and state elections, compared with the latter's 53,763.[79] The grand total of 283,525 votes cast for socialist candidates represented nearly a threefold increase over the comparable total for 1900.[80] Illinois was at the vanguard of the ascending movement and would, by 1904, boast more party members than any other state.[81] But socialism's reach extended well beyond this committed core. Between 1899 and 1902, for example, the Chicago-based Charles H. Kerr Publishing House sold more than 500,000 copies in its Pocket Library of Socialism series, "little red books," priced at 5 cents a copy, which contained essays by leading radical reformers.[82]

Looking to quash this rising socialist menace, Leo XIII selected James Edward Quigley to be the new archbishop of Chicago.[83] During his five-year tenure as the bishop of Buffalo, New York, Quigley had made a name for himself as a tough proponent of the Vatican's policy on industrial questions. When it appeared in early 1902 that socialists were making headway within that city's German trade unions, he rushed into the fray. Quigley forbade his flock to read the *Arbeiter Zeitung* and meanwhile issued an episcopal letter condemning socialism, which was read aloud in the vernacular in every German Catholic parish in the city. The following week he called a mass meeting in East Buffalo, which attracted several thousand trade unionists. There he reiterated the Church's support for workingmen, citing *Rerum Novarum* and hailing Leo as "the truest friend of labor the world has ever seen." But he focused especially on the nefarious consequences of socialism, raising at one point the specter of ever-more godless Germany. "Berlin has a population of 1,800,000 souls and returns a solid delegation of social democrats to the Reichstag," Quigley declared, going on to point out, "There are today only fifty-nine churches of all Christian denominations in Berlin." In his own assessment, the meeting had the desired effect. In his debut interview with the *Chicago Tribune*, the incoming archbishop reflected on the episode and said, with a self-satisfied smile, "We won."[84]

In Chicago, Quigley once more set about "winning" with a vengeance. He began his assault on socialism before he even arrived in the city, dispatching lieutenants to strategic parishes like the near West Side's Church of the Holy Family, where "there had been much discussion of the subject of socialism among the younger members," the *Tribune* reported. In early January 1903 the Reverend Edward Gleeson delivered a series of lectures at this, Chicago's largest English-speaking parish, with the hope of setting these wayward youths straight.[85] But as he had done in Buffalo, Quigley focused especially on eradicating socialism within the city's German communities. He was not the first to try. During the winter of 1901–1902, Theodore B. Thiele, a prominent leader within the German Catholic Societies of Illinois, had spearheaded an effort to gather workers into Church-sanctioned unions. Thiele explained the rationale to the press, saying, "The difficulty today is that labor is disposed to listen to the high sounding phrases of the Socialists without studying to see the motive that prompts them. We want to see workmen think and reason for themselves, not go after false gods."[86] This initiative soon fizzled, but the worry motivating it did not.

Consequently, when in February 1903 Quigley commissioned his subordinate, the Reverend Anton Heiter, to lead a "crusade" against socialism in Chicago's German parishes, many within the local hierarchy rejoiced.[87] The 53-year-old Heiter was an immigrant himself, having left Rülzheim in 1876, and had played a leading role in the 1902 anti-socialist campaign in his home diocese of Buffalo.[88] Upon arriving in Chicago, he coordinated with Thiele's organization as well as the city's German priests to set up an intensive week of speaking engagements. The anxieties fueling the whole enterprise were palpable. One of the archdiocese's leading German priests commented, "Every address will deal with some phase of socialism, which is prevalent in the trades unions of Chicago."[89] Dillon's successor at the *New World,* Charles J. O'Malley, elaborated further, declaring, "This is a battle for the church . . . this city is regarded as a rallying point for socialists. This is the only place in the United States where they have their socialistic Sunday schools." Thiele, meanwhile, was quick to clarify: "We are going to warn our people against socialism in unions, not unions themselves. We don't want our people compelled, because they have affiliated with organized labor, to be led unwittingly into socialism."[90]

Heiter commenced his lecture tour on 10 February. Over the course of a grueling seven days he spoke in German churches all over the city: at St. Martin's in Washington Park; St. Paul's in Pilsen; St. Alphonsus' in Lincoln Park; St. Boniface in West Town; St. Michael's in Old Town; St. Anthony's in Bridgeport; and Handel Hall in the Loop. His speeches, delivered entirely in German, were not rigorously argued. In his address at St. Martin's he declared, for example, "[Socialism] has sought to reduce the toiler to abject want"; and also, "Socialism has come and laid its cuckoo egg in the nest prepared by organized labor and expects you men to hatch it out."[91] His anti-radical harangues were laced, moreover, with anti-Semitism. At St. Alphonsus' he pronounced, "[Marx] really was a Jew, but no Jew could hold office in England, so he dropped his faith. He knew religion only in a degenerate form and blamed it for not making an end of the slavery of the masses."[92] Heiter was not only against socialism; he was for capitalism. While he never outright condemned unions, he spent the entire evening at St. Michael's deconstructing the labor theory of value and defending corporate privilege. At various point he proclaimed, "Labor [is] useless without the leadership of those men—those captains—who direct the armies of peace to the most profitable achievements"; and "it is untrue that the employer as a class oppresses the employee or withholds from him his due."[93] By the end of the week at least two thousand persons had likely heard Heiter speak and many times that number had been caught up in the excitement surrounding his visit.[94] But the crusade had nevertheless failed to achieve its primary goal.

Far from defeated, Chicago's socialists were abuzz. The news of Quigley's appointment provoked a sarcastic retort from Algie Simons. In the *Chicago Socialist*, the successor to the *Workers' Call*, he wrote, "If he is as successful here as he was in Buffalo there will be no cause of complaint, as his 'victory' there is confirmed by an increased Socialist vote as the November elections show. Come along, Bishop, we will not grudge you any future victories of this sort you may obtain here."[95] When Quigley finally arrived in Chicago on 10 March, the Danish socialist paper *Revyen* struck a more poignant note. Relaying that the new archbishop had traveled to the city in a luxurious Pullman sleeping car, the editor wrote, "He, whom the bishop is supposed to represent, and whose teachings he supposedly proclaims, came riding into Jerusalem on an ass and did not even have anything on which he might rest his head. He lived for and felt for the small ones in society, and scolded the rich and unjust."[96] Some radicals' criticisms were not so Christocentric. When the editor of the *Arbeiter Zeitung*, Rudolph Grossmann, got wind of Heiter's coming visit, he wrote a letter to the priest, the *Tribune* reported, "in which he declare[d] that religion is the curse of the laboring classes."[97] But such thoroughgoing anti-clericalism was more the exception than the rule.

In fact, prominent spokespersons within Chicago's diverse radical communities insistently challenged Quigley's notion that "Catholic" and "socialist" were mutually exclusive identities.[98] Simons hammered home this point in lengthy responses to both Fathers Gleeson and Heiter in the pages of the *Chicago Socialist*. He quoted Richard Ely, "Socialism is simply applied Christianity," and the *Encyclopedia Britannica*, "the ethics of Socialism are identical with the ethics of Christianity," to bolster his case. Simons went on to write in his own words, "the Socialist wants peace. He wants it made possible that he may sit under his own vine and fig tree—he wants the Kingdom of God on Earth."[99] A month after Heiter's campaign ended, meanwhile, another Catholic came from afar to speak on the relation of the Church to socialism: Father Thomas McGrady, the renowned socialist priest, who just four months previously had been forced to resign from his Bellevue, Kentucky, parish.[100] When J. B. Smiley, the chair of the meeting, introduced McGrady to the crowd gathered in the Loop's Auditorium on 26 March, the scene was reminiscent of Debs at Battery D several years before. Smiley described McGrady as "the man who has defended the cause of socialism against the attacks of Fathers Heiter and

Sherman." The next morning's *Tribune* noted, "The names of the two distinguished ecclesiastics brought forth from the audience a volley of jeers."
McGrady went on to declare, "A Catholic can be a socialist, for socialism
stands for the moral teachings of Christ, and the repudiation of socialism
is the repudiation of Christianity."[101]

Such spirited resistance only confirmed the hierarchy's growing
worry that radicals were stealing the Church's sheep. Under Quigley
and O'Malley's editorial direction, the *New World* soon became obses-
sively anti-socialist. In the first several years of the new archbishop's
tenure, especially, nearly every issue featured a contribution on the dangers of radicalism.[102] Editorials continued to insist that socialism was
intrinsically atheistic and therefore inimical to the Catholic faith.[103] The
English-language *New World* had a heavily Irish readership, but clergy
serving other immigrant groups made sure that the message went out to
their flocks as well.[104] Both in Chicago and in Rome, church authorities
envisioned parishes and parochial schools as bulwarks against the rising
socialist tide within communities of the foreign-born, a hope shared by
government officials as well.[105]

But still the tide rose. Chicago's socialists relentlessly returned
the Church's fire. Anti-Catholic sentiment spread through German,
Bohemian, Italian, and Polish circles, in particular, with much of the
focus on the Church's hypocrisy.[106] An article in the Polish *Dziennik
Ludowy* entitled, "Love Thy Neighbor as Thyself," began, "We hear these
words almost every Sunday, thrown at us from the pulpit by people
who never practice what they preach."[107] Meanwhile, Simons and other
contributors to the *Chicago Socialist* continued to criticize the hierarchy's position and moreover to blur the line between Christianity and
socialism.[108] When socialists made gains in the wider world, leading
Catholics' anxieties rose to fever pitch. In the wake of socialism's good
showing in the 1904 election, the *New World* ran editorials entitled,
"The Approach of Radicalism," "The Socialist Peril," and "Is Socialism
Incurable?" Sounding the alarm, O'Malley wrote: "We sincerely hope
those good people have their eyes opened now. If they have not they
never will. Forty-five thousand votes in Chicago—one hundred and
fifty thousand in the state—what more will they have? Will they wait
until they are struck by lightning?"[109]

Thus, at the turn of the century developments on the ground had
Chicago's Roman Catholic elite deeply concerned. With socialists seemingly expanding their movement's foothold in Chicago and across the

nation, church leaders found themselves in a bind: how could they protect their working-class flock from radicalism without appearing to be on the wrong side of the industrial war? The pope had addressed this very difficulty in *Rerum Novarum* by calling for the formation of specifically Catholic unions, but archdiocesan leaders were justifiably pessimistic about the prospects for these in a city as pluralistic as Chicago. Fortunately for them, conservative trade unionists were even then in the process of constructing a suitable alternative.

7

"Social Christianity Becomes Official"

THE RISE OF A MIDDLE-CLASS SOCIAL GOSPEL

IN THE FIRST decade of the twentieth century, "Social Christianity [became] official."[1] Or at least this was how one of the first historians of the movement, Charles Hopkins, described the startling developments of those years. It was then that, in denomination after denomination, progressive faith began to gain new institutional expression. In 1903 alone the Presbyterian Church founded a Department of Church and Labor, and the Congregational and Episcopal churches empowered commissions to investigate industrial problems. The Methodists established a Federation for Social Service in 1907 and soon thereafter endorsed a "Social Creed" that called "for equal rights and complete justice for all men in all stations of life," and more specifically "for the abolition of child labor"; "for the suppression of the 'sweating system'"; and "for a living wage in every industry."[2] The Federal Council of Churches (FCC) ratified that creed shortly after its founding in 1908. Meanwhile, in 1910 the American Federation of Catholic Societies sent its first fraternal delegate to the AFL's national convention. For working people, who had fought so long to reform the churches, these were heady times.[3]

A parallel set of developments unfolded on the ground in Chicago. As late as 1900, the city's trade unions could count few friends in the clergy's ranks; in the years immediately following, that number increased dramatically. Working people keyed the change. Their long-standing protest had, by the turn of the century, generated intense worries among the Christian elite about the possibility of a working-class exodus from the churches. That anxiety soon became the engine driving the emergence within the institutional churches of a middle-class Social Gospel, which was also, in an indirect sense, "union made."

The ascendance of conservative labor reformers within the AFL made it easier for the churches to embrace labor during these years. In distinguishing sharply between trade unionism and radicalism, the women and men of the AFL won to their side Catholic leaders whose support for labor had long been contingent upon its total disassociation from socialism. At the same time, the building of a massive coalition behind "pure-and-simple unionism" strengthened the hand of young, reforming Protestant ministers who sought to repair their churches' relationship to the working classes. Indeed, over the course of the decade following 1900, many Chicago clergymen would come to see the answer to the churches' workingman problem and to the nation's industrial crisis as one and the same: champion conservative labor reform.

Ecclesial support remained uneven and contingent, however, as the divergent reactions to two mid-decade strikes make clear. Throughout the packinghouse strike of 1904, the union remained disciplined, both in its street presence and in its public messaging. Union leaders spun the strike's purpose in ways that resonated with the city's middle classes, including a wide variety of church leaders. While many denominational officials remained neutral, priests and ministers on the ground rushed to defend the strikers and their cause. By contrast, in 1905, when the teamsters went out on a sympathetic strike against Montgomery Ward, expressing their solidarity with terminated garment workers, the Christian elite insisted that the walkout was entirely unjustified. Because the gambit sprung from no apparent injury to the teamsters themselves and moreover entailed the breaking of contracts, leading Christians wanted no part of it. When working people across the city showed support for the drivers by stalling and assaulting their replacements, leading Protestants and Catholics reflected that their initial reservations had been vindicated. Notably, however, when the teamsters' nemeses in the Employers' Association announced that they aimed to break the union altogether, influential Christians across the city argued that capital had crossed the line. Their ardent support for trade unionism in the general case—if not this particular one—underscores that, by the first decade of the twentieth century, social Christianity had finally and much belatedly gained a foothold in the churches themselves.

The origins of the American Federation of Labor lay in the early 1880s, when a desire for better coordination among the labor organizations scattered across the nation prompted conversations about the formation of a larger confederation. These culminated in a convention in Pittsburgh in 1881, where Samuel Gompers, a young leader within the International Cigarmakers' Union and chairman of the convention's Committee on Organization, proposed that the new association be called "The Federation of Organized Trades Unions of the United States of America and Canada." The proposed name smacked of exclusivity to many delegates, who hoped for an amalgamation of all workers, not just skilled craftsmen. One Mr. Pollinger declared, "We recognize neither creed, color nor nationality but want to take into the folds of this organization the whole labor element of this country, no matter of what calling; for that reason the name should read, 'Trades and Labor Unions.'" The proponents of inclusivity carried the day and the fledgling association was named the Federation of Organized Trades and Labor Unions of the United States and Canada. [4]

In 1886 the organization changed its name to the American Federation of Labor, but through the mid-1890s it continued to be a diverse body, readily incorporating workers of all different political orientations, as well as women, immigrants, and African Americans. Growing the membership was the leadership's first priority during these years. At the time of its founding, the AFL encompassed only 12 unions and roughly 50,000 trade unionists; by 1890 its membership—36 unions, 200,000 trade unionists—had surpassed that of the fading Knights of Labor.[5] The organization's openness to all different varieties of wage earners proved the engine of this rapid growth. In 1888 Gompers, who served as the AFL's president from 1886 until his death in 1924, chartered Federal Labor Union No. 2703, founded by Elizabeth Morgan and other Chicago-based women, most of whom were socialists or former Knights. Meanwhile, on the question of African American inclusion, as historian Bruce Laurie writes, "[Gompers] reprimanded racist field staff and rarely let an early AF of L convention pass without a lecture on reaching across the racial divide." As late as 1890, he remained tolerant also of socialists within the AFL's ranks. Emphasizing the pragmatic sources of this posture, Gompers remarked to a fellow organizer that national leaders "disposed to be dictatorial" would "soon find none to dictate to."[6]

In the mid-1890s, however, this policy of toleration gave way when the AFL's national leadership embraced a strategy of "prudential unionism." Whereas the federal government's intervention in the Pullman strike had pushed Debs in a more radical direction, it had only reinforced for Gompers the merits of a "pure and simple" strategy, which sought incremental gains in the workplace, not an overhaul of the economic system. From that point forward AFL leaders frowned upon unskilled and semi-skilled workers, who were predominantly foreign-born and more liable to participate in the mass strikes that invited unwanted government attention. The leadership moreover declined to challenge surging chauvinism and racism in its member unions, even as it engineered the formal marginalization of socialists within the Federation. At the AFL's annual convention in December 1894, a decisive majority of the delegates rejected a radical platform in favor of the conservative agenda thrust forward by Gompers and his associates.[7] Throughout this season of conservative triumph the AFL's growth slowed considerably, but in the years between 1897 and 1904 its membership expanded at a phenomenal rate.[8] In 1897 the organization counted 264,825 members or roughly 60% of all American trade unionists. By 1900 the rank-and-file had almost doubled in size, numbering 500,000, and in the ensuing four years it went on to more than triple. In 1904 the AFL boasted 1,676,200 members—fully 80% of the nation's organized wage earners—and had become the leading institutional voice of the American worker.[9]

In Chicago, meanwhile, prominent labor leaders such as the *Eight-Hour Herald's* Michael J. Carroll increasingly eschewed radical reform, preferring to advance their agenda through partnerships with the middle-class progressives who ran the Civic Federation and the Municipal Voters League. There was no clearer evidence for the conservative turn than the 1896 merger that created the CFL. When the strident Labor Congress joined forces with the far more moderate Trades and Labor Assembly, the ranks of organized labor moved toward the mainstream.[10] James Barrett writes that by 1903, "Nearly every union in Chicago was a constituent of the powerful Chicago Federation of Labor and . . . these unions had organized over half of the city's entire labor force, including many unskilled immigrants and more than 35,000 women."[11] There could be no doubt: conservative labor reform was on the move.

In building a massive coalition behind prudential unionism, the AFL and its affiliates forged a brand of labor reform that the Roman Catholic Church could support.[12] In Chicago, influential Catholics responded enthusiastically to the conservatives' ascendance within the Federation. By the turn of the century, in fact, the *New World*, the archdiocesan weekly, doubled as an unofficial mouthpiece of pure-and-simple unionism, regularly reproducing AFL circulars, leaflets, and speeches in its pages.[13] But as its coverage of the 1898 AFL national convention in Kansas City made clear, the Church's support for labor remained contingent upon its complete disassociation from radicalism. Reporting on the socialist faction's latest failure to rally the majority behind its platform, an editor remarked that this "sweeping" rejection illustrated the delegates' "sagacity."[14] But what if the convention had played out differently? Or what if, at some point in the future, socialistic labor reformers found a way to dislodge their conservative counterparts' hold over the organization?

For the Catholic hierarchy in Chicago these were very real fears. Consequently, the *New World* viciously denounced groups such as the American Labor Union and the Industrial Workers of the World—or Industrial "Shirkers" of the World, in one editor's preferred phrase—as well as radical leaders such as Debs, Haggerty, and Simons. It moreover urged its readers to boycott labor unions and publications that it deemed "unsafe."[15] But all the while, archdiocesan officials insisted that they supported the true interests of labor. "All over America just now Socialist sheets are declaring Catholicism opposed to the interests of the working-man," *New World* editor O'Malley wrote in 1905, "yet within a twelvemonth [sic] the American Federation of Labor has been commended by Cardinal Gibbons, Archbishop Messmer, Archbishop Ireland, Bishop Matz of Denver, Bishop Spaulding of Peoria, and Bishop McFaul of Trenton, to cite only a few well-known names."[16]

Eager to reinforce conservatives' strength within organizations such as the AFL, the United Mine Workers (UMW), and the CFL, Catholic leaders threw their collective weight behind Samuel Gompers, John Mitchell, and John Fitzpatrick. When they were attacked from either the Right or the Left, the *New World* rushed to their defense, calling Gompers, for one, "a sane, safe man and a foe of violence of every kind."[17] It was the conservatives' fierce opposition to socialism that especially endeared them to the hierarchy. The *New World* reprinted a speech by Wisconsin Archbishop Sebastian Messmer, in which he declared, "I have only words of commendation for the American Federation of Labor and the work of those excellent men, Samuel Gompers and John Mitchell, who have done great work for the laboring man, not only in aiding and protecting him in his interests, but in fighting the socialistic tendency."[18] O'Malley wrote in the same vein, "It is gratifying to note that the Chicago Federation of Labor, through its official organ, has protested against the entrance of the alleged American Labor Union into the local field. The latter is asserted to be distinctly a socialistic organization and has recently moved its headquarters... to this city in order the better to spread its peculiar gospel."[19] Influential Catholics did whatever they could to aid conservatives in their fight. When the delegates of the Cook County Branch of the AFL met at the Grand Pacific Hotel in July 1904, Archbishop Quigley showed up to bless their work.[20] Meanwhile, the New World continued to reproduce articles by trade unionists themselves with titles like, "Labor Wars on Socialism."[21]

The ample evidence of such synergy illustrates that conservatives' ascendance within the American Federation of Labor helped the hierarchy to resolve its dilemma regarding how to navigate the nation's industrial conflicts. By rallying nearly two million workers behind pure-and-simple unionism, Gompers, Mitchell, and allied reformers presented the Church with the option to be both anti-socialist and pro-labor. It was a precarious settlement, to be sure, and one that would be severely tested by the relentless strikes that beset Chicago in the first decade of the twentieth century.

Some of Chicago's leading Protestants were much slower to warm to organized labor during these years, and in fact some never did. Consider what happened at Pullman Presbyterian Church in the wake of the working-class walkout that dramatically shrank the congregation during the summer of 1894. In the months that followed, it became apparent that this uprising had only strengthened the position of George Pullman's allies within the church. When the Reverend Oggel's term expired, the congregation selected the Reverend Granville R. Pike to succeed him. Pike was deeply interested in the question of how to bring workingmen back into the churches—over the course of the ensuing decade, he would become nationally known as something of an expert on the matter—but he was at the same time a fierce critic of organized labor. In the autumn of 1895, at a gathering of Chicago's Presbyterian ministers, Pike gave a talk entitled, "A View at First Hand," in which he reprised his predecessor's interpretation of the conflict at Pullman, stoutly defending the company and contending the strikers had been in the wrong all along.[22]

Pike had plenty of company in turn-of-the-century Chicago, as Protestant churches with direct ties to the industrial elite typically remained antagonistic toward trade unions. This was true regardless of their theological orientation. Anti-unionism continued to be in vogue within nondenominational strongholds of "liberal" religion such as the People's Church; within fashionable mainline cathedrals such as First Congregational; within evangelical flagships such as the Moody Church; and within institutional churches such as Union Christian.[23] Ministers at churches like these were very much caught up in a perceived crisis of working-class attrition and yet, unwilling to modify their stance on industrial questions, they pursued alternative means of luring the men back.

The Reverend Frank W. Gunsaulus exemplified this stance. His illustrious Chicago career spanned three and a half decades, during which he presided over two of the city's wealthiest churches, Plymouth Congregational (1887–1899) and the Central Church (1899–1919). But Gunsaulus is best remembered for his pivotal role in the founding of the Armour Institute of Technology.[24] At Plymouth Congregational in the early 1890s, he delivered his "million-dollar sermon," in which he outlined the reforms he would pursue if he had the money. The oration so moved meatpacking mogul Philip D. Armour that he donated this princely sum for the founding of a school where young men of all classes could learn the practical arts.[25] Armour's one condition was that Gunsaulus serve as the Institute's president, which he did from its opening in 1893 until shortly before his death in 1921. The school embodied a major vein of Protestant outreach to working-class men: help the hard-working to help themselves. Indeed, a year after its doors opened, the Presbyterian *Interior* published a lengthy feature on it, gushing: "Sons of millionaires study in Armour institute, side by side with country lads who are working their way. Puritan stock jostles Africa's children, and all who may have any ideas about superiority of position or birth are taught the lesson of the brotherhood of man, and made to see that the only thing recognized where that spirit prevails, is superiority of merit."[26] In light of Gunsaulus's devotion to this meritocratic enterprise, many in his circles regarded him as a leading reformer and friend of working people. In fact, however, the story is much more complicated.

Like Pike, Gunsaulus was deeply committed to the uplift and Christianization of the city's working classes. But his approach to this project reflected hopes and prejudices befitting his Prairie Avenue address.[27] In addition to his work with the Armour Institute, he championed scientific charity and reviled the saloon.[28] During his first year at the Central Church, Gunsaulus suggested that it keep its doors open into the later evening on Sundays, so that young men in search of alternatives to drink could come and listen to classical music and engaging lectures. This was the kind of idea guaranteed to arouse the empathy and open the pocketbooks of the church's aristocratic membership, which included men like Abram Pence, one of the most eminent attorneys in Chicago, and A. C. Bartlett, vice-president of one of the city's largest wholesalers. Sure enough, the *Tribune* reported, "tumultuous applause broke forth from the congregation, and after the sermon several of the trustees consulted with the pastor with reference to carrying out the idea."[29]

Gunsaulus's outlook on the nation's industrial crisis only further ingratiated him to Chicago's Protestant upper crust. Following in the footsteps of his predecessors at the Central Church—the Reverends David Swing and Newell Hillis—he proved a determined foe of organized labor. To be sure, Gunsaulus emulated his nineteenth-century forebears in exalting "labor" in the abstract as "sacred."[30] But he would, in the same breath, assault the fundamental ideas underlying trade unionism. More than ten years after the Haymarket affair and five years after the Pullman strike and boycott, Gunsaulus was among those who still refused to admit a fundamental distinction between capital and labor. In one 1899 sermon he declared, "Capital is coined labor, and when labor strikes at capital it does not vanquish capital, but in reality commits suicide."[31] Such logic had seemed more defensible in the antebellum period, when Whigs had earnestly hoped for a republic spurred onward by artisans and entrepreneurs; but at the turn of the century, with corporate capitalism having been entrenched for a generation, this older line of thought amounted to little more than ideological cover for anti-unionism. Gunsaulus had problems with trade unions in the concrete as well, lamenting their deleterious effects upon technical education and low standards for membership.[32] More radical forms of working-class protest seemed entirely beyond the pale.[33] Gunsaulus did occasionally reprimand capital, but his calls for the wealthy to observe the Golden Rule did not exactly strike fear into the heart of his well-heeled congregation. They were, after all, almost always accompanied by reassurances that he stood firmly behind corporate privilege: "I believe in the rights of capital and in the power of capital," he declared at one point, while proclaiming at another, "I cannot help but feel that the corporation has been put into the hearts of men by God."[34]

In addition to those with strong ties to the industrial elite, Protestant ministers within a variety of northern European immigrant churches tended to remain antagonistic toward organized labor. To be sure, in the decades following the Pullman strike and boycott, there were a few Scandinavian ministers who took stands on behalf of working people. In 1905 the Reverend C. W. Finwall, pastor at Logan Square's Norwegian Baptist Church, became a vocal proponent of a servant girls' union, citing the oppressive conditions that these women braved.[35] Four years later, a Swedish Unitarian divine, the Reverend August Dallgren, came out in public support of a general strike back home in Sweden.[36] But these were voices crying out in a wilderness. Only in 1912 did the Dutch Christian Reformed Church officially relax its prohibition on union membership, when the Classis Illinois—the local governing body—declared it would "tolerate" unionized workers. But even into the 1950s a debate persisted within that denomination as to whether a churchgoer could belong to the CIO or AFL and still remain in good standing.[37]

Immigrant churches' enduring anti-unionism sprung from a variety of sources, including venerable worries about secret societies and more contemporary ones about assimilation. For still others, the cash nexus was close to the heart of the matter. When in 1903 a leader in one retail clerks' local approached a Swedish minister, asking him to endorse a boycott on Sunday morning purchases so that merchants would close their stores and employees could go to church, the divine refused: he dare not cross local retailers, he explained, as their advertisements funded his monthly news-letter.[38] In contrast with such pragmatism, some church leaders charted a fiercely bourgeois course on principle. Paul Petter Waldenström was a case in point. One of the founding spirits of the *Missionsförbundet*—a pietist offshoot of the Swedish Lutheran Church, which by the turn of the century had made significant inroads in Chicago—Waldenström proved a determined foe of trade unionism. When in 1897 lumber workers back in Sweden cast their strike as an outgrowth of their evangelical faith, he moved immediately to squelch this working-class gospel. Following his lead, the Church's annual meeting passed a resolution denying that "the religious movement contained within it socialism and communism," these being the rubrics under which it classified trade unionism. The statement went on, "the Swedish Mission Covenant, for its part, denies such connection, partly on the ground of the heartiest distaste, that any true Christian worker should allow himself to be led into such affairs, partly on the ground of extreme dislike of any attempt to exert pressure through so-called 'strikes' to better economic conditions."[39] Nor did the ensuing decade of labor strife disabuse leading Covenanters of these ideas. In 1909, with a general strike ongoing in Sweden, Waldenström once more leveraged his influence against working-class activism, send-ing a telegram to his fellow believers in Chicago, urging them to send no aid to the strikers.[40] So long as he had his way, the Swedish Mission Covenant Church would be no friend of organized labor.

But if one pole of leading Protestant opinion remained deeply antago-nistic to trade unionism, another more moderate pole gradually emerged in Chicago in these same years, as a number of ministers began to voice support for unions. This new voice was in fact many different voices, which varied greatly in the extent of their support for working-class organizations.

Some saw strikes as legitimate, others did not; some championed compulsory arbitration, others recoiled at the same. Notwithstanding such distinctions, they had in common a willingness to compromise in order to stay connected to the respectable working classes. The stakes were high: if the churches were to stay a power within city and nation, the reasoning went, they had to regain their footing among the people. Unlike their conservative counterparts, these moderates sought out personal relationships with union leaders in the conservative American Federation of Labor's orbit. In addition, these more accommodating Protestants began to acknowledge publicly that the wage-earning classes had legitimate grievances that demanded redress. But there remained hard limits on how far these moderates were willing to go: almost to a man they condemned sympathetic strikes, boycotts, closed shops, and interference with strikebreakers, and this unwieldy group remained united also in its fierce opposition to all forms of radicalism. Its more progressive gospel was, then, a noteworthy new creation, but far from revolutionary.

Bishop Samuel Fallows, who was for nearly fifty years rector of Union Park's St. Paul's Reformed Episcopal Church, stood near the center of this fractious moderate wing.[41] A veteran of the Union army and a lifelong Republican, Fallows was one of Chicago's most widely respected ministers. Throughout his career he took a deep interest in labor issues, insistently positioning himself, as well as the broader church, as a friend of the workingman.[42] This was never truer than in the wake of the violence at Andrew Carnegie's Homestead steel plant in the summer of 1892. Fallows made a point of stopping in Pennsylvania on his way back from a conference in New York and then, upon returning to Chicago, advocated vigorously for the Homestead workers. "[The law] should protect the workman in his moral right, which should be a legal right," Fallows declared. "The workman has to sell his labor for what he can get. The law is wrong in making a free man a serf—his employer an autocrat."[43] This was an audacious stand for Fallows to take. He was, after all, the minister of a church underwritten by many of Union Park's finest citizens. Notably, he would never go so far again.[44]

Over the course of the ensuing decades Fallows never relinquished the view that there was a legitimate place for trade unions in industrializing America. In one Labor Day sermon he remarked, "At the head of all the great processions of workmen which shall signalize throughout the land is the carpenter of Nazareth. . . . He has glorified toil. He has linked the highest heaven with the work of the lowliest artisan."[45] In Fallows's case, this was more than just talk: especially in cases where employers refused to arbitrate, he championed workers' campaigns.[46] But increasingly he also warned of the "evils connected with federations and unions."[47] Most strikingly, within two years of Homestead he had subordinated all language about a worker's "moral right" to the Christian establishment's contractual line: men had a right to sell their labor at whatever price they saw fit, Fallows now insisted, and so any coercive means of holding the picket line contravened not only human but also divine law.[48] By the turn of the century, he stood at the fore of a growing bloc of middle-aged Protestant ministers who condoned conservative trade unionism even while problematizing many of labor's signature tactics.[49]

In the first decade of the twentieth century, meanwhile, a number of Protestant ministers strove to push their respective denominations in more decidedly progressive directions. Several African American divines built on the legacy of those who had aided striking black waiters in the 1890s. The Reverend John F. Thomas of Olivet Baptist Church had been involved in those earlier efforts and went on to become, in the summer of 1901, one of the lead organizers of a union of black Pullman porters.[50] The Reverend Reverdy C. Ransom (figure 7.1) did not arrive in Chicago until 1896, but throughout his eight years in the city he proved a tireless advocate for a growing community of black workers.[51] In his first year of ministry at Bethel African Methodist Episcopal Church Ransom preached a sermon on "The Industrial and Social Conditions of the Negro," in which he rued that "we have been forced in the North, in Chicago, as well as in the South, into a condition that may truly be termed industrial serfdom."[52] Ransom saw that white Christians were fully complicit in this state of affairs, declaring, "I believe that it should be one of the missions of the colored churches in our land to take their stand against American Christianity and compel recognition at its hands."[53] He would go on to decry the structural racism that barred blacks from employment in so many of Chicago's industries and membership in so many of its unions. With respect to the latter, Ransom wrote, "The great army of toilers who have been crying out against our present social and industrial conditions have steadily refused to recognize the cause of the Negro workmen as one with theirs. This penniless freedman has had to contend against the frown and active opposition of organized labor for a chance to win his bread."[54]

Ransom's support for black workers went well beyond words. Like so many white ministers, he worried that the churches were drifting away

FIGURE 7.1 The Reverend Reverdy C. Ransom and his wife, Emma Ransom, standing on the steps of the Institutional Methodist Church, 4 May 1903

Credit: DN-0000555, Chicago Daily News negatives collection, Chicago History Museum.

from the masses and so in 1900 he left Bethel to found the Institutional Church and Social Settlement, which sought "to meet and serve the moral, social, and industrial need of [the people]" by offering a variety of services, ranging from a kindergarten to an employment bureau.[55] The endeavor garnered immediate support from white, middle-class reformers, including Jane Addams, Graham Taylor, and Mary McDowell, and produced unexpected benefits for black wage earners.[56] Ransom would later recall that some local union leaders were so impressed with the Church that they "recognized and admitted colored men to membership."[57] When countless others did not, he joined with leading African American ministers, including even his sometimes nemesis, the well-known Reverend Archibald J. Carey, in standing up for the basic rights of black strikebreakers, who were frequently the victim of violent assaults.[58]

Among Chicago's white Protestant denominations, Methodism produced the largest crop of rabble-rousers, some of whom continued the work they had begun in the months surrounding the Pullman strike and boycott. Nearly six years after he spoke at an American Railway Union (ARU) rally, the Reverend Herbert G. Leonard hijacked an April 1900 debate among the city's Methodist ministers on the permissibility of amusements. Excoriating denominational leaders—"bishops and editors who . . . hold down fat jobs with enormous salaries"—he went on to exclaim, "I would rather have the young people of my church dance, play cards, go to theaters, and do almost anything else than to lie and play the role of hypocrites."[59] Meanwhile, William Carwardine continued to cultivate a close relationship with the city's respectable working classes. In the wake of his spirited 1894 campaign on behalf of the ARU, Debs's *Railway Times* went so far as to publish a notice, "For a True Friend," urging its readers to send contributions to shore up the faltering finances of Carwardine's church.[60] In the ensuing years and until his death in 1929, Carwardine remained one of Chicago's most vocal Protestant advocates for the right of workingmen to organize. Notably, he never mustered the same enthusiasm for the mobilization of working women, arguing that it besmirched their virtue and moreover hampered men's efforts to achieve higher wages.[61] Yet few were as insistent as Carwardine in calling the church to "keep itself in touch with the heart of the masses"; nor were many as influential, especially after 1905, when he began a quarter-century-long tenure as religion editor for the *Herald and Examiner*, a post that offered him an ideal platform from which to propound the principles of "applied Christianity."[62]

Other Methodist reformers first made a name for themselves in the early years of the twentieth century. Among these was the Canadian-born Reverend John Clayton Youker, who used his Oak Park pulpit to challenge the churches' obsequious relationship to the wealthy. In the wake of Phillip Armour's death, and even as Gunsaulus and other leading Protestants delivered sentimental eulogies, Youker critiqued the millionaire's philanthropic legacy, declaring it would be better for the money of "financial kings" to end up "in the pay envelopes of their employes [sic]."[63]

Another young critic, Harry Ward, was converted to social Christianity by his experience in Packingtown. In 1901 the 27-year-old minister was called to serve the 47th Street Methodist Episcopal Church in the Back of the Yards, where he was confronted by a conspicuous lack of workingmen in the pews. Ward wasted little time in tearing out the gaudy pulpit chairs and joining the packinghouse workers' union himself. His successor later reflected, "One couldn't preach in that church if he didn't believe in the union."[64] While still in Chicago, Ward went on in 1907 to become one of the founders of the Methodist Federation for Social Service, an institutional bulwark of the rising middle-class Social Gospel.[65]

More perhaps than any of the above, the ministry of the Reverend Charles Stelzle illustrates the ways in which the middle-class Social Gospel was "union made." Stelzle was the son of German immigrants. He worked in a sweatshop as a boy and went on to learn the machinist's trade, before leaving that vocation in order to enter the ministry at the age of 24. Like countless others of this era, he worried about the churches' rocky relationship with the nation's workingmen; more than most, he worked assiduously to achieve reconciliation. Recall that, while stationed in St. Louis in 1901, Stelzle had conducted a survey of disaffected wage earners, seeking to understand why they had lost interest in the church. He took the results of this investigation straight to the leaders of the national Presbyterian Church, which in 1902 appointed him to its Home Mission Board, prompting one religious paper to comment that Stelzle's "past career and present views of society and religion make him an acceptable pioneer in a very important new phase of Protestant church activity. He was formerly a wage-earner. He knows how to play the part of mediator and interpreter."[66]

Sure enough, Stelzle threw himself into the work. In response to his ongoing agitation, the Presbyterian Church in 1903 appointed him the head of a newly founded Workingman's Department, whose mission was "to interpret the Church to working men, to interpret workingmen to the Church, and to interpret employer and employee to each other."[67] Based out of a new office in downtown Chicago, Stelzle soon became known as of the nation's leading experts on two questions near the fore of many a minister's mind: What was to be done about the labor question, and how could the churches attract workingmen back into the pews? In his communication with other religious leaders, he insisted that the questions were linked and the answer to both the same—the churches must take up workingmen's cause as their own. He wrote at one point: "Has it not been commonly said by workingmen that the churches are only for the rich? Is it not logical to address ourselves specifically to these working-men and say to them, very plainly: 'The Church of Jesus Christ makes no class distinctions—its privileges are also for you?' "[68] He declared at another: "We should indicate to workingmen that we are not offering them the gospel as a sop, but are offering the same to their employers. The labor union has come to stay and that fact had better be recognized. We should insist that the church does not stand for the present system of society if it is wrong."[69] In his quest to soften the Christian elite's attitude toward labor, Stelzle was the direct beneficiary of a long history of working-class protest against the churches, which had generated the anxiety into which he so effectively tapped.

At the same time, Stelzle bolstered his credibility among leading churchmen by deepening his relationship with workingmen themselves, especially those who congregated in the respectable AFL. He made head-lines in 1904 when he petitioned to be made a fraternal delegate to the Chicago Federation of Labor, observing in a letter to its secretary, "that for various reasons the ministry is not in as close touch with the labor movement as it should be." Some within the Federation objected to the proposal, but in the end the organization admitted Stelzle so long as he promised, among other things, to have "no sympathy with the fleecers of labor."[70] The following year the AFL invited Stelzle to address its conven-tion in Pittsburgh, where it moreover passed a resolution calling for "all affiliated state and central bodies [to] exchange fraternal delegates with the various state and city ministerial associations, wherever practicable, thus insuring a better understanding on the part of the church and clergy of the aims and objects of the labor union movement of America." Stelzle touted such gains in communications to church leaders, writing in the *Interior*, for example, that the Pittsburgh convention had "passed measures with reference to the church which were unique and epoch-making."[71] His office moreover published a leaflet entitled "Personal Paragraphs from Labor Leaders," which showcased the relationships he had managed to build with union officials across the country.[72] Meanwhile, Stelzle broad-ened his outreach to AFL workers themselves by publishing columns in trade union journals with titles such as "Is the Church Opposed to Workingmen?"; "How the Church and Labor May Cooperate"; and "Jesus Christ—Union Carpenter." By 1910 Stelzle, who had moved once again, this time to New York City, was regularly syndicated in at least 350 differ-ent labor publications.[73]

The Presbyterian reformer was no revolutionary. He vehemently opposed socialism, and moreover denounced violence, sympathetic strikes, and the abrogation of labor contracts. These positions made him more palatable to a wide range of church leaders. One clergyman in Omaha, Nebraska, having hosted Stelzle for ten days, wrote a glowing report to the *Interior*, in which he declared, notably, that "[Stelzle] proposes no fanatical, chimerical scheme as a panacea."[74] At the same time his moderate views on the labor question dovetailed with those of AFL leaders, whose pure-and-simple strategy only strengthened Stelzle's contention that the churches could support labor without contributing to disorder. If his ministry was far from radical, it nevertheless captures the ways in which the middle-class Social Gospel represented a break with what had gone before. Indeed, his peripatetic labors in the first decade of the twentieth century yielded tangible changes in the Presbyterian denomination's approach to working people, both in Chicago and across the nation.

The response of Chicago's Christian elite to two major strikes in the first decade of the twentieth century helps to clarify what exactly had and had not changed in terms of the churches' outlook on the labor question. The first of these is the packinghouse strike of 1904. In the spring of that year the Amalgamated Meat Cutters and Butcher Workmen of North America stipulated that, going forward, all employers would have to pay common laborers at a rate of twenty cents per hour. In Chicago, the packers refused to comply and so on 12 July 1904, 28,000 Packingtown workers went on strike. The walkout enjoyed strong support from the CFL and was, on the whole, disciplined and orderly. The three-month-long affair involved a number of sympathetic strikes by employees not directly affected by the disputed terms; moreover, socialists held 30 to 40 rallies every week, often at the busy corner of 47th and Halsted Streets. But union leaders were careful to disassociate their protest from any kind of radicalism. They posted signs in six languages around the neighborhood urging workers to remain peaceful and, meanwhile, pled their case with the public, arguing that the strike's primary aim was to gain for the neighborhood's impoverished residents a decent standard of living.[75]

Remarkably, this massive, disruptive strike generated little backlash from Chicago's Christian leaders. The Archdiocese called for all parties to refrain from violence and moreover championed widespread calls for arbitration. On the question of whether the packers or the strikers were in the right, it remained persistently neutral, with one column in the *New*

World remarking, "It is not our province to meddle in the unfortunate dispute."[76] Protestant pundits struck similar notes. Editorials in the *Christian Century*, the *Northwestern Christian Advocate*, and the *Interior* called for peaceable conduct and immediate arbitration, and hoped for a rapid end to a strike that impinged directly on the day-to-day lives of countless Chicagoans.[77]

On the ground, meanwhile, local ministers flocked to the strikers' side. Across Packingtown Catholic priests of many ethnicities joined with the archdiocese in condemning violence and yet declared in no uncertain terms their support for the union. To be sure, they were not, to a man, enthusiastic about the strike. One Boehmian priest, Father Thomas J. Bobal, condemned it outright, while several Irish clergymen elected to mention it only in prayer. Yet even some of those who had reservations chose to support the workers. The minister at St. Rose de Lima, Father Dennis Hayes, reflected, "Personally, I do not believe in strikes. They seldom seem to accomplish any good. But I realize that the men must keep together to maintain the principles of their union." At St. Gabriel's parish, Father Maurice J. Dorney answered similarly when asked to weigh in on the stock handlers' sympathetic strike. Knowing full well that one-quarter of the men in his congregation were implicated in the decision, he declared, "It is to be regretted. . . . The men are the best paid and the most considerately treated in the yards, and have no fault to find. It must be admitted, however, that such a step is sometimes necessary in order to maintain the cohesiveness of union labor." Still other priests threw caution to the wind. One Polish cleric insisted that the strikers were merely "fighting for their rights," while another personally escorted a non-unionized worker to the union hall so that he could sign up. Meanwhile, one Father Ryan announced, "We are helping those who are in need, and thus lending the arm of the church to what we believe is a righteous cause. It is natural that our sympathy is with the men."[78]

Located almost entirely outside of the Back of the Yards neighborhood, Protestant ministers did not comment much on the strike, with the notable exception of Bishop Fallows, who cheered the union. In one early August sermon he declared: "I can speak with sufficient authority to say that the great majority of the ministry, both in the Protestant and Catholic communion, have a profound sympathy with the workingmen of all classes. They proclaim both to employer and employee the principle of Christianity, 'The laborer is worthy of his hire.' " Nor was Fallows satisfied to deal in platitudes. He went on, "It is a palpable violation of

these principles to pay men having wives and families to support an average of $5 or $7 a week the year round." Toward the strike's conclusion
he returned to these themes once more, asking, "May we not hope that
employers will remember they are dealing with human beings when they
call them into their service; that every social, moral, and religious consideration demands that a fair living wage should be paid them?"[79]

The Christian elite's response to the teamsters' strike of 1905
offers a study in contrast. In early April, and at the CFL's behest, the
International Brotherhood of Teamsters presented Montgomery Ward
and Company with a demand that it rehire striking garment workers
whom it had replaced. When the company refused, the teamsters went
out on sympathetic strike, mandating that drivers make no deliveries
to or from Montgomery Ward. The union's tactics bespoke its commitment to class solidarity and in Chicago—where, in 1905, fully 30,000
of its 45,000 members resided—it had the strength to carry this militant strategy out. But the conflict's terrain shifted rapidly when the
Employers' Association came to Montgomery Ward's defense, urging
all State Street department stores to fire any worker participating in
the strike. In an attempt to break the union altogether, the Association
moreover encouraged retailers to refuse to hire striking drivers back.
Even as the affected employers joined forces, countless working-class
citizens took to the streets to support the teamsters, interfering with
replacement drivers and in some cases even assaulting them as they
attempted to make deliveries. Unlike the disciplined packinghouse
walkout of 1904, the teamsters' strike introduced considerable disorder
into the city's highways and byways.[80]

The clergy reacted with dismay. Catholics and Protestants alike
deplored the resort to violence. In mid-April the *New World* complained.
"some wretch has introduced a new feature—that of flinging into the struggling hordes egg shells filled with muriatic acid."[81] Some divines called
for voluntary arbitration, while others insisted that the parties should be
required to come to the bargaining table.[82] All bemoaned the strike's negative impact upon everyday Chicagoans. At St. Paul's Reformed Episcopal
Bishop Fallows declared, "The long, suffering, law abiding public is being
ground between the upper and lower millstones in such labor conflicts as
that now being waged."[83]

Moreover, nearly every Christian leader who voiced an opinion
inveighed against the practice of sympathetic strikes. "The garment workers may have had a just cause to strike, but why should the teamsters go

out?" an editorial in the *New World* asked in the early days of the conflict. As the battle dragged on the archdiocesan weekly became more pointed in its criticisms, pronouncing matter-of-factly at one point, "The firmest friend of labor unions in America is the Catholic Church, but it does not believe in the sympathetic strike."[84] The city's Protestant ministers echoed this latter sentiment, with one Lutheran decrying "the opportunity [the sympathetic strike] gives to anarchists and rioters to get in their work." At the People's Church, meanwhile, Dr. E. A. White proclaimed: "The strike was in its beginning unjustifiable. It began in a sympathetic strike and broken contracts." Protestant pundits echoed such claims, occasionally allowing superlatives to creep into their critique. "There has perhaps never been in Chicago, which is noted for labor strikes, a strike so devoid of jus-tification as the present teamsters' strike," an editor for the *Northwestern Christian Advocate* declared.[85]

But, crucially, the author of that same column took to task "repre-sentatives of employers who declare . . . that this is a bitter struggle for the destruction of unions," contending that "[they] are making a serious blunder."[86] While both Catholics and Protestants persisted in denouncing sympathetic strikes, even many of the latter articu-lated robust support for trade unions. Fallows rued the conduct of the strike and yet insisted, "Unionism itself, let it be clearly understood, has not been on trial, nor have its principles suffered defeat."[87] Even the Reverend Joseph A. Milburn, the minister at fashionable Plymouth Congregational, Gunsaulus's one-time pulpit, mustered qualified sup-port for working-class protest. "I sympathize, as does every clergyman in this city, with every legitimate effort on the part of the workingman to increase his wage or to better his life conditions." The key question, of course, was what constituted "legitimate." Protestants had long lauded labor in the abstract even while opposing it in all the particulars. Milburn broke with this pattern, announcing, "I believe also in the method of the strike as an instrument of industrial amelioration." He went so far as to say, "the strike in its ideal operation is a force of righteousness," though quickly added, "when it is associated with violence, with brute force, with slugging, with the boycott, and with anarchy, it is a curse, a menace to the peace of the community, and a disgrace to labor." Whatever the caveats, the very fact that the pastor of one of the city's wealthiest con-gregations could imagine a scenario in which a strike would be "a force of righteousness" left little doubt that a new day had dawned in the rela-tionship between church and labor.[88]

The clergy's contrasting responses to the packinghouse and teamster strikes illuminated the character of that new day. On the one hand, much remained the same. The Christian elite continued to look askance at not only radicalism but also violence, the closed shop, the breaking of contracts, enforcement of the picket line, the sympathetic strike, and a host of other working-class tactics. On the other hand, something very significant had changed: in most, though not all, of Chicago's churches, ministers had finally come around to see what workers had known for decades—that one could be a Christian and a trade unionist too.

Epilogue

IN 1913 ONE of the nation's leading Social Gospel ministers, Walter Rauschenbusch, declared, "Under the pressure of the social awakening the churches are officially seeking to get in touch with organized labor."[1] Rauschenbusch was right, though he underestimated the extent to which this "pressure" had been applied by labor itself. Having spearheaded the rise of social Christianity in cities like Chicago, working people continued to propound social gospels in the early decades of the twentieth century.

Indeed, the workers who preached on Labor Sunday in 1910 were participants in a growing tradition. Prior to Eugene Debs's speeches at Erie Street Methodist in 1896, it was unheard of for a representative of organized labor to teach or preach *inside* one of Chicago's churches. But in the years that followed, this phenomenon became much more common. There was Peter Miller—a Scottish harness-maker and card-carrying socialist—who assumed the pulpit at nearby Evanston's Emmanuel Methodist in December 1897 and, in the *Tribune*'s words, "expressed the conviction that something must be done for the laboring man by the capitalist."[2] Five years later, in 1902, Evanston's First Congregational Church invited Miller to give a series of talks to its Bible class. In one of these, he declared, "The church can aid society only by applying the principles of Christianity to everyday business life, and this it cannot do with its present economic environment."[3] Algie Simons cheered the occasion in the pages of the *Chicago Socialist*, writing, "Comrade Miller was thus pelting the Bible class with chunks of common sense."[4] When the class later took up the "servant girl problem," Simons wrote, "We suggest that Peter Miller, the Evanston Socialist harness maker get around there and tell that crowd a few things calculated to disabuse their minds of the idea that the 'children of the poor' were specially treated to do them menial service."[5]

That same year Merrill Methodist Church asked Simons to address its congregation on the subject of the anthracite coal strike then ongoing in Pennsylvania. Simons accepted the invitation and went on to chide an assembly of middle-class Englewood residents, saying: "I have no use for the man who waits until his coal bin is empty before he takes an interest in the strike. . . . If you are with the side of social progress you must lend your strength to the miners."[6] Leopold P. Straube, the secretary of the Allied Printing Trades Council, deployed an equally aggressive tone when, in 1906, the pastor at First Methodist invited him to speak on the theme, "The Golden Rule in Church and Labor." "The church of today, friends, has degenerated into a mercantile institution," Straube asserted, "in which your chances of salvation are dependent on the size of your contribution. It is nothing more nor less than a rich man's club, from which the poor and those the Master professed to serve are excluded." Working people had been making these kinds of claims for more than a generation but Straube, standing behind the pulpit at one of Chicago's most respectable churches, did so with new authority. He went on, "You may be surprised to hear it, but I have been much interested in the Bible in what time I have to study it, and nothing in it has impressed more than the driving of the money changers out of the temple. Why," Straube asked, "if the church member is a follower of Christ, doesn't he take this example to heart and purge the church of those who are desecrating it?" He paused here long enough for a feeble voice, sounding forth from somewhere beneath the balcony, to chime, "Amen!"[7]

Some of the city's more militant workers had given up on the church, but kept alive a more radical and secular gospel akin to the one the Haymarket anarchists had preached. One direct line of continuity ran through Lucy Parsons (figure E.1), who was present at the founding convention of the Industrial Workers of the World (IWW) in Chicago in 1905. The Wobblies, as they came to be called, disapproved of both the exclusivity and the moderation of the AFL and sought to create instead "One Big Union" of all wage earners, which could finally put capital in its place. The institutional churches seemed, if anything, an obstacle to their ambitions. As another of the IWW's founding spirits, Mother Jones, declared: "What is it to us if the church bell tolls each Easter morning and announces the resurrection of the Christ? It has never yet tolled for the resurrection of Christ's children from their long dark tomb of slavery."[8] Yet some Wobblies would

FIGURE E.I Lucy Parsons
Credit: The Newberry Library.

find inspiration for their activism in the example of the "Hobo Carpenter from Nazareth, whose call, stripped of the mystical and mythical veil of Constantine and his successors, and clothed in the original garb of communism and brotherhood, continues to sound intermittently across the ages."[9] Parsons herself was actually arrested outside the Newberry Library in 1909 for preaching (out of the third chapter of Genesis) without a permit. At police headquarters she informed the press, "I have some decided opinions on the matter of religion and I do not think the police have any right to interfere with me so long as I am not infringing on the rights of others."[10]

During these same years conservative labor reformers also took to Chicago's streets, Bibles in hand. The words of holy writ came up time and again, for example, in early twentieth-century campaigns for the six-day week. In a lengthy petition submitted to grocery and market proprietors in 1906, a teamsters' local quoted several choice scriptural passages, including one from Exodus that read "six days shalt thou labor and do all thy work; but the seventh day is the Sabbath of the Lord thy God; in it thou shalt not do any work."[11] Grocery clerks took a more confrontational approach in a 1910 push for Sunday closings, as 300 disgruntled workers knocked on the doors of one noncompliant store after another. If the owner answered, the union's president, J. W. Koeppen, would kick off the conversation with a question, "Do you believe in the Bible?" to which at least one proprietor grumbled in protest, "What are you doing? Starting a prayer meeting?"[12]

As it turned out, some of Chicago's working people did believe prayer meetings and Bible studies were still relevant to their cause. When in 1907 City Treasurer John R. Thompson informed Elizabeth Maloney, a key leader within the waitresses' union, that "nothing short of the Bible" would convince him to permit the organization of workers in his lunchrooms, she vowed, "Then we'll use the Bible." The Irish-Catholic Maloney, who kept a picture of the Madonna hanging in union headquarters, went on to put 250 waitresses through a crash course in scripture studies.[13] Later that same year, meanwhile, a gathering of striking telegraph operators morphed easily into a kind of church service when E. M. Moore, the chairman of the union's executive board, approached the platform, Bible in hand, and declared, "To those of you who don't recognize this book let me say it is the strongest weapon we have in this fight." Even as Moore went on to deliver an impromptu sermon, relating the operators' strike to the Genesis story of how Esau sold his birthright, a number of young women strikers hummed softly in the background the hymn, "We'll All Be Happy in the Sweet By and By."[14] There could be little doubt that in their view the spirit of the gospel dovetailed seamlessly with the aims of the labor movement.

As these stories suggest, in the early years of the twentieth century, women began to wield more influence within Chicago's trade union circles. While a number of female workers had determinedly organized and agitated throughout the Gilded Age, men long obstructed their efforts to join the labor movement.[15] As late as 1910, only 73,800 American women belonged to unions, less than 1% of the nation's 8,075,000 employed females.[16] The creation of the Women's Trade Union League (WTUL) by an alliance of working- and middle-class women in 1903 augured new possibilities, and in the years that followed the League successfully enlisted more women into unions. It would moreover succeed in carving out a permanent place and voice for women within an enduringly chauvinistic labor movement. While the going was often painfully slow, there were signs of progress. In 1907 the League sent fraternal delegates to the AFL convention, where President Gompers went so far as to invite Agnes Nestor to preside over part of the meeting. In Chicago, meanwhile, the organizers of the local chapter of the Women's Trade Union League (CWTUL) cultivated a close working partnership with John Fitzpatrick and the other male leaders of the CFL.[17]

In the first decades of the twentieth century, church leaders, too, sought out women such as Agnes Nestor. A force within both the Glove Workers' Union and the CWTUL, Nestor was a devout Catholic whose faith motivated her activism, though she did not often speak publicly about the connections between the two.[18] Nor did she follow many of her male counterparts in vituperatively criticizing the clergy. The CWTUL's position within the larger labor movement remained too precarious for Nestor and her fellow organizers to risk alienating the Christian elite. But when religious leaders invited her to address their people, as they increasingly did—to widespread incredulity—Nestor would, carefully, speak her mind.[19] On Labor Sunday in 1910, she crafted a message designed to resonate with the Victorian mores of the middle-class congregants at Winnetka Congregational, asserting, "It is the work of the church to take an active instead of passive interest in the welfare of the mothers of to-morrow and lend its strength toward a betterment of conditions." Nestor proceeded to declare, "With such support the piecework evil could be eradicated and ultimately an eight-hour day provided for all toilers."[20] She would go on in later decades to become one of the leading female proponents of social Christianity within the American Catholic Church, serving as vice-president of the U.S. Catholic Conference on Industrial Problems and as chairwoman of the National Council of Catholic Women's Committee on Women in Industry.[21]

Just months after Nestor's Labor Sunday sermon, meanwhile, striking women in the garment industries collaborated with some of their middle-class counterparts to launch the first ever "Sweatshop Sunday." On Sunday, 22 January 1911, some 1,200 women spent the morning knocking on doors and visiting churches to raise funds for the strikers and their families.[22] The *Tribune* reported that they would be "putting [biblical] passages into practice":

> With such pleas as 'Not for ourselves, but for our weaker comrades,' 'Thou shalt love thy neighbor as thyself,' 'Inasmuch as ye have done it unto one of the least of these, my brethren, ye have done it unto

me,' 'I was an hungered and ye gave me meat; I was thirsty and ye gave me drink; I was a stranger and ye took me in; naked and ye clothed me; I was sick and ye visited me; I was in prison and ye came unto me,' these women will knock at your door.[23]

Donations rolled in from some likely sources, including $7.00 from the Methodist Federation for Social Service and $115.00 from the Paulist Fathers, whose superior, Father P. J. O'Callaghan, was among the foremost clerical champions of the WTUL; but these were amply supplemented by more than seventy-five other gifts from a diverse array of Christian congregations and societies.[24] Crucially, women's religious activism over the course of the strike also yielded a handful of churchly endorsements. At one Episcopal church, the priest first ceded his pulpit to Ellen Gates Starr and then went on to make his own "personal appeal for the strikers."[25] Working women had been preaching social gospels for a generation, but never before to such manifestly great effect.

Yet in the early twentieth century, it was workingmen who won disproportionate institutional clout within the churches, as they continued to capitalize on the clergy's growing anxieties about feminization. Such worries prompted one Chicago church to hire an investigator to figure out why men in the neighborhood were so religiously apathetic. They moreover fueled the national Men and Religion Forward Movement, which drew over a million people to its meetings in 1911 and 1912.[26] Having stoked these anxieties for decades, workingmen now took full advantage, as can be seen in the story of a blacksmith by the name of James W. Kline (figure E.2).

Kline had grown up in eastern Pennsylvania's Lehigh Valley, where he was steeped in an artisan milieu. His ancestors emigrated from Germany in the mid-1740s and soon scattered throughout the Valley's villages, establishing farms and shops.[27] It was in rural Upper Milford township that Kline's father, Henry, learned the art of carpentry. When he and his young wife Diana set off to neighboring Lower Saucon on their own in the late 1850s, they had little in the way of worldly possessions.[28] But over the course of the ensuing decade Henry flourished as a coach-maker. The changes in his household reflected his newfound success: by 1870 it incorporated not only three children but also a younger kinsman and apprentice, David Kline, as well as three boarders, including a blacksmith and a carriage trimmer, who likely worked in his shop.[29] It was almost certainly there that James, born in 1860, first practiced at the anvil. He went

FIGURE E.2 James W. Kline, fifth in line from the left, is pictured here with other labor leaders following a 1922 meeting with President Harding

Credit: Library of Congress Prints and Photographs Division, Washington, DC. LC-DIG-hec-31713 (digital file from original negative).

on to work as a railroad clerk for a brief stint in his teens, but then fled the Valley in the early 1880s to find a better life.[30] Resettling eventually in Kansas City, Kansas, Kline secured employment as a blacksmith in a railroad shop and moreover joined the Knights of Labor. He was affiliated with Local Assembly 3694 until the early 1890s, when he became a founding member of the International Brotherhood of Blacksmiths Local 66.[31] His ensuing rise to the top of the International was quick. Kline attained the rank of trustee in 1901, second vice-president in 1904, and president in 1905. Shortly thereafter he relocated, along with his wife Amelia and their four children, to Chicago.

It was upon arriving in Chicago that Kline, a faithful Methodist and longtime Bible class attendee, first made a splash in religious circles.[32] It began with a dispute between the Western Methodist Book Concern and the Typographical Union, which had been ongoing for nearly three years and seemed nowhere near resolution. At the heart of this fight was the printers' demand for a closed shop, which the Book Concern categorically rejected, citing a conviction that every man has a right "to work when, where, and for whom he pleases."[33] Recriminations flew freely in both directions. In response to Methodist leaders' insistent claim that their church "has ever been known as the church of the people," the editor of the Chicago Federation of Labor's flagship journal resorted indignantly to holy writ: "Sermon after sermon may be preached and speech after speech may be made to the effect that the church is the true friend of labor; but so long as its attitude in practice is one of hostility to labor, it stands condemned as a whited sepulcher that 'outwardly appears righteous unto men, but within is full of hypocrisy and iniquity.'"[34] In January 1907, the Federation escalated the conflict, distributing 300,000 posters that called for union men across the country to boycott Methodism altogether.[35] The movement caught on and in the months that followed more than 5,000 Methodist printers reportedly left the church.[36]

Invited to address Chicago's Methodist clergy regarding the conflict in April 1908, Kline followed the Federation in deploying the gospel against its ministers. Summing up his speech, the *Typographical Journal* declared, "[he] told the preachers that if they had in them the spirit of Christ they would not now be in the humiliating position of fighting organized labor."[37] In the wake of Kline's address, the Reverend Harry F. Ward, then serving as pastor of the Union Avenue church, introduced a resolution calling for an investigation of the Book Concern. Another minister seconded the proposal, but the venerable Reverend Matthew M. Parkhurst—in his fifty-first year of ministry—soon galvanized the opposition. The fiery septuagenarian blamed labor unions for the plague of industrial violence that had so long beset the nation. Bickering ensued, but by all accounts it was Kline's words that proved decisive: the resolution passed by a vote of 40–3.[38]

The following year the Methodist Federation for Social Service, one of the leading institutional expressions of the Social Gospel, elected Kline to its board, demonstrating the extent to which working-class critics of the churches—especially those in the line of Andrew Cameron, who looked askance at radicalism and the saloon—were finally being heard and heeded.[39] Yet the struggle was far from over. When the *Northwestern Christian Advocate* published an unfavorable report on a strike in which Kline was directly involved, he responded with a four-page letter setting the facts straight. Its last line: "We believe God is on the side of the man instead of the dollar."[40] Meanwhile, Kline joined the Methodist preaching circuit, delivering addresses at a number of churches, including Halsted Street Institutional and Western Avenue Methodist.[41] In October 1913 he preached to a throng of workingmen, as well as the Methodist clergy of Chicago and northern Illinois, who were gathered for their annual meeting in the town of Freeport. The theme of the evening's session was "The Working Man and the Church," and Kline began in good evangelical fashion, reading aloud from the New Testament: "Behold the hire of the laborers who have reaped down your fields, which is of you kept back by fraud, crieth; and the cries of them which have reaped are entered into the ears of the Lord of Sabaoth." Staring out at the crowd, he went on, "I believe that I can see the conditions of our day depicted in the fifth Chapter of James, and would like to hear a few sermons preached from that chapter," adding, pointedly, "I have never heard an interpretation."

Kline did not hesitate to proffer his own. In a lengthy address he indicted the nation for allowing "men of large wealth" to become an "Invisible Government" and then rebuked the churches for "tak[ing] on the spirit of Caesar." The speech built toward a climactic litany:

> Behold! The National Beef Packers Association at their banquet at the Congress Hotel, in Chicago, where possibly $75,000 was spent on an extravagant dinner. Did you read the account of it?

> Behold! They have kept back by fraud the hire of their laborers working in their packing houses as low as 15¢ an hour, which makes it possible for them to waste it in extravagant living.

> Behold! The hire of the laborers in the steel mills at Gary, Ind., with Mr. Gary at the head, donating back in charity that which should be given them in wages, and building memorial churches with the money kept back by fraud.

After pronouncing judgment on the United States Steel Corporation, as well as the cotton, mining, and retail industries, he concluded with this salvo: "Behold! The hire of the laborers who have done all this so that others could live in pleasure and wickedness. . . . Their gold and their silver is cankered. It is burning their flesh like fire."[42] That night in Freeport, labor's gospel appeared triumphant.

But in private, Kline and his allies harbored ongoing frustrations. In 1917 he confided in the Reverend Ward, his closest friend and colleague within the Federation, "I want to say in the first place, Brother Ward, that I am pretty well discouraged." He went on to confess: "The General Conference was an eye-opener to me. . . . It is mighty aggravating to me to have ministers in our church, tell me that we are right and when the opportunity arises they fail to improve that opportunity by using their voice and influence."[43] Kline was alluding to a 1916 Methodist gathering, where a resolution had come to the floor regarding the dispute between the Book Concern and the typographical union, which was, remarkably, still unfolding. Ward had done his best to rally support for the printers' cause. He wrote labor leaders across the country, soliciting their "observation[s] concerning the effect of our Book Concern controversy with the Allied Printing Trades on the attitude of organized labor toward the church in general, and our church in particular." As he went on to admit—in words that drive home the fundamental dynamics motivating the rise of the middle-class Social Gospel—"Some of our laymen will not be impressed with this thing until we give them some evidence that it has meant a loss to the church."[44]

For the time being, they remained insufficiently impressed. The resolution Ward championed, which called for the publishing house to show merely "a preference" for union printers, was voted down 447 to 280. Once more, the enemies of the closed shop proved more powerful. Nevertheless, Ward urged Kline not to give in to despair, saying, "You must not forget that the other crowd has been in control a long time, and we have been at this job only a little while." Patience would, indeed, be required: the dispute between the printers and the Book Concern would not be resolved until 1932, when the latter finally agreed to unionize its operations.[45]

By that point social Christianity was, in some sense, finally "made." Thanks in no small part to the activism of countless working people, a pro-labor faith had taken root in many of the nation's Christian churches, which would go on to become crucial players in the New Deal coalition. Catholic wage earners could tout Pope Pius XI's 1931 encyclical, *Quadragesimo Anno*, as robust evidence that—now more than ever—the Vatican was on their side. Moving well beyond the positions staked out in *Rerum Novarum*, this latest papal pronouncement took direct aim at laissez-faire policies, declaring, "The right ordering of economic life cannot be left to a free competition of forces. For from this source, as from a poisoned spring, have originated and spread all the errors of individualist economic teaching."[46] Even the Episcopalian Franklin D. Roosevelt cheered the encyclical in the run up to the 1932 election, declaring to a large audience in Detroit that it was "just as radical as I am."[47] Roosevelt would find fast friends in a rising generation of labor priests, including the influential John Ryan, who became known in some quarters as the "Right Reverend New Dealer" following his controversial public endorsement of FDR's 1936 re-election bid.[48] In Chicago, Archbishop George Mundelein and Auxiliary Bishop Bernard Sheil rallied to the side of those workers who championed industrial unionism during the Great Depression, surging into the ranks of the upstart Congress of Industrial Organizations (CIO).[49] When in 1939 Sheil stood on a platform alongside CIO chief John Lewis and urged 16,000 packinghouse workers to fight for a living wage, even the *Tribune* declared it a new day.[50]

Meanwhile, across the United States many leading Protestants also cheered the changing shape of the New Deal state. The year after the promulgation of *Quadragesimo Anno* the Federal Council of Churches (FCC) decided it was time to bring its own teaching up to date. Whereas the original Social Creed had stipulated "the right of employees and employers alike to organize," the 1932 version both clarified and strengthened this provision to read, "The right of employees alike to organize for collective bargaining and social action." The revised document called moreover for the "subordination of speculation and the profit motive to the creative and cooperative spirit" and for "social planning and control of the credit and monetary systems and economic processes for the common good."[51] It was little wonder that FCC leaders reveled in Roosevelt's frenetic first hundred days. One hailed the New Deal as a "Third American Revolution," while another regarded it as the Social Gospel in practical form, an interpretation that resonated also with higher-ups in the Roosevelt administration.[52] Several members of the Cabinet were themselves steeped in the ideals of social Christianity and construed the cascade of legislation passing through Congress as a latter day realization of the Sermon on the Mount.[53] It was a new day indeed—and yet one that would not last long.[54]

By the late 1930s a number of historical processes that would, over time, erode social Christianity's popular base had already begun to unfold. In Detroit, Father Charles Coughlin was storming the radio waves with anti-CIO harangues.[55] In Los Angeles, businessman George Pepperdine was making plans for a Christian university that would offer a quality education free of any left-wing taint.[56] In the south, white enthusiasm for the New Deal was fading, as many began to harbor worries that the rising strength of both the federal government and organized labor might eventually upset the Bible Belt's apartheid regime.[57] Meanwhile, across the nation, fundamentalists were building vast institutional and associational networks within which Christian mission was reduced almost entirely to winning converts. For a growing number of militantly conservative believers, social reform reeked of the "Red" social gospel.[58]

To be sure, some American workers would long continue to find in Christianity grounds for resistance. Pro-labor gospels galvanized organizing campaigns well into the twentieth century and even beyond: among Kentucky coal miners and Missouri tenant farmers, among pecan shellers in San Antonio, auto workers in Detroit, and grape pickers in California's Central Valley.[59] Just weeks before his assassination in the spring of 1968, Martin Luther King, Jr., roused striking sanitation workers in Memphis, Tennessee, with a stirring address on "the dignity of labor." King's masterful performance left no doubt that the Bible, when rightly interpreted, retained the power to bring workers to their feet. Invoking the New Testament story of the rich man and Lazarus, he declared, "You know Jesus reminded us in a magnificent parable one day that a man went to hell because he didn't see the poor. His name was Dives." The members of the local branch of the American Federation of State, County and Municipal Employees (AFSCME) shouted, "Yeah, right!" King went on to interpret the parable, proclaiming:

> Dives went to hell because he passed by Lazarus every day, but he never really saw him. (Applause) Dives went to hell because he allowed Lazarus to become invisible. Dives went to hell because he allowed the means by which he lived to outdistance the ends for which he lived. Dives went to hell because he maximized the minimum and minimized the maximum. (Long applause) Dives finally went to hell because he sought to be a conscientious objector in the war against poverty. (Applause)

Then came one of the speech's many climactic lines, as raucous cheers greeted King's declaration: "And I come by here to say that America, too, is going to hell if she doesn't use her wealth. If America does not use her vast resources of wealth to end poverty and make it possible for all of God's children to have the basic necessities of life, she, too, will go to hell."[60]

Ironically, the Great Society era in which King delivered that speech appears in retrospect as not only the most affluent but also the most economically egalitarian period in modern American history. As Nobel Prize winning economist Joseph Stiglitz writes, "For thirty years after World War II, America grew together—with growth in income in every segment, but with those at the bottom growing faster than those at the top."[61] King did not live to see what was just around the corner: a resurgence of deeply conservative politics, buttressed in many cases by Christian faith. Mainline and Catholic churches never renounced their social teachings but in the closing decades of the twentieth century they carried less and less weight outside of denominational headquarters. By the end of the Cold War, millions of people in the pews had come to see free enterprise as a Christian imperative.[62] Meanwhile, hundreds of thousands more flocked to churches that taught that prosperity came not through gritty organizing efforts but through individual access to divine power.[63] Having flourished first at the grassroots, social Christianity withered there too.

Now, in the early decades of the twenty-first century, American capitalism appears once more poised to overwhelm American democracy. Affirmations of equality ring increasingly hollow in a society in which one family—the Waltons, heirs to the Wal-Mart fortune—boasts as much wealth as that of the poorest 48.8 million families combined.[64] It remains to be seen whether present-day believers will quietly abide this state of affairs, or whether it will at some point call forth a generation of prophets comparable to those that visited Gilded Age Chicago.

Notes

INTRODUCTION

1. "Hoodwinking Clergymen," *Cook County Herald*, 2 September 1910. Post's paid article ran in a variety of other papers ranging from the *Tahlequah Herald* (Oklahoma) to the *Times Dispatch* (Virginia) to the *Arizona Republican*.

2. George H. Nash III, "Charles Stelzle: Apostle to Labor," *Labor History* 11, no. 2 (1970): 167.

3. "Approve Labor Sunday Idea," *Chicago Daily Tribune*, 1 September 1910.

4. "'Labor Sunday' Fills Pulpits," *Chicago Daily Tribune*, 4 September 1910.

5. For record of the CFL's preparations for Labor Sunday in 1910, see "Labor Men Want Pulpits," *Chicago Daily Tribune*, 6 June 1910; "Report of Committee on Labor Sunday," Chicago Federation of Labor Minutes, 19 June 1910, Chicago History Museum, Chicago, IL; "Workingwomen to Preach?" *Chicago Daily Tribune*, 20 June 1910; "Reports of Special Committees," Chicago Federation of Labor Minutes, 29 June 1910; "Chicago Federation of Labor: Official Proceedings of the meetings of Aug. 7 and 21, 1910," *Union Labor Advocate* 11, no. 9 (September 1910): 8–9, 11; "Girl Labor Leader to Occupy Pulpit," *Inter Ocean*, 4 September 1910; and the Reverend Edwin F. Snell to Miss Agnes Nestor, 3 August 1910 and 6 August 1910; and J. W. F. Davies to Miss Agnes Nestor, 29 August 1910, Papers of the Women's Trade Union League and its principal leaders [microform], Agnes Nestor Papers, Reel 1, Chicago History Museum, Chicago, IL. For earlier, less successful attempts to rally support for Labor Sunday in the city, see "'Labor' Sunday on March 10," *Chicago Daily Tribune*, 24 February 1907; "Date Set for Labor Sunday," *Chicago Daily Tribune*, 24 April 1908; and "Blacksmith in the Pulpit," *Chicago Daily Tribune*, 11 May 1908.

6. "'Labor Sunday' is Observed in Church," *Inter Ocean*, 5 September 1910.

7. This was the title of an *American Journal of Sociology* article, published a decade before by a Chicago Baptist minister. H. Francis Perry, "The Workingman's Alienation from the Church," *American Journal of Sociology* 4, no. 5 (March 1899): 621–629.

8. "'Labor Sunday' is Observed in Church."

9. "First Labor Sunday; Unionists Tell Aims," *Chicago Record-Herald*, 5 September 1910.

10. "In Factory Girl Plea; Piecework is Scored," *Chicago Record-Herald*, 5 September 1910. Other worker-preachers this day included Oscar F. Nelson, president of the Post Office Clerks' Union, at the Olivet Institute; and Emmett Flood, AFL organizer, at Endeavor Presbyterian.

11. "Plea that Labor Recognize Negro," *Inter Ocean*, 5 September 1910.

12. "Says Church Must Solve All Industrial Problems," *Inter Ocean*, 5 September 1910.

13. Separate reports in the *Tribune, Record-Herald, Inter Ocean,* and *Examiner* name twenty-four churches where ministers preached on the theme, including St. Paul's Reformed Episcopal, Ravenswood Presbyterian, St. Ann's Episcopal, Grace Methodist Episcopal, Onward Presbyterian, Wesley Methodist Episcopal, the Cathedral of Saints Peter and Paul, St. Stephen's Lutheran, Humboldt Park Parish of the New Jerusalem, St. Barnabas Episcopal, Erie Chapel Presbyterian, Washington Park Baptist, First Roseland Baptist, St. Simon's Mission, Jackson Boulevard Christian, South Congregational, South Englewood Methodist, St. Mark's Episcopal, Crerar Memorial Presbyterian, Western Avenue Methodist, First Swedish Unitarian, Olivet Memorial Church, California Avenue Congregational, and St. James (Catholic) Pro-Cathedral in Rockford. The last of these is the only Roman Catholic church mentioned explicitly, though the *Tribune* report from 5 September declares, "Roman Catholic churches also joined in observing the day." See "Labor Leaders in City Pulpits To-Day," *Chicago Examiner*, 4 September 1910; "Workers and Divines Share Pulpits on 'Labor Sunday,'" *Chicago Examiner*, 5 September 1910; "'Labor Sunday' Fills Pulpits"; and "Gospel of Unions Told in Pulpits," *Chicago Daily Tribune*, 5 September 1910.

14. "Gospel of Unions Told in Pulpits."

15. These ties were dense across the industrializing north. E. Digby Baltzell, *The Protestant Establishment: Aristocracy and Caste in America* (New Haven, CT: Yale University Press, 1987); Tyler B. Flynn, "Calvinism and Public Life: A Case Study of Western Pennsylvania 1900–1955" (PhD diss., Pennsylvania State University, 2007); Timothy E. W. Gloege, *Guaranteed Pure: Fundamentalism, Business, and the Making of Modern Evangelicalism* (Chapel Hill, NC: University of North Carolina Press, 2015); Frederick Jaher, *The Urban Establishment: Upper Strata in Boston, New York, Charleston, Chicago, and Los Angeles* (Urbana: University of Illinois Press, 1982); and Thomas F. Rzeznik, *Church and Estate: Religion*

and Wealth in Industrial-Era Philadelphia (University Park: Pennsylvania State University Press, 2013).

16. "Approve Labor Sunday Idea."

17. "In Factory Girl Plea; Piecework is Scored."

18. On this point, Aaron Abell's classic works remain incisive. See "The Reception of Leo XIII's Labor Encyclical in America, 1891–1919," *Review of Politics* 7, no. 4 (October 1945): 464–495; and *American Catholicism and Social Action: A Search for Social Justice* (New York: Hanover House, 1960).

19. "Archbishop Quigley and Chicago Priests Go to Montreal Congress," *Chicago Daily Journal*, 5 September 1910; and "Labor is Warned by Bishop," *Record-Herald*, 5 September 1910.

20. "Labor Sees a New Era Here," *Chicago Daily Journal*, 5 September 1910.

21. On the difficulties of a more precise definition, as well as for a helpful discussion of the historiography, see Gary Scott Smith, *The Search for Social Salvation: Social Christianity and America, 1880–1925* (New York: Lexington Books, 2000), 1–64.

22. Abell, *American Catholicism and Social Action*; Charles Howard Hopkins, *The Rise of the Social Gospel in American Protestantism 1865–1915* (New Haven, CT: Yale University Press, 1940); and Henry F. May, *Protestant Churches and Industrial America* (New York: Harper & Brothers Publishers, 1949).

23. Examples include Ellen Blue, *St. Mark's and the Social Gospel: Methodist Women and Civil Rights in New Orleans, 1895–1965* (Knoxville: University of Tennessee Press, 2011); Wendy J. Deichmann Edwards and Carolyn De Swarte Gifford, *Gender and the Social Gospel* (Chicago: University of Illinois Press, 2003); Evelyn Brooks Higginbotham, *Righteous Discontent: The Women's Movement in the Black Baptist Church, 1880–1920* (Cambridge, MA: Harvard University Press, 1993); Ralph E. Luker, *The Social Gospel in Black and White: American Racial Reform, 1885–1912* (Chapel Hill: University of North Carolina Press, 1991); John Patrick McDowell, *The Social Gospel in the South: The Woman's Home Mission Movement in the Methodist Episcopal Church, South, 1886–1939* (Baton Rouge: Louisiana State University Press, 1982); and Ronald C. White, Jr., *Liberty and Justice for All: Racial Reform and the Social Gospel* (San Francisco: Harper and Row, 1990).

24. One exception to this rule is Ken Fones-Wolf, *Trade Union Gospel: Christianity and Labor in Industrial Philadelphia 1865–1915* (Philadelphia: Temple University Press, 1989). Currently, the field is in the midst of a major transition, as several scholars have begun to unearth the working-class origins of social Christianity. See David Burns, *The Life and Death of the Radical Historical Jesus* (New York: Oxford University Press, 2013); Heath W. Carter, "Scab Ministers, Striking Saints: Christianity and Class Conflict in 1894 Chicago," *American Nineteenth Century History* 11, no. 3 (September 2010): 321–349; and Janine Giordano Drake, "Between Religion and Politics: The Working Class Religious

Left, 1886–1920" (PhD diss., University of Illinois, 2012). In addition to these studies, which explicitly situate working people within the history of social Christianity, there are a number of others that emphasize the more radical and progressive bent of some working-class Christianities. For recent examples, see Richard Callahan, Jr., *Work and Faith in the Kentucky Coal Fields: Subject to Dust* (Bloomington: Indiana University Press, 2009); Erik Gellman and Jarod Roll, *The Gospel of the Working Class* (Urbana: University of Illinois Press, 2011); Dan McKanan, *Prophetic Encounters: Religion and the American Radical Tradition* (Boston: Beacon Press, 2011); William A. Mirola, *Redeeming Time: Protestantism and Chicago's Eight-Hour Movement, 1866–1912* (Urbana: University of Illinois Press, 2015); and Jarod Roll, *Spirit of Rebellion: Labor and Religion in the New Cotton South* (Urbana: University of Illinois Press, 2010).

25. "The Labor Turmoil," *Alliance* 1, no. 4 (3 January 1874): 2.

26. Christopher H. Evans, *The Kingdom is Always but Coming: A Life of Walter Rauschenbusch* (Grand Rapids, MI: William B. Eerdmans Publishing Company, 2004), xviii.

27. On "lived religion," see Robert A. Orsi, *The Madonna of 115th Street: Faith and Community in Italian Harlem, 1880–1950* (New Haven, CT: Yale University Press, 2002), ix–xxxviii; and David D. Hall, ed., *Lived Religion in America: Toward a History of Practice* (Princeton, NJ: Princeton University Press, 1997). In underscoring working people's intellectual contributions to American Christianity, this book reinforces the central insight of Herbert G. Gutman's groundbreaking article "Protestantism and the American Labor Movement: The Christian Spirit in the Gilded Age," *American Historical Review* 72, no. 1 (October 1966): 74–101.

28. For more on this theme, see Paul Boyer, *Urban Masses and Moral Order in America, 1820–1920* (Cambridge, MA: Harvard University Press, 1978).

29. See Kevin J. Christiano, *Religious Diversity and Social Change* (Cambridge: Cambridge University Press, 1987); Gail Bederman, " 'The Woman Have Had Charge of the Church Work Long Enough': The Men and Religion Forward Movement of 1911–1912 and the Masculinization of Middle-Class Protestantism," *American Quarterly* 41, no. 3 (September 1989): 432–465; and Anne Braude, "Women's History *is* American Religious History," in Thomas Tweed, ed., *Retelling U.S. Religious History* (Berkeley: University of California Press, 1997), 87–107.

30. For exemplary studies in this vein, see Darren Dochuk, *From Bible Belt to Sunbelt: Plainfolk Religion, Grassroots Politics, and the Rise of Evangelical Conservatism* (New York: Norton, 2011); Kevin Kruse, *One Nation under God: How Corporate America Invented Christian America* (New York: Basic Books, 2015); and Bethany Moreton, *To Serve God and Wal-Mart: The Making of Christian Free Enterprise* (Cambridge, MA: Harvard University Press, 2009).

31. The only Christianly inflected response that compares in importance during this era is populism. For two excellent books on its religious underpinnings,

see Joe Creech, *Righteous Indignation: Religion and the Populist Revolution* (Urbana: University of Illinois Press, 2006); and Michael Kazin, *A Godly Hero: The Life of William Jennings Bryan* (New York: Anchor Books, 2006).

32. As Catherine A. Brekus and W. Clark Gilpin write, "Christians have infused American society with an extensive repertoire of stories, symbols, and ethical ideals that have been among the defining terms of American cultural debate." See *American Christianities: A History of Dominance and Diversity* (Chapel Hill: University of North Carolina Press, 2011), 2. See also David Sehat, *The Myth of American Religious Freedom* (New York: Oxford University Press, 2011).

33. Mark 12:31. All scriptural quotations are from the King James Version, which was widely used in late nineteenth-century America.

34. Luke 10:7; and Luke 6:24.

35. Which is to say, at the very center of the nation's history. See Alice Kessler-Harris, "Capitalism, Democracy, and the Emancipation of Belief," *Journal of American History* 99, no. 3 (December 2012): 725–740.

36. This represents a vast sphere of human activity, in which ordinary persons have played decisive, albeit oft neglected, roles. Historians of the working classes might well regard the history of world Christianity as a pressing frontier for further study. Its promise as such is attested throughout Lamin Sanneh, *Disciples of All Nations: Pillars of World Christianity* (New York: Oxford University Press, 2008).

37. Hugh McLeod, *Piety and Poverty: Working-Class Religion in Berlin, London and New York, 1870–1914* (New York: Oxford University Press, 2003); and Bruce C. Nelson, "Revival and Upheaval: Religion, Irreligion, and Chicago's Working Class in 1886," *Journal of Social History* 25, no. 2 (Winter 1991): 233–253.

38. The paucity of sources for late nineteenth-century Catholic Chicago and especially for lay Catholics has proven particularly frustrating, given the demographics of the city and its labor movement. Everything I have found is included in the book. The evidence suggests the continuity I describe above, though the sources are less revealing of the ways that Catholics reconciled their faith and labor politics than I would like.

39. For more on the longer history of this theme, see, for example, Peter Brown, *Through the Eye of a Needle: Wealth, the Fall of Rome, and the Making of Christianity in the West, 350–550 AD* (Princeton, NJ: Princeton University Press, 2012).

40. Philip McCann, *Modern Urban and Regional Economics*, 2d ed. (New York: Oxford University Press, 2013), 289.

41. C. A. Bayly, *The Birth of the Modern World: 1780–1914* (Oxford: Blackwell Publishing, 2004); William Cronon, *Nature's Metropolis: Chicago and the Great West* (New York: W. W. Norton & Company, 1991); Eric Hobsbawm, *The Age of Capital: 1848–1875* (New York: Vintage Books, 1975); and Peter N. Stearns, *The Industrial Revolution in World History*, 3d ed. (Boulder, CO: Westview Press, 2007).

42. Here I have in mind: (1) The earlier, progressive bent of many working-class Christianities. See note 24 above. (2) Long-standing churchly hostility to labor, stemming from Protestant ties to capital and Catholic anxieties about socialism. See notes 15 and 18 above. And (3) the Christian elite's anxiety about losing working people and in particular working men. See Bederman, "The Woman Have Had Charge of the Church Work Long Enough."

43. See, for example, Paul Krugman, "Why We're in a New Gilded Age," *New York Review of Books*, 8 May 2014. For analyses of contemporary economic inequality, see Joseph E. Stiglitz, *The Price of Inequality: How Today's Divided Society Endangers Our Future* (New York: W. W. Norton & Company, 2012); and Thomas Piketty, *Capital in the Twenty-First Century* (Cambridge, MA: Belknap Press of Harvard University Press, 2014).

CHAPTER 1

1. See Robert Ozanne, "Union Wage Impact: A Nineteenth-Century Case," *Industrial and Labor Relations Review* 15, no. 3 (April 1962): 351.

2. "Is the Laborer Worthy of His Hire?" *Chicago Press and Tribune*, 14 July 1858.

3. This was true at the federal level. Some states continued to have established churches. Massachusetts became the last state to cut ties with the church in 1833. For more on this, see Patricia Bonomi, *Under the Cope of Heaven: Religion, Society, and Politics in Colonial America* (New York: Oxford University Press, 2003).

4. "Duty of the Church to Support the Ministry," *Zion's Herald and Wesleyan Journal*, 23 April 1851.

5. Compare E. Brooks Holifield, *God's Ambassadors: A History of the Christian Clergy in America* (Grand Rapids, MI: Eerdmans Publishing Company, 2007), 130; and Bruce Laurie, *Artisans into Workers: Labor in Nineteenth-Century America* (Urbana: University of Illinois Press, 1989), 56–61.

6. Holifield, *God's Ambassadors*, 130–131.

7. See "Preachers—To the Rescue," *Independent*, 21 April 1853.

8. For a helpful definition of the evangelical tradition, see Mark A. Noll, *The Rise of Evangelicalism: The Age of Edwards, Whitefield, and the Wesleys* (Downers Grove, IL: InterVarsity Press, 2003), 13–26. The literature on evangelicalism's rise is vast. See, for example, the selected bibliography in Noll, *The Rise of Evangelicalism*, 295–317. For an account of evangelicalism's improbable convergence with republicanism and common sense moral philosophy, see Mark A. Noll, *America's God: From Jonathan Edwards to Abraham Lincoln* (New York: Oxford University Press, 2002). For more on the marketing dimension, see both Nathan Hatch, *The Democratization of American Christianity* (New Haven, CT: Yale University Press, 1989); and R. Laurence Moore, *Selling God: American Religion in the Marketplace of Culture* (New York: Oxford University Press, 1995).

9. See Jon Butler, *Awash in a Sea of Faith: Christianizing the American People* (Boston: Harvard University Press, 1990); and Hatch, *The Democratization of American Christianity*. Religious historians have long cited the early national period as a crucial turning point in the Christianization of the people. For a classic account that focuses particularly on the significance of disestablishment, see Sidney Mead, *The Lively Experiment: The Shaping of Christianity in America* (New York: Harper & Row, 1963).

10. See Roger Finke and Rodney Stark, *The Churching of America, 1776–1990: Winners and Losers in Our Religious Economy* (New Brunswick, NJ: Rutgers University Press, 1992), 15–16.

11. "Is the Laborer Worthy of His Hire?"

12. This shift can be seen as part of a much wider "reorientation" of the nation's evangelical churches away from the revivalism that had so deeply informed their earlier development. See James D. Bratt, "The Reorientation of American Protestantism, 1835–1845," *Church History* 67, no. 1 (March 1998): 52–83.

13. John B. Jentz and Richard Schneirov, *Chicago in the Age of Capital: Class, Politics, and Democracy during the Civil War and Reconstruction* (Urbana: University of Illinois Press, 2012), 23–24.

14. Bessie Louise Pierce, *A History of Chicago*, Vol. 1: *The Beginning of a City, 1673–1848* (New York: Alfred A. Knopf, 1937), 201.

15. Pierce, *A History of Chicago*, 1:65.

16. Quotations from contemporary accounts, cited in Pierce, *A History of Chicago*, 1:204.

17. Charles Butler to Chicago Historical Society, 17 December 1881, Autograph Letters, XXXI (*Ms.* Chicago Historical Society), quoted in Pierce, *A History of Chicago*, 1:49.

18. Ibid., 1:50–51.

19. Wolf's Point is a still-visible outcrop of land near where the Chicago River splits into north and south branches.

20. See "Churches and Church Choirs in Chicago," *Chicago Magazine: The West as It Is*, Vol. 1 (J. Gager & Company for Chicago Mechanics' Institute, 1857), 344; and Alfred Theodore Andreas, *History of Chicago*, Vol. 1 (Chicago: A. T. Andreas Company, 1884), 288.

21. See Mrs. John H. Kinzie, *Wau-Bun* (Philadelphia, 1873), 149, quoted in Pierce, *A History of Chicago*, 1:223. For more on Kinzie—one of early Chicago's most formidable women—and particularly about her seminal role within the city's St. James Episcopal Church, see Rima Lunin Schultz, *The Church and the City: A Social History of 150 Years at Saint James, Chicago* (Chicago: Cathedral of St. James, 1986), 17–38.

22. Andreas, *History of Chicago*, 1:325.

23. Quoted in Gilbert Joseph Garraghan, *The Catholic Church in Chicago, 1673–1871* (Chicago: Loyola University Press, 1921), 50.

24. For a description of the building, see Andreas, *History of Chicago*, 1:290. By 1837, when St. Cyr moved on, the congregation counted more than 2,000 persons of American, Irish, French, and German stock. See Pierce, *History of Chicago*, 1:226.

25. Andreas, *History of Chicago*, 1:315.

26. Ibid., 1:300–301.

27. See Schultz, *The Church and the City*, 25–29; and Pierce, *A History of Chicago*, 1:194.

28. Schultz, *The Church and the City*, 30.

29. Pierce, *A History of Chicago*, 1: 128.

30. See Cronon, *Nature's Metropolis*, 91.

31. Class stratification was, of course, as old as the city itself. In 1831, one resident observed that there were "about ten or twelve families . . . who consider themselves even above the common class." Quoted in Pierce, *A History of Chicago*, 1:186.

32. The Federal Census of that year enumerated 29,963 persons, 15,682 of whom were foreign-born. See Pierce, *A History of Chicago*, 1:179. For more on early Bridgeport, see ibid., 13.

33. For more on the common background of these families, see, for example, Jaher, *The Urban Establishment*, 453–576.

34. See Schultz, *The Church and the City*, 27–28.

35. See Pierce, *A History of Chicago*, 1:139–140.

36. Andreas, *History of Chicago*, 1:335.

37. This was part of a much larger migration of churches from Washington Avenue, an early hub of religious life, to Wabash Avenue. See Daniel Bluestone, *Constructing Chicago* (New Haven, CT: Yale University Press, 1991), 62–103.

38. Andreas, *History of Chicago*, 1:301–302.

39. Ibid., 305.

40. For more on the wages for various trades during these years, see Pierce, *A History of Chicago*, 1:194–198.

41. On the bricklayers, see Bessie Louise Pierce, *A History of Chicago*, Vol. 3: *The Rise of a Modern City, 1871–1893* (Chicago: University of Chicago Press, 1857), 240. For Patterson's wages, see Thomas Butler Carter and John C. Grant, *The Second Presbyterian Church of Chicago* (Chicago: Knight, Leonard, & Co, 1892), 20.

42. See Andreas, *History of Chicago*, 1:339; and "How Preachers Are Paid," *Chicago Daily Tribune*, 7 June 1874. There are countless other examples. First Presbyterian hired Flavel Bascom to be its minister in 1840 for $1,000/year. In 1850 it upped the ante to $1,500 in order to attract Harvey Curtis away from his pulpit in Madison, Indiana. By 1859 it took $3,000 to get the Reverend

Z. M. Humphrey to move from Milwaukee and then, less than a decade later in 1868, $5,000 to lure Arthur Mitchell from Morristown, New Jersey. See Philo Adams Otis, *The First Presbyterian Church: A History of the Oldest Organization in Chicago* (Chicago: Clayton F. Summy Co, 1900), 17–30. Olivet Presbyterian hired its first pastor for $1,300 a year; its second for $2,000 in 1863; and its third for $4,000 in 1867. See Andreas, *History of Chicago*, 1:314–315. While earlier salary figures are not available for many other denominations, the trend was hardly confined to the Presbyterians, as made clear by the 1874 *Tribune* report (cited above) on ministers' salaries.

43. See Andreas, *History of Chicago*, 1:291.

44. On efforts to secure funds from elsewhere, see, for example, Garraghan, *The Catholic Church in Chicago*, 122–123, 173; and Alfred Theodore Andreas, *History of Chicago*, Vol. 1 (Chicago: A. T. Andreas Company, 1884).

45. Andreas, *History of Chicago*, 1:294.

46. Ibid., 1:297.

47. Ibid., 1:401–403.

48. "Progress of Chicago," *Chicago Daily Tribune*, 4 January 1856.

49. Holifield, *God's Ambassadors*, 130–131.

50. There were a handful of experimental "free churches" founded during this era. See, for example, "Episcopal Free Church on the West Side," *Chicago Press and Tribune*, 25 June 1859.

51. See, for example, "Rental of Pews—First Baptist," *Chicago Tribune*, 24 December 1867.

52. "Brooklyn News: Annual Renting of Pews of Plymouth Church," *New York Times*, 4 January 1865.

53. John Floyd, "The Catholic Clergy and Laiety," *Chicago Daily Tribune*, 13 March 1857. Catholic building campaigns were criticized for different reasons by those outside the fold. As Ellen Skerrett astutely writes, "While newspapers generally applauded the efforts of wealthy Protestant congregations to finance brick or stone churches, opinion was sharply divided when it came to Irish parishes such as Holy Name. The disparate treatment accorded Protestants and Catholics reflected an underlying critical debate: should poor immigrant congregations spend limited resources on constructing beautiful houses of worship?" See "Creating Sacred Space in an Early Chicago Neighborhood," in Ellen Skerrett, ed., *At the Crossroads: Old Saint Patrick's and the Chicago Irish* (Chicago: Loyola University Press, 1997), 30.

54. R. W. M., "Plea for the Suffering Poor," *Chicago Press and Tribune*, 4 August 1859. See also "The Sunday Question," *Chicago Press and Tribune*, 20 July 1859; and "A Lay Member's Views of the Sunday Question," *Chicago Press and Tribune*, 4 August 1859." In the last of these, the author noted, "A great handle has been made in this controversy of the aristocracy of the Churches, etc. I purposely omit all that. Every one has a right to what they pay for. It would, however, be a great blessing if there were some free Churches."

55. See the discussion in Noll, *America's God*, 195–202.

56. This way of framing the story mediates between two conflicting schools of thought. Scholars such as Paul Johnson, Sean Wilentz, and Charles Sellers argue that evangelicalism functioned as a new means of social control within a rapidly industrializing society. See Paul Johnson, *A Shopkeeper's Millennium: Society and Revivals in Rochester, New York, 1815–1837* (New York: Hill and Wang, 1978); Charles Sellers, *The Market Revolution: Jacksonian America, 1815–1846* (Oxford: Oxford University Press, 1991); and Paul Johnson and Sean Wilentz, *The Kingdom of Matthias: A Story of Sex and Salvation in 19th-Century America* (Oxford: Oxford University Press, 1994). I agree that the tradition's emphasis on individual moral discipline did, in many cases, blind believers to the systemic dimensions of emerging social problems. However, I reject the notion, present in some of this literature, that shopkeepers and factory owners foisted evangelical religion upon their employees. Here I agree with Daniel Howe, among others, that working people embraced it of their own accord. See Daniel Walker Howe, *What Hath God Wrought: The Transformation of America, 1815–1848* (New York: Oxford University Press, 2007), 191–195, 579–580. In the end, though, I do not accept Howe's admittedly sunny view of these developments, springing as it does from his assumption—expressed in a spring 2008 colloquium at the University of Notre Dame—that "material progress begets moral progress."

57. William R. Sutton drives this point home in his compellingly argued review essay, "Tied to the Whipping Post: New Labor History and Evangelical Artisans in the Early Republic," *Labor History* 36, no. 2 (1995): 251–281.

58. Sean Wilentz, *Chants Democratic: New York City and the Rise of the American Working Class, 1788–1850*, Twentieth-Anniversary Edition (Oxford: Oxford University Press, 2004), 81–82.

59. See William R. Sutton, *Journeymen for Jesus: Evangelical Artisans Confront Capitalism in Jacksonian Baltimore* (University Park: Pennsylvania State University Press, 1998), 215–258.

60. Jama Lazerow, *Religion and the Working Class in Antebellum America* (Washington, DC: Smithsonian Institute Press, 1995); and Teresa Ann Murphy, *Ten Hours' Labor: Religion, Reform, and Gender in Early New England* (Ithaca, NY: Cornell University Press, 1992).

61. Lazerow, *Religion and the Working Class in Antebellum America*, 71.

62. Peter Way recounts these episodes and others in "Evil Humors and Ardent Spirits: The Rough Culture of Canal Construction Laborers," *Journal of American History* 79, no. 4 (March 1993): 1397–1428.

63. See Patrick Staunton and Patrick Roe, "Treatment of Laborers by the Wisconsin and Chicago Railroad Company," *Western Tablet* 11, no. 7 (19 March 1853): 5; and for other examples, John Kelly, "The Ill. Central R.R. Co. and their Agent," *Western Tablet* 1, no. 30 (30 October 1852): 3; Patrick, "'Laborers Wanted!!',"

Western Tablet 1, no. 32 (13 November 1852): 4; An Observer, "Illinois Central Railroad," *Western Tablet* 1, no. 47 (25 December 1852): 4–5; A Friend to the Poor, "More Railroad Outrages," *Western Tablet* 2, no. 44 (3 December 1853): 8. The *Tablet* also reproduced a similar kind of notice from the *Boston Pilot*. See "Laborers," *Western Tablet* 1, no. 33 (18 September 1852): 4.

64. As Eric Foner writes, "Only those who profited from the work of others, or whose occupations were largely financial or promotional, such as specula-tors, bankers, and lawyers, were excluded from this definition." See *Free Soil, Free Labor, Free Men: The Ideology of the Republican Party before the Civil War* (New York: Oxford University Press, 1995), 15.

65. Ibid., 32.

66. Another significant prop was the moral indignation that welled up in many a northern Christian when she paused to reflect upon the most obvious alterna-tive: the dreaded slave system of the fire-eating South. See ibid.; and Amy Dru Stanley, *From Bondage to Contract: Wage Labor, Marriage, and the Market in the Age of Slave Emancipation* (Cambridge: Cambridge University Press, 1999).

67. Pierce, *History of Chicago*, Vol. 2: *From Town to City, 1848–1871* (Chicago: University of Chicago Press, 1940), 160–167; Richard Schneirov, *Labor and Urban Politics: Class Conflict and the Origins of Modern Liberalism in Chicago, 1864–1897* (Urbana: University of Illinois Press, 1998), 32.

68. "One Hundred and Forty-Eighth Anniversary of the Birth of Benjamin Franklin," *Chicago Daily Tribune*, 18 January 1855.

69. For more on Lunt's myriad civic commitments, see John Moses and Joseph Kirkland, *History of Chicago, Illinois* (Chicago: Munsell & Company, 1895), 646.

70. For a more in-depth description of Wabash Avenue Methodist, see George Searle Phillips, *Chicago and Her Churches* (Chicago: E. B. Myers and Chandler, 1868), 300. The Colored Baptist Church down the street cost, by comparison, $3,500. See *A Review of the Commerce of Chicago, Her Merchants and Manufacturers* (Chicago: Scripps, Bross, and Spears, 1855), 7. As pricey as Wabash Avenue Methodist's building was, it still paled in comparison to the Briggs house, which was valued at $110,000 upon completion in 1855. "The Briggs House," *Chicago Daily Tribune*, 24 May 1855.

71. See the Federal Census for 1860, as well as E. Brooks Holifield, "The Penurious Preacher? Nineteenth Century Clerical Wealth: North and South," *Journal of the American Academy of Religion* 58, no. 1 (Spring 1990): 17–36.

72. I have estimated Cox's salary based on a previous pastor's, set at $600 in 1857. Because the Panic of 1857 coincided with the building project, the church was experiencing financial struggles during these years that would likely have pre-cluded any more lucrative offer. The fact that Cox and his family enjoyed free use of the parsonage did lend them a considerable edge over the average com-positor, however. See Andreas, *History of Chicago*, 1:329. On the printers' pay scale, see Pierce, *A History of Chicago*, 2:160–161.

73. "Chicago Typographical Union," *Chicago Daily Tribune*, 18 January 1861.
74. Ibid.

CHAPTER 2

1. The average white male worker earned roughly $300 a year in 1860. See Laurie, *Artisans into Workers*, 127.
2. See "A Valuable Gift," *Lee County Journal* 2, no. 22 (18 July 1867): 1; and "Methodist News: Personal," *Northwestern Christian Advocate* 15, no. 30 (24 July 1867): 237.
3. Pierce, *A History of Chicago*, 2:174; Schneirov, *Labor and Urban Politics*, 33.
4. A similar bill, establishing the eight-hour day for federal employees and enjoying strong support from an unwieldy coalition of Northern Democrats and Radical Republicans, passed the House of Representatives in March 1867 but never made its way out of committee in the Senate that spring. Only in 1868 did it become law. See Eric Foner, *Reconstruction: America's Unfinished Revolution, 1863–1877* (New York: Perennial Classics, 1988), 480–481.
5. In the antebellum era, most Republicans opposed legislation that would shorten the workday. See Foner, *Free Soil, Free Labor, Free Men*, 26. In the postbellum era, they were generally more sympathetic, seeing it as a means to uplift free labor, though as Schneirov points out they were less than enthusiastic. This helps to explain the relative weakness of Illinois's first eight-hour law, which was filled with exceptions: for example, it did not regulate labor paid by the week, month, or year, and it moreover allowed employers to enforce longer daily hours so long as they were stipulated in a contract. See Schneirov, *Labor and Urban Politics*, 33–34; Pierce, *History of Chicago*, 2:175.
6. "The Eight-Hour Movement," *Chicago Tribune*, 2 May 1867; "On the Lake Shore," *Chicago Tribune*, 2 May 1867; "The Labor Question," *Christian Freeman* 1, no. 6 (9 May 1867): 2; Pierce, *A History of Chicago*, 2:177–178.
7. "The Eight Hour Movement," *Lee County Journal*, 27 April 1867.
8. *Lee County Journal*, 11 May 1867.
9. See "The Eight Hour Demonstration," *Lee County Journal*, 4 May 1867; "The Labor Question," *Chicago Republican*, 9 May 1867; "Meeting of the Late Employees of the I.C.R.R. at Keeling's Hall," *Lee County Journal*, 11 May 1867; and "The Eight-Hour Question," *Chicago Republican*, 12 May 1867.
10. The Amboy Methodist church counted some 100 members, drawn from all ranks of respectable society. On a given Sunday morning, one might find the families of Abel Burham, a farm laborer, George Mingle, a shoemaker, and Henry Badger, a miller whose $28,000 fortune rivaled that of the highest-ranking Chicago professionals. In Chicago only 28.6% of lawyers, 11.9% of physicians, and 4.7% of engineers boasted more than $20,000 in property in 1870. See

Thomas Goebel, "The Uneven Rewards of Professional Labor: Wealth and Income in the Chicago Professions, 1870–1920," *Journal of Social History* 29, no. 4 (Summer 1996): 752. For a brief history of the church, see *History of Lee County* (Chicago: H. H. Hill & Company, 1881), 335–337. I matched the aforementioned names of members here with the 1860 and 1870 US federal censuses. In 1870, Holmes informed the census taker that he owned $3,000 worth of real estate and $600 of other property. His total wealth put him just slightly above the northern white mean of $2,921 in 1870. See the 1870 US federal census; and Edward Bubnys, "Nativity and the Distribution of Wealth: Chicago 1870," *Explorations in Economic History* 19, no. 2 (1982): 106.

11. See names mentioned in *Lee County Journal*, 11 May 1867; "The Eight-Hour Movement," *Chicago Daily Tribune*, 23 May 1867; and "A Valuable Gift," *Lee County Journal*, 18 July 1867. I matched these with the US federal census. In addition, I found mention of Corcoran in association with the local Catholic parish in *History of Lee County*, 341.

12. "The Labor Question," *Christian Freeman* 1, no. 6 (9 May 1867): 2.

13. "Labor and Wages," *Christian Times and Witness* 14, no. 37 (9 May 1867): 3.

14. Ibid.

15. "Editorial Items," *Northwestern Christian Advocate* 15, no. 19 (8 May 1867): 148.

16. Schneirov, *Labor and Urban Politics*, 34–35; Pierce, *A History of Chicago*, 2:178–179.

17. In the middle decades of the nineteenth century, those who ended up in Chicago most often hailed from Germany, Ireland, and other parts of the Old Northwest. In 1860 the city was comprised of roughly half native- and half foreign-born persons. That year migrants from the Old Northwest comprised 57.58% of the native-born population, while the Germans and Irish comprised 40.70% and 36.41% of the foreign-born, respectively. In 1870 the overall ratio of native- to foreign-born remained relatively stable. Persons from the Old Northwest comprised 65.59% of the native-born population, while the Germans and Irish comprised 41.02% and 27.66% of the foreign-born population, respectively. See Pierce, *History of Chicago*, 2:482.

18. Schultz, *The Church and the City*, 57.

19. For more on rising municipal costs, see Pierce, *A History of Chicago*, 2:345–346.

20. See ibid., 2:331.

21. See ibid., 2:333.

22. By the early 1870s, from downtown one could easily go south to 55th Street, or south and then all the way west to the Union Stockyards near 43rd and Ashland in the neighboring Town of Lake; alternatively, one could travel due west to the city limits at aptly named Western Avenue, or north to Irving Park Road, two miles beyond the northerly boundary at Fullerton. See Dominic A. Pacyga, *Chicago: A Biography* (Chicago: University of Chicago Press, 2009), 73–74. For

more on the difficulties occasioned by horse-dependent travel, see Perry R. Duis, *Challenging Chicago: Coping with Everyday Life, 1837–1920* (Urbana: University of Illinois Press, 1998), 17–18.

23. For more on the character of shock cities, see, for example, the discussion of Manchester in Asa Briggs, *Victorian Cities* (Berkeley: University of California Press, 1963), 88–138.

24. See Theodore J. Karamanski, *Rally 'Round the Flag: Chicago and the Civil War* (New York: Rowman and Littlefield, 2006), 167.

25. As Jaher notes, "in 1848 the railroad had not yet appeared in Chicago; four years later a line connected it with the East, and in 1856 it was the hub of ten trunk lines with 2,033 miles of track." See Jaher, *The Urban Establishment*, 453–454; Foner, *Reconstruction*, 18–19; and Karamanski, *Rally 'Round the Flag*, 165–166.

26. Cronon, *Nature's Metropolis*, 229–230.

27. See Schneirov, *Labor and Urban Politics*, 22–24. For a classic look at the post-bellum evolution of the national economy down these same lines, see Alfred D. Chandler, Jr., *The Visible Hand: The Managerial Revolution in American Business* (Cambridge, MA: Harvard University Press, 1977).

28. On wages during these years, see Pierce, *History of Chicago*, 2:155–159.

29. See Schneirov, *Labor and Urban Politics*, 19–25.

30. Karamanski, *Rally 'Round the Flag*, 176; and Jentz and Schneirov, *Chicago in the Age of Capital*, 66.

31. Pierce, *History of Chicago*, 2:160–167; Schneirov, *Labor and Urban Politics*, 32. At the national level, meanwhile, as Jentz and Schneirov write, "in 1864, the number of trade unions in the United States multiplied almost three-and-one-half times." Jentz and Schneirov, *Chicago in the Age of Capital*, 67.

32. Pierce, *History of Chicago*, 2:162. Quoted in James Green, *Death in the Haymarket: A Story of Chicago, The First Labor Movement and the Bombing that Divided Gilded Age America* (New York: Pantheon Books, 2006), 21.

33. Pierce, *History of Chicago*, 2:168–169; Schneirov, *Labor and Urban Politics*, 32–33.

34. "Dignity of Labor," *Chicago Tribune*, 11 April 1866.

35. Robert Collyer, "The Ministry at Large," *Chicago Press and Tribune*, 3 March 1859.

36. See John Haynes Holmes, *The Life and Letters of Robert Collyer, 1823–1912*, Vol. 1 (New York: Dodd Mead and Company, 1917), 199–200.

37. Karamanski, *Rally 'Round the Flag*, 93, 100.

38. "Trades Assembly Lectures," *Workingman's Advocate* 2, no. 43 (19 May 1866): 4.

39. John Haynes Holmes, *The Life and Letters of Robert Collyer, 1823–1912*, Vol. 2 (New York: Dodd Mead and Company, 1917), 104.

40. "Dr. Collyer's Lecture," *Workingman's Advocate* 2, no. 41 (5 May 1866): 3.

41. "Trades Assembly Lectures," *Workingman's Advocate* 2, no. 44 (26 May 1866): 4.

42. "Lecture to Working Men," *Chicago Tribune*, 11 May 1866.

43. "The Groves Were God's First Temples," *Workingman's Advocate* 3, no. 5 (25 August 1866).

44. In all the extant issues between the founding of the *Workingman's Advocate* in 1864 and the general strike of 1867, this is in fact the only such column I have found. The trend would swiftly reverse in the wake of the strike, however.

45. For a description of the building, see Phillips, *Chicago and Her Churches*, 300. Recall from chapter 1 that in the earlier 1860s the Reverend Henry Cox—guest of honor at the Typographical Union's 1861 banquet—had presided at this church.

46. "Wabash Avenue Methodist Church," *Chicago Republican*, 25 February 1867.

47. This talk is mentioned in "A Small Stream from a Large Fountain," *Workingman's Advocate* 4, no. 9 (21 September 1867), though there is no indication of when Everts gave it.

48. At the Trades Assembly's Fourth of July rally in 1865, one of the speakers, Detroit-based Richard Trevellick, president of the International Ship Carpenters' and Caulkers' Union, articulated this very conviction. The *Tribune* paraphrased, "He desired to see the States accept eight hour's labor as a legal days work. The principle was based upon the biblical record. 'Six days did the Lord labor and the seventh did he rest from his labor.' The Supreme Being has thus exemplified the necessity for rest and recreation." See "The City," *Chicago Tribune*, 6 July 1865.

49. Perhaps the closest parallel was an observation in the 8 May edition of the *Northwestern Christian Advocate* that "a cogent argument for caution has been furnished by the known readiness of the Dearborn Light Artillery for shotted interference," but the writer added, "We trust and expect that no bloodshed will occur." *Northwestern Christian Advocate*, 8 May 1867.

50. "The Labor Movement," *Northwestern Christian Advocate*, 22 May 1867.

51. See Bubnys, "Nativity and the Distribution of Wealth."

52. Eric L. Hirsch, *Urban Revolt: Ethnic Politics in the Nineteenth-Century Chicago Labor Movement* (Berkeley: University of California Press, 1990), 9.

53. Ibid.

54. See "Andrew Carr Cameron," *Artist Printer* 3, no. 10 (July 1892): 417–419.

55. See Schneirov, *Labor and Urban Politics*, 55; and Philip S. Foner, *History of the American Labor Movement in the United States*, Vol. 1: *From Colonial Times to the Founding of the American Federation of Labor* (New York: International Publishers, 1998), 413.

56. See, for example, "Appeal to Workingmen," *Evening Journal*, 6 May 1867. Twenty of the other twenty-four signatories on the document, issued by the Workingmen's Central Executive Committee, had Anglo surnames, underscoring the balance of power within labor's ranks. The following year, with momentum building once more behind campaigns for shorter hours and higher wages, Cameron and other labor leaders steered clear of a strike, which they feared would culminate in another riot. Instead they organized a procession "to show the strength of the trade unions to the strange workmen now here

and to induce them to unite with their brethren." Quoted in Schneirov, *Labor and Urban Politics*, 51.

57. "When finished," one of Everts's contemporaries wrote admiringly of the 13,800 square-foot Gothic structure, "it will not be surpassed in magnificence of internal finish by any church in the city." See Phillips, *Chicago and Her Churches*, 396–398; and Andreas, *History of Chicago*, 2:434.

58. See "Labor and Christianity," *Chicago Republican*, 16 September 1867; and "A Small Stream from a Large Fountain," *Workingman's Advocate* 4, no. 9 (21 September 1867).

59. See "James E. Tyler," *Biographical Sketches of the Leading Men of Chicago* (Chicago: Wilson & St. Clair, 1868), 256.

60. "A Small Stream from a Large Fountain," *Workingman's Advocate* 4, no. 9 (21 September 1867).

61. "The Working Men of the Present Day," *Advance* 1, no. 4 (26 September 1867): 1.

62. "Autor Ultra Crepidam!" *Workingman's Advocate*, 28 September 1867.

63. Ibid.

64. In one of the four columns, Cameron aimed this critique directly at Patton, writing, "Now, doctor, as we have a homely way of our own in passing judgment upon all such sophistry, allow us to place you in the position occupied by hundreds of thousands of our mechanics, and see how this argument would apply to yourself." He went on to argue that, had Patton known personally the adverse circumstances common to workingmen, he would never have come to entertain such ideas. See "The 'Advance' Movement," *Workingman's Advocate*, 12 October 1867.

65. "A Parting Salute," *Workingman's Advocate* 4, no. 13 (19 October 1867).

66. "The 'Advance' in a Retrograde Movement," *Workingman's Advocate* 4, no. 11 (5 October 1867).

67. "Autor Ultra Crepidam!"

68. Ibid.

69. Ibid.

70. "A Parting Salute."

71. Eileen Yeo, "Christianity in Chartist Struggle: 1839–1942," *Past & Present* 91, no. 1 (1981): 123–124.

72. For the complete lyrics of "Sons of Poverty Assemble," see E. P. Thompson, *The Making of the English Working Class* (New York: Vintage Books, 1966), 399. For more on these themes, see also Harold Faulkner, *Chartism and the Churches: A Study in Democracy* (New York: Columbia University Press, 1916).

73. Leslie C. Wright, *Scottish Chartism* (London: Oliver and Boyd Ltd., 1953), 39–40.

74. Hugh McLeod, *Religion and the Working Class in Nineteenth-Century Britain* (London: Macmillan, 1984), 48; and Wright, *Scottish Chartism*, 100.

75. For the classic analysis of this tradition, see Wilentz, *Chants Democratic*.

76. Foner, *Reconstruction*, 385.

77. "Have We Slave Drivers in Chicago?" *Workingman's Advocate* 12, no. 29 (13 October 1877): 2.

78. "The Wrongs of the Seamstress," *Workingman's Advocate* 12, no. 16 (9 December 1876): 2. Cameron's defense of the seamstresses sprung in part from his sense that their unjust employers were impinging upon their virtue, another gendered construction with a longer history. On its antebellum precedents, see, for example, Murphy, *Ten Hours' Labor*, 197–200.

79. For the classic treatment of this theme, see David R. Roediger, *The Wages of Whiteness: Race and the Making of the American Working Class* (London: Verso, 1991).

80. See Karamanski, *Rally 'Round the Flag*, 106–108.

81. See Foner, *Reconstruction*, 395–402.

82. "Colored Labor," *Workingman's Advocate* 10, no. 10 (7 February 1874): 23. Compare with the text of Galatians 3:28 (New Revised Standard Version): "There is no longer Jew or Greek, there is no longer slave or free, there is no longer male and female; for all of you are one in Christ Jesus."

83. See, for example, "The Chinese Problem," *Workingman's Advocate* 10, no. 17 (28 March 1874): 2; and "The Chinese Problem," *Workingman's Advocate* 11, no. 50 (6 May 1876): 2; and also, Foner, *Reconstruction*, 479; and Matthew Frye Jacobson, *Barbarian Virtues: The United States Encounters Foreign Peoples at Home and Abroad* (New York: Hill and Wang, 2000), 74–81.

84. Foner, *Reconstruction*, 561. By 1870, the *Advocate* boasted at least 5,000 subscribers. See *The Men Who Advertise* (New York: George P. Rowell & Company, 1870), 633. Even beyond such official readership numbers, the paper carried extra weight by virtue of its position, throughout the late 1860s and early 1870s, as the official voice of the National Labor Union. See Green, *Death in the Haymarket*, 34. As one reads through the extant issues, the paper's national reach is underscored by the correspondence—originating in all corners of the nation—that Cameron received and published in its pages.

85. See "Rev. Dr. Westwood," *Workingman's Advocate* 5, no. 27 (30 January 1869): 2; and "The Religious Press," *Workingman's Advocate* 8, no. 25 (27 April 1872): 2. For other examples, see also "A Pliant Judge," *Workingman's Advocate* 6, no. 20 (18 December 1869): 2; and "The Religious (?) Press and the Labor Platform," *Workingman's Advocate* 8, no. 20 (23 March 1872): 2.

86. See "The Church vs. Trades Unions," *Workingman's Advocate* 9, no. 33 (12 July 1873): 2; and "Cowardice vs. Principle," *Workingman's Advocate* 9, no. 40 (30 August 1873): 2. In the process of raging against Montreal's Bishop Bourget, Cameron offered this praise to the local Catholic hierarchy: "The Chicago Typographical Union—a trades organization second to none in the country—has recently purchased a burial lot in Calvary Cemetery, consecrated by a Catholic bishop and with the consent and approbation of an honored pillar of the Church, the Rev. Thos. Foley, Bishop of the Diocese of Chicago."

87. "A Windy Bellow," *Workingman's Advocate* 5, no. 21 (12 December 1868): 2. See also, for example, "A Daniel Come to Judgment," *Workingman's Advocate* 7, no. 24 (11 February 1871): 2.

88. Phillips, *Chicago and Her Churches*, 271–272.

89. See Holmes, *The Life and Letters of Robert Collyer*, 1:228–229; and "The Church," *Chicago Daily Tribune*, 4 May 1873.

90. This number includes both his salary from the church, which in 1871, the year of the great fire, was $5,000; as well as his estimated income from lectures, books, etc., which as early as 1868 was already some $2,000 a year. See Holmes, *The Life and Letters of Robert Collyer*, 2:104, 165. In striking contrast, in 1873 the preacher at Dickson Street Methodist church made $600 and had no parsonage.

91. For a letter from one minister articulating the need for the discount, see, for example, William D. Skelton, "Ministers' Half-Fare," *Chicago Daily Tribune*, 20 August 1873.

92. "City Matters," *Workingman's Advocate* 9, no. 39 (23 August 1873): 3.

93. F.B., "Working Women," *Chicago Daily Tribune*, 31 May 1874.

94. See "Educating Woman: Meeting in Behalf of the Industrial and Educational Aid Society," *Chicago Daily Tribune*, 21 November 1874.

95. Bueth, "Another Woman on Mr. Collyer's 'Poor-House,'" *Chicago Daily Tribune*, 29 November 1874.

96. Miranda Meane, "Another Letter on the Same Subject," *Chicago Daily Tribune*, 13 December 1874.

97. For more on the Darker family's life in Quorndon, see various records from the village's marvelous digitized archive, http://www.quornmuseum.com/. For record of Maria and Legrand's marriage, see Richard Wynkoop, *Wynkoop Genealogy in the United States of America* (New York: Knickerbocker Press, 1904), 157–158. Legrand was a member of the local Methodist church's board of trustees in the 1840s. See Frank E. Stevens, *History of Lee County*, Vol. 1 (Chicago: S. J. Clarke Publishing Company, 1914), 361. He was elected a member of Dixon's first-ever Board of Trustees in 1853. See *History of Lee County* (Chicago: H. H. Hill and Company, 1881), 106.

98. It is not entirely clear when the group disbanded, but I found no mention of it after 1 October 1874.

99. Mrs. M. D. Wynkoop, "The Advocates of Justice," *Chicago Daily Tribune*, 21 February 1874.

100. "Organizing," *Chicago Daily Tribune*, 18 February 1874. For more on the Advocates of Justice, see also "The Workingmen Organizing," *Chicago Daily Tribune*, 18 February 1874; "Now for the Workingmen," *Republican Banner*, 21 February 1874; "Advocates of Justice," *Chicago Daily Tribune*, 26 February 1874; "Advocates of Justice," *Chicago Daily Tribune*, 8 March 1874; Mrs. M. D. Wynkoop, "The Advocates of Justice," 11 March 1874; "Local Items," *Chicago Daily Tribune*, 12 March 1874; "Advocates of Justice," *Chicago Daily Tribune*, 15 March 1874; J. W. Powers, "The Advocates of Justice," *Chicago Daily Tribune*,

29 March 1874; and "The Social Science Congress," *Manchester Guardian*, 1 October 1874.

101. "Rags," *Chicago Daily Tribune*, 11 October 1874.

102. Mrs. M. D. Wynkoop, "The Labor Question," *Chicago Daily Tribune*, 1 March 1874.

103. H.G.C., "Views of a Mechanic's Wife," *Chicago Daily Tribune*, 15 March 1874.

104. "Religious News," *Chicago Daily Tribune*, 15 February 1874. In a similar letter published a couple of years before, "A Workingman" wrote, in part, "If your churches are very desirous of gaining our attendance, they will have to show us better examples than being great marts for fashionable people to display their silks, satins, and jewelry in, or in being houses of raillery." See "The Working Classes, Religion, and Sunday Recreation," *Chicago Tribune*, 28 April 1872.

105. "Christianity a Failure," *Workingman's Advocate* 4, no. 42 (9 May 1868): 2.

106. "Liberal Christianity," *Workingman's Advocate* 4, no. 17 (16 November 1867): 2.

107. "A Pliant Judge," *Workingman's Advocate* 6, no. 20 (18 December 1869): 2.

108. "Thanksgiving," *Workingman's Advocate* 11, no. 33 (27 November 1875): 2.

109. For example, in 1870 Cameron reprinted a six-part article on "Views of the Labor Movement" by reforming Catholic thinker T. Wharton Collens, who had first published it in New York's *Catholic World*. See T. Wharton Collens, "Views of the Labor Movement," *Workingman's Advocate* 6, no. 31 (12 March 1870) and 6, no. 36 (16 April 1870). For more on Collens, see Robert C. Reinders, "T. Wharton Collens: Catholic and Christian Socialist," *Catholic Historical Review* 52, no. 2 (July 1966): 212–233; and Robert C. Reinders, "T. Wharton Collens and the Christian Labor Union," *Labor History* 8, no. 1 (1967): 53–70. Cameron also recommended *Ave Maria*, a Catholic publication, to his readership, and reprinted a sermon from English Cardinal Henry Manning on the "Dignity of Labor." See *Workingman's Advocate* 10, no. 27 (6 June 1874): 2; and "Cardinal Manning on the Dignity of Labor," *Workingman's Advocate* 9, no. 49 (22 April 1876): 4.

110. "Liberal Christianity," *Workingman's Advocate* 4, no. 17 (16 November 1867): 2.

111. "'Working People and their Employers,'" *Workingman's Advocate* 12, no. 8 (26 August 1876): 2.

CHAPTER 3

1. One 1867 editorial in the *Christian Freeman*, the denomination's Chicago flagship, declared, for example, "the churches are too good, too much carving, too much frescoing, too many chandeliers, and cushions, and carpets. They were never built for men that could not command a Sunday suit, and such men do not occupy them." "Churches and Church-Goers," *Christian Freeman* 1, no. 26 (26 September 1867): 2.

2. See, for example, "Church of the Holy Communion," *Chicago Press and Tribune*, 8 February 1859; "Episcopal Free Church on the West Side," *Chicago Press and Tribune*, 25 June 1859; "The Episcopal Free Church of the South Division," *Chicago Tribune*, 15 March 1864; "Free Church Dedication," *Chicago Tribune*, 6 January 1866; and "New Free Church," *Chicago Tribune*, 10 November 1866.

3. "Churches for Rich and Poor," *Advance* 1, no. 44 (2 July 1868): 4.

4. E. P. Goodwin, "The Cost of Churchgoing," *Advance*, 22 April 1869.

5. Consider that in 1873 its fourteen-member governing council boasted at least one prominent attorney, two influential physicians, two insurance moguls, two lumber tycoons, and two grain commissioners, including Charles E. Culver, the president of the Board of Trade. Among the other five members were two influential religious figures. I have deduced this by matching the church's directory from that year, which has been digitized and is thus available through WorldCat, with listings in the various city directories and digitized publications available through Google Books.

6. By 1874, Goodwin's salary was $5,000/year. See "How Preachers are Paid in Chicago," *Chicago Daily Tribune*, 7 June 1874; and Bruce, *1877*, 44. Goodwin's connection to the financial elite paid off in countless other ways as well. He received, for one, good investment advice. In a letter dated 25 June 1887, Thomas M. Avery, member at First Congregational and leading man on the Board of Trade, congratulated Goodwin on a forthcoming dividend check from Elgin National Watch Company, of which Avery was the president. "[It's] a good nest egg, for a preacher and I congratulate you upon your having invested in this instead of in mines," the letter read. See Thomas M. Avery to Edward P. Goodwin, 25 June 1887, The Goodwin Family Papers, Box 1, Folder 11, The Newberry Library, Chicago, IL.

7. By decade's end more than half of the city's 503,185 residents hailed from outside the United States. See Pierce, *History of Chicago*, 3:515–516.

8. For a more in-depth description of the neighborhood's changing demographics, see Richard Sennett, *Families Against the City: Middle Class Homes of Industrial Chicago, 1872–1890* (Cambridge, MA: Harvard University Press, 1984), 25–43.

9. "A Good Movement," *Chicago Tribune*, 3 June 1865.

10. An 1876 city directory locates the Cameron family at 529 Park Avenue, which on the city's current grid, puts them on Maypole Street just west of Western Avenue. See the *Lakeside Annual Directory for the City of Chicago* (Chicago: Chicago Directory Co, 1876), 230. The Wynkoops lived just a block or so from the Camerons, a block west of Western Avenue on Lake Street. See "Organizing," *Chicago Daily Tribune*, 18 February 1874.

11. In 1870, 38% of Chicagoans worked outside the home, and 64% of those were foreign-born. See Pacyga, *Chicago*, 71. By 1880 the foreign-born accounted for 65.39% of workers in the manufacturing and mechanical trades, 55.85% of workers in domestic and personal service, and 66.9% of workers in agriculture.

Meanwhile, the native-born overwhelmingly predominated in trade, and in professional and clerical services. There was a more even split in the field of transportation and communication, as well as in public services. See Pierce, *A History of Chicago*, 3:518.

12. The most seminal study of upper-class mobilization in this period is Sven Beckert, *The Monied Metropolis: New York City and the Consolidation of the American Bourgeoisie, 1850–1896* (Cambridge: Cambridge University Press, 1993). For an in-depth look at this process in Chicago, see Jentz and Schneirov, *Chicago in the Age of Capital*. The literature on the consolidation of the American bourgeoisie has very little to say about the role and significance of the churches in this process, a conspicuous gap which this chapter only begins to fill.

13. "Communism in Chicago," *Standard* 11, no. 14 (1 January 1874): 4.

14. "Are We to Have a Commune?" *Northwestern Christian Advocate* 21, no. 53 (31 December 1873): 420; "Communism—From What It Comes," *Advance* 7, no. 331 (8 January 1874): 8; "Communism—To What It Leads," *Advance* 7, no. 331 (8 January 1874): 8.

15. For more on Chicago's experience of the panic, see Pierce, *A History of Chicago*, 3:194–196, 240–243.

16. Quoted in Karen Sawislak, *Smoldering City: Chicagoans and the Great Fire, 1871–1874* (Chicago: University of Chicago Press, 1995), 267.

17. For more on American reactions to the Commune, see Philip M. Katz, *From Appomattox to Montmartre: Americans and the Paris Commune* (Cambridge, MA: Harvard University Press, 1998).

18. "The French Rebellion," *Chicago Tribune*, 11 April 1871.

19. This theory took off after the *Times* published a lengthy confession purportedly written by the Communard. Though fictitious, it was not regarded as such by many Chicagoans at the time. For more on this episode, see Sawislak, *Smoldering City*, 46–48.

20. "Communism—To What It Leads," *Advance* 7, no. 331 (8 January 1874): 8. See also "Communism in Chicago," *Standard* 11, no. 14 (1 January 1874): 4.

21. Schneirov, *Labor and Urban Politics*, 54.

22. "Communism in Chicago," *Standard* 11, no. 14 (1 January 1874): 4; "Communism—To What It Leads," *Advance* 7, no. 331 (8 January 1874): 8; and "Are We to Have a Commune?" *Northwestern Christian Advocate* 21, no. 53 (31 December 1873): 420.

23. Jentz and Schneirov, *Chicago in the Age of Capital*, 117-154.

24. *Standard* 11, no. 7 (13 November 1873): 8.

25. "Communism in Chicago," *Standard* 11, no. 14 (1 January 1874): 4.

26. "Communism—To What It Leads," *Advance* 7, no. 331 (8 January 1874): 8; and "Are We to Have a Commune?" *Northwestern Christian Advocate* 21, no. 53 (31 December 1873): 420.

27. Sawislak, *Smoldering City*, 267–268.

28. Ibid., 269.

29. The Board of Director's roster is available in *Chicago Relief: First Special Report of the Chicago Relief and Aid Society* (Chicago: Culver, Page, Hoyne & Co., 1871), 32.

30. For an excellent discussion of this theme, see Kathleen D. McCarthy, *Noblesse Oblige: Charity and Cultural Philanthropy in Chicago, 1849–1929* (Chicago: University of Chicago Press, 1982).

31. "Are We to Have a Commune?" *Northwestern Christian Advocate* 21, no. 53 (31 December 1873): 420.

32. "Events of the Week," *Advance* 7, no. 330 (1 January 1874): 5; "Are We to Have a Commune?" *Northwestern Christian Advocate* 21, no. 53 (31 December 1873): 420.

33. "Communism in Chicago," *Standard* 11, no. 14 (1 January 1874): 4.

34. "Are We to Have a Commune?" *Northwestern Christian Advocate* 21, no. 53 (31 December 1873): 420.

35. "The Labor Turmoil," *Alliance* 1, no. 4 (3 January 1874): 2.

36. Sawislak, *Smoldering City*, 119, 270–272.

37. Mrs. M. D. Wynkoop, "The Commune—England and the United States," *Chicago Daily Tribune*, 11 January 1874.

38. Mrs. M. D. Wynkoop, "The Labor Question," *Chicago Daily Tribune*, 28 December 1873.

39. "Great Outpouring of Labor," *Workingman's Advocate* 10, no. 5 (27 December 1873, and 3 January 1874): 3. See also his column, "Idleness and Starvation," *Workingman's Advocate* 10, no. 4 (20 December 1873): 2.

40. "The Workingmen's Demonstrations," *Chicago Daily Tribune*, 26 December 1873.

41. Jack Flake, "Letters from the People," *Chicago Daily Tribune*, 30 December 1873. For another letter in this same vein, see C. O. Lundberg, "Capital and Labor," *Chicago Daily Tribune*, 2 January 1874.

42. For in-depth analysis of these developments, see Schneirov, *Labor and Urban Politics*, 38; and John B. Jentz, "Class and Politics in an Emerging Industrial City: Chicago in the 1860s and 1870s," *Journal of Urban History* 17, no. 3 (May 1991): 236–237.

43. Quoted in Schneirov, *Labor and Urban Politics*, 52. For more on these developments, see also pp. 50–52.

44. Quoted in Foner, *Reconstruction*, 413.

45. Quoted in Schneirov, *Labor and Urban Politics*, 55.

46. Pierce, *History of Chicago*, 3:308.

47. *Tribune* editor Horace White's comment in the wake of the fire captured the spirit of the strategy: "We must no longer decide our fire policy by counting noses," he declared. Quoted in Schneirov, *Labor and Urban Politics*, 56.

48. Quoted in Schneirov, *Labor and Urban Politics*, 58.

49. Jentz and Schneirov, *Chicago in the Age of Capital*, 169.

50. For a general account of the 1877 railroad riots, see Robert V. Bruce, *1877: Year of Violence* (New York: Ivan R. Dee, 1989).

51. Jentz and Schneirov, *Chicago in the Age of Capital*, 186–197.

52. For a synopsis of Parson's remarkable early life journey, including a discussion of Lucy Parson's contested origins, see Paul Avrich, *The Haymarket Tragedy* (Princeton, NJ: Princeton University Press, 1984), 3–15.

53. For accounts of the way the upheaval unfolded in Chicago, see Pierce, *A History of Chicago*, 3:244–252; Bruce, *1877*, 230–260; Schneirov, *Labor and Urban Politics*, 70–76; and Richard Schneirov, "Chicago's Great Upheaval of 1877: Class Polarization and Democratic Politics," in David O. Stowell, ed., *The Great Strikes of 1877* (Urbana: University of Illinois, 2008).

54. For mention of "Father Dunn," see "At the Bridge," *Chicago Daily Tribune*, 27 July 1877. For more on him, see also Rev. Msgr. Harry C. Koenig, S.T.D., *A History of the Parishes of the Archdiocese of Chicago* (Chicago: Archdiocese of Chicago, 1980), 38–39.

55. See "Die Strikes," *Katholisches Wochenblatt*, 25 July 1877. Translated by Alex Meyer, University of Chicago.

56. "Biblical Bullets," *Chicago Times*, 30 July 1877.

57. "A Strike Against Strikers," *Chicago Times*, 30 July 1877.

58. "Rev. H. M. Paynter: Some Reflections on the Strike," *Chicago Daily Tribune*, 30 July 1877.

59. "Striking Lessons," *Inter Ocean*, 30 July 1877. Such sentiments were not unique to Caldwell. They reflected the consensus also in the Protestant press, which decried the authorities' purported restraint, wishing that more of the "mob" had been killed. See, for example, "Outlook," *Interior* 8, no. 381 (26 July 1877): 1; "The Revolt," *Northwestern Christian Advocate* (1 August 1877): 4; "A Week of Excitement," *Advance* 11, no. 517 (2 August 1877): 216; *Interior* 8, no. 382 (2 August 1877): 4; "The Communist," *Standard* 24, no. 44 (2 August 1877): 4; "A Life for a Life," *Standard* 24, no. 45 (9 August 1877): 4.

60. Out of all those gathered, only one man raised an objection—or "a slight sibilant demonstration," as the *Times* called it—to Caldwell's words. "Biblical Bullets," *Chicago Times*, 30 July 1877.

61. The best-paid minister in Chicago as of 1874 was the Reverend William A. Bartlett of Plymouth Congregational, who made $7,000 a year. Strobridge's salary fell squarely in the middle of the local Methodist pay scale, however. In 1874 the minister at Dickson Street Methodist Church earned a measly $600 salary, making him the lowest-paid Methodist divine in the city; during the same year the highest paid was the Reverend Jonas O. Peck of Centenary Church, who received a $4,000 salary in addition to the use of a luxurious parsonage. See "How Preachers are Paid in Chicago," *Chicago Daily Tribune*, 7 June 1874.

62. The minister's salary, in particular, became the subject of much bitterness and infighting within the congregation, and this was aired over the course of a couple years in two trials covered by the *Tribune*. One can find a concise summary of the drama in "The Ada Street Church," *Chicago Daily Tribune*, 16 August 1874. The new building included many of the trappings of upper-class church life, including crimson-upholstered, ash-and-walnut pews and a $4,500 organ. Even then, the $145,000 that Ada Street spent on two different buildings—one constructed in 1870 and the latter in 1873—was just over half of what the First Congregational Church spent on its two. See "Dedication of Ada Street Church—Sermon by Dr. Hatfield," *Chicago Tribune*, 11 June 1870; and "Another New Church," *Chicago Daily Tribune*, 28 June 1873.

63. "Ada Street Church," *Chicago Tribune*, 3 November 1876.

64. See both Ada Street Methodist Church Directory, 1877; and "Numbered with the Dead," *Chicago Daily Tribune*, 11 September 1895.

65. For more on the changing demographics of the Union Park neighborhood in this period, see Richard Sennett, *Families Against the City*.

66. Matching the church directory with the US Census for 1880, as well as the records available through Google Books, I was able to track down the occupations of 119 of Ada Street's 332 members. Of the 119 identified, 60 belonged to white-collar families. Of these 60, fully 40 were merchants, entrepreneurs, etc., with the other 20 working as clerks, bookkeepers, and the like. My contention that those in the petit bourgeoisie outnumbered those in the upper-middle classes thus rests on the presumption that the latter are dramatically overrepresented in the sample of identified families. Of the 119 identified members, 59 worked in blue-collar occupations. Having conducted my own analysis of the class composition of this congregation, I later stumbled upon another independent account of the same. In his dissertation, Timothy R. Morriss asserts that the church's members were 42.9% working class, 11.3% professional, 13.5% proprietors, and 32.3% commercial employees. See Timothy R. Morriss, "'To Provide for All Classes': The Methodist Church and Class in Chicago, 1871–1939" (PhD diss., Yale University, 2007), 42. Our analyses thus more or less corroborate one another.

67. In saying hundreds I am taking into account not just members but also the non-members—likely half of the crowd—who were in attendance at Ada Street that day.

68. "Biblical Bullets," *Chicago Times*, 30 July 1877. I do not assume the sex of the one protester. The report indicates that it was a male.

69. For more on the demographics of the congregation during this period, see Thomas Wakefield Goodspeed, *The University of Chicago Biographical Sketches*, Vol. 1 (Chicago: University of Chicago Press, 1922), 343–344.

70. "The Workingmen's Conflict," *Chicago Times*, 30 July 1877.

71. "Communistic Tendencies of Trade Unions, *Chicago Daily Tribune*, 6 August 1877. The Reverend Galusha Anderson hit on the same theme at Second Baptist Church. See "A Strike Against Strikers," *Chicago Times*, 30 July 1877.

72. "The Revolt," *Northwestern Christian Advocate* (1 August 1877): 4; "A Week of Excitement," *Advance* 11, no. 517 (2 August 1877): 216; "The Labor Question," *Interior* 8, no. 382 (2 August 1877): 4; "The Great Strike," *Standard* 24, no. 44 (2 August 1877): 8; "The City," *Standard* 24, no. 44 (2 August 1877): 8.

73. "Outlook," *Interior* 8, no. 382 (2 August 1877): 1.

74. "A Strike Against Strikers," *Chicago Times*, 30 July 1877. See also, for example, "Railroad Troubles," *Standard* 24, no. 43 (26 July 1877): 4; "The Unanimous Verdict," *Advance* 11, no. 518 (9 August 1877): 232; "The Workingmen's Conflict," *Chicago Times*, 30 July 1877; and "The Churches," *Chicago Daily Tribune*, 30 July 1877.

75. Some problematized even an individual's right to strike. See, for example, "A Strike Against Strikers," *Chicago Times*, 30 July 1877; and "Striking Lessons," *Inter Ocean*, 30 July 1877.

76. "A Strike Against Strikers," *Chicago Times*, 30 July 1877.

77. "Communistic Tendencies of Trade Unions, *Chicago Daily Tribune*, 6 August 1877. See also, for example, "The Unanimous Verdict," *Advance* 11, no. 518 (9 August 1877): 232.

78. "Outlook," *Interior* 8, no. 382 (2 August 1877): 1; *Chicago Times*, 7 August 1877.

79. "Christianity and Strikes," *Chicago Times*, 30 July 1877. Gray wrote in the same vein, "railroad presidents may offer what wages they choose." See "Outlook," *Interior* 8, no. 382 (2 August 1877): 1.

80. "Railroad Troubles," *Standard* 24, no. 43 (26 July 1877): 4.

81. "A Dollar a Day for Bread and Water," *Northwestern Christian Advocate* (8 August 1877): 4.

82. "Outlook," *Interior* 8, no. 382 (2 August 1877): 1. A few Protestants rejected this explanation, attributing low wages to market forces. At Second Baptist, for example, the Reverend Anderson avowed, "These wages have not been reduced by the caprice of employers, but by the action of the immutable laws of commerce; and we might as well rebel against the law of gravitation as to revolt against them." See "A Strike Against Strikers," *Chicago Times*, 30 July 1877. Anderson was in the decided minority on this point, however.

83. "Outlook," *Interior* 8, no. 382 (2 August 1877): 1.

84. "Rev. H. M. Paynter: Some Reflections on the Strike," *Chicago Daily Tribune*, 30 July 1877.

85. See "Calvary Tabernacle: An Undenominational Church," *Chicago Daily Tribune*, 2 July 1877.

86. "The Workingmen's Conflict," *Chicago Times*, 30 July 1877.

87. "The Churches," *Chicago Daily Tribune*, 30 July 1877. Patton had served as pastor of First Congregational from 1857 to 1868, and editor of the *Advance*

from 1867 to 1873. For more Protestant criticism of railroad executives, see, for example, "Topics of the Times," *Advance* 11, no. 517 (2 August 1877): 209.

88. "The Labor Riot," *Northwestern Christian Advocate* (1 August 1877): 5. See also, for example, "The Strike," *New Covenant* 30, no. 31 (2 August 1877): 2–3; "The Great Strike," *Standard* 24, no. 44 (2 August 1877): 8; and "The City," *Standard* 24, no. 44 (2 August 1877): 8.

89. "Pulpit Lessons," *Inter Ocean*, 30 July 1877.

90. "Christianity and Strikes," *Chicago Times*, 30 July 1877.

91. "The Workingmen's Conflict," *Chicago Times*, 30 July 1877.

92. See "The Great Strike," *Workingman's Advocate* 12, no. 28 (28 July 1877): 2.

93. "The Struggles of a Poor Man," *Chicago Daily News*, 21 August 1877.

CHAPTER 4

1. "The Thief on the Cross," *Chicago Daily Tribune*, 21 November 1887.

2. For the reference to "blasphemous comparisons," see "They Must Hang," *Los Angeles Times*, 8 October 1886.

3. *August Spies' Auto-Biography; His Speech in Court, and General Notes* (Chicago: Niña Van Zandt, 1887), 77–80.

4. For examples, see "With Thankful Hearts," *Chicago Daily Tribune*, 25 November 1887.

5. See the account in "Hanged," *Western Catholic* 11, no. 5 (12 November 1887): 3.

6. "Religious Beliefs of the Dead Men," *Chicago Daily Tribune*, 12 November 1887.

7. "The Thief on the Cross."

8. On the *Knights of Labor*'s booming circulation, see Schneirov, *Labor and Urban Politics*, 223.

9. A Christian Woman, *Knights of Labor* 1, no. 34 (27 November 1886): 10. See also another letter, presumably from the same source: A Christian Woman, "A Lady's View," *Knights of Labor* 1, no. 31 (6 November 1886): 10. Her letter alluded to a confrontation, previously reported in the paper, between an unnamed woman and an elder at Chicago's prestigious Fourth Presbyterian church. The woman asked this leading layman, who was in his professional life a real estate agent, "Don't you think we ought to pray for these condemned anarchists?" He replied, "No, Hell is too good for them," to which she inquired, "But did not Christ die for them too, and should we not pray for them?" He responded, "No, send them to Hell first and pray for them afterward." See "Without Benefit of Clergy," *Knights of Labor* 1, no. 31 (6 November 1886): 7.

10. C. M. Clark, *Knights of Labor* 1, no. 36 (11 December 1886): 10–11.

11. F. A. Bascom, "A 'George' Man—No Anarchist," *Labor Enquirer* 1, no. 41 (15 October 1887): 3. For other examples, see H. J. Wibel, "Crucify Them," *Knights of Labor* 1, no. 36 (11 December 1886): 11; and H.J.H., "To the Ministers," *Labor Enquirer* 1, no. 42 (22 October 1887): 3; and "An Open Letter to Judge Gary,"

American Nonconformist, included on Reel 1 of the Albert R. Parsons Papers, Wisconsin Historical Society.

12. "Auch ein Martyrer," *Vorbote* 13, no. 17 (28 April 1886): 2 (translated by Joela Zeller, PhD candidate in Germanic Studies at the University of Chicago).

13. "The Counsel of the Artisan Association," *Svenska Amerikanaren* 10, no. 24 (12 June 1886): 8 (translated by Stina Bäckström, PhD candidate in Philosophy at the University of Chicago).

14. See Pierce, *A History of Chicago*, 3:50.

15. Ibid., 20–63. For exact numbers, see also the chart on p. 516.

16. The proportion of native-born Chicagoans rose from 51.65% in 1870 to 59.02% in 1890. Ibid., 21–22.

17. Reproduced in Bessie Louise Pierce, ed., *As Others See Chicago: Impressions of Visitors, 1673–1933* (Chicago: University of Chicago Press, 2004), 230.

18. Ibid., 146; and Cronon, *Nature's Metropolis*, 311.

19. Pierce, *A History of Chicago*, 3:55–56.

20. See Jentz and Schneirov, *Chicago in the Age of Capital*, 220–245.

21. Schneirov, *Labor and Urban Politics*, 168.

22. Ibid., 173–179.

23. Ibid., 194.

24. Nell Painter, *Standing at Armageddon: A Grassroots History of the Progressive Era* (New York: W. W. Norton & Company, 2008), 44.

25. On the number of strikes, see Schneirov, *Labor and Urban Politics*, 183; on the socioeconomic roots of the Great Upheaval, see ibid., 184–191.

26. Ibid., 168–173. Schneirov points out that Harrison's appointment of Bonfield—an Irish Republican—was a clear attempt to shore up his electoral support among that demographic, which had been faltering in its allegiance.

27. Painter, *Standing at Armageddon*, 46.

28. Accounts of the events at Haymarket abound. In constructing this account, I have drawn especially on a recent and eminently readable version of the story. See Green, *Death in the Haymarket*.

29. See "Socialism," *Chicago Daily Tribune*, 20 May 1878; "Moral Suasion as a Means of Repressing Communism," *Chicago Daily Tribune*, 27 May 1878; "Communism," *Chicago Daily Tribune*, 10 February 1879; "Prof. Bierbower," *Chicago Daily Tribune*, 17 June 1878; "The Character of Communism," *Chicago Daily Tribune*, 24 June 1878; and for other examples, "The Labor Problem," *Chicago Daily Tribune*, 3 June 1878; "Socialism," *Chicago Daily Tribune*, 24 June 1878; and "The Red Flag," *Chicago Daily Tribune*, 24 June 1878.

30. "Communism," *Chicago Daily Tribune*, 15 July 1878.

31. Available at http://www.vatican.va/holy_father/leo_xiii/encyclicals/documents/hf_l-xiii_enc_28121878_quod-apostolici-muneris_en.html.

32. For a much more in-depth account, see Richard Scheirov, "Free Thought and Socialism in the Czech Community in Chicago, 1875–1887," in Dick

Hoerder, ed., *"Struggle a Hard Battle": Essays on Working Class Immigrants* (Dekalb: Northern Illinois University Press, 1986).

33. See, for example, *The Western Catholic* 18, no. 23 (6 December 1884): 5; and "Editorial Passing Comment," *Northwestern Christian Advocate* 34, no. 17 (28 April 1886): 1. After the bomb exploded in Haymarket Square, many leading religious figures joined the business elite in arguing that the city's tolerance of the anarchists was to blame. See "Editorial Passing Comment," *Northwestern Christian Advocate* 34, no. 19 (12 May 1886): 1; "The Riot and Its Results," *Advance* 21, no. 974 (13 May 1886); "Communism in the West," *Standard* 33, no. 37 (13 May 1886): 4; and "The Red Flag," *Living Church*, 15 May 1886.

34. "The Churches," *Chicago Daily Tribune*, 6 July 1885.

35. For a few examples of comparably violent rhetoric, see "The World," *Interior* 16, no. 792 (9 July 1885): 1; "The Great Strike," *Advance* 20, no. 929 (9 July 1885): 449; "Editorial Passing Comment," *Northwestern Christian Advocate* 34, no. 16 (21 April 1886): 1; and *Advance* 21, no. 967 (25 March 1886): 184.

36. See "Church-Absenteeism," *Chicago Daily Tribune*, 1 December 1878; Rev. Chas. S. Daniel, "Why the Masses Do Not Go to Church," *Living Church*, 23 October 1886; and Rev. A. H. Bradford, D.D., "A Success in Reaching the Artisan Classes with the Gospel," *Advance* 21, no. 971 (22 April 1886): 243; and "The Non-Churchgoers: Why So Many New York Pews Are Empty Sundays," *Chicago Daily Tribune*, 16 December 1888.

37. See "Chicago," *Interior* 16, no. 811 (19 November 1885): 8; "Ministers' Meeting," *Standard* 33, no. 21 (21 January 1886): 4; and "What the Pastors Said," *Chicago Daily Tribune*, 14 February 1887.

38. P.S., "Satan on the West Side," *Interior* 16, no. 805 (8 October 1885): 2.

39. On the hopeful end, see, for example, "The Bohemians in Chicago," *Interior* 16, no. 816 (24 December 1885): 1 and 8. As for the resigned, see, for example, untitled notes in *Interior* 16, no. 794 (23 July 1885): 4; and *Interior* 16, no. 805 (8 October 1885): 4.

40. See "The Bible and the Poor," *Interior* 16, no. 791 (16 April 1885); and "The People and the Churches," *Interior* 16, no. 807 (22 October 1885): 4.

41. For such an endorsement, see the untitled note in *Standard* 33, no. 41 (10 June 1886): 4.

42. See Gloege, *Guaranteed Pure*, 21–23.

43. Quoted in Ibid., 51, 55.

44. Ibid., 57.

45. Quoted in Ibid., 59–60.

46. Quoted in Ibid., 44.

47. C. H. Zimmerman, "How to Reach the Masses," *Interior* 16, no. 790 (9 April 1885): 1.

48. For some other examples of Zimmerman's work, see "Competition vs. Competition," *Advance* 20, no. 904 (15 January 1884): 33–34; "Labor and

Monopolies," *Interior* 16, no. 790 (25 June 1885): 1; "Labor Unions," *Interior* 16, no. 792 (9 July 1885): 1. For critical responses published alongside his columns in the *Interior*, see D.C.W., "Rank Socialism," *Interior* 16, no. 794 (14 May 1885): 2; *Interior* 16, no. 790 (25 June 1885): 4; J. M. Swift, "Labor and Capital," *Interior* 16, no. 792 (8 July 1885): 2; and "Labor and Capital," *Interior* 16, no. 795 (30 July 1885): 2.

49. "Ministers' Meetings," *Chicago Daily Tribune*, 18 May 1886. The *Interior* often advanced this view, as did a number of influential northern European believers. See, for example, the *Interior* 16, no. 793 (16 July 1885): 793; "Secret Associations," *Svenska Amerikanaren* 10, no. 8 (20 February 1886): 4 (translated by Stina Bäckström, PhD candidate in Philosophy at the University of Chicago); *Sandebudet*, 14 July 1886 (translated by Stina Bäckström, PhD candidate in Philosophy at the University of Chicago); and also the *Advance* 21, no. 996 (14 October 1886): 655.

50. "Leading Thoughts from Pulpit and Rostrum," *Knights of Labor* 1, no. 6 (15 May 1886): 3.

51. See "The Strikers Restive," *Chicago Daily Tribune*, 14 October 1886; "Father Flanagan Succumbs to Pneumon," *New World* 16, no. 2 (7 September 1907): 10; and Schneirov, *Labor and Urban Politics*, 107–108.

52. See, for example, "The Labor Question," *Catholic Home* 1, no. 10 (March 1886): 164; *Northwestern Christian Advocate*, 31 March 1886; "Labor Agitation," *Catholic Home* 1, no. 11 (April 1886): 181; John R. Walsh, "Eight Hours a Day," *Chicago Daily Tribune*, 11 April 1886; and "Hon. Frank Lawler on the Labor Question," *Catholic Home* 1, no. 12 (May 1886): 192; "Child Labor," *Knights of Labor* 2, no. 13 (7 May 1887): 6; "Voices from the Pulpit," *Knights of Labor* 2, no. 13 (7 May 1887): 12; and "Favor Sunday Closing," *Chicago Daily Tribune*, 23 September 1889.

53. "Eight Hours Per Day," *Interior* 17, no. 835 (6 May 1886): 4. On the eight-hour movement and its variations in mid-1880s Chicago, see Schneirov, *Labor and Urban Politics*, 194–199. For more on the concerted clerical opposition to eight hours work for ten hours pay, see, for example, F. W. Sassman, "Labor and Labor Topics," *Chicago Daily Tribune*, 26 April 1886; and "The Sunday Pulpits," *Chicago Daily Tribune*, 24 May 1886. For more on clerical support for the movement, see, for example, the *Tribune* report on the Methodist ministers' discussion of the issue: "Preachers on Labor," *Chicago Daily Tribune*, 13 April 1886.

54. See "Preachers on Labor," *Chicago Daily Tribune*, 13 April 1886.

55. See, for example, "Editorial Passing Comment," *Northwestern Christian Advocate* 34, no. 15 (14 April 1886): 1; *Advance* 21, no. 971 (22 April 1886): 251; *Standard* 33, no. 33 (20 May 1886): 4; "G.M.W. Powderly and the Church," *Western Catholic* 21, no. 11 (15 October 1887): 4.

56. On Powderly's poor relationship with the Chicago Knights, see Schneirov, *Labor and Urban Politics*, 220–224. The Knights' national leadership worked

assiduously throughout these years to head off a rumored ban by the Catholic hierarchy, which was nervous especially about the KOL's secretive ethos. Some priests in Chicago mobilized against the Knights, but they had a strong champion in Archbishop Feehan, who opposed any top-down decree against the KOL throughout the 1880s. For a full account of this story, see Henry J. Browne, *The Catholic Church and the Knights of Labor* (Washington, DC: Catholic University of America Press, 1949); on the approach of the Chicago hierarchy, in particular, see pages 85, 99, 147–148, 163, 219, 206, and 232. For more on the Protestant posture toward organized labor in this era, see Carl Griffiths, "Some Protestant Attitudes on the Labor Question," *Church History* 11, no. 2 (June 1942): 138–148.

57. See, for example, "Strikes," *Interior* 16, no. 797 (13 August 1885): 4; "Strikes, Violence, and Boycotting," *Northwestern Christian Advocate* 34, no. 12 (24 March 1886): 8; and "The Labor Strikes," *Advance* 21, no. 969 (8 April 1886): 216.

58. "Christianity and Socialism," *Northwestern Christian Advocate,* 11 March 1885. This distinction between good and bad labor was ubiquitous in church leaders' rhetoric during the Great Upheaval. For just a few of the countless Protestant examples, see "The Churches," *Chicago Daily Tribune,* 14 September 1885; *Interior* 16, no. 808 (29 October 1885): 4; *Advance* 21, no. 963 (25 February 1886): 120; "The Chivalry of Labor," *Standard* 33, no. 29 (18 March 1886): 3–4; "The Rev. Dr. Thomas on the Labor Question," *Chicago Daily Tribune,* 29 March 1886. Catholics made such distinctions as well. See, for example, the *Western Catholic* 18, no. 23 (6 December 1884): 5; "Labor Agitation," *Catholic Home* 1, no. 11 (April 1886): 181; and the report on Bohemian and Polish priests decision not to preach on anarchy in the wake of the riots because "their people who went to church participated in none of the anarchist movements, and sermonizing on the subject was only a waste of time," in *Chicago Daily Tribune,* 10 May 1886. In the Catholic case, the distinction between "honest" and "dangerous" labor was less bound up in questions about the saloon or nativity, and much more tied to the issue of radicalism.

59. *Interior* 17, no. 320 (21 January 1886): 4. Such rhetoric evinced the staying power of Whig ideals within the city's Protestant elite. For other examples of anti-monopoly rhetoric, see, for example, "The Struggle for Bread," *Northwestern Christian Advocate,* 25 March 1885; and "The Coal Monopoly," *Advance* 21, no. 996 (14 October 1886): 654.

60. For just a handful of the dozens of examples, see *Progressive Age* 1, no. 20 (16 July 1881): 4; *Progressive Age* 1, no. 22 (30 July 1881): 5; "Bourgeoise Civilization," *Alarm* 1, no. 16 (7 February 1885): 2; "The Rev. J. H. Worcester Pleads for the Poor—A Possible Danger," *Knights of Labor* 1, no. 7 (22 May 1886): 5; "A Catholic Bishop's View," *Knights of Labor* 1, no. 8 (29 May 1886): 12; "The Right to Strike: A Sermon by Rev. J. Coleman Adams," *Knights of Labor* 1, no. 33 (20 November 1886): 10; "The Undercurrents of Life," *Labor Enquirer* 1, no. 10

(26 March 1887): 3; "A Plea for the Poor," *Labor Enquirer* 2, no. 25 (5 November 1887): 12.

61. "Nothing to Prevent Them," *Progressive Age* 3, no. 12 (20 May 1882): 1. For more on *The Progressive Age* and its Bohemian-born editor, Joseph Gruenhut, see Schneirov, *Labor and Urban Politics*, 128, 147–150.

62. The resolution read, "We, the ministers of the Baptist Pastors' Conference, having listened with pleasure to the presentation by members of the eight-hour league, and being satisfied that it is no movement in favor of state socialism, or an assault on individual rights or the fundamental principles of America, we heartily express our approbation, in general, of the aims of the organization and do cordially commend the reform to the good people of the community, capitalists and laborers together; desiring also that in a humble way we may be able to further its progress." See "Ministers' Meeting," *Standard* 33, no. 31 (1 April 1886): 5. For some of the many news reports on the resolution, see *Interior* 17, no. 831 (8 April 1886): 8; "Agitators before Baptist Ministers," *Svenska Amerikanaren* 10, no. 14 (3 April 1886): 8 (translated by Stina Bäckström, PhD candidate in Philosophy at the University of Chicago); and "Die Pfaffen und die Achtstundenfrage," *Vorbote* 13, no. 14 (7 April 1886): 2 (translated by Joela Zeller, PhD candidate in Germanic Studies at the University of Chicago).

63. Jacob Henry Dorn, *Washington Gladden: Prophet of the Social Gospel* (Columbus, OH: Ohio State University Press, 1966): 209–211. Gladden tried out some of these same ideas on the city's Presbyterian ministers in March 1886. For reports of that visit, see "Chicago Sundries," *Standard* 33, no. 29 (18 March 1886): 8; "Chicago" and "An Evening on Labor," *Interior* 17, no. 828 (18 March 1886): 8; and "Editorial Passing Comment," *Northwestern Christian Advocate* 34, no. 12 (24 March 1886): 1. Not surprisingly, the Interior was most interested in the anti-socialist aspects of Gladden's thought. "Christian Socialism," *Interior* 17, no. 830 (1 April 1886): 4.

64. "Applied Christianity," *Knights of Labor* 2, no. 8 (2 April 1887): 5.

65. "Compromising on Beer," *Chicago Daily Tribune*, 2 May 1886.

66. "Arbitration," *Chicago Daily Tribune*, 28 May 1883.

67. "Aspects of the Social Question," *Unitarian Review* 30, no. 2 (August 1888): 169.

68. "Minutes of Meeting," 9 May 1886, Records of the Chicago Typographical Union no. 16, Chicago History Museum, Chicago, IL.

69. On the relationship between radicalism and irreligion in Chicago, see especially Nelson, "Revival and Upheaval"; and Bruce C. Nelson, *Beyond the Martyrs: A Social History of Chicago's Anarchists, 1870–1900* (New Brunswick, NJ: Rutgers University Press, 1988): 165–170.

70. Burns, *The Life and Death of the Radical Historical Jesus*, 12–13.

71. "The Religion of Mammon," *Alarm* 1, no. 5 (1 November 1884): 4. For other editorials in this vein, see, for example, "Bourgoisie Morality," *Alarm* 1, no. 24

(13 June 1885): 2; "Pulpit and Rostrum," *Alarm* 2, no. 10 (26 December 1885): 2; and "Trinity Church," *Alarm* 2, no. 15 (6 March 1886): 2.

72. "The Pope of Rome," *Alarm* 1, no. 14 (13 January 1885): 3. See also, for example, his criticism of Bishop John Ireland in " 'The Powers That Be,' " *Alarm* 1, no. 8 (22 November 1884): 3. The *Alarm* would continue to publish criticisms of the churches with a distinctly constructive edge even after Parsons's imprisonment and eventual execution in 1887. See, for example, the *Alarm* 1, no. 18 (14 July 1888): 2; "Christian Liberty," *Alarm* 1, no. 19 (21 July 1888): 2; and "A Strange Gospel," *Alarm* 1, no. 12 (7 April 1888): 2.

73. See Lucy Parsons, "A Christmas Story," reproduced in Gale Ahrens, ed., *Freedom, Equality, and Solidarity: Writings and Speeches, 1878–1937* (Chicago: Charles H. Kerr Publishing Company, 2004), 46–51.

74. "In Church," *Alarm* 2, no. 4 (3 October 1885): 4.

75. By anti-clerical here I refer to those who opposed religion qua religion, regardless of its social or economic orientation. For a sampling of anti-clerical rhetoric, see *Chicagoer Arbeiter Zeitung*, 20 October 1882; "Most, the Anarchist," *Chicago Daily Tribune*, 29 December 1882; "Belief," *Alarm* 1, no. 21 (18 April 1885): 2; *Die Fackel*, 1 November 1885 (translated by Ian Rinehart, German major at Northwestern University); and *Vorbote* 13, no. 23 (23 June 1886): 3 (translated by Joela Zeller, PhD candidate in Germanic Studies at the University of Chicago).

76. "How the Americans Care for Chicago's Bohemians. We are Infamous Heathens According to an American Missionary Society," *Svornost*, 16 September 1884 (available through the WPA Foreign-Language Press Survey).

77. See "Ich bin ein christlicher Sozialist," *Vorbote* 12, no. 27 (8 July 1885): 1; and "Einer der Prediger," *Vorbote* 12, no. 28 (15 July 1885): 3 (both translated by Joela Zeller, PhD candidate in Germanic Studies at the University of Chicago).

78. "Ein wandernder Zimmermannsgeselle," *Vorbote* 13, no. 16 (21 April 1886): 1. *Vorbote* directed such criticisms against Catholic leaders as well. In one 1885 article a columnist wrote, "Three years ago, the pastor of the local [St.] Stanislaus Church (Polish) got several hundred fellow countrymen to work for 75 cents a day for the North Chicago salt factory, and the original workers who earned $1.50 a day were fired. Of course the ways of the Lord are wonderful." See "Man darf den," *Vorbote* 12, no. 28 (15 July 1885): 4 (both translated by Joela Zeller, PhD candidate in Germanic Studies at the University of Chicago).

79. "Ein wandernder Zimmermannsgeselle."

80. "Allerlei Trostgrunde," *Vorbote* 13, no. 22 (16 June 1886): 13.

81. "Jones, der grosse Harlequin des Evangeliums," *Vorbote* 13, no. 23 (23 June 1886): 1.

82. See "The Methodist Ministers of Chicago Resume the Discussion of Socialism," *Chicago Daily Tribune*, 21 May 1878; and for another example, see the report on Spies's attendance at the Ministers' Union in "News from the Churches," *Advance* 20, no. 954 (31 December 1885): 862.

83. "A Lasting Monument," *Chicago Daily Tribune*, 14 December 1882.

84. "Ready for Business," *Chicago Daily Tribune*, 30 April 1885.

85. "The Overshadowing Issue," *Northwestern Christian Advocate*, 6 May 1885; and the *Interior* 16, no. 783 (7 May 1885): 4.

86. See *August Spies' Auto-Biography*, 77–80.

87. "Autobiography of Albert R. Parsons," in Philip S. Foner, ed., *The Autobiographies of the Haymarket Martyrs* (New York: Pathfinder, 1969), 78.

88. Quoted in Carolyn Ashbaugh, *Lucy Parsons: American Revolutionary* (Chicago: Charles H. Kerr Publishing Company, 1976), 169–170.

89. For excellent national perspective on this theme, see Robert E. Weir, *Beyond Labor's Veil: The Culture of the Knights of Labor* (University Park: Pennsylvania State University Press, 1996), 67–102.

90. L. S. Oliver, "Troops for the 'Riff-Raff,'" *Knights of Labor* 1, no. 31 (6 November 1886): 10. Goodwin was one of countless ministers the Knights singled out in this way. For just a few examples, see "Clergymen and Politicians on Labor Problems," *Progressive Age* 3, no. 18 (1 July 1882): 2; "Creed or Deed?" *Knights of Labor* 1, no. 32 (13 November 1886): 11; John Thompson, "George's Theory Denounced," *Knights of Labor* 1, no. 36 (11 December 1886): 15; "Prof. Swing 'Rastles' with one of the Ten Commandments," *Knights of Labor* 2, no. 27 (19 November 1887): 8; and Psycho, "In the Churches," *Labor Enquirer* 1, no. 48 (3 December 1887): 1. For a more general denunciation of the clergy as a class see, for example, Justus, *Progressive Age* 1, no. 10 (7 May 1881): 4.

91. Mrs. B. R. Root, "The Ministers," *Labor Enquirer* 1, no. 50 (17 December 1887): 4. For similar criticisms of wealthy laypeople, see, for example, "Defrauding Customers," *Progressive Age* 3, no. 9 (29 April 1882): 1; "A Short Sermon to Chicago Clergymen," *Knights of Labor* 2, no. 24 (29 October 1887): 8; and John H. Allen, "Why the Poor Don't Attend the Churches," *Knights of Labor* 3, no. 8 (22 February 1888): 5. More generally, on the corruption of churches by wealth see the damning poem, "The Church Walking with the World," *Knights of Labor* 1, no. 27 (9 October 1886): 12; as well as, in the same issue, the satirical contribution by Deacon Allmoney, "A Soliloquy," *Knights of Labor* 1, no. 27 (9 October 1886): 12.

92. J. V. Farwell, "Our Government and Laborers," *Knights of Labor* 1, no. 16 (24 July 1886): 8. For more on Trumbull, see Ray Boston, "General Matthew Mark Trumbull Respectable Radical," *Journal of the Illinois State Historical Society* 66, no. 2 (Summer 1973): 159–176.

93. Wheelbarrow, "A Reply to Mr. Farwell," *Knights of Labor* 1, no. 18 (7 August 1886): 2.

94. E. J. Paul, "The Influence of the Church," *Knights of Labor* 1, no. 27 (9 October 1886): 2. For other letters in this lengthy and wide-ranging exchange, see J. V. Farwell, "A Few Facts and a Little Advice for Labor Organizations," *Knights of Labor* 1, no. 18 (7 August 1886): 2–3; Bert Stewart, "A Reply to Mr. Farwell,"

Knights of Labor 1, no. 19 (14 August 1886): 2; George Dean, "An Answer from Pullman," *Knights of Labor* 1, no. 19 (14 August 1886): 3; Wheelbarrow, "More from Wheelbarrow," *Knights of Labor* 1, no. 19 (14 August 1886): 3–4; J. V. Farwell, "Is 'Wheelbarrow' a Workingman and A Christian?" *Knights of Labor* 1, no. 19 (14 August 1886): 2.; J. V. Farwell, "Plug Hatted Anarchism vs. Bomb-Throwing Anarchism," *Knights of Labor* 1, no. 20 (21 August 1886): 2; Wheelbarrow, "Wheelbarrow to Mr. Farwell," *Knights of Labor* 1, no. 21 (28 August 1886): 2; Bert Stewart, "Bert Stewart Gives Figures," *Knights of Labor* 1, no. 22 (4 September 1886): 2–3; and J. V. Farwell, "Where Strikes and Boycotts Would Be Legitimate," *Knights of Labor* 1, no. 31 (6 November 1886): 9.

95. *Progressive Age* 2, no. 22 (29 July 1882).

96. "Creed or Deed?" *Knights of Labor* 1, no. 32 (13 November 1886): 11.

97. See "A Short Sermon to Chicago Clergymen," *Knights of Labor* 2, no. 24 (29 October 1887): 8; "Aristocratic Religion," *Progressive Age* 1, no. 21 (23 July 1881): 1; and for yet another example, this one in verse, the *Progressive Age* 1, no. 15 (11 June 1881): 2.

98. "Religion," *Labor Enquirer* 1, no. 23 (16 July 1887): 3.

99. Ibid. See also "George's Theory Denounced," *Knights of Labor* 1, no. 36 (11 December 1886): 15; *Knights of Labor* 1, no. 37 (18 December 1886): 1.

100. John H. Allen, "Why the Poor Don't Attend the Churches," *Knights of Labor* 3, no. 8 (22 February 1888): 5. For other examples, see "Rev. E. M. Clark and the Universalist," *Knights of Labor* 1, no. 24 (18 September 1886): 8; and "By Their Fruits Ye Shall Know Them," *Knights of Labor* 1, no. 27 (9 October 1886): 8.

101. "Why Are the Laboring Classes Leaving the Churches?" *Knights of Labor* 3, no. 4 (1 February 1888): 4.

CHAPTER 5

1. The Civic Federation brought together religious, labor, and other civic leaders under the umbrella of a reform organization that long strove to eliminate corruption and improve the plight of the city's poor. For more on Stead's role in founding the Federation, as well as its larger legacy, see William T. Stead, *If Christ Came to Chicago* (Chicago: Laird and Lee, 1894); Smith, *The Search for Social Salvation*, 65–86; and Schneirov, *Labor and Urban Politics*, 333–335.

2. See Stead, *If Christ Came to Chicago*, 389–405.

3. As sociologist Kevin Christiano reports, "Total church membership grew 60 percent nationally between 1890 and 1906, and increased more than 87 percent in the cities. . . . Church membership expressed as a percentage of population registered a healthy increase as well. By 1906, 39 percent of Americans belonged to some church, while over 46 percent of city residents were affiliated with a local congregation." Christiano, *Religious Diversity and Social Change*, 20.

4. See the clipping from a January 1893 issue of the *Washington Post* entitled "Open it on Sunday," in the Thomas J. Morgan Collection, Box 1, Folder 9, Illinois Historical Survey, Urbana, IL. While Sunday closing campaigns sometimes brought ministers and workers together, this one did just the opposite: in organized labor's view, the clergy's calls for a strict observance of the Sabbath were offensive because they threatened to effectively bar many six-day-a-week wage earners from the wondrous Fair's gates. For more on this, see William A. Mirola, "Shorter Hours and the Protestant Sabbath: Religious Framing and Movement Alliances in Late-Nineteenth-Century Chicago," *Social Science History* 23, no. 3 (Autumn 1999): 419–423; and Alexis McCrossen, *Holy Day, Holiday: The American Sunday* (Ithaca, NY: Cornell University Press, 2000), 71–78.

5. See Thomas J. Morgan, "Labor's Need and W. T. Stead's Suggestion," Thomas J. Morgan Collection, Box 1, Folder 13, Illinois Historical Survey, Urbana, IL.

6. "Not to Chicago," *Railway Times* 1, no. 10 (15 May 1894): 2.

7. Rev. S. E. Price, "The Church and the Workingman," *Standard* 42, no. 47 (19 July 1894): 1–2.

8. "Need the Help of the Clergy," *Chicago Daily Tribune*, 13 July 1891.

9. Quote from "The Church and the Laborer," *Age of Labor* 1, no. 14 (15 July 1892): 8. See also Price, "The Church and the Workingman"; "Milwaukee Preachers on the Masses," *Chicago Daily Tribune*, 17 February 1891; "The Gap between Labor and the Church," *Rights of Labor* 6, no. 269 (14 March 1891); and Rev. Hugh Price Hughes, "Jesus Christ and the Masses," *Northwestern Christian Advocate* 42, no. 32 (8 August 1894): 3–4.

10. "The Church and the Laborer," *Age of Labor*.

11. Bederman, "The Women Have Had Charge of the Church Work Long Enough," 435.

12. As Bederman incisively writes, "The crisis of cultural 'effiminacy' developed in part because feminized religion, tailored for laissez-faire capitalism, no longer answered the needs of the new modern society. 'Feminine' religion no longer balanced 'male' self-interest in American society. Now, 'she' threatened to overwhelm 'him.' The 'ladylike' voice of higher morality remained embedded in men's overworked superegos, urging thrift, hard work, and self denial—increasingly irrelevant values in a corporate, consumer society." Ibid., 437.

13. See, for example, Hortense J. Holland, "Working-Girls and the Church," *Chicago Daily Tribune*, 20 March 1891; and Rena A. Michaels, "Church and People," Chicago Daily Tribune, 15 January 1893; "Sabbath Services," *Daily Inter-Ocean*, 26 May 1894; "Sabbath Services," *Daily Inter-Ocean*, 2 June 1894; and "Church Notices," *Daily Sun*, 8 September 1894.

14. See, for example, "Out of Touch with Working People," *Chicago Daily Tribune*, 14 June 1892. And for related conversations, "Dr. Thompson's Idea is Indorsed,"

Chicago Daily Tribune, 27 November 1891; and "Duty of the Church to Laborers," *Chicago Daily Tribune*, 4 June 1894.

15. "Ministers Speak for the Laborers," *Chicago Daily Tribune*, 17 May 1892.

16. "Zero Weather Here," *Chicago Daily Tribune*, 25 January 1894.

17. T. J. Jackson Lears, *Rebirth of a Nation: The Making of Modern America, 1870–1920* (New York: Harper, 2009), 172; "Hard Luck Stories: Chicago's Unemployed Retail Their Sad Experiences," *Chicago Daily Tribune*, 10 December 1893.

18. Pierce, *A History of Chicago*, 3:469.

19. "Recall Old Times: Congregational Club Members Celebrate Forefathers' Day," *Chicago Daily Tribune*, 20 December 1892.

20. Two of these are singled out in Rand McNally's *Handy Guide to Chicago and World's Columbian Exposition* (Chicago and New York: Rand, McNally, & Company, 1893), 114.

21. *The Chronicle: A Journal Devoted to the Interests of Insurance*, 1 January–30 June 1894, vol. 53, 114.

22. This account of the evening's events is drawn from several accounts, including "Church is Criticised: L. W. Rogers' Plain Talk to the Congregational Club," *Chicago Daily Tribune*, 23 January 1894, 8; as well as "The Congregational Club" and "Labor and the Church," *Railway Times* 1, no. 3 (1 February 1894): 3. The *Railway Times*'s coverage includes the full text of Rogers's speech.

23. Stead, *If Christ Came to Chicago*, 397, 467.

24. Hirsch, *Urban Revolt*, 93.

25. The CLU had splintered off from the TLA in 1884. See Hirsch, *Urban Revolt*, 115; Schneirov, *Labor and Urban Politics*, 174.

26. "Draws a Race Line," *Chicago Daily Tribune*, 19 June 1894.

27. "Church is Criticised"; "Labor and the Church."

28. "Church is Criticised"; "Labor and the Church."

29. "Church is Criticised"; and "The Congregational Club."

30. "Workingmen and the Church," *Christian Intelligencer* 65, no. 10 (7 March 1894): 1.

31. "The Church and Labor," *Interior* 25, no. 1237 (8 February 1894): 163–164.

32. See "Representative Religious Journalists," *Frank Leslie's Sunday Magazine* 27 (January–June 1885): 158.

33. The number of subscribers had reportedly climbed from fewer than 5,000 in 1871 to more than 20,000 by 1885. See "Representative Religious Journalists." While the exact circulation in 1894 is unknown, the *Review of Reviews* reported in 1895 that the Interior had "an external beauty and a circulation which surpass those of any of its Presbyterian rivals." See George P. Morris, "Religious Journalism and Journalists," *Review of Reviews* 12, no. 1 (July 1895): 424.

34. "Representative Religious Journalists," p. 158, col. 2.

35. By 1894 Gray co-owned the publication along with the McCormick estate. See Andreas, *History of Chicago*, 3:709.

36. See ibid.; and also, "Purcell, Charles A," *The Book of Chicagoans: A Biographical Dictionary of Leading Living Men of the City of Chicago* (Chicago: A. N. Marquis & Company, 1911), 553.

37. "The Congregational Club."

38. "Reply from the Church," *Railway Times* 1, no. 4 (15 February 1894): 2.

39. For an introduction to the near West Side's history, see Dominic A. Pacyga and Ellen Skerrett, *Chicago, City of Neighborhoods: Histories and Tours* (Chicago: Loyola University Press, 1986), 199–219.

40. "The Pride of the Order," *Chicago Daily Tribune*, 23 March 1889, 3.

41. William T. Stead, "My First Visit to America," *Review of Reviews* (English ed.) 9 (January–June, 1894), reprinted in Pierce, *As Others See Chicago*, 360–361.

42. Stead, *If Christ Came to Chicago*, 397.

43. "Will Found a Workingman's Church: Trade Unionists Adopt a Plan for Preaching at Bricklayers' Hall," *Chicago Daily Tribune*, 9 February 1894.

44. John Trevor, "The Labor Church," published in William Dwight Porter Bliss, ed., *The Encyclopedia of Social Reform* (New York and London: Funk & Wagnalls Company, 1897), 781. For more on the animating convictions of this movement, see Mark Bevir, "The Labour Church Movement, 1891–1902," *Journal of British Studies* 38, no. 2 (April 1999): 217–245.

45. William Dwight Porter Bliss, "The Church of the Carpenter and Thirty Years After," *Social Preparation for the Kingdom of God* 9, no. 1 (January 1922): 12–15, quoted in Hopkins, *The Rise of the Social Gospel in American Protestantism*, 178.

46. For more on the relationship between Bliss and Casson, see William Fitzhugh Brundage, *A Socialist Utopia in the New South: The Ruskin Colonies in Tennessee and Georgia, 1894–1901* (Urbana and Chicago: University of Illinois Press, 1996), 55–56.

47. Quoted in Hopkins, *The Rise of the Social Gospel in American Protestantism*, 86–87.

48. Pacyga and Skerrett, *Chicago, City of Neighborhoods*, 311.

49. "Labor Church Opens: Auspicious Beginning of the Modern Ecclesiastical Idea," *Chicago Daily Tribune*, 12 February 1894.

50. See "New Labor Church," *Railway Times* 1, no. 5 (1 March 1894): 2; "The Sunday-Gossip," *Die Fackel*, 11 March 1894. Translated by Ian Rinehart, Northwestern University.

51. "Topics of the Time," *Advance* 28, no. 1475 (15 February 1894): 101.

52. The full text of Pomeroy's address was published under the title "Stacks and Steeples" and can be found in the Thomas J. Morgan Collection, Box 1, Folder 15, Illinois Historical Survey, Urbana, IL.

53. "The Modern Church: A Lively Debate Occupies One Session," *Railway Times* 1, no. 6 (15 March 1894): 1; "Church as an Issue: It is Discussed by a Labor Leader and a Preacher," *Chicago Daily Tribune*, 26 February 1894; Stead, *If Christ Came to Chicago*, 398; and "The Pulpit," *Advance* 28, no. 1477 (1 March 1894): 135.

54. In most cases this was because, lacking the support of greater institutions, they depended heavily upon the time and talents of a charismatic leader. When sickness, weariness, or the allure of other opportunities drew the founder away, the organization floundered. Herbert Casson's congregation in Lynn, Massachusetts, survived for six years—an exceptional tenure to be sure—but, in keeping with the trend, his resignation in 1900 hastened the church's decline. See William Dwight Porter Bliss, ed., *The New Encyclopedia of Social Reform* (London and New York: Funk & Wagnalls Company, 1909), 677; also, Hopkins, *The Rise of the Social Gospel in American Protestantism*, 86–87.

55. Lears, *Rebirth of a Nation*, 181–182; and Charles Postel, *The Populist Vision* (New York: Oxford University Press, 2007), 211–212.

56. *Tenth Annual Report of the Commissioner of Labor* (Washington, DC: Government Printing Office, 1896), 248–260.

57. See "Dr M'Pherson on Industrial Armies," *Chicago Daily Tribune*, 30 April 1894. Barrows may have been earning even more. As early as 1885, he was drawing a salary of $8,000 a year, following a $1,000 raise he received that December. See "Church Meetings: The First Presbyterian Society Raises Pastor Barrows' Salary," *Chicago Daily Tribune*, 10 December 1885. In 1890—before the depression put a serious dent in wages—the average factory worker earned only $448 per year. See A. P. Winston, review of *L'anarchisme aux Etats Unis*, by Paul Ghio, and *History of Socialism in the United States*, by Morris Hillquit, *Journal of Political Economy* 13, no. 1 (December 1904): 119.

58. "Industrial Armies and Industrious Citizens," *Interior* 25, no. 1247 (19 April 1894): 487; "The Strike," *Interior* 25, no. 1249 (3 May 1894): 549.

59. "Industrial Armies and Industrious Citizens"; "Editorial Topics," *Interior* 25, no. 1249 (3 May 1894): 555; "Unsuccessful Men," *Interior* 25, no. 1250 (10 May 1894): 585. The Congregationalist *Advance* seconded such sentiments, painting Coxey and his kindred as "tramping armies of dupes and deadbeats," and expressing an almost pained incredulity at the fact that "socialistic theories . . . have seized the imagination of the people." "The Meaning of It," *Advance* 28, no. 1485 (26 April 1894): 261–262.

60. On the ascendance of nativism in the postbellum period, see John Higham, *Strangers in the Land: Patterns of American Nativism, 1860–1925*, 6th ed. (London: Rutgers University Press, 2004), 35–105.

61. "Petitions in Boots and Bummery," *Advance* 28, no. 1486 (May 3, 1894): 277–278.

62. For an erudite account of this process, see Stanley, *From Bondage to Contract*.

63. "Lockout the Theme of Sermons: Bishop Fallows Sees No Cause for Alarm in Labor Contests," *Chicago Daily Tribune*, 16 April 1894.

64. "Labor Trouble Possible," *Northwestern Christian Advocate* 42, no. 15 (11 April 1894): 8.

65. See "Saint Gabriel Church, Diamond Jubilee Souvenir Program," housed in the Archives of the Archdiocese of Chicago, Chicago, IL. For more on Dorney, see

Schneirov, *Labor and Urban Politics*, 104–105; as well as Michael F. Funchion, "Irish Chicago: Church, Homeland, Politics, and Class—The Shaping of an Ethnic Group, 1870–1900," in Melvin G. Holli and Peter d'A Jones, eds., *Ethnic Chicago: A Multicultural Portrait* (Grand Rapids, MI: William B. Eerdmans Publishing, 1995), 64.

66. See "The Shepherds and their Flock," *Chicagoer Arbeiter Zeitung*, 7 September 1887, accessed via the Chicago Foreign Language Press Survey.

67. "Trouble in Pennsylvania," *New World* 2, no. 22 (3 February 1894): 6. This more hospitable attitude to the foreign-born sprung naturally from the fact that the Catholic Church in Chicago was overwhelmingly comprised of the same. See Charles Shanabruch, *Chicago's Catholics: The Evolution of an American Identity* (South Bend, IN: University of Notre Dame Press, 1981), 31–104, 234.

68. "Trouble in Pennsylvania," *New World* 2, no. 22 (3 February 1894): 6.

69. For criticism of the editor's perspective on the coal strikes, see "Correspondence," *New World* 2, no. 43 (30 June 1894): 10.

70. Cited in Abell, "The Reception of Leo XIII's Labor Encyclical in America, 1891–1919," 466.

71. "Tribute of Church," *Chicago Daily Tribune*, 4 September 1893.

72. For a more in-depth discussion of the complex reasons why the encyclical's failed to inspire a grass-roots movement, see Abell, "The Reception of Leo XIII's Labor Encyclical"; as well as Jay Dolan, *The American Catholic Experience: A History from Colonial Times to the Present* (Garden City, NY: Doubleday, 1985), 334–336.

73. See "Society of Polish Catholic Workers in Chicago," 27 March 1894, and "Labor Meeting," *Dziennik Chicagoski*, 6 April 1894, both accessed via the Chicago Foreign Language Press Survey; and on a related note, "Offered to Go to Work," *Chicago Daily Tribune*, 1 July 1891.

74. For my account of events leading up to the strike I have relied primarily upon Stanley Buder, *Pullman: An Experiment in Industrial Order and Community Planning, 1880–1930* (New York: Oxford University Press, 1967), 147–162. See also Almont Lindsay, *The Pullman Strike: The Story of a Unique Experiment and of a Great Labor Upheaval* (Chicago: University of Chicago Press, 1964).

75. Ibid.

76. "What the Ministers Said," *Daily News*, 14 May 1894.

77. *New World* 2, no. 37 (19 May 1894): 1.

78. "Says Both Sides Are to Blame: The Rev. Frank M. Bristol Preaches on the Trouble at Homestead," *Chicago Daily Tribune*, 11 June 1892.

79. "Strikes as Seen from the Pulpit: The Rev. Frank Bristol Declares Them Un-American and of No Avail," *Chicago Daily Tribune*, 14 May 1894.

80. See Buder, *Pullman*, 172, 179–180.

81. See ibid., 181–183.

82. *New World* 2, no. 43 (30 June 1894): 8.

83. "Passing Comment," *Northwestern Christian Advocate* 42, no. 27 (4 July 1894): 1; "Topics of the Time," *Advance* 28, no. 1495 (5 July 1894): 421.

84. "Editorial Summary," *Standard* 41, no. 45 (5 July 1894): 4.

85. This account is drawn primarily from Lindsay, *The Pullman Strike*.

86. See "Letter from the Archbishop," *New World* 2, no. 45 (14 July 1894): 8; "Church Notices," *Daily Sun*, 7 July 1894; *Daily Inter Ocean*, 7 July 1894; and "Law and Order Mass-Meeting Sunday," *Chicago Daily Tribune*, 7 July 1894.

87. "Passing Comment—Almost Civil War," *Northwestern Christian Advocate* 42, no. 28 (11 July 1894): 1.

88. "Editorial Summary," *Standard* 41, no. 46 (12 July 1894): 4.

89. "The Great Strike," *New World* 2, no. 44 (7 July 1894): 8.

90. "Why Not Arbitrate?" *New World* 2, no. 45 (14 July 1894): 8.

91. "A Way Out of the Difficulty," *New World* 2, no. 45 (14 July 1894): 8. The *Gazeta's* view is reproduced in "Mysli z powodu strajkow," *Dziennik Chicagoski*, 12 July 1894 (translated by Jessica Szafron, University of Illinois, Chicago).

92. "Modes of Enforcing the Law," *New World* 2, no. 45 (14 July 1894): 8.

93. See "Down on Mob Work," *Chicago Daily Tribune*, 16 July 1894; "Speaks as a Patriot," *Daily Inter Ocean*, 16 July 1894; "Ireland Condemns It," *Evening Journal*, 16 July 1894.

94. See Dolan, *American Catholic Experience*, 308–315.

95. "Speaks as a Patriot," *Daily Inter Ocean*, 16 July 1894.

96. "Passing Comment—An Advance," *Northwestern Christian Advocate* 42, no. 28 (11 July 1894): 1.

97. "News and Notes," *Living Church* 17, no. 15 (14 July 1894): 251; "Treasonous Leadership," *Advance* 28, no. 1496 (12 July 1894): 438.

98. "Law and Order in America," *Standard* 41, no. 46 (12 July 1894): 4.

99. See "The Pulpit," *Advance* 28, no. 1497 (19 July 1894): 455; "Camp Services at Pullman," *Chicago Times*, 16 July 1894; and *Standard*, 2 August 1894.

100. "Lessons of the Time: Rev. Dr. Barrows Preaches on the Recent Strike," *Daily Inter Ocean*, 16 July 1894.

101. "The Church and the Unemployed," *Northwestern Christian Advocate* 42, no. 2 (10 January 1894): 2–3; "Social Functions of the Church," *Northwestern Christian Advocate* 42, no. 13 (28 March 1894): 3; "Arbitration of Labor Troubles," *Northwestern Christian Advocate* 42, no. 31 (1 August 1894): 2.

102. "Tell of Their Work," *Chicago Daily Tribune*, 12 June 1894.

103. This was how Henry May described the crises that ultimately destabilized the antebellum Protestant consensus. See May, *Protestant Churches and Industrial America*.

104. "Protest of a Pastor," *Chicago Times*, 15 July 1894.

105. Charles B. Atwell, ed., *Northwestern University Alumni Record of the College of Liberal Arts* (Evanston, IL: Northwestern University, 1903), 201–202.

106. "Moses as the Father of Socialism: The Rev. H. G. Leonard Arraigns Fellow Pastors on the Labor Problem," *Chicago Daily Tribune*, 20 February 1894.

107. See Buder, *Pullman*, 53, 119–122.

108. "A Clergyman Hits Hard," *Railway Times* 1, no. 11 (1 June 1894): 1.

109. See "Should Pull Together: Strike Lessons as Urged by the Rev. J. M. Lockhart," *Chicago Times*, 30 July 1894.

110. Renown came in response especially to his book, discussed below, which was reviewed in far-flung publications. See, for example, "The Pullman Strike," *Literary News*, New York, October 1894; *Post-Intelligencer*, Seattle, Washington, 3 September 1894; and "The Pullman Strike," *Times-Star*, Cincinnati, OH, 6 September 1894. Clippings of these reviews can be found in the Pullman Strike Scrapbooks, 1894–1897, Pullman Palace Car Company Collection, Reels 14–16, The Newberry Library, Chicago, IL.

111. The *Mail* testified to the strikers' enthusiastic reception of him, declaring, "The dominie is the most popular man in town." See "Pullman Taken Ill," *Chicago Mail*, 22 May 1894. This article is included in the Pullman Strike Scrapbooks, 1894–1897.

112. "A Minister Favors the Strike: Pastor Carwardine Commends the Pullman Workmen for their Action," *Chicago Inter-Ocean*, 18 May 1894; "Strikers Pack Kensington Hall," *Chicago Dispatch*, 18 May 1894; "Hard Blows at Pullman," *Daily News*, 17 May 1894; "Consider Him a Foe: George M. Pullman Denounced from the Pulpit," *Chicago Tribune*, 21 May 1894. These articles are included in the Pullman Strike Scrapbooks, 1894–1897.

113. "Pastor vs. Pullman," *Chicago Daily Tribune*, 23 July 1894. See also "Bitterly Arraigns Mr. Pullman," *Chicago Daily Tribune*, 16 June 1894; "He Spoke of Pullman," *Chicago Times*, 16 June 1894; "Carwardine on Pullman Again," *Chicago Herald*, 16 June 1894; and "Debs to be Re-Elected President," *Chicago Daily Tribune*, 21 June 1894. These articles are included in the Pullman Strike Scrapbooks, 1894–1897.

114. William H. Carwardine, *The Pullman Strike* (Chicago: Charles H. Kerr & Co, 1894), 13–14.

115. Wm. H. Carwardine to Mr. and Mrs. Lloyd, 6 July 1894. Reproduced in Henry Demarest Lloyd Papers, Reel 5, Correspondence, General, 1893 Sept. 1–1894 Dec. 31, State Historical Society of Wisconsin.

116. See, for example, "The Preacher and Mr. Pullman," *Evening Journal*, 21 May 1894.

117. For a selection of a number of these letters from ordinary persons, see "Pullman Stays Away," *Chicago Times*, 25 June 1894. In addition, the Central Strike Committee issued its own endorsement of Carwardine's book, declaring, "Carwardine is a man of sterling ability, a clear thinker, an eloquent speaker," the notice began, going on to say, "He is respected by all and loved by many. We heartily indorse all that he writes about the present strike and the

Town of Pullman." The signatories on the document included T. W. Heathcote, R. W. Brown, and J. W. Jacobs, the Committee's president, vice-president, and acting secretary. The endorsement was written on official Strike Committee stationery. Both the original and copies of it can be found in the unsorted box of Carwardine materials at United Library, Garrett-Evangelical Theological Seminary, Evanston, IL.

118. Robert P. Swierenga, *Dutch Chicago: A History of the Hollanders in the Windy City* (Grand Rapids, MI: William B. Eerdmans Publishing, 2002), 640–641.

119. "He Gave Up the Church," *Chicago Daily Tribune*, 31 July 1891.

120. "Had to Make a Choice," *Chicago Daily Tribune*, 1 August 1891; "Labor War Declared for Roseland," *Chicago Daily Tribune*, 4 August 1891.

121. "Seek Pulpit Aid," *Chicago Times*, 29 May 1894; "More Men Go Out," *Chicago Times*, 30 May 1894; "Strikers are Joyful," *Chicago Times*, 31 May 1894; "Shy of Patrimonium," *Chicago Record*, 31 May 1894.

122. Swierenga, *Dutch Chicago*, 313.

123. See ibid., 328–329.

124. *Fosterlandet*, no. 20 (16 May 1894): 4 (translation by Stina Bäckström, University of Chicago).

125. "Pastor Takes No Striker's Advice," *Chicago Daily Tribune*, 25 July 1894.

126. Ibid.

127. "Food Must Be Worked For," *Chicago Daily Tribune*, 27 July 1894.

128. "Pullman Industrial System," *Chicago Record*, 14 May 1894.

129. "Chided by a Pastor: Pullman Employees Are Criticised by the Rev. Mr. Oggel," *Chicago Tribune*, 14 May 1894.

130. Matching church and census records, one can determine the national origins of the church's members. Not surprisingly, it primarily attracted those hailing from Scotland, Holland, England, Wales, and Switzerland, all nations steeped in the Reformed tradition.

131. McLachlan had previously served in the mid-1880s as a foreman of masonry and sewage at Pullman Works. His contracts included those for the Market Hall, as well as the Roman Catholic and Swedish church buildings. See George William Warvelle, *A Compendium of Freemasonry in Illinois: Embracing a Review of the Introduction, Development, and Present Condition of All Rites and Degrees* (1897), 487.

132. The churches records dating back to its founding in 1882 have been preserved. See the "Register of Communicants" and "Minutes of Session," Archive, Pullman Presbyterian Church, Chicago, IL.

133. "Pullman Taken Ill"; "The Big Strike," *Advertiser*, 19 May 1894.

134. "Taxes but no Bread," *Chicago Journal*, 30 May 1894.

135. "Register of Communicants."

136. I obtained these results by cross-referencing the "Register of Communicants," on the one hand, and both the Chicago city directory for 1894 and the

US Census of 1900, on the other. It is not possible to identify the occupations of all those who left, as some were not listed and others had very common names.

137. Calvin F. and Mary Swingle represent an intriguing exception to this rule. Calvin F. Swingle had served as the Chief Engineer at Pullman Works for several years, until his relationship with the Company suddenly terminated in 1894. One surmises that he may have had a falling out with management, which would also explain his disillusionment with this church, though it is impossible to know for certain.

138. Again, I have uncovered these names and occupations by matching the Register of Communicants with the 1894 city directory, the 1900 census, and old issues of the *Chicago Tribune*. While it is impossible to track down all of the church's congregants, these findings confirm a newspaper report stating that many who stayed were department heads and other high-ranking employees at Pullman. See "Pullman Taken Ill."

139. A post-mortem on the situation in the *Interior* admitted as much, relating that some members, "imagining the church not to be in sympathy with their attitude, withdrew." See "Chicago," *Interior* 25, no. 1273 (18 October 1894): 1357. Perhaps the most plausible alternative explanation for the church's dramatic loss of members is the lack of an immediate full-time replacement for Oggel. However, the short duration of the interim period—a new pastor was installed by autumn—and the church's stability through several other interim periods make this a weaker theory. The *Interior* chalked up part of the losses to people moving away, yet as I make clear in this paragraph, the vast majority stayed in close proximity to the church.

140. See "Register of Communicants." While E. Myrtle Plant and Annie Masterbrook may have joined other churches, they are listed as moving on only to Valparaiso, IN, and Roseland, IL, respectively.

141. Ibid. An attachment to the Reformed tradition likely prevented more from joining Carwardine's church. While some were willing to cross denominational lines, most were reticent to abandon their theological heritage. Only three families reaffiliated with non-Reformed churches.

142. "Pullman Stays Away."

CHAPTER 6

1. "Go Wild Over Debs," *Chicago Daily Tribune*, 23 November 1895.

2. See Eugene V. Debs, *Debs: His Life, Writings and Speeches* (Chicago: Charles H. Kerr & Company, 1908), 327–344; and "Church Is Not Against Labor," *Chicago Daily Tribune*, 2 December 1895.

3. "Touches Up Debs and the Politicians," *Chicago Daily Tribune*, 30 November 1894.

4. "Rap at the Church," *Chicago Daily Tribune*, 24 September 1895.

5. "A Thrust at the Church," *New World* 4, no. 13 (30 November 1895): 10.

6. See "Debs and the Church," *Chicago Daily Tribune*, 1 December 1895; and "Church Is Not Against Labor," *Chicago Daily Tribune*, 2 December 1895.

7. For more on the neighborhood, see Steven Essig, "West Town," in James R. Grossman, Ann Durkin Keating, and Janice L. Reiff, eds., *The Encyclopedia of Chicago* (Chicago: University of Chicago Press, 2004), 873; and Pacyga and Skerrett, *Chicago, City of Neighborhoods*, 165–173.

8. For more on Wilson's longer trajectory, see, for example, Douglas Firth Anderson, "J. Stitt Wilson and Herronite Socialist Christianity," in Jacob H. Dorn, ed., *Socialism and Christianity in Early 20th Century America* (Westport, CT: Greenwood Press, 1998), 41–64.

9. "May Tie Up the Pabst Brewery," *Chicago Daily Tribune*, 5 December 1895; "Dates Are Made for Debs," *Chicago Daily Tribune*, 4 January 1896; "Debs Makes Three Addresses," *Chicago Daily Tribune*, 11 April 1896; "Debs to Speak at the University," *Chicago Daily Tribune*, 22 April 1896.

10. "Debs Makes Three Addresses," *Chicago Daily Tribune*, 11 April 1896. For more on Debs's own religious trajectory, see Burns, *The Life and Death of the Radical Historical Jesus*, 162–197.

11. For an obituary, along with expressions of sympathy from the Old-Time Printer's Association, Typographical Union no. 16, and the Press Club of Chicago, see "Andrew Carr Cameron," *Artist Printer*, 417–419.

12. For more on this, see Nelson, "Revival and Upheaval," 233–253.

13. For comparative perspective, see, for example, McLeod, *Piety and Poverty*.

14. See clipping entitled, "I Am Only a Working Girl," Thomas J. Morgan Collection, Book 2, Illinois Historical Survey, Urbana, IL. For more on Morgan, see Tax, *The Rising of the Women*, 47–48.

15. J. B. Maynard, "The Theology of Labor," *Railway Times* 2, no. 9 (1 May 1895): 4.

16. See J. Robert Constantine, ed., *Letters of Eugene V. Debs*, Vol. 1: *1874–1912* (Urbana: University of Illinois Press, 1990): 95.

17. "W. J. Bryan on Toil," *Chicago Daily Tribune*, 8 September 1896. For more on Bryan's distinctive blend of faith and politics, see Kazin, *A Godly Hero*. For the authoritative treatment of Populist Christianity at the grassroots, see Creech, *Righteous Indignation*.

18. There was, for example, a history of religious and labor leaders working together on Sabbatarian campaigns. For in-depth discussion of this, see Mirola, "Shorter Hours and the Protestant Sabbath," 395–433.

19. See, for example, "Hail Labor as an Ally," *Chicago Daily Tribune*, 30 June 1898; "Congress of Religions Open," *Chicago Daily Tribune*, 13 December 1899; *Living Church*, 11 November 1905; "Trade Unions and Temperance," *Northwestern Christian Advocate* 54, no. 40 (3 October 1906); "Moved to Pity Child Toilers,"

Chicago Daily Tribune, 16 March 1903; "Ministers Unite to Rescue Girls," *Chicago Daily Tribune*, 7 February 1908.

20. See "Pulpit and the Barber," *Chicago Daily Tribune*, 8 July 1895; "Signs of Sunday Rest," *Chicago Daily Tribune*, 23 December 1895; and "Clergymen Oppose Sunday Labor," *Chicago Daily Tribune*, 24 December 1895.

21. *Eight-Hour Herald* 4, no. 97 (28 December 1895): 4.

22. "Sunday as a Day of Rest," *Eight-Hour Herald* 5, no. 93 (4 January 1896): 1.

23. Pierce, *A History of Chicago*, 3: 48.

24. On the class profile of black churches prior to the Great Migration, see Wallace Best, *Passionately Human, No Less Divine: Religion and Culture in Black Chicago, 1915–1952* (Princeton, NJ: Princeton University Press, 2005).

25. See "A Remarkable Sermon," *Chicago Daily Tribune*, 22 August 1887; and "The Pulpit Again," *Labor Enquirer* 1, no. 34 (27 August 1887): 1.

26. See Margaret Garb, *Freedom's Ballot: African American Political Struggles in Chicago from Abolition to the Great Migration* (Chicago: University of Chicago Press, 2014): 117–146. For coverage in the *Tribune*, see also "Colored Waiters May Strike Monday," *Chicago Daily Tribune*, 8 May 1890; "Worrying the Old Bosses," *Chicago Daily Tribune*, 13 May 1890; "Hotels Are Giving In," *Chicago Daily Tribune*, 22 May 1890; "Announcements," *Chicago Daily Tribune*, 24 May 1890; "Agree to Stand by their Fellows," *Chicago Daily Tribune*, 28 May 1890; "Waiters Run Against a Snag," *Chicago Daily Tribune*, 29 May 1890; "Want Better Wages," *Chicago Daily Tribune*, 17 February 1893; "Waiters Will Demand Higher Wages," *Chicago Daily Tribune*, 25 April 1893; "Colored Waiters Demand Better Pay," *Chicago Daily Tribune*, 28 April 1893; "Waiters to Strike," *Chicago Daily Tribune*, 1 May 1893; "Offer to Arbitrate," *Chicago Daily Tribune*, 5 May 1893.

27. See US Strike Commission, *Report on the Chicago Strike of June–July, 1894*, 53rd Cong., 3d sess., 448–449.

28. "Methodists Indorse Carwardine," *Chicago Daily Tribune*, 11 September 1894.

29. "Presentation to Rev. W. H. Carwardine," *Northwestern Christian Advocate*, Chicago, IL, 19 September 1894.

30. As Hugh McLeod writes, "All his life [Hardie] was both an ardent Christian and a severe critic of the churches. . . . Hardie was representative of a good many working-class Christians of the later Victorian period, who adopted a highly practical form of religion that gave a high priority to the achievement of a just and equal society, and who came to believe that labour and socialist organizations were doing more than the churches to bring about the kind of world that they wanted." McLeod, *Religion and the Working Class in Nineteenth-Century Britain*, 35.

31. "He Shows His Venom," *Chicago Daily Tribune*, 10 September 1895; and "Keir Hardie before Preachers," *New York Times*, 10 September 1895.

32. "Ask Hardie to Talk," *Chicago Daily Tribune*, 3 September 1895.

33. "He Shows his Venom."

34. See Jane Preston, "Chicago Commons," in Grossman, Keating, Reiff, eds., *Encyclopedia of Chicago*, 133.

35. "Conditions," *Railway Times* 2, no. 11 (1 June 1895): 1. J. Pierpont Morgan's Trinity Episcopal Church in New York City was one of the editor's favorite targets. He called it, among other things, an "abnormal abomination" and "the devil's strongest stronghold in Gotham." See *Railway Times* 2, no. 7 (1 April 1895): 2; "A Bishop as a Labor Arbitrator," *Railway Times* 2, no. 11 (1 June 1895): 2; and for yet another example, *Railway Times* 2, no. 6 (15 March 1895): 2.

36. "Church and Labor Get Redhot," *Chicago Daily Tribune*, 11 December 1895.

37. See "Labor Leaders Give Their Views," *Chicago Daily Tribune*, 16 February 1896.

38. For one of countless examples, see "Says Poor are Crowded," *Chicago Daily Tribune*, 1 October 1900.

39. "Union Labor Holds Funeral," *Chicago Daily Tribune*, 24 December 1900.

40. "First of 'Workingmen's Dinners,'" *Chicago Daily Tribune*, 13 April 1895.

41. Hopkins, *The Rise of the Social Gospel in American Protestantism*, 84.

42. Abell, *Urban Impact on American Protestantism*, 61–62; and Dorn, *Washington Gladden*, 211–212.

43. Perry, "The Workingman's Alienation from the Church," 621–629.

44. "Workingmen and the Church," *Chicago Daily Tribune*, 30 July 1901. See also "Workingmen and the Church," *New York Times*, 22 January 1901.

45. "Find Flaws in Church," *Chicago Daily Tribune*, 3 October 1902. For an initial report announcing the planned survey, see "Trainmen Vote for More Pay," *Chicago Daily Tribune*, 16 September 1902.

46. See also, for example, "Workers Blame the Church," *Chicago Daily Tribune*, 14 March 1901; and "Few Toilers in Churches," *Chicago Daily Tribune*, 6 February 1911. One 1903 survey of the clergy by an Evanston Congregationalist found that "churches in the middle west are not allowing laboring men to drift away from them," making it a definite outlier. See "Artisans Go to Church," *Chicago Daily Tribune*, 26 January 1903.

47. "Unions Rebuke Pulpit Critics," *Chicago Daily Tribune*, 3 June 1901. Until it ceased publication the *Eight-Hour Herald* continued to apply pressure in its pages as well. See, for example, "Labor and the Church," *Eight-Hour Herald* 5, no. 133 (3 September 1896): 3; "Not the Sermon on the Mount," *Eight-Hour Herald* 6, no. 169 (11 May 1897): 4; and "The Poor Not Wanted," *Eight-Hour Herald* 7, no. 203 (6 January 1898): 3.

48. *Social Democrat* 4, no. 23 (28 October 1897): 2. Letters from readers and other correspondents convey the wider reach of these views. See, for example, E. E. Smith, "The Socialism of Christ," *Social Democrat* 5, no. 4 (27 January 1898): 2; R. Fletcher Gray, "The Social Teaching of Jesus," *Social Democrat* 5, no. 9 (3 March 1898): 2; Stanley Savage, "A Preachers View of the Golden Rule," *Social*

Democrat 5, no. 11 (17 March 1898): 2; C. W. Minor, "Christianity—Socialism," *Social Democrat* 5, no. 11 (17 March 1898): 2

49. Quoted in Kent and Gretchen Kreuter, *An American Dissenter: The Life of Algie Martin Simons, 1870–1950* (Lexington: University of Kentucky Press, 1969): 16.

50. "Snap Shots by the Wayside," *Workers' Call* 3, no. 113 (4 May 1901): 2.

51. See *Workers' Call* 2, no. 53 (10 March 1900): 2; and for similar examples, "Arouses Class Fury," *Workers' Call* 2, no. 103 (23 February 1901): 2; and "Snap Shots by the Wayside," *Workers' Call* 3, no. 134 (28 September 1901): 2. For more criticism of clerical salaries, see, for example, "Clerical Salaries," *Workers' Call* 3, no. 114 (11 May 1901): 2; and also *Workers' Call* 3, no. 138 (26 October 1901): 2; and "Don't Know Where He's At," *Workers' Call* 2, no. 103 (23 February 1901): 1.

52. See "Pulpit Puerilities," *Chicago Daily Socialist* 4, no. 160 (29 March 1902): 1. Within a year of Gunsaulus's 1887 arrival in Chicago, he was making an annual salary of $8,000. I have found no record of his salary in later years, but it is almost certain that between his work at the Armour Institute and his church he made well in excess of $10,000. See "Highway and Byway," *Chicago Daily Tribune*, 3 June 1890. For more examples in which Gunsaulus is criticized, see also "'Heaven,' 'New Jerusalem,' 'Chicago,'" *Chicago Daily Socialist* 5, no. 255 (23 January 1904): 2; and Henry J. Wiegel, "Dots and Dashes on the Class Struggle," *Chicago Daily Socialist* 6, no. 276 (18 June 1904): 1. Among Simons's other modernist victims was the Reverend Hiram Thomas, pastor at the People's Church. See "Dr. Thomas," *Workers' Call* 1, no. 7 (22 April 1899): 1, 3; and *Workers' Call* 1, no. 7 (22 April 1899): 2.

53. "If They 'Do Good,'" *Workers' Call* 2, no. 101 (9 February 1901): 1. For the report in the *Tribune*, see "Begin the Work with Prayer," *Chicago Daily Tribune*, 29 January 1901.

54. The paper was published from 1901 to 1906, when it merged with the *Svenska Tribunen*. See Ernst Wilhelm Olson, Martin J. Engberg, and Anders Schön, *History of the Swedes of Illinois* (Chicago: Engberg Holmberg Publishing Company, 1908), 825.

55. "Labor Unions and the Church," *Svenska Nyheter*, 22 December 1903. This reforming zeal shone through again when a devout reader in nearby Batavia, Albert Gustafson, wrote to discontinue his subscription on the grounds that "you are criticizing the church and its ministers unjustly." Malmquist's response to Gustafson, published alongside the text of his letter, read in part, "Cheerfully do we admit that we have criticized the ministers, criticized them because they do not live in accordance with their teachings; criticized them because they proved far speedier on their feet in running the errands of Mammon than the errands of the God they propose to serve." *Svenska Nyheter*, 19 January 1904. The paper's editorial page did regularly highlight church-related scandals, including some, to be fair to Gustafson, which were likely little more than salacious rumor. For some examples, see, "Judge Not, That Ye Be Not Judged,"

Svenska Nyheter, 18 August 1903; "Friendliness of the Catholic Church to Labor," *Svenska Nyheter,* 22 September 1903; "They Are Going Too Far," *Svenska Nyheter,* 18 December 1903; *Svenska Nyheter,* 23 February 1904; and *Svenska Nyheter,* 26 April 1904. All of these articles can be accessed via the Chicago Foreign Language Press Survey.

56. "Religion and Socialism," *Chicago Daily Socialist* 6, no. 289 (17 September 1904): 2–3.

57. See "Dutch Pastor Speaks Out," *Workers' Call* 3, no. 120 (22 June 1901): 3; "Mogens A. Sommer Dead," *Revyen,* 2 March 1901; *Scandia,* 9 March 1912; and "Scandia," *Scandia,* 31 August 1912. The latter two articles can be accessed via the Chicago Foreign Language Press Survey.

58. See "Why Converts Join the Episcopalian Church," *New World* 8, no. 35 (28 April 1900): 8; and "Making More Nothingarians," *New World* 12, no. 26 (27 February 1904): 16.

59. "President Gompers and the Churches," *New World* 4, no. 50 (15 August 1896): 8.

60. See, for example, "The Church of the Poor," *New World* 8, no. 46 (14 July 1900): 8; "The Church and the Classes," *New World* 12, no. 28 (12 March 1904): 17; and "'The Church of the Classes," *New World* 15, no. 34 (20 April 1907): 15. For more articles that exalt Catholic ties to the poor, frequently with comparison to Protestants and sometimes to Jews, see also "The 'Non-Church-Going Masses'" *New World,* 28 August 1897; John McIntosh, "Bishop Potter's Startling Prediction," *New World* 13, no. 23 (6 February 1904): 10–11; "Three Prelates Discuss Labor," *New World* 13, no. 23 (6 February 1904): 16; "Labor Chased to its Lair," *New World* 12, no. 30 (26 March 1904): 16; "All Christianity Arraigned," *New World* 12, no. 33 (16 April 1904): 17; "The Churches Losing Ground," *New World* 13, no. 21 (21 January 1905): 16; "Topics of the Hour," *New World* 13, no. 40 (3 June 1905): 3; "The Churches and the Workingman," *New World* 13, no. 47 (22 July 1905): 16; "Topics of the Hour," *New World* 14, no. 6 (5 October 1905): 3; "The Wail of the Protestant Preacher," *New World* 14, no. 13 (25 November 1905): 3.

61. See "The Real Danger in Labor Injunctions," *New World* 6, no. 5 (2 October 1897); "Judges and Injunctions," *New World* 6, no. 4 (26 September 1897); "The Eight Hour Day," *New World* 6, no. 6 (9 October 1897); and *New World* 6, no. 15 (11 December 1897): 3.

62. "Lessons of the Labor War," *New World* 8, no. 42 (16 June 1900): 8.

63. One of the Strikers, "The Merits of the Strike," *New World* 2, no. 46 (21 July 1894): 10. For mention of the backlash against the paper's position on the Pullman affair, see "Debs on the Great Strike," *New World* 3, no. 32 (13 April 1895): 8.

64. For their exchange, see W. J. Thomas, "The Ethics of Strikes," *New World* 4, no. 51 (22 August 1896): 8; "The Freedom of Labor," *New World* 5, no. 1

(5 September 1896): 8; and W. J. Thomas, "The Ethics of Strikes," *New World* 5, no. 1 (5 September 1896): 10.

65. "Burns Captured the Meeting," *Railway Times* 4, no. 9 (1 May 1897): 3.

66. Available at http://www.vatican.va/holy_father/leo_xiii/encyclicals/documents/ hf_l-xiii_enc_28121878_quod-apostolici-muneris_en.html.

67. Reproduced in David M. Byers, ed., *Justice in the Marketplace: Collected Statements of the Vatican and the United States Catholic Bishops on Economic Policy, 1891–1984* (Washington, DC: United States Catholic Conference, 1985), 21.

68. Ibid., 19.

69. For more on the encyclical's reception in the United States, see Abell, "The Reception of Leo XIII's Labor Encyclical in America, 1891–1919," 464–495.

70. Available at http://www.papalencyclicals.net/Leo13/l13grcom.htm.

71. On the Czechs, see the discussion in chapter 4. On the Irish, see, for example, "The Knights' of Labor Ticket," *Western Catholic* 20, no. 32 (5 March 1887): 4; "Father Conway on Socialism," *Chicago Daily Tribune*, 20 February 1888; and "The Abject Slavery of Laborers to Trade Unions," *Chicago Daily Tribune*, 26 March 1888.

72. See "Priest Denounces Circular," *Chicago Daily Tribune*, 21 April 1899. For the full text of the circular, see "Catholicism and Socialism," *Workers' Call* 1, no. 11 (20 May 1899): 3.

73. D.R.A., "Book Notes," *New World* 9, no. 38 (18 May 1901): 14.

74. "Rickaby on Socialism," *Workers' Call* 3, no. 143 (30 November 1901): 1.

75. See S.T., "A Plea for Socialism," *New World* 8, no. 27 (3 March 1900): 10; S.T., "Trusts and the Remedy," *New World* 8, no. 29 (17 March 1900): 10; and S.T., "Further Plea for Socialism," *New World* 8, no. 32 (7 April 1900): 10.

76. See M. J. Weis, "The Class Struggle," *New World* 9, no. 3 (15 September 1900): 10; and "The Industrial Problem," *New World* 9, no. 5 (29 September 1900): 10. According to the American Almanac, Weis was a member of the Cook County Socialist Central Committee by 1904. He was likely serving in that capacity even earlier. See *The American Almanac, Year-Book, Cyclopaedia and Atlas*, Vol. 2 (New York: Hearst's Chicago American and San Francisco Examiner, 1904), 846.

77. "'Beyond the Black Ocean': A Plea for Socialism," *New World* 9, no. 47 (20 July 1901): 10.

78. With respect to socialism's marginality, consider that in 1900 the AFL boasted half a million members, the Socialist Labor Party 1,400, and the Social Democratic Party 10,000. In the presidential election that year, socialists failed to collectively capture even 1% of the vote, despite having two candidates in the field—Social Democracy's Debs and Socialist Labor's Joseph Malloney. See Marc Karson, *American Labor Unions and Politics, 1900–1918* (Carbondale: Southern Illinois University Press, 1958), 27–28.

79. See "Socialism," in Daniel Coit Gilman, Harry Thurston Peck, and Frank Moore Colby, eds., *The New International Encyclopaedia*, Vol. 18 (New York: Dodd, Mead, and Company, 1905), 300.

80. 97,000 had been cast for socialists in 1900 elections. Kreuter, *An American Dissenter*, 88.

81. Ibid., 86.

82. Allen Ruff, *"We Called Each Other Comrade": Charles H. Kerr & Company, Radical Publisher* (Urbana: University of Illinois Press, 1997), 85.

83. For more on the various dynamics inflecting Quigley's selection, see Shanabruch, *Chicago's Catholics*, 107–110.

84. See "Interesting Personality of the New Archbishop of Chicago," *Chicago Daily Tribune*, 21 December 1902; and "Ban on Socialism," *New World* 10, no. 26 (1 March 1902): 25. The focus of the lengthy *Tribune* interview underscored the nature of the reputation that preceded the new archbishop: more than half of the article was devoted to an account of Quigley's crusade against socialists in Buffalo.

85. See "Priest Foe to Socialism," *Chicago Daily Tribune*, 5 January 1903; and "Socialists Are Found Wanting," *Chicago Chronicle*, 26 January 1903. For more on Holy Family's near West Side location, see Pacyga and Skerrett, *Chicago, City of Neighborhoods*, 207.

86. See "War on Bridwell Labor," *Chicago Daily Tribune*, 13 November 1901; and "Aim to Fight Socialism," *Chicago Daily Tribune*, 21 January 1902.

87. Heiter denied that Quigley had sent him, but the *Tribune* thought otherwise. Both the timing and the close relationship between the two men corroborate the paper's account. See "Opens Crusade on Socialism," *Chicago Daily Tribune*, 11 February 1903; and "Will Root Out Socialism," *Chicago Daily Tribune*, 6 February 1903.

88. See "In Brief," *Congregationalist and Christian World*, 22 March 1902.

89. "Will Root Out Socialism," *Chicago Daily Tribune*, 6 February 1903.

90. "Christian War on Socialism," *Chicago Daily Tribune*, 7 February 1903.

91. "Opens Crusade on Socialism," *Chicago Daily Tribune*, 11 February 1903. See also "Town Chronicle Social Question," *Dziennik Chicagoski*, 11 February 1903, in the Chicago Foreign Language Press Survey.

92. "Attacks Doctrine of Marx," *Chicago Daily Tribune*, 13 February 1903.

93. "Labor Must Be Aided," *Chicago Chronicle*, 16 February 1903.

94. I have based this conservative estimate of attendees on the fact that three hundred persons attended the lecture at St Michael's. See "Opens Crusade on Socialism." Heiter's lectures were also published and at least 10,000 copies distributed. See letter from A. Heiter to Rev. Dr. Mueller, 24 March 1903, housed with the Chancery Correspondence at the Archive of the Archdiocese of Chicago. There may have been a simultaneous campaign in non-German parishes as well, though if so, it was not covered in the newspapers. It seems far

from coincidental that in February 1903 a small South Side parish, St. Bride's, published a synopsis of the Rev. T. E. Sherman's lecture against socialism. See "Synopsis of Rev. T. E. Sherman's S.J. Lecture on Socialism," *Monthly Record of St. Bride's Parish* 1, no. 5 (February 1903). Available in the Chicago Parishes Folder of the Archdiocese of Chicago Collection at the Archives of the University of Notre Dame.

95. "Snap Shots by the Way Side," *Chicago Socialist* 4, no. 200 (3 January 1903): 2; see also "Bishop Quigley's Advisers," *Chicago Socialist* 4, no. 200 (10 January 1903): 3. Simons had earlier been deeply critical of Quigley's anti-socialist campaign in Buffalo. See, for example, "Religion vs. Socialism," *Chicago Socialist* 4, no. 157 (8 March 1902): 1; and "Open Letter to Bishop Quigley," *Chicago Socialist* 4, no. 179 (9 August 1902): 1.

96. "Train De Luxe Brings Archbishop Quigley to Fight Socialism," *Revyen*, 21 March 1903.

97. "Opens Crusade on Socialism," *Chicago Daily Tribune*, 11 February 1903.

98. In Buffalo, Quigley had apparently declared, "No man can be a Catholic and a social democrat." See "Anti-Socialist War," *Chicago Socialist* 4, no. 208 (28 February 1903): 3.

99. See "Catholicism Attacks Socialism," *Chicago Socialist* 4, no. 207 (21 February 1903): 1; and "Rev. Anton Heiter is Answered," *Chicago Socialist* 4, no. 208 (28 February 1903): 1, 3. For more response to Heiter in the *Chicago Socialist*, see "Snap Shots by the Way Side," *Chicago Socialist* 4, no. 206 (14 February 1903): 2; and the Right Rev. Pius Clarke, "The Priest and the Hornets," *Chicago Socialist* 5, no. 211 (21 March 1903): 2. See also "Socialist Makes a Reply," *Chicago Chronicle*, February 1903.

100. This was not McGrady's first speaking engagement in Chicago. In earlier visits the priest had gotten favorable reviews from local socialists. See, for example, *Socialist Spirit* 1, no. 7 (March 1902): 31; and "Father M'Grady's Speech," *Chicago Socialist* 3, no. 156 (1 March 1902): 2.

101. "Ex-Priest as a Socialist," *Chicago Daily Tribune*, 27 March 1903.

102. These anti-socialist contributions were vast and varied. O'Malley reprinted sermons and tracts written by leading American bishops such as Metz, Spalding, and Messmer. See "The Socialist Paradise," *New World* 13, no. 18 (2 January 1904): 12; "Socialism Will Perish," *New World* 13, no. 21 (23 January 1904): 8; "Socialism and Labor," *New World* 13, no. 23 (6 February 1904): 6–7; "The Social Question," *New World* 12, no. 24 (13 February 1904): 6–7, 11; "The Social Question," *New World* 12, no. 25 (20 February 1904): 6–8; "The Social Question," *New World* 12, no. 26 (27 February 1904): 6–7); "The Social Question," *New World* 12, no. 27 (5 March 1904): 13–14; "The Social Question," *New World* 12, no. 28 (12 March 1904): 13; "The Social Question," *New World* 12, no. 29 (19 March 1904): 12–13; and "The Church and Socialism," *New World* 13, no. 2 (10

September 1904): 7. The *New World* also regularly featured commentary by other anti-socialist priests and laymen. See "Destructive Socialism," *New World* 12, no. 35 (30 April 1904): 7; Charles Coppens, S.J., "What do Socialists Want?" *New World* 12, no. 38 (21 May 1904): 8; Cecil Calvert, "Socialism and Cripple Creek," *New World* 12, no. 42 (18 June 1904): 12; Morris Cliggett, "The Christianity of Socialism," *New World* 12, no. 45 (9 July 1904): 11; P. P. Carroll, "Why Socialism Exists," *New World* 13, no. 27 (4 March 1905): 7–8; John McIntosh, "Socialism in America," *New World* 13, no. 27 (4 March 1905): 14; John McIntosh, "The Church's Care for Labor," *New World* 13, no. 28 (11 March 1905): 10; August M. Mueller, "Socialism in the United States," *New World* 13, no. 31 (1 April 1905): 6–7; Rev. P. F. Mueller, "Building the Revolution," *New World* 13, no. 39 (27 May 1905): 9; Rev. William Stang, "False Theories in Modern Life," *New World* 13, no. 40 (3 June 1905): 6; Rev. William Stang, "The Trade Guilds of the Middle Ages," *New World* 13, no. 41 (10 June 1905): 6–7; Charles Coppens, S.J., "The Real Claims of Socialism," *New World* 13, no. 44 (1 July 1905): 8–9; Rev. Henry Day, S.J., "Conditions under Socialism," *New World* 14, no. 3 (16 September 1905): 7; and Ralph M. Easley, "Socialism in Great Secular Colleges," *New World* 14, no. 8 (21 October 1905): 23.

103. "Unfamiliar with Their Own Prophets," *New World* 12, no. 48 (30 July 1904): 16; "What Is Marxian Socialism?" *New World* 13, no. 12 (19 November 1904): 10; "Irreligious American Socialism," *New World* 13, no. 14 (3 December 1904): 17; "An American Admission," *New World* 13, no. 31 (1 April 1905): 16; "What Is American Socialism?" *New World* 13, no. 44 (1 July 1905): 16–17; "A New Agent of Destruction," *New World* 13, no. 48 (29 July 1905): 15; and "Another Serpent and the Old File," *New World* 14, no. 2 (9 September 1905): 15.

104. German- and Polish-Catholic leaders were especially vigilant on this front. See, for example, *Narod Polski* 5, no. 38 (18 September 1901); "Yellow Journal Declared Bad for Church or Home," *Chicago Daily Tribune*, 27 May 1903; "Polish Catholic Congress in Pittsburgh," *Narod Polski* 8, no. 31 (3 August 1904); "From the Life of Poles in America," *Dziennik Chicagoski* 16, no. 72 (27 March 1905); "The Agitation between the Socialist Party and the Nationalist League Amidst Polish America," *Narod Polski* 9, no. 14 (5 April 1905); and "Allegiance to Pope Renewed," *Chicago Daily Tribune*, 19 February 1906; *Chicago Daily Tribune*, 23 September 1908; and *Chicago Daily Tribune*, 8 August 1913. The *Narod Polski* and *Dziennik Chicagoski* articles are available via the Chicago Foreign Language Press Survey. For more on the Polish Resurrectionists' anti-socialism in particular, see George S. Pabis, "The Polish Press in Chicago and American Labor Strikes: 1892 to 1912," *Polish American Studies* 48, no. 1 (Spring 1991). John Radzilowski advances a contrasting and ultimately less persuasive interpretation in "Rev. Wincenty Barzynski and a

Polish Catholic Response to Industrial Capitalism," *Polish American Studies* 58, no. 2 (Autumn 2001): 23–32.

105. See, for example, "Envoy of Pope Talks," *Chicago Chronicle*, 31 July 1905, in the Chicago Foreign Language Press Survey; "Socialism Peril to Nation," *Chicago Daily Tribune*, 13 February 1908; and "Poles Dedicate Huge School," *Chicago Daily Tribune*, 10 May 1908.

106. Much anti-clerical literature focused on purported scandals involving clergy. For examples of this sub-genre and others, see "Churches on Decline," *Svornost*, 29 March 1899; *Svenska Nyheter*, 22 September 1903; *Svenska Nyheter*, 26 April 1904; "How Churches are Built," *Dziennik Ludowy*, 20 May 1907; "Evangelistic Racket," *La Parola dei Socialisti*, 18 April 1908; "Roman and Polish Slaves," *Dziennik Ludowy* 2, no. 177 (30 July 1908); "Letter from a Priest Housekeeper to Bicz Bozy," *Bicz Bozy* 4, no. 4 (21 January 1912); "This and That," *Bicz Bozy* 4, no. 24 (9 June 1912); "Isn't That Terrible?" *Bicz Bozy* 4, no. 25 (16 June 1912); "Sinister Activities of Clerical Swine," *La Parola dei Socialisti*, 28 June 1913; and "The Infiltration of the Black-Frocked Sect into the Hull House," *La Parola Dei Socialisti*, 10 January 1914.

107. "Love They Neighbor as Thyself," *Dziennik Ludowy*, 9 April 1907.

108. See, for example, "Condemns Socialism," *Chicago Socialist* 5, no. 211 (21 March 1903): 3; "Scattering Paragraphs," *Chicago Socialist* 5, no. 216 (25 April 1903): 4; Father Thomas Hagerty, "Economic Discontent," *Chicago Socialist* 5, no. 219 (16 May 1903): 1; Father Thomas Hagerty, "Catholic Workingmen and their Relation to the Socialist Movement," *Chicago Socialist* 5, no. 234 (29 August 1903): 2–3; Ernest Untermann, "Religious Ethics vs. Class Ethics," *Chicago Socialist* 5, no. 257 (6 February 1904): 1; "Priest Denounces Socialism," *Chicago Socialist* 6, no. 266 (9 April 1904): 2; "Catholics Fight Socialism," *Chicago Socialist* 6, no. 275 (11 June 1904); "Jesuit Calls Socialism Evil," *Chicago Socialist* 6, no. 283 (6 August 1904): 2; "Our Catholic Critics," *Chicago Socialist* 6, no. 307 (21 January 1905): 2; "The Church and the Workers," *Chicago Socialist* 6, no. 363 (17 February 1906): 4; "Cardinal Gibbons on Equality," *Chicago Socialist* 6, no. 368 (24 March 1906): 4; "Socialism and the Catholic Church," *Chicago Socialist* 6, no. 381 (23 June 1906): 1; and "Archbishop Ireland and Socialism," *Chicago Socialist* 6, no. 402 (17 November 1906): 4.

109. For post-election coverage, see "The Approach of Radicalism," *New World* 13, no. 11 (12 November 1904): 17; August Bebber, "Socialism Attacks the Church," *New World* 13, no. 28 (11 March 1905): 14–15; "One Bishop and a Strike," *New World* 13, no. 15 (10 December 1904): 10; "The Socialist Peril," *New World* 13, no. 16 (17 December 1904): 6; and "Is Socialism Incurable?" *New World* 13, no. 19 (7 January 1905): 14–15.

CHAPTER 7

1. Hopkins, *The Rise of the Social Gospel in American Protestantism*, 280.

2. Among many other things. For the full text of the Creed, see David Nelson Duke, *In the Trenches with Jesus and Marx: Harry F. Ward and the Struggle for Social Justice* (Tuscaloosa: University of Alabama Press, 2003), 60–61.

3. See Hopkins, *The Rise of the Social Gospel in American Protestantism*, 280–317; and Abell, *American Catholicism and Social Action*, 137–188.

4. See Foner, *History of the Labor Movement in the United States*, 1:518–524.

5. See Laurie, *Artisans into Workers*, 183.

6. Ibid., 185–198.

7. For a fuller discussion of Gompers, prudential unionism, and the trajectory of the AFL, see Laurie, *Artisans into Workers*, 176–210.

8. In 1890 the AFL boasted 200,000 members; in 1897, it counted only 264,825. See Laurie, *Artisans into Workers*, 183; and Foner, *History of the Labor Movement in the United States*, 1:27.

9. Ibid., 26–28.

10. See Richard Schneirov, "Labor and the New Liberalism in the Wake of the Pullman Strike," in Richard Schneirov, Shelton Stromquist, and Nick Salvatore, eds., *The Pullman Strike and the Crisis of the 1890s: Essays on Labor and Politics* (Urbana: University of Illinois Press, 1999), 219–222.

11. James R. Barrett, "Unity and Fragmentation: Class, Race and Ethnicity on Chicago's South Side, 1900–1922," *Journal of Social History* 18, no. 1 (August 1984): 49.

12. The Federation had good reason to cultivate the Church's support: its members were overwhelmingly Catholic. See Foner, *History of the Labor Movement in the United States*, 1:112.

13. See, for example, "Trade Unions," *New World* 7, no. 45 (8 July 1899): 14; "American Federation of Labor," *New World* 8, no. 9 (28 October 1899): 16; "Federation of Labor," *New World* 8, no. 10 (4 November 1899): 16; "Federation of Labor and Central Unions," *New World* 8, no. 11 (11 November 1899): 16; and "Federation of Labor," *New World* 8, no. 13 (25 November 1899): 16. Also, consider that an 1897 editorial in the *New World* cited the AFL's *American Federationist* against Debs's experiment in "cooperative colonization." "Mr. Debs' Experiment," *New World* 5, no. 50 (7 August 1897): 8.

14. "Current Topics," *New World* 7, no. 17 (24 December 1898): 3. Catholic leaders celebrated other failed socialist takeovers. See, for example, *New World* 12 (23 January 1904): 1; *New World* 12, no. 45 (9 July 1904): 3; "Another Rejection of Socialism," *New World* 13, no. 13 (26 November 1904); M. I. Boarman, S.J. "Socialism Crushed in Massachusetts," *New World* 14, no. 10 (4 November 1905).

15. "A Socialistic Organization," *New World* 13, no. 22 (30 January 1904): 16; "The Agitators at Home," *New World* 13, no. 23 (6 February 1904): 16; "The

Church the Friend of Labor," *New World* 12, no. 26 (27 February 1904): 12, 24; *New World* 12, no. 36 (7 May 1904): 3; "An Outbreak of Anarchy," *New World* 12, no. 41 (11 June 1904): 17; "The Conflict in Colorado," *New World* 12, no. 42 (18 June 1904): 16; "A New Economic Devilfish," *New World* 13, no. 20 (14 January 1905): 17; "An Insidious Enemy of Labor," *New World* 13, no. 28 (11 March 1905): 17; "Still Assailing the Church," *New World* 13, no. 30 (25 March 1905): 16; *New World* 13, no. 34 (22 April 1905): 17; "Merely Fishing for Gudgeons," *New World* 13, no. 41 (10 June 1905): 16; "Topics of the Hour," *New World* 13, no. 44 (1 July 1905): 3; "And Now the Industrial Shirkers," *New World* 13, no. 45 (8 July 1905): 16; and "The Manufacture of Blue Wool," *New World* 14, no. 1 (2 September 1905): 14.

16. "An Insidious Enemy of Labor," *New World* 13, no. 28 (11 March 1905): 17.

17. See, for example, "Topics of the Hour," *New World* 13, no. 38 (20 May 1905): 3; "Topics of the Hour," *New World* 13, no. 22 (30 January 1904): 3; and "Attacking Honest John Mitchell," *New World* 16, no. 43 (20 June 1908): 14.

18. "A War on Socialism Begun," *New World* 12, no. 47 (23 July 1904): 11.

19. "Topics of the Hour," *New World* 12, no. 45 (9 July 1904): 3.

20. "Federation of Labor," *New World* 12, no. 45 (9 July 1904): 26.

21. See, for example, "John Mitchell on Strikes," *New World* 12, no. 36 (7 May 1904): 16; Samuel Gompers, "Labor and Socialism War?" *New World* 13, no. 24 (11 February 1905): 11; and Hugh McGregor, "Labor Wars on Socialism," *New World* 13, no. 41 (10 June 1905): 8.

22. For more on Pike's expertise, including a report that he won a national prize for a sermon on the theme, "Compel Them to Come In," see George Whitefield Mead, *Modern Methods in Church Work: The Gospel Renaissance* (New York: Dodd, Mead and Company, 1897), 35; and the *Christian Work and Evangelist* 74 (1903): 506. "He Shows His Venom," *Chicago Daily Tribune*, 10 September 1895. Pike elaborated the reasons for his more general opposition to trades unionism in an 1899 book. See Granville Ross Pike, *The Divine Drama: The Manifestation of God in the Universe* (London: MacMillan & Company, 1899), 221–273.

23. See, for examples, "Ministers Discuss Labor Day," *Chicago Daily Tribune*, 5 September 1898; "Some Lessons of Labor Day," *Chicago Daily Tribune*, 4 September 1899; "Pulpit Talks on Labor," *Chicago Daily Tribune*, 26 March 1900; "Points out Labor's Foes," *Chicago Daily Tribune*, 27 April 1903; "Religion a Cure for Strikes," *Chicago Daily Tribune*, 8 June 1903; "Gospel Offers a Solution," *Chicago Daily Tribune*, 15 June 1903; "Preaches for Open Shop," *Chicago Daily Tribune*, 19 October 1903; "Pastors Call for Peace," *Chicago Daily Tribune*, 23 November 1903; "Church Has Strike Cure," *Chicago Daily Tribune*, 16 November 1903; and "'Bums' Drawn into Church," *Chicago Daily Tribune*, 12 August 1907.

24. The Armour Institute merged with the Lewis Institute in 1940 to form what is now the Illinois Institute of Technology.

25. This was not the only occasion upon which Gunsaulus's oratory powerfully affected Armour. He wrote to Gunsaulus in a letter dated May 11, 1895, "I am sorry I will not be at Plymouth Church to-morrow, as I always feel much better and greatly rested after listening to your voice; and I might add about all the rest I have had for the past year is the little relief I get every Sunday at Plymouth Church and the Armour Mission." See Philip D. Armour to F. W. Gunsaulus, IIT Archive, Box 1, Folder 6, number 1998.24. For more on the "Million-Dollar Sermon," see article entitled, "Frank Wakeley Gunsaulus, the Poet-Preacher," by Rev. J. W. Luccock, contained in the Gunsaulus collection at the IIT archives, item number1991.10.

26. Clara E. Laughlin, "The Armour Institute," *Interior* 25, no. 1243 (22 March 1894): 369–372.

27. The 1900 census lists Gunsaulus's address as 2618 Prairie Avenue. The neighborhood had already passed its glory days and Gunsaulus's house lay several blocks south of the most impressive mansions, but this address still had considerable cachet at the turn of the century.

28. On his support for scientific charity, see, for example, "Rob in Misery's Cloak," *Chicago Daily Tribune*, 16 February 1897.

29. "Planning to Save Young Men," *Chicago Daily Tribune*, 25 September 1899.

30. Ibid. See also "Labor Is Honorable to All," *Chicago Daily Tribune*, 3 February 1902.

31. "Take Trusts for Text," *Chicago Daily Tribune*, 18 September 1899.

32. Frank W. Gunsaulus, "Triumph of American Labor," *Chicago Daily Tribune*, 28 June 1903; and "City Seen from Pulpits," *Chicago Daily Tribune*, 28 September 1903.

33. For examples of Gunsaulus's career-long opposition to all forms of radicalism, see "Another View of the Case," *Chicago Daily Tribune*, 31 October 1887; "Argument as Against the Pope," *Chicago Daily Tribune*, 25 November 1887; "Justice in Sorry Plight," *Chicago Daily Tribune*, 26 November 1906; "Wants Schools in Churches," *Chicago Daily Tribune*, 31 December 1907; "Bible Opposed to Socialism," *Chicago Daily Tribune*, 25 March 1908; and "Socialist Menace Worst in the U.S.," *Chicago Daily Tribune*, 9 November 1908.

34. "Voice of Pulpit in Miners' Cause," *Chicago Daily Tribune*, 6 October 1902; and "Justice in Sorry Plight," *Chicago Daily Tribune*, 26 November 1906. See also "Pulpit Praise of Armour," *Chicago Daily Tribune*, 14 January 1901; "Abraham a Model Employer," *Chicago Daily Tribune*, 17 March 1902; and "Religion a Cure for Strikes," *Chicago Daily Tribune*, 8 June 1903.

35. Notably, his support was not unqualified. He declared, "I should advocate the forming of servant girl unions, provided they are directed by sane and Christian leaders." See "Urges a Servants' Union," *Chicago Daily Tribune*, 16 October 1905.

36. "Toilers Praised by Clergy," *Chicago Daily Tribune*, 6 September 1909.

37. In the 1912 decision the Classis added that a CRC member who joined a union could not hold any office within the church, and furthermore that the member must resign from the union if it authorized violence or other "violations of God's commandments." For more on the CRC's evolving attitudes toward unions, see Swierenga, *Dutch Chicago*, 640–649.

38. See "Labor Unions and the Church," *Svenska Nyheter*, 22 December 1903.

39. The resolution's language offered yet another illustration of how hegemonic the discourse of contractual freedom had become: the annual meeting justified its stance in terms not only of scripture but also of "the nature of free contract." For more on the *Missionsförbundet*—a still-active denomination known in the United States as the Evangelical Covenant Church—and labor protest, see Zenos Hawkinson, "An Interpretation of the Background of the Evangelical Mission Covenant Church of America," *Swedish Pioneer* 2, no. 1 (Summer 1951): 3–14.

40. "Toilers Praised by Clergy," *Chicago Daily Tribune*, 6 September 1909.

41. Fallows served this church from 1875 until his death in 1922. See "Public Funeral on Friday for Bishop Fallows," *Chicago Daily Tribune*, 6 September 1922.

42. See especially "Time for Real Help," *Chicago Daily Tribune*, 29 August 1893; "Is the Church Decadent?" *Chicago Daily Tribune*, 28 January 1900; and "Church Friend to Labor," *Chicago Daily Tribune*, 27 July 1903.

43. "Bishop Fallows on Labor Problems," *Chicago Daily Tribune*, 17 July 1892; and "Bishop Fallows Supports Labor," *Chicago Daily Tribune*, 25 July 1892. Fallows talk of the worker's "moral right" was reminiscent of the sentiments Pope Leo XIII expressed in his ground-breaking encyclical *Rerum Novarum* the previous year.

44. For a roster of the prominent men who comprised the vestry early in Fallows tenure, see Alice Katharine Fallows, *Everybody's Bishop: The Life and Times of the Right Reverend Samuel Fallows, D.D.* (New York: J. H. Sears & Company, 1927), 282. It is not clear whether he came under the censure of his vestry or his political party, but what is clear is that he had a change of heart in the years after 1892.

45. "Labor Day Text for Sermons," *Chicago Daily Tribune*, 7 September 1903. In this same sermon, he cast the fact of Labor Day as a measure of the exceptionality of American civilization, saying, "Heathenism has no Labor day. Barbarism has none. Mohammedanism, with its unspeakable Turks and allied fierce peoples, knows of no such demonstration."

46. See, for example, "In the Cause of Labor," *Chicago Daily Tribune*, 30 March 1896; "Plan for a 'Miner's Day' in the Chicago Churches," *Chicago Daily Tribune*, 30 August 1902; "Arbitration by Compulsion Is Fallows' Plea," *Chicago Examiner*, 4 September 1916.

47. "Lockout the Theme of Sermons," *Chicago Daily Tribune*, 16 April 1894.

48. For more on Fallows's worries, see, for example, "Lockout the Theme of Sermons"; "Five-Minute Talk on 'Strikes,' " *Chicago Daily Tribune*, 13 May 1895; "Pulpit on City's Perils," *Chicago Daily Tribune*, 10 May 1897; "On Christianity and Labor," *Chicago Daily Tribune*, 4 September 1899; "Pulpit Talks on Labor," *Chicago Daily Tribune*, 26 March 1900.

49. In a similar vein, many Protestant moderates endorsed unions but rejected any move toward the closed shop. See, for example, "Preaches for the Open Shop," *Chicago Daily Tribune*, 21 September 1903. They more predictably recoiled at vandalism, violence, and the violation of contracts. See, for just one example, "Labor Day Text for Sermons," *Chicago Daily Tribune*, 7 September 1903.

50. "Car Porters in Revolt," *Chicago Daily Tribune*, 4 August 1901.

51. By 1900, Chicago counted 30,150 African Americans. See Milton C. Sernett, *Bound for the Promised Land: African American Religion and the Great Migration* (Durham, NC: Duke University Press, 1997), 155.

52. Reverdy C. Ransom, *The Industrial and Social Condition of the Negro: A Thanksgiving Sermon* (Chicago: Conservator Print, 1896).

53. Ibid.

54. See Reverdy C. Ransom, "The Negro and Socialism," in Anthony B. Pinn, ed., *Making the Gospel Plain: The Writings of Bishop Reverdy C. Ransom* (Harrisburg, PA: Trinity Press International, 1999), 188.

55. Annetta Louise Gomez-Jefferson, *The Sage of Tawawa: Reverdy Cassius Ransom, 1861–1959* (Kent, OH: Kent State University Press, 2003), 66–67, 69.

56. Reverdy C. Ransom, "The Institutional Church and Social Settlement," in Pinn, ed., *Making the Gospel Plain*, 254.

57. Quoted in Gomez-Jefferson, *The Sage of Tawawa*, 67.

58. See "Want Negro Vote Used," *Chicago Daily Tribune*, 19 August 1899; "Preaches on Race Chasm," *Chicago Daily Tribune*, 20 August 1900; "Inquiry on City Negroes," *Chicago Daily Tribune*, 14 July 1902; "Ministers' Meetings," *Advance*, 12 May 1904; "Negroes Protest Against Race Prejudice in Strike," *Chicago Daily Tribune*, 10 May 1905; "Cease to Support Striking Drivers," *Chicago Daily Tribune*, 27 May 1905; and Terrel Dale Goddard, "The Black Social Gospel in Chicago, 1896–1906: The Ministries of Reverdy C. Ransom and Richard R. Wright, Jr," *Journal of Negro History* 84, no. 3 (Summer 1999): 237, 242. Ransom later remembered playing a key role in the resolution of a 1902 stockyards strike, though I have been unable to corroborate his account. See "The Institutional Church and Social Settlement," in Pinn, ed., *Making the Gospel Plain*, 256–257; and Reverdy C. Ransom, *The Pilgrimage of Harriet Ransom's Son* (Nashville, TN: Sunday School Union, 1949), 113–114. On Ransom's troubled relationship with Carey, see *The Pilgrimage of Harriet Ransom's Son*. For more on the over-all shape of black life in Chicago during these years, see Christopher Robert Reed, *Black Chicago's First Century*, Vol. 1: *1833–1900* (Columbia: University of Missouri Press, 2005), 337–444.

59. "At Outs on Amusements," *Chicago Daily Tribune*, 24 April 1900. See also "Church and Labor," *Chicago Daily Tribune*, 16 September 1895.

60. "For a True Friend," *Railway Times* 2, no. 18 (16 September 1895): 4. In a similar vein, Debs singled Carwardine out as one of only a handful of pro-labor ministers in all the American churches. See, for example, the undated clipping entitled "Pulpit and Labor," Thomas J. Morgan Collection, Box 1, Folder 17, Illinois Historical Survey, Urbana, IL.

61. "Woman's Place at Home," *Chicago Daily Tribune*, 19 August 1901.

62. "W. H. Carwardine on Miners' Strike," *Chicago Daily Tribune*, 9 August 1897. For other examples of Carwardine speaking up for workers, see, for example, "Carwardine on Labor Unions," *Chicago Daily Tribune*, 16 August 1897; "W. H. Carwardine on Riches," *Chicago Daily Tribune*, 23 August 1897; "Denounces Governor Tanner," *Chicago Daily Tribune*, 6 September 1897; "Labor Day Text for Sermons," *Chicago Daily Tribune*, 7 September 1903; "Pastors Call for Peace," *Chicago Daily Tribune*, 23 November 1903; "Chicago and Vicinity," *Northwestern Christian Advocate*, 3 August 1904. See also Carwardine's hundreds of contributions to the newspaper, which are readily accessible via the Chicago Public Library's electronic resources page.

63. "Pulpit Praise of Armour," *Chicago Daily Tribune*, 14 January 1901. For more examples, see also "Pulpit Talks on Labor," *Chicago Daily Tribune*, 26 March 1900; "For Shirt Waists in Church," *Chicago Daily Tribune*, 19 August 1901; and "Sway of Gold in Church," *Chicago Daily Tribune*, 21 October 1901.

64. See Duke, *In the Trenches with Jesus and Marx*, 51–52.

65. Ibid., 59–61.

66. "Presbyterian Labor Envoy," *Congregationalist and Christian World*, 22 March 1902.

67. Quoted in Nash III, "Charles Stelzle," 155.

68. Charles Stelzle, "Evangelism among the 'Class-Conscious,'" *Interior* 36, no. 1806 (5 January 1905): 7–8.

69. "Church Clings to its Old Creed," *Chicago Daily Tribune*, 24 May 1905. In addition to calling for a shift in the churches' attitude toward labor, Stelzle also spearheaded a variety of concrete initiatives, including a Presbyterian Labor Sunday and evangelistic outreaches in factories and shops. For some of the myriad examples of his outreach to churchmen, see also *Interior* 35, no. 1755 (14 January 1904): 59; Charles Stelzle, "World's Fair Evangelistic Campaign," *Interior* 35, no. 1795 (20 October 1904); Charles Stelzle, "The Presbyterian Church and Workingmen," *Interior* 36, no. 1842 (14 September 1905): 1157–1158; Charles Stelzle, "Echoes from Labor Day Sunday," *Interior* 36, no. 1844 (28 September 1905): 1216–1217; Charles Stelzle, "Working Men and 'Tainted' Money," *Congregationalist and Christian World*, 16 September 1905; Charles Stelzle, "A Shop Campaign," *Interior* 36, no. 1846 (12 October 1905): 1279–1280; Charles Stelzle, "Some Methods of Approach," *Interior* 36,

no. 1848 (26 October 1905): 1345; *Interior* 36, no. 1848 (26 October 1905): 1365; and Charles Stelzle, "The Friendly Attitude toward Unionism," *Interior* 36, no. 1856 (21 December 1905): 1672–1673.

70. For more on the CFL's internal process, see "Minutes of Meeting," Chicago Federation of Labor, 20 March, 17 April, and 1 May 1904, Chicago History Museum, Chicago, IL. For more on the considerable controversy the petition generated, see "War on a Preacher," *Chicago Daily Tribune*, 21 March 1904; "Newspapers and Pulpits," *Chicago Daily Tribune*, 22 March 1904; *Independent*, 24 March 1904; "Labor Chased to its Lair," *New World* 12, no. 30 (26 March 1904): 16; "Ministers as Walking Delegates," *Public Opinion* 36, no. 13 (31 March 1904): 407–408; *Interior* 35, no. 1766 (31 March 1904): 398; "Preachers and Labor," *Northwestern Christian Advocate* 52, no. 14 (6 April 1904): 3–4; "Labor Scorns a Pastor," *Chicago Daily Tribune*, 11 April 1904; and "All Christianity Arraigned," *New World* 12, no. 33 (16 April 1904): 17.

71. See Charles Stelzle, "Federated Labor's Response," *Interior* 36, no. 1853 (30 November 1905): 1540; and in a related vein, "Labor and the Church," *Congregationalist and Christian World*, 15 December 1906. Similarly, in framing the importance of Labor Sunday in 1906, he declared, "On Sunday, September 2nd, then, the workingmen of this country have an appointment to go to church." Charles Stelzle, "'Labor Sunday,'" *Northwestern Christian Advocate*, 15 August 1906.

72. See "Personal Paragraphs from Labor Leaders," in Box 14, Folder 1 of the Charles Stelzle Papers, housed in the Rare Book and Manuscript Library at Columbia University.

73. See Charles Stelzle, "Is the Church Opposed to Workingmen?" *Blacksmiths Journal* 6, no. 11 (November 1905): 33; Charles Stelzle, "How the Church and Labor May Cooperate," *Motorman and Conductor* 13 (February 1906): 29; Charles Stelzle, "Jesus Christ—Union Carpenter," *Blacksmiths Journal* 8, no. 5 (May 1907): 9; and Nash, "Charles Stelzle," 156.

74. Newman Hall Burdick, "Some Impressions Mr. Stelzle Makes," *Interior* 36, no. 1818 (30 March 1905): 386. See also "Rev. Charles Stelzle," *Interior* 35, no. 1769 (21 April 1904): 496; and "Calls Socialism Church Usurper," *Chicago Daily Tribune*, 25 March 1908.

75. For more on the context for and progress of the strike, see James Barrett, *Work and Community in the Jungle: Chicago's Packinghouse Workers, 1894–1922* (Urbana: University of Illinois Press, 1987): 165–182.

76. "The Strikers Are Not Socialists," *New World* 12, no. 50 (13 August 1904): 17. For more *New World* coverage of the packinghouse strike, see "The Great Strike Begins," *New World* 12, no. 46 (16 July 1904): 16; "The Great Strike Settled," *New World* 12, no. 47 (23 July 1904): 16; "Settle the Great Strike," *New World* 12, no. 48 (30 July 1904): 17; "The Catholic Press on the Strike," *New World* 12, no. 49 (6 August 1904): 8; "The Progress of the Strike," *New World* 12, no. 49 (6 August

1904): 16; *New World* 12, no. 50 (13 August 1904): 3; "Not the Right Spirit," *New World* 12, no. 51 (20 August 1904): 17; "Should the President Interfere?" *New World* 12, no. 51 (20 August 1904): 17; and *New World* 13, no. 1 (3 September 1904): 3.

77. See, for example, "The Packers' Strike," *Northwestern Christian Advocate*, 20 July 1904; "The Packers & the Strikers," *Christian Century* 21, no. 29 (21 July 1904): 656; "The Stock Yards Strike," *Northwestern Christian Advocate*, 27 July 1904; *Interior* 35, no. 1783 (28 July 1904): 993; *Interior* 35, no. 1787 (25 August 1904): 1095–1096; and *Interior* 35, no. 1790 (15 September 1904): 1207.

78. For more on Catholic priests' varied reactions to the strike, see "Strikers Have Stocks of Food," *Chicago Daily Tribune*, 24 July 1904; "Drivers' Council Against Strike," *Chicago Daily Tribune*, 25 July 1904; "Bring in More Workers," *Chicago Daily Tribune*, 26 July 1904; and "Clergymen Pray Unions May Win," *Chicago Daily Tribune*, 8 August 1904.

79. See "Clergymen Pray Unions May Win"; and "Preach on the Strike," *Chicago Daily Tribune*, 12 September 1904.

80. For more on the teamsters' strike of 1905, see David Witwer, "Unionized Teamsters and the Struggle over the Streets of the Early-Twentieth-Century City," *Social Science History* 24, no. 1 (2000): 183–222.

81. "Violence Always a Great Mistake," *New World* 13, no. 33 (15 April 1905): 16–17. For other examples of denunciations of violence, see, for example, "Chicago Strike," *Christian Century* 22, no. 17 (27 April 1905); and "'Strike' Is Sermon Topic," *Chicago Daily Tribune*, 1 May 1905. As in times past, Protestants lambasted the municipal authorities for not aggressively defeating the mob. The Reverend David Beaton declared, "as for the idea of a city government permitting the rioters, thugs and mercenaries to usurp the streets to the lasting disgrace of the city, that is so preposterous and ludicrous a condition." See "'Strike' Is Sermon Topic," *Chicago Daily Tribune*, 8 May 1905.

82. The *New World* was especially dogged in calling for compulsory arbitration. The *Christian Century* also espoused this view, while the *Interior* remained less than enthused about it. Bishop Fallows advocated for "compulsory investigation" and voluntary arbitration, a proposal also favored by the *Northwestern Christian Advocate*. See "Would Compulsory Arbitration Avail?" *New World* 13, no. 36 (6 May 1905): 17; "Some Things It Would Do," *New World* 13, no. 37 (13 May 1905): 16; "The Spread of the Strike," *New World* 13, no. 39 (27 May 1905): 16; "Topics of the Hour," *New World* 13, no. 42 (17 June 1905): 3; "Chicago Strike," *Christian Century* 22, no. 17 (27 April 1905); "The Strike Evil," *Interior* 36, no. 1822 (27 April 1905): 512; "'Strike' Is Sermon Topic," 8 May 1905; and "The Teamsters' Strike in Chicago," *Northwestern Christian Advocate*, 3 May 1905, 5–6. When the mayor eventually appointed an arbitration committee, it included the progressive Reverend Graham Taylor, who denounced the union leadership in the papers. See the materials

in "Teamsters Strike of 1905—memoranda, manuscript notes and typewritten," in Series 5, Box 32, Folder 1814 of the Graham Taylor Papers, Newberry Library, Chicago, IL.

83. "'Strike' Is Sermon Topic," *Chicago Daily Tribune*, 1 May 1905. For other examples of religious leaders coming to the public's defense, see "Certain to Injure All," *New World* 13, no. 35 (29 April 1905): 17; "Topics of the Hour," *New World* 13, no. 37 (13 May 1905); "Teamsters' Strike," *Christian Century* 22, no. 18 (4 May 1905); and "The Strike," *Christian Century* 22, no. 20 (18 May 1905): 492.

84. "The Catholic Press on the Strike," *New World* 13, no. 50 (12 August 1905): 12. See also "Topics of the Hour," *New World* 13, no. 43 (24 June 1905): 3; and "Topics of the Hour," *New World* 13, no. 47 (22 July 1905): 3.

85. See "'Strike' Is Sermon Topic," *Chicago Daily Tribune*, 8 May 1905; "The Strike in Chicago," *Northwestern Christian Advocate*, 10 May 1905; and also, for other examples, "Labor's Worst Foe," *Northwestern Christian Advocate* 53, no. 20 (17 May 1905); "The Strike," *Christian Century* 22, no. 20 (18 May 1905): 492; "The Teamsters' Strike," *Northwestern Christian Advocate*, 7 June 1905; "The Teamsters' Strike Ended," *Northwestern Christian Advocate*, 26 July 1905; "End of the Strike," *Interior* 36, no. 1835 (27 July 1905): 939; *Interior* 36, no. 1835 (27 July 1905): 942; *Living Church*, 29 July 1905; and "A Strike Fiasco," *Christian Century* 22, no. 31 (3 August 1905).

86. "The Strike in Chicago."

87. "Strike Lessons a Text," *Chicago Daily Tribune*, 24 July 1905.

88. "'Strike' Is Sermon Topic," 1 May 1905.

EPILOGUE

1. Walter Rauschenbush, *Christianizing the Social Order* (New York: McMillan Company, 1913), 12.

2. "Harnessmaker in the Pulpit," *Chicago Daily Tribune*, 20 December 1897.

3. "Bible Class Hears Socialist," *Chicago Daily Tribune*, 10 November 1902.

4. *Chicago Socialist* 4, no. 193 (15 November 1902): 2.

5. *Chicago Socialist* 4, no. 194 (22 November 1902): 2.

6. "Voice of Pulpit in Miners' Cause," *Chicago Daily Tribune*, 6 October 1902.

7. "Declares Riches Control Church," *Chicago Daily Tribune*, 18 June 1906.

8. Quoted in Elliott J. Gorn, *Mother Jones: The Most Dangerous Woman in America* (New York: Hill and Wang, 2001), 147.

9. Quoted in Melvyn Dubofsky, *We Shall Be All: A History of the Industrial Workers of the World*, ed. Joseph A. McCartin (Urbana: University of Illinois Press, 2000), 95. See also Donald E. Winters, Jr., *The Soul of the Wobblies: The I.W.W., Religion, and American Culture in the Progressive Era, 1905–1917* (Westport, CT: Greenwood Press, 1985).

10. "Arrest Hits New Religion," *Chicago Daily Tribune*, 30 August 1909.

11. "Labor Plea Cites Bible," *Chicago Daily Tribune*, 24 May 1906.

12. "Use Bible to Shut Groceries Sunday," *Chicago Examiner*, 13 June 1910.

13. "Civic Branch Body Here," *Chicago Daily Tribune*, 15 January 1907. For mention of Maloney's hanging of the Madonna, see Debra Campbell, "American Catholic Women, 1900–1965," in Rosemary Skinner Keller, Rosemary Radford Reuther, and Marie Cantlon, eds., *Encyclopedia of Women and Religion in North America*, Vol. 1 (Bloomington: Indiana University Press, 2006), 189.

14. "Bible as a Strike Weapon; Impresses Idle Operators," *Chicago Daily Tribune*, 29 September 1907.

15. For more on women's organizing in Gilded Age Chicago, see Meredith Tax, *The Rising of the Women: Feminist Solidarity and Class Conflict, 1880–1917* (Urbana: University of Illinois Press, 2001), 13–72.

16. Philip S. Foner, *History of the Labor Movement in the United States*, Vol. 3: *The Policies and Practices of the American Federation of Labor, 1900–1909* (New York: International Publishers, 1964), 232.

17. Nestor later wrote of the CFL's longtime president, for example, "John Fitzpatrick was my great friend and counselor." See Agnes Nestor, *Woman's Labor Leader: An Autobiography of Agnes Nestor* (Rockford, IL: Bellevue Books Publishing Co, 1954), 44. For more on the above, see Maureen Flanagan, *Seeing with Their Hearts: Chicago Women and the Vision of the Good City, 1871–1933* (Princeton, NJ: Princeton University Press, 2002); Tax, *The Rising of the Women*; and Patricia A. Lamoureux, "Irish Catholic Women and the Labor Movement," *U.S. Catholic Historian* 16, no. 3 (Summer 1998): 24–44.

18. Nestor attended mass faithfully. As a young woman she diligently recorded her attendance in her diary; on those occasions when she could not make it, she made sure to give a reason. What remains extant of the diary can be found in the Agnes Nestor Papers, Reel 1, Chicago History Museum, Chicago, IL. While Nestor remained often quiet on the question of her faith's relationship to her activism, others would be more effusive, especially later in her life and as her accomplishments became more widely recognized. In 1929, Loyola University Chicago presented her with an honorary Doctor of Laws degree for her "outstanding work as a citizen and a pioneer for industrial betterment." When news of the honor got out, many admirers wrote to congratulate her, including one Rose J. McHugh, who remarked, "I know few women who have done more to preserve and secure us certain essential conditions of Catholic living than have you." See Frederick Siedenberg to Miss Agnes Nestor, 16 May 1929, Agnes Nestor Papers, Reel 3; and Rose J. McHugh to Miss Nestor, 7 June 1929, Agnes Nestor Papers, Reel 3. The one point at which Nestor did tout her Catholic faith was in her 1928 campaign for the office of state representative. Eager to court the vast Catholic vote, she paid for dozens of advertisements in parish bulletins. At the bottom of most every one of these was the clause, "Member of Our Lady of Lourdes Parish." One exception was that, in the ad she placed in St. Vincent's

Church bulletin, she highlighted instead, "Former Member of St. Vincent's Parish for sixteen years." See the numerous parish bulletins included in the campaign materials in the Agnes Nestor Papers, Reel 6. For more on the faith of Nestor and some of her colleagues, see Lamoureux, "Irish Catholic Women and the Labor Movement." For a more comprehensive treatment of the crucial role Irish-Catholic women played in Chicago's early twentieth-century labor movement, see Suellen Hoy, "The Irish Girls' Rising: Building the Women's Labor Movement in Progressive-Era Chicago," *Labor: Studies in Working-Class History of the Americas* 9, no. 1 (Spring 2012): 77–100. Of course, not all the League's women found inspiration in Christian faith. In her autobiography Mary Anderson recalled standing outside many a Catholic church early on Sunday morning to distribute leaflets, but made clear, "I did not go to church myself." See Mary Anderson, *Woman at Work: The Autobiography of Mary Anderson as told to Mary N. Winslow* (Westport, CT: Greenwood Press, 1951), 48, 69.

19. Consider these incredulous headlines: "Workingwomen to Preach?" *Chicago Daily Tribune*, 20 June 1910; "One Preacher is a Girl," *Chicago Examiner*, 5 September 1910; and "One Woman to Preach," *Chicago Daily Tribune*, 4 September 1910. She spoke also, for example, to the Catholic Woman's League in 1907; at St. Paul's Universalist Church in 1908; and at Jenkin Lloyd Jones's church at Lincoln Center in 1909. See Rose A. Trainor to Agnes Nestor, 14 February 1907, Agnes Nestor Papers, Reel 1; W. H. MacPherson to Miss Agnes Nestor, 29 October 1907, Agnes Nestor Papers, Reel 1; and Nestor, *Woman's Labor Leader*, 119.

20. See "Workers and Divines Share Pulpits on 'Labor Sunday,'" *Chicago Examiner*, 5 September 1910.

21. Lamoureux, "Irish Catholic Women and the Labor Movement," 40.

22. "Formulate Task for Arbitrators," *Chicago Daily Tribune*, 23 January 1911.

23. Harriet Ferrill, "Society and Club Women to Canvass City in Aid of Garment Strikers," *Chicago Daily Tribune*, 15 January 1911.

24. For more on O'Callaghan's support of the WTUL, see "Sermon by Father O'Callaghan," *Union Labor Advocate* 8 (December 1908); and letter from Margaret Robins to Raymond Robins, April 28, 1908, Papers of the National Women's Trade Union League, Reel 52, Chicago History Museum. I am deeply grateful to noted historian Suellen Hoy for first calling my attention to these sources. For a list of all donations from churches and religious societies, see "Official Report of the Strike Committee: Chicago Garment Workers' Strike, October 29, 1910–February 18, 1911" (Chicago: Women's Trade Union League, 1911), 47–49.

25. "Milk is Promised for Strike Babies," *Chicago Daily Tribune*, 28 November 1910.

26. See "Ask Why Men 'Backslide,'" *Chicago Daily Tribune*, 18 December 1911; and Bederman, "'The Woman Have Had Charge of the Church Work Long Enough,'" 432.

27. See the section on the Kline family in *History of Lehigh County, Pennsylvania, and a Genealogical and Biographical Record of its Families* (Northampton County, PA: Lehigh Valley Publishing Company, 1914), 679–685. There is no mention of Harrison or James Kline in this history of the family, but there is a paragraph on Daniel Kline, a farmer in Upper Milford township. This corresponds to the 1850 census, which lists Harrison—then 17—as living with this branch of the Kline family.

28. The 1860 census stipulates that Kline was a carpenter and that he owned no real estate, and moreover values the family's personal estate at $330.

29. As reported in the 1870 census.

30. The *Blacksmiths Journal* reports that Kline fled "during the panic of '78," but the 1880 census lists him still at home with Henry and Diana. See *Blacksmiths Journal* 4, no. 11 (November 1903): 19.

31. See ibid.; as well as Peter J. Albert and Grace Palladino, eds., *The Samuel Gompers Papers*, Vol. 8: *Progress and Reaction in the Age of Reform, 1909–13* (Urbana: University of Illinois Press, 2001), 540.

32. His Bible class appears to have enthusiastically supported his involvement in the labor movement. Even after he left Chicago, his friends in that class kept in touch. When they heard that Kline was in San Francisco and engrossed in negotiations regarding a pending railroad strike, they sent, by unanimous vote, a telegram that read, "God bless you in your efforts to do that for which the Master came, and in your future course, if such a peace cannot be honorably achieved. We remembered you to-day to the Divine Superintendent." See *Wesleyan Advocate*, September 1911. I thank Christopher Cantwell for sharing this piece of evidence with me from his excellent work on the social history of fundamentalism in Chicago. See Christopher D. Cantwell, "The Bible Class Teacher: Piety and Politics in the Age of Fundamentalism," (PhD diss., Cornell University, 2012).

33. "Methodism and Labor," *Northwestern Christian Advocate*, 18 April 1906.

34. "Are Methodists Hypocrites?" *Union Labor Advocate* 6, no. 12 (August 1906): 24.

35. "Boycotting Methodism," *Northwestern Christian Advocate*, 30 January 1907.

36. "Refuse a Raise to Drivers," *Chicago Daily Tribune*, 12 April 1908.

37. "Chicago, ILL.," *Typographical Journal* 32, no. 5 (May 1908): 545.

38. See ibid.; as well as "Preachers in Hot Debate over Politics and Labor," *Chicago Daily Tribune*, 7 April 1908.

39. For Kline on the saloon and radicalism, respectively, see, for example, "Labor's New Alignment," *Association Men* 41, no. 12 (September 1916): 680; and "President Kline Delivers Talk," *International Brotherhood of Blacksmiths, Drop Forgers, and Helpers Monthly Journal* 22, no. 12 (December 1920): 46–47.

40. See letter from J. W. Kline to the Editor of the *Northwestern Christian Advocate*, in "The Church and Labor Correspondence and Clippings—Part 2," Records of the Methodist Federation for Social Action, Methodist Collection—Drew University, Madison, New Jersey.

41. For record of his sermons, see "Blacksmith in the Pulpit," *Chicago Daily Tribune*, 11 May 1908; "Church and Trades Unionism," *Blacksmiths Journal* 10, no. 6 (June 1909): 17–22; James W. Kline, "Labor's Opportunity," *Blacksmiths Journal* 8, no. 11 (November 1907): 12–13; and "Can Be Unionists to Grave," *Chicago Daily Tribune*, 9 June 1909.

42. James W. Kline, "The Working Man and the Church," *Blacksmiths Journal* 15, no. 11 (November 1913): 12–16; and "Conference Labor Rally," *Daily Bulletin*, 3 October 1913, and "Bishop M'Dowell Urges Ministers to Strive," *Record Herald*, 3 October 1913, and "Labor Leader Warns Church," *Freeport Daily Standard*, 3 October 1913, all included in "Scrapbook—Part I," Records of the Methodist Federation for Social Action, Methodist Collection—Drew University, Madison, New Jersey.

43. See James W. Kline to the Reverend Harry F. Ward, 5 February 1917, Records of the Methodist Federation for Social Action, Methodist Collection—Drew University, Madison, New Jersey.

44. See various letters in "Correspondence—Part 2," Records of the Methodist Federation for Social Action, Methodist Collection—Drew University, Madison, New Jersey.

45. See James W. Kline to the Reverend Harry F. Ward, 5 February 1917; and Harry F. Ward to Mr. James W. Kline, 9 February 1917, Folder 17, Records of the Methodist Federation for Social Action, Methodist Collection—Drew University, Madison, New Jersey. On the outcome at the 1916 General Conference, see "Lost Cause of Unions," *Los Angeles Times*, 14 May 1916; and on the final resolution see "Methodists Agree to Unionize Printing," *New York Times*, 25 November 1932. For another instance of a frustrated Kline battling against conservatives within the Methodist denomination, see the exchange of letters between he and W. H. Van Benschoten in the *Christian Advocate* 96, no. 15 (14 April 1921): 488; and the *Christian Advocate* 96, no. 18 (5 May 1921): 570.

46. Quoted in John McGreevy, *Catholicism and American Freedom: A History* (New York: W. W. Norton & Company, 2003), 150.

47. Ibid., 151.

48. On labor priests, see Mary Harrita Fox, *Peter E. Dietz: Labor Priest* (Notre Dame, IN: University of Notre Dame Press, 1953); and Kimball Baker, *Go to the Worker: America's Labor Apostles* (Milwaukee, WI: Marquette University Press, 2010). Ryan had first made a name for himself with the publication of his book *A Living Wage* in 1906. He went on to direct the National Catholic Welfare Conference's Social Action Department. For more on his life and work, see Neil Betten, *Catholic Activism and the Industrial Worker* (Gainesville: University Presses of Florida, 1976); and McGreevy, *Catholicism and American Freedom*, 127–165.

49. Betten, *Catholic Activism and the Industrial Worker*, 75, 89.

50. "Bishop Sheil Appeals for Labor's Rights," *New World*, 21 July 1939; and "C.I.O. Threatens Packer Strike on Wage Pacts," *Chicago Daily Tribune*, 17 July 1939.

51. Paul A. Carter, *The Decline and Revival of the Social Gospel: Social and Political Liberalism in American Protestant Churches, 1920–1940* (Ithaca, NY: Cornell University Press, 1954), 149–150; and Ronald C. White, Jr., and C. Howard Hopkins, *The Social Gospel: Religion and Reform in Changing America* (Philadelphia: Temple University Press, 1976), 202–213.

52. Carter, *The Decline and Revival of the Social Gospel*, 167.

53. David M. Kennedy, *Freedom from Fear: The American People in Depression and War, 1929–1945* (New York: Oxford University Press, 2005), 145–146; John Evans, "Wallace Calls on Churches to Back New Deal," *Chicago Daily Tribune*, 8 December 1933; and "New Deal is Based on Christ's Tenets, Ickes Says in Talk," *Chicago Daily Tribune*, 24 May 1934.

54. For a provocative and related analysis of the New Deal itself as a "long exception," see Jefferson Cowie and Nick Salvatore, "The Long Exception: Rethinking the Place of the New Deal in American History," *International Labor and Working-Class History* 74 (Fall 2008): 1–32.

55. Matthew Pehl, "'Apostles of Fascism,' 'Communist Clergy,' and the UAW: Political Ideology and Working-Class Religion in Detroit, 1919–1945," *Journal of American History* 99, no. 2 (September 2012): 450–454.

56. Dochuk, *From Bible Belt to Sunbelt*, 66–76.

57. Ira Katznelson, *Fear Itself: The New Deal and the Origins of Our Time* (New York: Liveright Publishing Corporation, 2013), 131–224.

58. Joel A. Carpenter, *Revive Us Again: The Reawakening of American Fundamentalism* (New York: Oxford University Press, 1997), 66, 78.

59. See, for example, Callahan, *Work and Faith in the Kentucky Coal Fields*; Mario T. García, ed., *The Gospel of César Chávez: My Faith in Action* (New York: Sheed & Ward, 2007); Erik S. Gellman and Jarod Roll, *The Gospel of the Working Class: Labor's Southern Prophets in New Deal America* (Urbana: University of Illinois Press, 2011); Pehl, "'Apostles of Fascism,' 'Communist Clergy,' and the UAW: Political Ideology and Working-Class Religion in Detroit, 1919–1945"; Roll, *Spirit of Rebellion*; as well as a number of the essays in Christopher D. Cantwell, Heath W. Carter, and Janine Giordano Drake, eds., *Between the Pew and the Picket Line: Christianity and the Working Class in Industrial America* (forthcoming with University of Illinois Press).

60. Martin Luther King, Jr., *"All Labor Has Dignity,"* ed. Michael K. Honey (Boston: Beacon Press, 1963), 167–178.

61. Stiglitz, *The Price of Inequality*, 4. In 1970 the top 10% of American income earners commanded only 35% of total income, a modest figure compared to the nearly 50% they commanded in both the late 1920s and the mid-2000s. Piketty, *Capital in the Twenty-First Century*, 291.

62. Dochuk, *From Bible Belt to Sunbelt*; Moreton, *To Serve God and Wal-Mart*; and Kruse, *One Nation under God*.

63. See Kate Bowler, *Blessed: A History of the American Prosperity Gospel* (New York: Oxford University Press, 2013).

64. Josh Bivens, "Inequality, Exhibit A: Walmart and the Wealth of American Families," The Economic Policy Institute Blog, http://www.epi.org/blog/inequality-exhibit-wal-mart-wealth-american/.

Bibliography

PRIMARY SOURCES
Archival Sources

Archives of the Archdiocese of Chicago. Chicago, Illinois.
    Chancery Correspondence.
    St. Gabriel's Church.
Archives of the University of Notre Dame. Notre Dame, Indiana.
    Archdiocese of Chicago Collection.
Chicago History Museum. Chicago, Illinois.
    Agnes Nestor Papers.
    Chicago Federation of Labor Minutes.
    Chicago Typographical Union No. 16 Collection.
    Papers of the Women's Trade Union League and its Principal Leaders.
Drew University. Madison, New Jersey.
    Records of the Methodist Federation for Social Action.
Illinois Historical Survey. Urbana, Illinois.
    Thomas J. Morgan Collection.
Illinois Institute of Technology. Chicago, Illinois.
    Frank W. Gunsaulus Collection.
Newberry Library. Chicago, Illinois.
    The Goodwin Family Papers.
    Graham Taylor Papers.
    Pullman Palace Car Company Collection.
Pullman Presbyterian Church. Chicago, Illinois.
Rare Book and Manuscript Library, Columbia University. New York City, New York.
    Charles Stelzle Papers.

State Historical Society of Wisconsin. Madison, Wisconsin.

  Henry Demarest Lloyd Papers.

  Albert R. Parsons Papers.

United Library, Garrett-Evangelical Theological Seminary. Evanston, Illinois.

  William H. Carwardine Papers (unsorted).

Church Directories

(Note: All of these churches were/are located in Chicago and all of these directories can be accessed digitally via WorldCat).

Ada Street Methodist Episcopal Church, 1877.

First Congregational Church, 1873.

New England Congregational Church, 1891.

St. Paul's Reformed Episcopal Church, 1876.

Second Presbyterian Church, 1892.

Government Documents

Bureau of the Census. *Statistical View of the United States, Embracing its Territory, Population—White, Free Colored, And Slave, Moral and Social Condition, Industry, Property, and Revenue; The Detailed Statistics of Cities, Towns and Counties; Being a Compendium of the Seventh Census.* Washington, DC: Beverly Tucker, 1854.

——. *Population of the United States in 1860; Compiled from the Original Returns of the Eighth Census.* Washington, DC: Government Printing Office, 1864.

——. *The Statistics of the Population of the United States: Embracing the Tables of Age, Race, Nationality, Sex, Selected Ages, and Occupations: To Which Are Added Statistics of School Attendance and Illiteracy, of Schools., Libraries, Newspapers and Periodicals, Churches, Pauperism and Crime, and of Areas, Families, and Dwellings, Compiled from the Original Returns of the Ninth Census (June 1, 1870).* Washington, DC: Government Printing Office, 1872.

——. *Statistics of the Population of the United States at the Tenth Census (June 1, 1880).* Washington, DC: Government Printing Office, 1884.

——. *Report on Population of the United States at the Eleventh Census: 1890.* Washington, DC: Government Printing Office, 1895.

——. *Census Reports for the Twelfth Census of the United States Taken in the Year 1900.* Washington, DC: Government Printing Office, 1903.

——. *Thirteenth Census of the United States Taken in the Year 1910.* Washington, DC: Government Printing Office, 1913.

——. *Fourteenth Census of the United States Taken in the Year 1920.* Washington, DC: Government Printing Office, 1922.

Tenth Annual Report of the Commissioner of Labor. Washington, DC: Government Printing Office, 1896.

United States Strike Commission. *Report on the Chicago Strike of June–July, 1894.* 53rd Cong., 3d sess.

Periodicals
General Papers

Advertiser
Chicago Chronicle
Chicago Daily News
Chicago Daily Tribune
Chicago Dispatch
Chicago Examiner
Chicago Herald
Chicago Journal
Chicago Mail
Chicago Press and Tribune
Chicago Record
Chicago Record-Herald
Chicago Republican
Chicago Times
Cook County Herald
Daily Sun
Evening Journal
Inter Ocean
Lee County Journal
Los Angeles Times
New York Observer and Chronicle
New York Times
Svenska Amerikanaren
Times-Star

Labor and Radical Papers

Age of Labor
Alarm
Artist Printer
Bicz Bozy (accessed through Chicago Foreign Language Press Survey)
Blacksmiths Journal
Chicago Daily Socialist
Chicagoer Arbeiter Zeitung (accessed through CFLPS)
Die Fackel
Dziennik Ludowy (accessed through CFLPS)
Eight-Hour Herald
International Brotherhood of Blacksmiths, Drop Forgers, and Helpers Monthly Journal
Knights of Labor

Labor Enquirer
La Parola dei Socialisti (accessed through CFLPS)
The Motorman and Conductor
Progressive Age
Railway Times
Revyen (accessed through CFLPS)
Scandia (accessed through CFLPS)
Social Democrat
Socialist Spirit
Svenska Nyheter
Svornost (accessed through CFLPS)
Typographical Journal
Union Labor Advocate
Vorbote
Workers' Call
Workingman's Advocate

Miscellaneous Papers

Association Men
Chronicle
Frank Leslie's Sunday Magazine
Independent
Literary News
Manchester Guardian
Public Opinion
Review of Reviews

Religious Papers

Advance
Alliance
Catholic Home
Christian Advocate and Journal
Christian Century
Christian Freeman
Christian Intelligencer
Christian Times and Witness
Congregationalist and Christian World
Dziennik Chicagoski
Fosterlandet
Interior

Katholisches Wochenblatt
Living Church
Narod Polski (accessed through CFLPS)
New World
Northwestern Christian Advocate
Post-Intelligencer
Sandebudet
Standard
Unitarian Review
Wesleyan Advocate
Western Catholic
Western Tablet
Zion's Herald and Wesleyan Journal

Published

The American Almanac, Year-Book, Cyclopaedia and Atlas. Vol. 2. New York: Hearst's Chicago American and San Francisco Examiner, 1904.

Anderson, Mary. *Woman at Work: The Autobiography of Mary Anderson as told to Mary N. Winslow*. Westport, CT: Greenwood Press, 1951.

Andreas, A. T. *History of Chicago: From the Earliest Period to the Present Time*. 3 vols. Chicago: A. T. Andreas Company, 1886.

Atwell, Charles B., ed. *Northwestern University Alumni Record of the College of Liberal Arts*. Evanston, IL: Northwestern University, 1903.

August Spies' Auto-Biography; His Speech in Court, and General Notes. Chicago: Niña Van Zandt, 1887.

"Autobiography of Albert R. Parsons." In Philip S. Foner, ed., *The Autobiographies of the Haymarket Martyrs*. New York: Pathfinder, 1969.

Biographical Sketches of the Leading Men of Chicago. Chicago: Wilson & St. Clair, 1868.

Bliss, William Dwight Porter, ed. *The New Encyclopedia of Social Reform*. London and New York: Funk & Wagnalls Company, 1909.

The Book of Chicagoans: A Biographical Dictionary of Leading Living Men of the City of Chicago. Chicago: A. N. Marquis & Company, 1911.

Carter, Thomas Butler, and John C. Grant. *The Second Presbyterian Church of Chicago*. Chicago: Knight, Leonard, & Co., 1892.

Carwardine, William H. *The Pullman Strike*. Chicago: Charles H. Kerr & Co., 1894.

Chicago Relief: First Special Report of the Chicago Relief and Aid Society. Chicago: Culver, Page, Hoyne & Co., 1871.

"Churches and Church Choirs in Chicago." In *Chicago Magazine: The West as it is*. Vol. 1. Chicago: J. Gager & Company for Chicago Mechanics' Institute, 1857.

Debs, Eugene V. *Debs: His Life, Writings and Speeches*. Chicago: Charles H. Kerr & Company, 1908.

Fallows, Alice Katharine. *Everybody's Bishop: The Life and Times of the Right Reverend Samuel Fallows, D.D.* New York: J. H. Sears & Company, 1927.

Gilman, Daniel Coit, Harry Thurston Peck, and Frank Moore Colby, eds. *The New International Encyclopaedia.* Vol. 18. New York: Dodd, Mead, and Company, 1905.

Goodspeed, Thomas Wakefield. *The University of Chicago Biographical Sketches.* Vol. 1. Chicago: University of Chicago Press, 1922.

Handy Guide to Chicago and World's Columbian Exposition. Chicago and New York: Rand, McNally, & Company, 1893.

History of Lee County. Chicago: H. H. Hill & Company, 1881.

History of Lehigh County, Pennsylvania, and a Genealogical and Biographical Record of its Families. Northampton County, PA: Lehigh Valley Publishing Company, 1914.

Holmes, John Haynes. *The Life and Letters of Robert Collyer, 1823–1912.* Vols. 1 and 2. New York: Dodd Mead and Company, 1917.

Lakeside Annual Directory for the City of Chicago. Chicago: Chicago Directory Co., 1876.

Mead, George Whitefield. *Modern Methods in Church Work: The Gospel Renaissance.* New York: Dodd, Mead and Company, 1897.

The Men Who Advertise. New York: George P. Rowell & Company, 1870.

Moses, John, and Joseph Kirkland. *History of Chicago, Illinois.* Chicago: Munsell & Company, 1895.

Nestor, Agnes. *Woman's Labor Leader: An Autobiography of Agnes Nestor.* Rockford, IL: Bellevue Books Publishing Co., 1954.

"Official Report of the Strike Committee: Chicago Garment Workers' Strike, October 29, 1910–February 18, 1911." Chicago: Women's Trade Union League, 1911.

Olson, Ernst Wilhelm, Martin J. Engberg, and Anders Schön. *History of the Swedes of Illinois.* Chicago: Engberg Holmberg Publishing Company, 1908.

Otis, Philo Adams. *The First Presbyterian Church: A History of the Oldest Organization in Chicago.* Chicago: Clayton F. Summy Co., 1900.

Perry, H. Francis. "The Workingman's Alienation from the Church." *American Journal of Sociology* 4, no. 5 (March 1899): 621–629.

Phillips, George Searle. *Chicago and Her Churches.* Chicago: E. B. Myers and Chandler, 1868.

Pike, Granville Ross. *The Divine Drama: The Manifestation of God in the Universe.* London: MacMillan & Company, 1899.

Ransom, Reverdy C. *The Industrial and Social Condition of the Negro: A Thanksgiving Sermon.* Chicago: Conservator Print, 1896.

———. *The Pilgrimage of Harriet Ransom's Son.* Nashville, TN: Sunday School Union, 1949.

Rauschenbusch, Walter. *Christianizing the Social Order.* New York: McMillan Company, 1913.

A Review of the Commerce of Chicago, Her Merchants and Manufacturers. Chicago: Scripps, Bross, and Spears, 1855.

Stead, William T. *If Christ Came to Chicago.* Chicago: Laird and Lee, 1894.

Stevens, Frank E. *History of Lee County.* Vol. 1. Chicago: S. J. Clarke Publishing Company, 1914.

Trevor, John. "The Labor Church." In William Dwight Porter Bliss, ed., *The Encyclopedia of Social Reform.* New York and London: Funk & Wagnalls Company, 1897.

Warvelle, George William. *A Compendium of Freemasonry in Illinois: Embracing a Review of the Introduction, Development, and Present Condition of All Rites and Degrees,* 1897.

Winston, A. P. Review of *L'anarchisme aux Etats Unis,* by Paul Ghio and *History of Socialism in the United States,* by Morris Hillquit. *Journal of Political Economy* 13, no. 1 (December 1904).

Wynkoop, Richard. *Wynkoop Genealogy in the United States of America.* New York: Knickerbocker Press, 1904.

SECONDARY SOURCES

Abell, Aaron I. "The Reception of Leo XIII's Labor Encyclical in America, 1891–1919." *Review of Politics* 7, no. 4 (October 1945): 464–495.

———. *American Catholicism and Social Action: A Search for Social Justice.* New York: Hanover House, 1960.

Ahrens, Gale, ed. *Freedom, Equality, and Solidarity: Writings and Speeches, 1878–1937.* Chicago: Charles H. Kerr Publishing Company, 2004.

Albert, Peter J., and Grace Palladino, eds. *The Samuel Gompers Papers,* Vol. 8: *Progress and Reaction in the Age of Reform, 1909–13.* Urbana, IL: University of Illinois Press, 2001.

Anderson, Douglas Firth. "J. Stitt Wilson and Herronite Socialist Christianity." In Jacob H. Dorn, ed., *Socialism and Christianity in Early 20th Century America.* Westport, CT: Greenwood Press, 1998: 41–63.

Ashbaugh, Carolyn. *Lucy Parsons: American Revolutionary.* Chicago: Charles H. Kerr Publishing Company, 1976.

Avrich, Paul. *The Haymarket Tragedy.* Princeton, NJ: Princeton University Press, 1984.

Baker, Kimball. *Go to the Worker: America's Labor Apostles.* Milwaukee, WI: Marquette University Press, 2010.

Baltzell, E. Digby. *The Protestant Establishment: Aristocracy and Caste in America.* New Haven, CT: Yale University Press, 1987.

Barrett, James R. "Unity and Fragmentation: Class, Race and Ethnicity on Chicago's South Side, 1900–1922." *Journal of Social History* 18, no. 1 (August 1984): 37–55.

———. *Work and Community in the Jungle: Chicago's Packinghouse Workers, 1894–1922.* Urbana: University of Illinois Press, 1987.

Bayly, C. A. *The Birth of the Modern World: 1780–1914*. Oxford: Blackwell Publishing, 2004.

Beckert, Sven. *The Monied Metropolis: New York City and the Consolidation of the American Bourgeoisie, 1850–1896*. Cambridge: Cambridge University Press, 1993.

Bederman, Gail. "'The Woman Have Had Charge of the Church Work Long Enough': The Men and Religion Forward Movement of 1911–1912 and the Masculinization of Middle-Class Protestantism." *American Quarterly* 41, no. 3 (September 1989): 432–465.

Best, Wallace. *Passionately Human, No Less Divine: Religion and Culture in Black Chicago, 1915–1952*. Princeton, NJ: Princeton University Press, 2005.

Betten, Neil. *Catholic Activism and the Industrial Worker*. Gainesville: University Presses of Florida, 1976.

Bevir, Mark. "The Labour Church Movement, 1891–1902." *Journal of British Studies* 38, no. 2 (April 1999): 217–245.

Bivens, Josh. "Inequality, Exhibit A: Walmart and the Wealth of American Families." The Economic Policy Institute Blog. http://www.epi.org/blog/inequality-exhibit-wal-mart-wealth-american/.

Blue, Ellen. *St. Mark's and the Social Gospel: Methodist Women and Civil Rights in New Orleans, 1895–1965*. Knoxville: University of Tennessee Press, 2011.

Bluestone, Daniel. *Constructing Chicago*. New Haven, CT: Yale University Press, 1991.

Bonomi, Patricia. *Under the Cope of Heaven: Religion, Society, and Politics in Colonial America*. New York: Oxford University Press, 2003.

Boston, Ray. "General Matthew Mark Trumbull Respectable Radical." *Journal of the Illinois State Historical Society* 66, no. 2 (Summer 1973): 159–176.

Bowler, Kate. *Blessed: A History of the American Prosperity Gospel*. New York: Oxford University Press, 2013.

Boyer, Paul. *Urban Masses and Moral Order in America, 1820–1920*. Cambridge, MA: Harvard University Press, 1978.

Bratt, James D. "The Reorientation of American Protestantism, 1835–1845." *Church History* 67, no. 1 (March 1998): 52–83.

Braude, Anne. "Women's History *is* American Religious History." In Thomas Tweed, ed., *Retelling U.S. Religious History*. Berkeley: University of California Press, 1997: 87–107.

Brekus, Catherine A., and W. Clark Gilpin, eds. *American Christianities: A History of Dominance and Diversity*. Chapel Hill, NC: University of North Carolina Press, 2011.

Briggs, Asa. *Victorian Cities*. Berkeley: University of California Press, 1963.

Brown, Peter. *Through the Eye of a Needle: Wealth, the Fall of Rome, and the Making of Christianity in the West, 350–550 AD*. Princeton, NJ: Princeton University Press, 2012.

Browne, Henry J. *The Catholic Church and the Knights of Labor*. Washington, DC: Catholic University of America Press, 1949.

Bruce, Robert V. *1877: Year of Violence*. New York: Ivan R. Dee, 1989.

Brundage, William Fitzhugh. *A Socialist Utopia in the New South: The Ruskin Colonies in Tennessee and Georgia, 1894–1901*. Urbana: University of Illinois Press, 1996.

Bubnys, Edward. "Nativity and the Distribution of Wealth: Chicago 1870." *Explorations in Economic History* 19, no. 2 (1982): 101–109.

Buder, Stanley. *Pullman: An Experiment in Industrial Order and Community Planning, 1880–1930*. New York: Oxford University Press, 1967.

Burns, David. *The Life and Death of the Radical Historical Jesus*. New York: Oxford University Press, 2013.

Butler, Jon. *Awash in a Sea of Faith: Christianizing the American People*. Boston: Harvard University Press, 1990.

Byers, David M., ed. *Justice in the Marketplace: Collected Statements of the Vatican and the United States Catholic Bishops on Economic Policy, 1891–1984*. Washington, DC: United States Catholic Conference, 1985.

Callahan, Richard, Jr. *Work and Faith in the Kentucky Coal Fields: Subject to Dust*. Bloomington: Indiana University Press, 2009.

Cantwell, Christopher D. "The Bible Class Teacher: Piety and Politics in the Age of Fundamentalism." PhD diss., Cornell University, 2012.

Cantwell, Christopher D., Heath W. Carter, and Janine Giordano Drake, eds. *Between the Pew and the Picket Line: Christianity and the Working Class in Industrial America*. Urbana: University of Illinois Press, forthcoming 2016.

Carpenter, Joel A. *Revive Us Again: The Reawakening of American Fundamentalism*. New York: Oxford University Press, 1997.

Carter, Heath W. "Scab Ministers, Striking Saints: Christianity and Class Conflict in 1894 Chicago." *American Nineteenth Century History* 11, no. 3 (September 2010): 321–349.

———. "Striking Out on Its Own: Labor and the Modern Church." *Chicago History* 37, no. 2 (Summer 2011): 4–19.

Carter, Paul A. *The Decline and Revival of the Social Gospel: Social and Political Liberalism in American Protestant Churches, 1920–1940*. Ithaca, NY: Cornell University Press, 1954.

Chandler, Alfred D., Jr. *The Visible Hand: The Managerial Revolution in American Business*. Cambridge, MA: Harvard University Press, 1977.

Christiano, Kevin J. *Religious Diversity and Social Change*. Cambridge: Cambridge University Press, 1987.

Constantine, J. Robert, ed. *Letters of Eugene V. Debs*, Vol. 1: *1874–1912*. Urbana: University of Illinois Press, 1990.

Cowie, Jefferson, and Nick Salvatore. "The Long Exception: Rethinking the Place of the New Deal in American History." *International Labor and Working-Class History* 74 (Fall 2008): 1–32.

Creech, Joe. *Righteous Indignation: Religion and the Populist Revolution.* Urbana: University of Illinois Press, 2006.

Cronon, William. *Nature's Metropolis: Chicago and the Great West.* New York: W. W. Norton & Company, 1991.

Dochuk, Darren. *From Bible Belt to Sun Belt: Plain-Folk Religion, Grassroots Politics, and the Rise of Evangelical Conservatism.* New York: W. W. Norton & Company, 2011.

Dolan, Jay. *The American Catholic Experience: A History from Colonial Times to the Present.* Garden City, NY: Doubleday, 1985.

Dorn, Jacob Henry. *Washington Gladden: Prophet of the Social Gospel.* Columbus: Ohio State University Press, 1966.

Drake, Janine Giordano. "Between Religion and Politics: The Working Class Religious Left, 1886–1920." PhD diss., University of Illinois, 2012.

Dubofsky, Melvyn. *We Shall Be All: A History of the Industrial Workers of the World.* Ed. Joseph A. McCartin. Urbana: University of Illinois Press, 2000.

Duis, Perry R. *Challenging Chicago: Coping with Everyday Life, 1837–1920.* Urbana: University of Illinois Press, 1998.

Duke, David Nelson. *In the Trenches with Jesus and Marx: Harry F. Ward and the Struggle for Social Justice.* Tuscaloosa: University of Alabama Press, 2003.

Edwards, Wendy J. Deichmann, and Carolyn De Swarte Gifford, eds. *Gender and the Social Gospel.* Chicago: University of Illinois Press, 2003.

Evans, Christopher H. *The Kingdom is Always but Coming: A Life of Walter Rauschenbusch.* Grand Rapids, MI: William B. Eerdmans Publishing Company, 2004.

Faulkner, Harold. *Chartism and the Churches: A Study in Democracy.* New York: Columbia University Press, 1916.

Finke, Roger, and Rodney Stark. *The Churching of America, 1776–1990: Winners and Losers in Our Religious Economy.* New Brunswick, NJ: Rutgers University Press, 1992.

Flanagan, Maureen A. *Seeing with Their Hearts: Chicago Women and the Vision of the Good City, 1871–1933.* Princeton, NJ: Princeton University Press, 2002.

Flynn, Tyler B. "Calvinism and Public Life: A Case Study of Western Pennsylvania 1900–1955." PhD diss., Pennsylvania State University, 2007.

Foner, Eric. *Reconstruction: America's Unfinished Revolution, 1863–1877.* New York: Harper & Row Publishers, 1988.

———. *Free Soil, Free Labor, Free Men: The Ideology of the Republican Party before the Civil War.* New York: Oxford University Press, 1995.

Foner, Philip S. *History of the Labor Movement in the United States,* Vol. 1: *From Colonial Times to the Founding of the American Federation of Labor.* New York: International Publishers, 1947.

———. *History of the Labor Movement in the United States,* Vol. 3: *The Policies and Practices of the American Federation of Labor 1900–1909.* New York: International Publishers, 1964.

Fones-Wolf, Ken. *Trade Union Gospel: Christianity and Labor in Industrial Philadelphia.* Philadelphia: Temple University Press, 1989.

Fox, Mary Harrita. *Peter E. Dietz: Labor Priest.* Notre Dame, IN: University of Notre Dame Press, 1953.

Funchion, Michael F. "Irish Chicago: Church, Homeland, Politics, and Class—The Shaping of an Ethnic Group, 1870–1900." In Melvin G. Holli and Peter d'A Jones, eds., *Ethnic Chicago: A Multicultural Portrait.* Grand Rapids, MI: William B. Eerdmans Publishing, 1995: 57–92.

Garb, Margaret. *Freedom's Ballot: African American Political Struggles in Chicago from Abolition to the Great Migration.* Chicago: University of Chicago Press, 2014.

García, Mario T., ed. *The Gospel of Cesar Chavez: My Faith in Action.* New York: Sheed & Ward, 2007.

Garraghan, Gilbert Joseph. *The Catholic Church in Chicago, 1673–1871.* Chicago: Loyola University Press, 1921.

Gellman, Erik, and Jarod Roll. *The Gospel of the Working Class.* Urbana: University of Illinois Press, 2011.

Gloege, Timothy E. W. *Guaranteed Pure: Fundamentalism, Business, and the Making of Modern Evangelicalism.* Chapel Hill, NC: University of North Carolina Press, 2015.

Goddard, Terrel Dale. "The Black Social Gospel in Chicago, 1896–1906: The Ministries of Reverdy C. Ransom and Richard R. Wright, Jr." *Journal of Negro History* 84, no. 3 (Summer 1999): 227–246.

Goebel, Thomas. "The Uneven Rewards of Professional Labor: Wealth and Income in the Chicago Professions, 1870–1920." *Journal of Social History* 29, no. 4 (Summer 1996): 749–777.

Gomez-Jefferson, Annetta Louise. *The Sage of Tawawa: Reverdy Cassius Ransom, 1861–1959.* Kent, OH: Kent State University Press, 2003.

Gorn, Elliott J. *Mother Jones: The Most Dangerous Woman in America.* New York: Hill and Wang, 2001.

Green, James. *Death in the Haymarket: A Story of Chicago, The First Labor Movement and the Bombing that Divided Gilded Age America.* New York: Pantheon Books, 2006.

Griffiths, Carl. "Some Protestant Attitudes on the Labor Question." *Church History* 11, no. 2 (June 1942): 138–148.

Grossman, James R., Ann Durkin Keating, and Janice L. Reiff, eds. *The Encyclopedia of Chicago.* Chicago: University of Chicago Press, 2004.

Gutman, Herbert G. "Protestantism and the American Labor Movement: The Christian Spirit in the Gilded Age." *American Historical Review* 72, no. 1 (October 1966): 74–101.

Hall, David D., ed. *Lived Religion in America: Toward a History of Practice.* Princeton, NJ: Princeton University Press, 1997.

Hatch, Nathan. *The Democratization of American Christianity.* New Haven, CT: Yale University Press, 1989.

Hawkinson, Zenos. "An Interpretation of the Background of the Evangelical Mission Covenant Church of America." *Swedish Pioneer* 2, no. 1 (Summer 1951): 3–14.

Higginbotham, Evelyn Brooks. *Righteous Discontent: The Women's Movement in the Black Baptist Church, 1880–1920.* Cambridge, MA: Harvard University Press, 1993.

Higham, John. *Strangers in the Land: Patterns of American Nativism, 1860–1925.* 6th ed. London: Rutgers University Press, 2004.

Hirsch, Eric L. *Urban Revolt: Ethnic Politics in the Nineteenth-Century Chicago Labor Movement.* Berkeley: University of California Press, 1990.

Hobsbawm, Eric. *The Age of Capital: 1848–1875.* New York: Vintage Books, 1975.

Holifield, E. Brooks. "The Penurious Preacher? Nineteenth Century Clerical Wealth: North and South." *Journal of the American Academy of Religion* 58, no. 1 (Spring 1990): 17–36.

———. *God's Ambassadors: A History of the Christian Clergy in America.* Grand Rapids, MI: Eerdmans Publishing Company, 2007.

Hopkins, Charles Howard. *The Rise of the Social Gospel in American Protestantism, 1865–1915.* New Haven, CT: Yale University Press, 1940.

Hopkins, C. Howard, and Ronald C. White, Jr. *The Social Gospel: Religion and Reform in Changing America.* Philadelphia: Temple University Press, 1976.

Howe, Daniel Walker. *What Hath God Wrought: The Transformation of America, 1815–1848.* New York: Oxford University Press, 2007.

Hoy, Suellen. "The Irish Girls' Rising: Building the Women's Labor Movement in Progressive-Era Chicago." *Labor: Studies in Working-Class History of the Americas* 9, no. 1 (Spring 2012): 77–100.

Jacobson, Matthew Frye. *Barbarian Virtues: The United States Encounters Foreign Peoples at Home and Abroad.* New York: Hill and Wang, 2000.

Jaher, Frederik. *The Urban Establishment: Upper Strata in Boston, New York, Charleston, Chicago, and Los Angeles.* Urbana: University of Illinois Press, 1982.

Jentz, John B. "Class and Politics in an Emerging Industrial City: Chicago in the 1860s and 1870s." *Journal of Urban History* 17, no. 3 (May 1991).

Jentz, John B., and Richard Schneirov, *Chicago in the Age of Capital: Class, Politics, and Democracy during the Civil War and Reconstruction.* Urbana: University of Illinois Press, 2012.

Johnson, Paul E. *A Shopkeeper's Millennium: Society and Revivals in Rochester, New York, 1815–1837.* New York: Hill and Wang, 1978.

Johnson, Paul E., and Sean Wilentz. *The Kingdom of Matthias: A Story of Sex and Salvation in 19th-Century America.* Oxford: Oxford University Press, 1994.

Karamanski, Theodore J. *Rally 'Round the Flag: Chicago and the Civil War.* New York: Rowman and Littlefield, 2006.

Karson, Marc. *American Labor Unions and Politics, 1900–1918.* Carbondale: Southern Illinois University Press, 1958.

Katz, Philip M. *From Appomattox to Montmartre: Americans and the Paris Commune.* Cambridge, MA: Harvard University Press, 1998.

Katznelson, Ira. *Fear Itself: The New Deal and the Origins of Our Time.* New York: Liveright Publishing Company, 2013.

Kazin, Michael. *A Godly Hero: The Life of William Jennings Bryan.* New York: Anchor Books, 2006.

Keller, Rosemary Skinner, Rosemary Radford Reuther, and Marie Cantlon, eds. *Encyclopedia of Women and Religion in North America.* Vol. 1. Bloomington: Indiana University Press, 2006.

Kennedy, David M. *Freedom from Fear: The American People in Depression and War, 1929–1945.* New York: Oxford University Press, 2005.

Kessler-Harris, Alice. "Capitalism, Democracy, and the Emancipation of Belief." *Journal of American History* 99, no. 3 (December 2012): 725–740.

King, Martin Luther, Jr., *"All Labor Has Dignity."* Ed. Michael K. Honey. Boston: Beacon Press, 1963.

Koenig, Rev. Msgr. Harry C. *A History of the Parishes of the Archdiocese of Chicago.* Chicago: Archdiocese of Chicago, 1980.

Kreuter, Kent, and Gretchen Kreuter. *An American Dissenter: The Life of Algie Martin Simons, 1870–1950.* Lexington: University of Kentucky Press, 1969.

Krugman, Paul. "Why We're in a New Gilded Age." *New York Review of Books,* 8 May 2014.

Kruse, Kevin. *One Nation under God: How Corporate America Invented Christian America.* New York: Basic Books, 2015.

Lamoureux, Patricia A. "Irish Catholic Women and the Labor Movement." *U.S. Catholic Historian* 16, no. 3 (Summer 1998): 24–44.

Laurie, Bruce. *Artisans into Workers: Labor in Nineteenth-Century America.* Urbana: University of Illinois Press, 1989.

Lazerow, Jama. *Religion and the Working Class in Antebellum America.* Washington, DC: Smithsonian Institute Press, 1995.

Lears, Jackson. *Rebirth of a Nation: The Making of Modern America, 1870–1920.* New York: Harper, 2009.

Lindsay, Almont. *The Pullman Strike: The Story of a Unique Experiment and of a Great Labor Upheaval.* Chicago: University of Chicago Press, 1964.

Luker, Ralph E. *The Social Gospel in Black and White: American Racial Reform, 1885–1912.* Chapel Hill, NC: University of North Carolina Press, 1991.

May, Henry F. *Protestant Churches and Industrial America.* New York: Harper & Brothers Publishers, 1949.

McCann, Philip. *Modern Urban and Regional Economics.* 2d ed. New York: Oxford University Press, 2013.

McCarthy, Kathleen D. *Noblesse Oblige: Charity and Cultural Philanthropy in Chicago, 1849–1929.* Chicago: University of Chicago Press, 1982.

McCrossen, Alexis. *Holy Day, Holiday: The American Sunday*. Ithaca, NY: Cornell University Press, 2000.

McDowell, John Patrick. *The Social Gospel in the South: The Women's Home Mission Movement in the Methodist Episcopal Church, South, 1886–1939*. Baton Rouge: Louisiana State University Press, 1982.

McGreevy, John. *Catholicism and American Freedom: A History*. New York: W. W. Norton & Company, 2003.

McKanan, Dan. *Prophetic Encounters: Religion and the American Radical Tradition*. Boston: Beacon Press, 2011.

McLeod, Hugh. *Religion and the Working Class in Nineteenth-Century Britain*. London: Macmillan, 1984.

———. *Piety and Poverty: Working-Class Religion in Berlin, London and New York, 1870–1914*. New York: Oxford University Press, 2003.

Mead, Sidney. *The Lively Experiment: The Shaping of Christianity in America*. New York: Harper & Row, 1963.

Mirola, William A. "Shorter Hours and the Protestant Sabbath: Religious Framing and Movement Alliances in Late-Nineteenth-Century Chicago." *Social Science History* 23, no. 3 (Autumn 1999): 395–433.

———. *Redeeming Time: Protestantism and Chicago's Eight-Hour Movement*. Urbana: University of Illinois Press, 2015.

Moore, R. Laurence. *Selling God: American Religion in the Marketplace of Culture*. New York: Oxford University Press, 1995.

Moreton, Bethany. *To Serve God and Wal-Mart: The Making of Christian Free Enterprise*. Cambridge, MA: Harvard University Press, 2009.

Morriss, Timothy R. " 'To Provide for All Classes': The Methodist Church and Class in Chicago, 1871–1939." PhD diss., Yale University, 2007.

Murphy, Teresa Ann. *Ten Hours' Labor: Religion, Reform, and Gender in Early New England*. Ithaca, NY: Cornell University Press, 1992.

Nash III, George H. "Charles Stelzle: Apostle to Labor." *Labor History* 11, no. 2 (1970): 151–174.

Nelson, Bruce C. *Beyond the Martyrs: A Social History of Chicago's Anarchists, 1870–1900*. New Brunswick, NJ: Rutgers University Press, 1988.

———. "Revival and Upheaval: Religion, Irreligion, and Chicago's Working Class in 1886." *Journal of Social History* 25, no. 2 (Winter 1991): 233–253.

Noll, Mark A. *America's God: From Jonathan Edwards to Abraham Lincoln*. New York: Oxford University Press, 2002.

———. *The Rise of Evangelicalism: The Age of Edwards, Whitefield, and the Wesleys*. Downers Grove, IL: InterVarsity Press, 2003.

Orsi, Robert A. *The Madonna of 115th Street: Faith and Community in Italian Harlem, 1880–1950*. New Haven, CT: Yale University Press, 2002.

Ozanne, Robert. "Union Wage Impact: A Nineteenth-Century Case." *Industrial and Labor Relations Review* 15, no. 3 (April 1962): 350–375.

Pabis, George S. "The Polish Press in Chicago and American Labor Strikes: 1892 to 1912." *Polish American Studies* 48, No. 1 (Spring 1991): 7–21.

Pacyga, Dominic A. *Chicago: A Biography.* Chicago: University of Chicago Press, 2009.

Pacyga, Dominic A., and Ellen Skerrett. *Chicago, City of Neighborhoods: Histories and Tours.* Chicago: Loyola University Press, 1986.

Painter, Nell. *Standing at Armageddon: A Grassroots History of the Progressive Era.* New York: W. W. Norton & Company, 2008.

Pehl, Matthew. "'Apostles of Fascism,' 'Communist Clergy,' and the UAW: Political Ideology and Working-Class Religion in Detroit, 1919–1945." *Journal of American History* 99, no. 2 (September 2012): 440–465.

Pierce, Bessie Louise. *A History of Chicago,* Vol. 1: *The Beginning of a City, 1673–1848.* New York: Alfred A. Knopf, 1937.

———. *A History of Chicago,* Vol. 2: *From Town to City, 1848–1871.* Chicago: University of Chicago Press, 1940.

———. *A History of Chicago,* Vol. 3: *The Rise of a Modern City, 1871–1893.* Chicago: University of Chicago Press, 1857.

———. *As Others See Chicago: Impressions of Visitors, 1673–1933.* Chicago: University of Chicago Press, 2004.

Piketty, Thomas. *Capital in the Twenty-First Century.* Cambridge, MA: Belknap Press of Harvard University Press, 2014.

Pinn, Anthony B., ed. *Making the Gospel Plain: The Writings of Bishop Reverdy C. Ransom.* Harrisburg, PA: Trinity Press International, 1999.

Postel, Charles. *The Populist Vision.* New York: Oxford University Press, 2007.

Radzilowski, John. "Rev. Wincenty Barzynski and a Polish Catholic Response to Industrial Capitalism." *Polish American Studies* 58, no. 2 (Autumn 2001): 23–32.

Reed, Christopher Robert. *Black Chicago's First Century,* Vol. 1: *1833–1900.* Columbia: University of Missouri Press, 2005.

Reinders, Robert C. "T. Wharton Collens: Catholic and Christian Socialist." *Catholic Historical Review* 52, no. 2 (July 1966): 212–233.

———. "T. Wharton Collens and the Christian Labor Union." *Labor History* 8, no. 1 (1967): 53–70.

Roll, Jarod. *Spirit of Rebellion: Labor and Religion in the New Cotton South.* Urbana: University of Illinois Press, 2010.

Ruff, Allen. *"We Called Each Other Comrade": Charles H. Kerr & Company, Radical Publisher.* Urbana: University of Illinois Press, 1997.

Rzeznik, Thomas F. *Church and Estate: Religion and Wealth in Industrial-Era Philadelphia.* University Park: Pennsylvania State University Press, 2013.

Sanneh, Lamin. *Disciples of All Nations: Pillars of World Christianity.* Oxford: Oxford University Press, 2008.

Sawislak, Karen. *Smoldering City: Chicagoans and the Great Fire, 1871–1874.* Chicago: University of Chicago Press, 1995.

Schneirov, Richard. "Free Thought and Socialism in the Czech Community in Chicago, 1875–1887." In Dick Hoerder, ed., *"Struggle a Hard Battle": Essays on Working Class Immigrants.* DeKalb: Northern Illinois University Press, 1986: 121–142.

———. *Labor and Urban Politics: Class Conflict and the Origins of Modern Liberalism in Chicago, 1864–1897.* Urbana: University of Illinois Press, 1998.

———. "Chicago's Great Upheaval of 1877: Class Polarization and Democratic Politics." In David O. Stowell, ed., *The Great Strikes of 1877.* Urbana: University of Illinois, 2008: 76–104.

———. "Labor and the New Liberalism in the Wake of the Pullman Strike." In Richard Schneirov, Shelton Stromquist, and Nick Salvatore, eds., *The Pullman Strike and the Crisis of the 1890s: Essays on Labor and Politics.* Urbana: University of Illinois Press, 1899: 204–231.

Schultz, Rima Lunin. *The Church and the City: A Social History of 150 Years at Saint James, Chicago.* Chicago: Cathedral of St. James, 1986.

Sehat, David. *The Myth of American Religious Freedom.* New York: Oxford University Press, 2011.

Sellers, Charles. *The Market Revolution: Jacksonian America, 1815–1846.* Oxford: Oxford University Press, 1991.

Sennett, Richard. *Families Against the City: Middle Class Homes of Industrial Chicago, 1872–1890.* Cambridge, MA: Harvard University Press, 1984.

Sernett, Milton C. *Bound for the Promised Land: African American Religion and the Great Migration.* Durham, NC: Duke University Press, 1997.

Shanabruch, Charles. *Chicago's Catholics: The Evolution of an American Identity.* Notre Dame, IN: University of Notre Dame Press, 1981.

Skerrett, Ellen, ed. *At the Crossroads: Old Saint Patrick's and the Chicago Irish.* Chicago: Loyola University Press, 1997.

Smith, Gary Scott. *The Search for Social Salvation: Social Christianity and America, 1880–1925.* New York: Lexington Books, 2000.

Stanley, Amy Dru. *From Bondage to Contract: Wage Labor, Marriage, and the Market in the Age of Slave Emancipation.* Cambridge: Cambridge University Press, 1999.

Stearns, Peter N. *The Industrial Revolution in World History.* 3d ed. Boulder, CO: Westview Press, 2007.

Stiglitz, Joseph E. *The Price of Inequality: How Today's Divided Society Endangers Our Future.* New York: W. W. Norton & Company, 2012.

Sutton, William R. "Tied to the Whipping Post: New Labor History and Evangelical Artisans in the Early Republic." *Labor History* 36, no. 2 (1995): 251–281.

———. *Journeymen for Jesus: Evangelical Artisans Confront Capitalism in Jacksonian Baltimore.* University Park: Pennsylvania State University Press, 1998.

Swierenga, Robert P. *Dutch Chicago: A History of the Hollanders in the Windy City.* Grand Rapids, MI: William B. Eerdmans Publishing, 2002.

Tax, Meredith. *The Rising of the Women: Feminist Solidarity and Class Conflict, 1880–1917*. Urbana: University of Illinois Press, 2001.

Thompson, E. P. *The Making of the English Working Class*. New York: Vintage Books, 1966.

Way, Peter. "Evil Humors and Ardent Spirits: The Rough Culture of Canal Construction Laborers." *Journal of American History* 79, no. 4 (March 1993): 1397–1428.

Weir, Robert E. *Beyond Labor's Veil: The Culture of the Knights of Labor*. University Park: Pennsylvania State University Press, 1996.

White, Ronald C., Jr. *Liberty and Justice for All: Racial Reform and the Social Gospel*. San Francisco: Harper and Row, 1990.

Wilentz, Sean. *Chants Democratic: New York City and the Rise of the American Working Class, 1788–1850*. Twentieth-Anniversary Edition. Oxford: Oxford University Press, 2004.

Winters, Donald E., Jr. *The Soul of the Wobblies: The I.W.W., Religion, and American Culture in the Progressive Era, 1905–1917*. Westport, CT: Greenwood Press, 1985.

Witwer, David. "Unionized Teamsters and the Struggle over the Streets of the Early-Twentieth-Century City." *Social Science History* 24, no. 1 (2000): 183–222.

Wright, Leslie C. *Scottish Chartism*. London: Oliver and Boyd Ltd., 1953.

Yeo, Eileen. "Christianity in Chartist Struggle: 1839–1842." *Past & Present* 91, no. 1 (1981): 109–139.

Index

CPSIA information can be obtained
at www.ICGtesting.com
Printed in the USA
BVHW030217021019
559953BV00002B/8/P